The Book Trade of the World

Volume II
The Americas, Australia, New Zealand

The Book Trade of the World

Volume I
Europe and
International Section

Volume II
The Americas
Australia, New Zealand

Volume III
Africa, Asia

The Book Trade of the World

Edited by
Sigfred Taubert

Volume II
The Americas
Australia, New Zealand

Wiesbaden / Gütersloh
London / New York
Verlag für
Buchmarkt-Forschung
André Deutsch
R. R. Bowker

English versions:
Frederick Plaat, London
Typography:
Hans P. Willberg, Frankfurt a. M.

© Verlagsgruppe Bertelsmann GmbH /
Verlag für Buchmarkt-Forschung,
Wiesbaden, Gütersloh 1976
Gesamtherstellung: Mohndruck
Reinhard Mohn OHG, Gütersloh
ISBN 3-578-04567-5
Printed in Germany

Distribution rights for North, Central and
South America: R. R. Bowker Company,
New York

Distribution rights for United Kingdom
and Commonwealth Countries (except Canada):
André Deutsch Ltd, London

Dedicated to the United Nations
Educational, Scientific and Cultural
Organization (UNESCO), Paris, in deep
appreciation of outstanding contributions
to the international free flow of books
and to the improvement of the book
situation in the developing countries

Contents

* Klaus Thiele contributed the following chapters as well: Bermuda, Costa Rica, Dominican Republic, El Salvador, French Guiana, Guadeloupe, Guatemala, Honduras, Martinique, Netherland Antilles, Nicaragua, Panama, Panama-Canal Zone, St. Pierre et Miquelon, Surinam, and Virgin Islands (USA).

The need for the first volume of this international handbook was gratifyingly borne out by the comments and compliments that followed its publication.

In the Foreword to Volume I we said we were attempting to make this book the means of supplying such information about the present state of the book trade, and the tasks, themes and problems connected with it, as are necessary for a world-wide understanding of the subject. This attempt has obviously been well received. A better knowledge of the foundations of each country's national book trade is in itself the prerequisite for an adequate understanding of the ever-growing international achievements, contacts and endeavours evident in the various fields of the book trade of our day.

A large proportion of the countries and territories contained in the present volume have never until now had the benefit of a systematic description of their book trade. The difficulties for the editor and the compilers of each chapter are further confounded by the fact that the evolution and revolution in the development of the trade in many of these countries is by no means complete. Thus in a number of chapters a certain amount of compromise has been inevitable. But in each case it has been our ambition to give as objective and considered a picture as possible. Inevitably there are gaps, particularly in the Caribbean territories. The original plan had been to treat this whole region as a single entity, but in view of the political developments towards division and independence we decided to try to treat each country separately.

As in Volume I, the editor underestimated the difficulties that he was to encounter in getting together the text for individual chapters, subsequently the time gap between the publication dates of Volumes I and II has widened. I must therefore crave the reader's indulgence for delays that arose out of problems which often rested my own patience to breaking point.

I wish to offer my cordial thanks at this point to my colleagues and all those who collaborated and advised me in producing the present volume. I am particularly indebted to Miss Beate Gottlob, Frankfurt a. M., who in her capacity as secretary did a great deal of the preparatory work on the book. I wish to reiterate an invitation to all users of *The Book Trade of the World*: I would welcome any discussion and criticism. These will be invaluable in further editions of this reference book, as well as in the compilation of the third, concluding volume (Africa and Asia) and a possible further volume including an overall index.

This volume is dedicated to UNESCO, Paris. The editor and his collaborators wish thus to express their great admiration for work which, emanating from Paris, benefits the book trade in every continent and which has acted as a mediator and sponsor of many effective innovations in the developing world's book trade–particularly since the establishment of regional UNESCO centres such as those now operating in Bogotá, Karachi and Tokio, and such further ones as will in the near future be established in Cairo and Yaoundé. So we gratefully reproduce here a reply from M. René Maheu, former Director General of UNESCO, in answer to our request to accept our dedication:

"Très sensible à votre initiative, qui honore l'Organisation, je l'accepte volontiers.

Le premier volume du manuel est bien connu à l'UNESCO et je tiens a vous adresser mes vœux pour le succès d'une entreprise qui présente un grand intérêt pour les professionels du livre des divers pays du monde."

Sigfred Taubert

Am Felsenkeller 26
D–6457 Maintal-Hochstadt
Federal Republic of Germany

Publishing and trading in books is an act of bridge-building between author and reader, country and country, continent and continent. Never before have all branches of the book trade had so great and promising a mission in uniting the nations as they have today. Books stream daily across hundreds of frontiers. They bridge the oceans to reach the remotest parts of the earth.

This task, with which the book trade is faced–of promoting peaceful encounters between countries and of establishing the presence of books in every conceivable place–demands from the publisher and the bookseller not only a knowledge of conditions in his own country but equally of circumstances in other lands. Even the "small" publisher and bookseller can no longer afford to limit his horizon. The book trade has drawn the inevitable consequences. There are numerous forms of international cooperation, both on an individual and an institutional basis; but in both cases experience often shows that negotiating partners know too little of the book trade in other countries. Useless repetition, consuming time and energy, in international discussions is often the result of a wrong or totally inadequate conception of the structure of the book trade in other countries.

The Book Trade of the World offers such assistance, and at the same time presents in comprehensible form information which, experience has shown again and again, is required in book-trade work at international level.

In order to present material that is reliable and up to date, the editor has been at pains to obtain well-known experts as authors for the chapters on their countries. He wishes to express his thanks to all collaborators for their contributions to this work.

Contributors were asked to present the information under 35 headings laid down by the editor, and each author is responsible for his own contribution. Only in unavoidable cases has the editor discussed technical alterations and additions with authors. It must be expressly stated that these never referred to fundamental passages connected with the book trade or with politics or ideologies. On the other hand, the individual authors are not necessarily expected to identify themselves with the editor's chapter entitled "International Section".

The space at the disposal of the various countries was related to the number of book-titles produced annually. As a result countries fell into one of three groups, and this meant that by and large the space offered was sufficient to cover individual demands. Some authors exploited their space to the full, others were more modest. Where there was nothing to report under some of the individual 35 headings, these have been omitted.

Only the most important items could be quoted under Bibliography. Where a work is not printed in the language(s) of the particular country, a note to this effect has been added. As far as possible an English translation of titles has been placed in parentheses after the original, as with the names of associations and institutions.

This volume is dedicated to the memory of Sir Stanley Unwin, the "Grand Old Man" of the international book trade, who died in 1968 at the age of 83. More than any other publisher of his generation, Sir Stanley devoted his inexhaustible and exemplary energy, both in deed and word, to the free flow of books, and thus created a precedent which this book has tried to emulate.

Latin America

1 General Information

The Latin American countries offer a number of markets of growing importance to international publishing and book-distributing activities. Nevertheless, for traditional and social reasons some of these nations are in many respects not up to international professional standards, and depend in many cases on foreign production and influences, mainly those of their former mother countries in colonial times. In this chapter we try to give a general view of the special problems in the book trade of this sub-continent as a whole, and of its international relations. The term "Latin America", sometimes used for all the continental (from Mexico to South America) and Caribbean countries and islands, is used here in the more current sense referring to the continental countries south of the Rio Grande, where Spanish and Portuguese are spoken as the official language. As the international business of these countries is to a great extent with organizations and companies outside the region, we will refer also, in respective chapters, to the most important developments in these foreign countries, as regards their contact with the Latin American book trade as a whole.

This is particularly the case with the bibliographical data given as a selection of the most important or most characteristic works for professional information. But the reader of *The Book Trade of the World* should also bear in mind a number of publications published outside the Latin American countries, especially in countries with a close contact with the South American continent, i.e. Spain, Portugal and the United States of America. Those interested in the Latin American book trade should thus consult the bibliographical information and the chapters on import and export concerning each of these countries ($\rightarrow$ BTW I and II).

No reference has been made, even when they are the only sources, to international publications in which Latin America is included. These can be found in the *International Section* of this handbook ($\rightarrow$ BTW I, pp. 10–54). There, the reader should look for the international problems of the book trade which are not characteristic of Latin American countries alone but of the profession and the book in general.

2 Past and Present

The historical background of the nations of Latin America still plays an important role in their book trade. Latin America, as part of the former Spanish colonial empire and, in the case of Brazil, of Portugal, cannot up to the present day meet all the needs for books for its educational, scientific and cultural development without importing such material, and the modern publishing and distribution techniques, from the former mother countries and from the United States of America and the industrialized European countries. The United States especially exerts continuously growing influences on local book markets, either by means of books in English or in Spanish and Portuguese. But there are a number of countries in Latin America, particularly the Argentina, Brazil and Mexico, which are steadily developing an autonomous standard in book production and distribution though they still afford a large market for North American, European, and, lateley, Asian books.

A kind of book trade, at least of publishing, already existed in the high cultures flowering before the arrival of the Europeans on the American continent, at the beginning of the sixteenth century. This is true firstly of the Mesoamerican cultures, among the Aztec and Mayan nations, where the invention of a bark paper led to the production of a kind of book in leporello form, written in a pictographic script. Partly written after the arrival of the Spanish, they record dates of the conquest as well as information about daily life before the discovery of America by Columbus.

Even when those "books" where used and guarded by the priests, there must have been a small "publishing industry"; paper production was concentrated in eighteen villages on the Mexican *altiplano;* the old chronicles report paper as an important part of the tributary payments to the Aztec emperor.

A similar fact has been reported about the Inca empire, where the so-called *kipu* (i.e. a system of knots in strings, signifying certain quantities and key words) served as correspondence and as accounts for tributes and taxes. However, this can hardly be called "publishing" or "book trade", since books or even complete texts have never been discovered.

Thus, the modern book trade in America began with the arrival of the European conquerors, followed by Catholic priests who where the first persons interested in the distribution of religious literature among the Indian tribes.

The colonial policy, however, and a certain lack of interest on the part of the first governors, restricted publishing activities severely. Furthermore, every colonial country had to rely on books almost solely from the homeland–bearing in mind that even during those years, when Gutenberg's invention of moveable type increased the distribution of literature in Europe enormously, the American colonies had very few persons interested in literature and in a position to buy it. The first printing press on American soil was founded in Mexico in 1536 through the initiative of the bishop *Zumárraga*, who obtained permission for *Juan Pablos*, assistant of the Sevillian, German-born, printer Johan Cromberger, to install it in the city of Mexico. During the sixteenth century printing spread through Mexico, Peru, Guatemala and to the Antilles. Book imports from the homelands increased, and the attention of the local authorities was drawn to the problem of book distribution, as can be seen in contemporary documents, where the selection of these books was broadly discussed.

Only after independence from the Spanish and Portuguese crowns, during the first half of the eighteenth century, could a truly local publishing and bookselling activity arise. It was the founding of the United States, made known in Latin America by way of American books and papers, which together with the ideas of the French revolution led to the independence struggle of the creoles against the Spanish crown.

The United States, from then on, retained the foremost place in America as publisher and exporter of books, though Spain, and to some extent Portugal, even after the independence of their American colonies, maintained a very strong place as suppliers of books to these countries, and many Latin American authors had to look for publishers there too. Only during the second half of the nineteenth century did the picture change, with a growing local publishing industry developing in Latin America, and due to changes in buying policies towards other countries (→27). These suppliers, in turn helped to create a new situation in the supply of books to Latin America, by producing books in Spanish and Portuguese; firstly textbooks for higher levels. The United States, but also Japan and lately some European countries, have followed this trend, while Spain is facing this situation by creating a number of facilities to their publishers for exports to Latin America, and by a policy of joining the Latin American international organizations (→4) as an ordinary, or at least observing, member.

During the nineteenth century, too, bookshops, founded by immigrants from neighbouring countries or from Europe, spread through Latin America; some of them attained European standard. In publishing, among the Latin American countries, Argentina, Brazil and Mexico head the list of producing countries, including a relatively dense network of bookshops and wholesalers handling national and imported and magazines. These countries, followed by Chile, Venezuela, Uruguay and some of the Central American states, have specialized bookshops and special book-distribution channels.

As will be shown in later chapters, the Latin American countries' great dependence on the foreign book still accounts for most of their special problems. But by following the example of North American and European firms, during the last decades the book trade in Latin America has been modernized and there are a number of international bookshops comparable to any sales outlet on any other continent. Figures of the growing battle for education in the Latin American region, of increasing book imports (in spite of the legal support, in some countries, to enable local publishers to confront the competition of the imported book →27) and growing local book production show, without doubt, that the Latin American countries will become one of the outstanding international book markets of our world.

Bibliography

Antiguos Privilegios y Documentos de las Viejas Ciudades de la América Española. Vol. I: Santiago del Nuevo Extremo. (Ancient privileges and documents of the old cities of Spanish America.) Madrid, Joyas Bibliográficas 1970. 75 pp.

A. Arias Larreta, *Literaturas aborígenes de América.* Azteca, Incaica, Maya-Qiché. (Aboriginal literatures of America.) 9th ed. Kansas City, Editorial Indoamerica 1968. VII, 304 pp.

H. Biedermann, *Altmexikos heilige Bücher.* (The sacred books of ancient Mexico.) Graz, Akademische Druck- und Verlagsanstalt 1971. 80 pp.

B. Christensen and S. Marti, *Brujerías y papel Precolombino. Witchcraft and Pre-Columbian paper.* (Bilingual). 2nd ed. México, D.F., Ediciones Euroamericanas 1972. 96 pp.

E. D. Church, *A catalogue of books related to the discovery and early history of North and South America.* 5 vols. New York 1907.

G. Furlong, *Origines del arte tipográfico en America.* (The origins of the typographical art in America.) Buenos Aires, Ed. Huarpes (1947). 225 pp.

A. E. Gropp, *A bibliography of Latin American bibliographies.* Metuchen, N.J., Scarecrow Press 1968. IX, 515 pp.

Among the 69 subject groups are: bibliography, books, booksellers and publishers, government publications, libraries, literature, and printing. This bibliography covers all publications with imprint dates before 1 January 1965.

V. W. von Hagen, *The Aztec and Maya papermakers.* New York, N.Y., J. J. Augustin 1944.

P. S. Jennison and W. H. Kurth, *El libro en América.* Estudio de las principales barreras al comercio del libro en América. (The book in America. Study of the principal barriers to the commerce of the book in America.) Washington, D.C., Panamerican Union 1960. XII, 172 pp.

H. Kropfinger–von Kügelgen, E. C. Morales and J. Specker, *Europäische Bücher in Neuspanien zu Ende des 16. Jahrhunderts.* (European books in New Spain at the end of the 16th century.) Wiesbaden, Franz Steiner 1973. VII, 145 pp.

I. A. Leonard, *Los libros del conquistador.* (The books of the conqueror.–Translation of "Books of the Brave", being an account of books and on men in the Spanish conquest and settlement of the 16th Century.) México, D.F., Fondo de Cultura Económica 1953. 399 pp.

I. A. LEONARD, *Romances of chivalry in the Spanish Indies*. With some lists of shipments of books to the Spanish colonies. Berkeley, Calif., University of California 1933. 155 pp.

J. T. MEDINA, *Historia de la imprenta en los antiguos dominios españoles de América y Oceanía*. (History of printing in the former Spanish dominions of America and Oceania.) 2 vols. Chile, Fondo Histórico y Bibliográfico José Toribio Medina 1958.

N. SARMIENTO, *Historia del libro y de las bibliotecas en América*. (History of the book and of the libraries in America.) Buenos Aires, Veggia 1930. 158 pp.

L. S. THOMPSON, *Printing in colonial Spanish America*. Hamden, Conn., Archon Books 1962. 108 pp.

J. TORRE REVELLO, *Un catálogo impreso de libros para vender en las Indias Occidentales en el siglo XVII*. (A printed catalogue of books for sale in the West Indies in the 17th century.) Madrid, Beltran 1930. 30 pp.

J. TORRE REVELLO, *El libro, la imprenta y el periodismo en América durante la dominación Española*. (The book, printing and journalism during the Spanish domination.) Buenos Aires, Peuser 1940.

R. H. VALLE, *Incunables del Imperio Español*. (Incunabula of the Spanish Empire.) In: "Americas", vol. I, no. 7, pp. 36. Washington, D.C., Panamerican Union 1949.

3 Retail Prices

The European fixed-price system (→BTW I, International Section 3) is unknown in Latin America, with the exception of fixed prices similar to those in the Socialist countries of Europe used in Cuba, and in Chile during the government of the "Unidad Popular".

Nevertheless, retail prices fixed by local publishers are generally respected, particularly with textbooks, which in many cases are published by government institutions. In the same way, discounts given to students or to libraries are often kept uniform by agreement with the local booksellers.

As in all Latin American countries the imported book plays a leading role (unless it is restricted by import regulations in order to save foreign exchange reserves). In examining the retail price systems, one has to refer to imported books. Booksellers' organizations in many Latin American countries have reached unified rates of exchange of foreign to local book prices. In other countries prices are fixed by the importers, and the situation may vary when distributors fix their prices, including high costs of importation and discount to local parties, while at the same time individual booksellers import the same titles in small quantities, often without being obliged to meer costly and longlasting customs regulations.

4 Organization

There have been many efforts to concentrate the publishers and booksellers of the various Latin American countries in regional international organizations. Apart from the participation of some professional associations in the *International Publishers' Association* (IPA, →BTW I, International Section 4) of which Argentina, Brazil, Mexico and Venezuela are members, no international institution has been successful in Latin America. Spanish publishers and booksellers have often participated in and initiated regional associations in Latin America, and the influences of that country's profession can be seen in the passing of many legal acts in favour of the book in the leading publishing countries of Latin America–namely in the Spanish-speaking area. For instance, the first *"Congreso Iberoamericana de Asociaciones y Cámaras del Libro"* (Spanish-American Congress of Book Trade Associations) was held in Mexico City in 1964, after similar congresses in Santiago de Chile and Buenos Aires in 1946 and 1947 respectively, with participation of the Instituto Nacional del Libro Español (Spanish National Book Institute, →BTW I, Spain 4). A number of declarations in favour of the publishing and distributing of books in Latin America have been published; and finally the congress decided to create the

Federación Iberoamericana de Instituciones
Editoriales y Libreras (FIEL)
(Ibero-American Federation of
Publishing and Bookselling Institutions)

whose activities have not yet begun. However, there is continous pressure to initiate such an organization (→Mexico 8). Recently, on the initiative of the Argentina *Cámara de Publicaciones* (Chamber of Publications), representatives of the professional organizations of the countries belonging to the

Latin American Free Trade Association
(ALALC)

met in Montevideo. Publishers from Argentina, Bolivia, Brazil, Colombia, Chile, Ecuador, Mexico, Paraguay, Peru, Uruguay and Venezuela, with observers from the

Centro Regional para el Fomento del Libro en
América Latina (CERLAL)
(Regional Centre for Book Development in
Latin America)
Calle 70 No. 9–52
CO Bogotá, Colombia

and of the

Confederación Latinoamericana de la
Industria Gráfica (CONLATINGRAF),
(Latin American Federation of the graphic
Industry)

Hotel Victoria Plaza, Of. 912
U Montevideo, Uruguay

participated.

The almost regular meetings of publishers and wholesalers of books and magazines from the ALALC countries involved a promise to form a first active cell for the creation of regional professional associations in Latin America. Above all, they concentrate on efforts to solve concrete and daily problems of the trade which affect the interchange of books and book-trade materials among the Latin American countries.

Among the two organizations mentioned above, the *Centro Regional para el Fomento del Libro en América Latina* (CERLAL), a UNESCO foundation, supported by the Columbian government with 10 member states (in 1973): Argentina, Bolivia, Colombia, Ecuador, El Salvador, Panama, Paraguay, Peru, Dominican Republic and Uruguay, will not only be an important training centre for the trade (→11), but its continous initiative will give an impulse to national as well as regional unions of trade groups in publishing and book distribution. One of its plans consists in a bi-annual exhibition of Latin American books (→29).

The objectives of the Centre are:

a) to develop and harmonize the book market, leading to a common market for books in Latin America;

b) to lower economic and transport barriers impeding the free flow of books into and within the countries of the region through agreements with organizations and authorities concerned;

c) to carry out training programmes in order to improve the knowledge and skills of staff in the various branches of the trade in Latin America;

d) to undertake research and make available statistics and documentation relating to the production, distribution and use of reading materials;

e) to serve as a regional clearing house of information and copyright;

f) to promote the reading habit of the masses through appropriate promotional campaigns, contests, exhibitions, etc.;

g) to encourage the planning and establishment of school and public library systems at the national level;

h) to strengthen the infrastructure of the book communities in the region through the setting-up of national organizations for book promotion and development;

i) to promote bibliographical work in Latin America including the use of electronic computers.

The achievement of these objectives is being pursued mainly through negotiations with governments and appropriate agencies and organizations; through studies and research at a regional level on problems impeding book development and free flow of information in the region; and, finally, through regional seminars and training courses in the various fields of book development such as publishing management, publishing techniques, distribution problems, librarianship, reading habits and buying capacity of the potential reading mass audience.

The Centre is governed by a Board (Junta). It is headed by a Director, appointed by the Board in agreement with the Government of Colombia and UNESCO. International experts are being provided through the United Nations Development Programme.

The Centre is financed jointly by contributions from the host Government, its Member States, the United Nations Development Programme and UNESCO.

Since July 1974 CERLAL publishes a *Boletín Bibliográfico* as a contribution to current Latin-American bibliography. The Centre is as well the publisher of numerous pamphlets, books, documents and reports. Since December 1972 the Centro Regional publishes a magazine called "Noticias del CERLAL". This periodical contains interesting material about the activities of this institution and about Latin American book problems.

At the invitation of UNESCO, experts on book production, distribution and promotion from 23 Latin American countries, including those of the Caribbean, attended a meeting in Bogotá (Colombia) in September 1969. The final report about this meeting discusses many problems of the Latin American book market. The conclusions and suggestions covered the following topics: development of book distribution and of book production including copyright, training and research; promotion, and, finally, proposals for the establishment of the Centro Regional.

In co-operation with the Federal Republic of Germany the first *Encuentro Latinoamericano entre Libreros y Editores Universitarios y Especialistas en la Reforma del Libro de Texto* has been held in 1974 in Mexico City.

Bibliography

Memoria a la Primera Reunión de Bibliotecarios de Universidades de Centroamérica. (On the First Reunion of Librarians of Universities of Central America.) San José, Universidad de Costa Rica 1962. 165 pp.

Memorias de Primer Congreso Iberoamericano de Asociaciones y Cámaras del Libro, celebrado en la ciudad de México del 19 al 23 de Mayo de 1964. (On the First Iberoamerican Congress of Associations and Chambers of the Book, held in the city of Mexico from 19 to 23 May 1964.) México, D. F., Instituto Mexicano del Libro 1964. 96 pp.

Proceedings of the Assembly of Librarians of the Americas. 12 May to 6 June 1947. Washington, D. C., Library of Congress 1948. IV, 314 pp.

UNESCO: *Meeting of Experts on Book Development in Latin America.* Final Report. Paris, UNESCO 1969. 30 pp.

5 Trade Press

Apart from a number of bulletins edited by local professional organizations (→ respective countries, 5), periodicals covering trade problems of all or various Latin American countries are very rare. Within the region there exists the

Fichero Bibliográfico Hispanoamericano
(Hispano-American Bibliographical File)
Chile 1441, piso 1º, Of. 3
RA Buenos Aires

It publishes a growing number of reports and articles on the Latin American countries, including a bibliography of new publications.

Another trade publication which covers Latin America in a special section is

El Libro Español
(The Spanish Book)
Santiago Rusiñol,
E Madrid 3

published by the Instituto Nacional del Libro Español (→ BTW I, Spain 5). It is not only important for Latin American book professionals because of the bibliographical information on books published in Spain, but also because it has regular commentaries on the book scene in Latin America.

(→ 4: "Noticias de CERLAL").

Bibliography

Fichero Bibliográfico Hispanoamericano. (Hispano-American Bibliographical File). Edited by Mary C. Turner. Buenos Aires, Turner Ediciones 1961 ff. Monthly.

Librería. (The Bookshop.) Edited by J. C. Abella. Barcelona, Gremio de Libreros de Barcelona 1968 ff. Bi-monthly.

El Libro Español. (The Spanish Book.) Madrid, Instituto Nacional del Libro Español 1958 ff. Monthly.

Livros de Portugal. (Books of Portugal.) Lisboa, Grémio Nacional dos Editores e Livreiros 1940 ff. Trimestral.

O Editor. (The Publisher.) Edited by J. M. López Barreto. Rio de Janeiro, Editora Metodos. Bi-monthly.

6 Book-Trade Literature

In view of the fact that book-trade manuals covering all aspects in Latin America are very rare, only a few bibliographical data are listed below. Further data should be taken from the different national contributions about the countries of the region and those with a strong professional influence in the region.

Bibliography

J. Cardenas N., *Manual del editor.* (Publisher's manual.) Cali, Norma 1969. 109 pp.

J. K. Gates, *Libros y bibliotecas.* Guía para su uso. (Books and libraries. Guide to their use.) Buenos Aires, Bowker Editores 1972. 360 pp.

Manual del Librero. Recopilación de artículos publicados en "Fichero Bibliográfico Hispanoamericano". (Booksellers' Manual. Summary of articles published in "Fichero Bibliográfico Hispanoamericano".) Buenos Aires, Bowker Editores 1968. 118 pp.

H. Marcos Pino, *Gestión y administración de la librería.* (Conduct and administration of the bookshop.) Madrid, Paraninfo 1970. 168 pp.

A. Palau Dulcet, *Manual del librero Hispanoamericano.* 23 vols. (Manual of the Hispanoamerican bookseller.) Madrid, Palau 1948–72. 12 200 pp.

F. Vindel, *Manual de conocimientos técnicos y culturales para profesionales del libro.* (Handbook of technical and cultural knowledge for book professionals.) 2nd. ed. Madrid, Góngora 1948. VII, 197 pp.

7 Sources of Information, Address Services

There is no special address service for the book trade, wether for the whole area or one or a number of the countries of Latin America. However, professional local organizations (→respective countries, 4) usually list their members for promotional purposes.

As for all Latin America, the only special directory is *La Empresa del Libro en América Latina*, published by Bowker Editores, Buenos Aires. A more or less complete list of publishers, booksellers and libraries in Latin America within the international directories is listed below (→BTW I, International Section 7).

Bibliography

Books and Libraries in the Americas. Libros y Bibliotecas en América. (Bi-lingual edition.) Washington, D.C., Panamerican Union 1963. VII, 287 pp.

Directorio de Librerías y Casas Editoriales en América Latina. (Directory of Bookshops and Publishers in Latin America.) 6th ed. Washington, D.C., Panamerican Union 1958. 160 pp.

La Empresa del Libro en América Latina. Guía seleccionada de editoriales, distribuidores y librerías de América Latina. (The Book in Latin America. Selected guide to publishers, distributors and bookshops in Latin America.) 2nd ed. Buenos Aires, Bowker Editores 1974. VIII, 306 pp.

J. E. SABOR, *Manual de fuentes de información.* (Handbook of sources of information.) 2nd ed. Buenos Aires, Kapelusz 1970. 359 pp.

8 International Membership

→BTW I, International Section 4.

10 Books and Young People

The promotion of books among the people beginning to read and those of student's age is usually provided by librarians and their organizations inside and outside of governmental bodies rather than by booksellers or publishers, with the exception of a number of individual and local but, under the circumstances, praiseworthy efforts. All these campaigns to spread reading habits and to popularize children's books, however, are mainly national activities which rarely go beyond the borders of the respective countries.

On the other hand, the literacy campaigns in many Latin American countries have some international programmes. There are, firstly, the programmes initiated by UNESCO jointly with national government institutions, and the alphabetization programmes organized by *Franklin Book Programs* (→USA 28) in the Western Hemisphere. The latter deserve special note, as they are specifically planned to guarantee publications which cover the needs of beginner readers, adults or young people, in places where there is no other contact with reading materials.

One has to bear in mind that in many Latin American countries it is as important to keep alive the knowledge of writing and reading among the population after primary school age, if not more so, as to help children make their first contact with the world of books.

11 Training

Professional training is nearly unknown in the Latin American book trade, except that given by individual publishing houses and bookselling companies to their own personnel. A European–type apprenticeship system does not exist.

Only in a few countries of the sub-continent schools or training courses have been installed, the majority of them unfortunately only temporarily. Thus the training courses for Argentine booksellers, given to young employees of the Buenos Aires area book trade and organized by the *Cámara del Libro* (→Argentina 4) in the same capital, existed between 1967 and 1969.

The graphic arts industry may be given here as an example of this, for in the leading producing countries, courses for printers have been held for many years, mainly in collaboration and with the financial support of the respective governments ($\rightarrow$34) as also those for young librarians.

Recently, new initiatives have been taken, stimulated by European examples (e.g., yearly courses in Brazil, with the participation of specialists from Europe). Also, in Europe, professional or government institutions are inviting Latin American booksellers and publishers to take part in their normal book-trade courses or in specially organized ones. The *Instituto Nacional del Libro Español* ($\rightarrow$ Spain, 4 and 11) has not only opened its three professional schools in Madrid, Barcelona and Valencia to young colleagues from the Spanish-speaking countries of America, but also recently installed special training courses for participants from these nations. The training courses organized by the *British Council*, London, for booksellers from the Third World are offered not only to students from former colonies of the British crown, but also to other Latin American, as well as African and Asian countries. Similarlily, West German initiatives, directed particularly at foreign booksellers, will start in the near future.

In some Latin American countries there are plans to begin or to re-open professional training courses. There is one regional organization which has begun to organize courses for book distribution and production, the *Centro Regional para el Fomento del Libro en América Latina* in Bogotá (CERLAL, UNESCO's Regional Center for Book Development in Latin America, $\rightarrow$ 4). It is intended to give these courses the character of a pioneer contribution to training in the Latin American book world. Further, some legislative concepts for a new "Book Law" in Latin American countries include plans for local training schools for young employees in the trade.

Bibliography

Guía de Escuelas y Cursos Bibliotecológicos en América Latina. (Guide to Schools and Courses of Librarianship in Latin America.) Compiled by Carmen Rovina. 3rd ed. Washington, D.C., Panamerican Union 1962. VII, 66 pp.

Primer Seminario del Libro Centroamericano. – Documento Final. (First Seminar on Books in Central America–Final document.) San José, Consejo Superior Universitario Centroamericano 1968. 28 pp.

Tercer Congreso de Editores e Livreros do Brasil, Río de Janeiro 1956. (Third Congress of Publishers and Booksellers of Brazil, Río de Janeiro 1956). Edited by the National Society of Book Publishers and the Brazilian Book Chamber. Rio de Janeiro, Ministerio de Educacão 1959. 239 pp.

12 Taxes

Commercial book-trade activities are subject to different types of tax, which, in Latin America, differ from one country to another ($\rightarrow$the respective national chapters.) However, it may be seen that nearly all Latin American governments show a high respect for the book and legislation with regard to it, by guaranteeing its unrestricted distribution.

Latin American governments intend to reduce their dependence on imported books and to support book exports. Subsidies are given for the development of the publishing industry and for the growth of its exports apart from official credits for the import of machinery, and sometimes of paper and other raw materials, and for the production of books where large foreign orders occur.

Latin America

14 Copyright

The copyright situation in Latin America has been presented in volume I of this Handbook (→BTW I, International Section 14). However, this may be the place to state once more that some of the Latin American nations have very advanced national copyright laws and take part in international conventions on the subject.

Bibliography

Copyright Protection in the Americas. 3rd ed. Washington, D.C., Panamerican Union 1962. IX, 175 pp.

W. GOLDBAUM, *Lateinamerikanische urheberrechtliche Gesetzgebung. (The copyright laws of Latin America.)* München, Verlag Dokumentation 1960. 101 pp.

C. MOUCHET and S. RADEALLI, *Los derechos del escritor y del artista.* (The rights of the writer and the artist.) Buenos Aires, Editorial Sudamericana 1957. 376 pp. Includes bibliography.

Union List of Basic Latin American Legal Materials. Edited by K. Wallach. South Hackensack, N.J., Rothmans 1971. 71 pp.

F. ZESATI ESTRADA, *Naturaleza jurídica del contrato de edición o reproducción.* (Legal nature of the contract of publishing or reproduction.) México, D.F., Facultad de Derecho, Universidad Nacional Autónoma de México (Thesis) 1966. 151 pp.

15 National Bibliography, National Library

The national bibliographies of Latin America are obviously much younger than those, e.g. of Europe, and there are still a number of countries which up to now have not got beyond the planning stage for a national bibliography. Where national bibliographies have been published–sometimes by private institutions–it is difficult for their editors to include all local production. More than in other regions, a good proportion of the books are privately published by authors and printers, and are never reported to the national libraries or the official bibliographical institutes. Furthermore, often legal deposit laws are not respected by commercial or even by official publishers.

The only attempts to record all Latin American (or, more exactly Spanish–language) publications are by private ventures. There are firstly the volumes of *Libros en Venta*, like the New York-based *Books in Print* (→USA 15), published by the Argentine sister company of the same publisher. These catalogues, published since 1964 and completed with bi-annual or annual supplements, together with the regular bibliography section of the magazine *Fichero Bibliográfico Hispanoamericano* (→5), are the most used regional sources, covering the main part of Latin America's (and Spanish) book production. Bearing in mind the above mentioned obstacles, it is doubtlessly a succesful bibliographic effort. Other bibliographies, sometimes on particular subjects only, have at least up to the moment not been able to reach the distribution and completeness of *Libros en Venta*. As for the library system in Latin America, there is at least a National Library or Documentation Centre in each country, and a relatively dense net of public libraries. It is in this field that many book promotions, reading campaigns and professional training courses are organized, which it must be admitted, are generally superior to similar efforts by the book trade. With wider official support, librarians' organizations have done far better than the book trade.

Bibliography

Boletín Bibliográfico (CERLAL) →4.

Fichero Bibliográfico Hispanoamericano. (Hispano-American Bibliographical File.) Buenos Aires, Turner Ediciones 1961 ff. Monthly. Contains monthly lists of new titles, and a preview of forthcoming books.

Many special numbers with extra bibliographies on particular subjects.

A. E. GROPP, *Guide to libraries and archives* in Central America, and West Indies, Panama, Bermuda and British Guiana. New Orleans, Tulan University 1961.

A. E. GROPP, *A bibliography of Latin American bibliographies*. Metuchen, N. J., Scarecrow Press 1968 IX, 515 pp.

Información Final del Segundo Seminario Bibliográfico Centro-Americano y del Caribe. (Final Information of the Second Seminar of Bibliography of Central America and the Caribbean.) Panamá, Ministerio de Educación 1958.

W. V. JACKSON, *Library needs of Latin America.* In: "Library Journal", 86/1961, pp. 3896–3900, November 1961. New York, N. Y., R. R. Bowker 1961.

C. K. JONES, *A bibliography of Latin American bibliographies.* 2nd ed. Washington, D. C., Government Printing Office 1942. 311 pp.

A. JORDAN (ed.), *Research library cooperation in the Caribbean.* Chicago, American Library, Association 1973. 145 pp.

Libros en Venta en Hispanoamerica y España. (Books for Sale in Spanish speaking America and Spain.) 2nd ed. 2 vol. Buenos Aires, Bowker Editores 1975.

Proceedings of the Assembly of Librarians of the Americas. 12 May to 6 June 1947. Washington, D. C., Library of Congress 1948. IV, 314 pp.

La UNESCO *en el Desarrollo Bibliotecario de América Latina.* (The UNESCO in the Library Development of Latin America.) La Habana, Lázaro Hnos. 1961. 20 pp.

J. ZIMMERMANN, *Current national bibliographies of Latin America.* Gainesville, Fla., University of Florida Press 1971. X, 139 pp.

16 Book Production

Book-production statistics from Latin American countries suffer the same disadvantages resulting from differences in definitions as we find in any international comparisons. (→BTW I, International Section 16.) Nevertheless, the UNESCO *Statistical Yearbook* (1972 edition), giving the figures of the continental countries of Latin America, offers the following information:

Latin American book production 1970
                              21,974 titles
Latin American book production 1971
                              21,226 titles.

These two years seem to prove that the book production in the Latin American countries are at a stand-still. However, there is definitely a constant increase in book production at least in the leading book nations of the subcontinent. For better information, consult the production statistics of each individual country (→national chapters, 16).

Bibliography

P. M. LE CACHEUX, *Meeting the demand for newsprint and other printing papers in Latin America.* Paris, UNESCO 1969. 41 pp. (Mimeogr.)

17 Translations

A large proportion of the translations on sale in the book markets of Latin America are from Spanish and Portuguese publishing houses. The UNESCO *Statistical Yearbook* (for the year 1970) shows a total of 1,448 translations published in Latin America–while Spain appears with 2,936, and Portugal with 648 titles translated from foreign languages in the same year. The main original language was English. The most active countries were Argentina (677), Brazil (427) and Mexico (289), the leading publishing nations of the subcontinent. Brazil publishes 40% of the world's translations into Portuguese.

Latin America

Bibliography

J. I. Mantecon, *Indice de las traducciones impresas en México 1959*. (Index of the translations printed in Mexico 1959.) México, Biblioteca Nacional 1966. 247 pp.

P. Ronai, *Escola de traductores*. (School of translators.) Río de Janeiro, São José 1956. 91 pp.

18 Book Clubs

Book clubs as varied as those that exist in Europe and the United States of America are unknown in Latin America.

There is a Spanish-based organization, Circulo de Lectores, S.A., with three branch offices in Mexico, Central and South America, which mainly offers special editions of regular titles published in the Spanish-speaking book markets, at reduced prices. It thus follows the example of its founder company, a leading German book club (→BTW I, Germany: FRG 18). There is constant expansion and further branch offices will open in the main countries of Latin America, with a steadily growing number of original titles and translations from foreign languages. This shows that book clubs which adjust their publishing and distribution policies to the situation in Latin America can find a big public in these countries.

On the other hand, there are the USA book clubs, which could win a good number of members for their publications in English, read by those who are better educated. As for books in Spanish and Portuguese, some active booksellers have formed their individual "book clubs" which, are, however, more a special promotion venture to increase book sales among regular customers, by offering certain books at a reduced price; sometimes customers of particular bookshops are asked to open an account for this purpose, with standing monthly payments.

19 Paperbacks

Paperback series are not only an important factor in Latin American book sales, but also in the book production of the subcontinent. Among imported books, paperbacks have become important because they are cheap and because this saves valuable foreign-currency reserves. As for books in foreign languages, mainly in English, paperbacks constitute the main proportion of the books sold.

Most Latin American titles are published in paperback, and there are a number of paperback series known not only in the local country but all over the subcontinent. There are also countries where nearly all books published are paper-bound, without being necessarily published within a series. This trend is still growing.

Bibliography

F. L. Schick, *The paperbound book in America*. New York, N.Y., R. R. Bowker 1968. XXIII, 262 pp.

Largely concerning North America. pp. 245–250: selected bibliography.

20 Book Design

In spite of the problems of insufficient raw materials, machinery and typographical standards, compared to international norms, there have been a number of books published in Latin America which display highly professional standards of editorial and typographical work. The vast majority, however, suffer from the lack of adequate printing facilities, so that typographical standards are often below those of other parts of the world.

Latin American publishers and illustrators have occasionally participated in international book-design competitions, but no national selection of the best-designed books exists as in many other countries (→BTW I, International Section 20).

It is to be hoped that the most active book producers among the Latin American countries will initiate local competitions for the best-designed books in the near future. This would help the region reach the international standards which it needs so urgently to fill the books needs of the respective countries, and to increase exports.

The training work of the *Centro Regional para el Fomento del Libro* (→4 and 11) may be expected to lead to the recognition of the importance of adequate standards, and will influence Latin American publishers and printers, in spite of the fact that the book producer's most important goal has to be quantity, rather than quality.

21 Publishing

Publishing in Latin America shows not only strong influences of the former dominant countries, especially Spain and the United States. As stated before (→11), publishing as a professional career is generally unknown in Latin America. This is to some extent compensated for in many companies by individual training and the activity of professionals who have immigrated from other countries.

Many of the publishing companies working in Latin America are branches of European or U.S. publishers–not only just importing the books of their head organization, but publishing more and more inside the country of residence, and in many cases participating in the book exports of those countries. This is not just a consequence of the efforts of many Latin American governments to strenghten local publishing and to lower book imports costly in foreign exchange. It also helps to cover the growing need for books in these countries, and to introduce higher European or United States distribution and production techniques among Latin American publishers. Furthermore, many Latin American publishing companies have owners and executives who began their career in one of the leading publishing countries outside the region, bringing with them the traditions and knowledge of their home countries. This has contributed to a steady improvement in Latin American publishing standards.

The leading countries of the region are Argentina, Brazil and Mexico. In these countries, private publishers are the rule. While even in these three many government organizations take part in publishing, in other countries of the subcontinent the governments are the leading publishers, and often the only ones to have been able to establish a book industry, because of advantages not available to private enterprise. This is especially the case when a country has an insufficient number of book readers. Government and official companies, for the same reasons, dominate textbook publishing. Together with them must be mentioned the university presses, who have done some outstanding work.

A high percentage of authors in Latin American countries, especially the smaller ones, publish and distribute their books privately. So a good part of the region's book production never comes into professional hands, to be edited and sold adequately, nor does it find its way into the bibliographies. This way of publishing, not totally unknown in other parts of the world, demonstrates not only the problems of the Latin American publishing industry, but also the need for a better public presentation of its character and possibilities. →23.

Bibliography

D. DE ABREU, *O livro e a indústria do conhecimento.* (The book and the knowledge industry.) Río de Janeiro, Centro de Bibliotecnia 1968. 50 pp.

D. BOONOCORE, *Bibliografía literaria* y otros temas sobre el editor y el libro. (Literary bibliography and other subjects concerning the publisher and the book.) 2nd ed. Santa Fe, Imprenta Universitaria y Nacional del Litoral 1956. 49 pp.

R. H. BOTTARO, *La edición de libros en Argentina*. (The publication of books in Argentina.) Buenos Aires, Troquel 1964. 104 pp.

J. CARDENAS H., *Manual del editor*. (Publisher's handbook.) Cali, Norma 1969. 109 pp.

J. CASTRO CEPEDA, *Implantación de un sistema de costos en una compañía editora impresora de libros*. (Installation of costing system in a book publishing-printing company.) México, D.F., Escuela Nacional de Comercio y Administración, Universidad Nacional Autónoma de México (Thesis) 1965. 92 pp.

A. LOPEZ LLENERAS, *Algunos aspectos de la industria editorial en México*. (Some aspects of the publishing industry in Mexico.) México, D.F., Escuela Nacional de Economía, Universidad Nacional Autónoma de México (Thesis) 1961. 322 pp.

G. MACEDIN, *Editores en América Latina*. (Publishers in Latin America.) In: "America", vol. 4 no. 11, p. 3, November 1952. Washington, D.C., Panamerican Union 1952.

G. MACEDIN and F. S. ROSENAU, *Editores en América Latina*. (Publishers in Latin America.) In: "America, vol. 7 no. 6, p. 42, November 1955. Washington, D.C., Panamerican Union 1955.

F. PENALOZA, *The Mexican book industry*. New York, N.Y., Scarecrow Press 1957.

22 Literary Agents

As mentioned in the International Section of this handbook (→BTW I, International Section 22), literary agents have a very limited role in Latin American book production. Their part is mainly taken over by the home offices of internationally active publishers through participation in international projects of co-production.

However, during the last years and not only as a consequence of the "boom of Latin American literature" in the United States and in Europe, a number of literary agents specializing in the interchange of translation rights between Latin America and Europe or the United States have started in South America or have opened branch offices there. As for the principal work of literary agencies–the introduction of the work of young authors–this is often done in Latin America by the local writers' associations.

23 Wholesale Trade

Because of geographical exigencies, i.e. the large distances in many Latin American countries, wholesale organizations which offer a complete service like some European companies cannot flourish.

The wholesale trade in books is characterized by distributors who cover one or a number of neighbour countries in the distribution of a publisher's, or a group of publisher's list. But there are some organizations based in the United States or in South America which cover all Latin America with a list of more than one hundred North American and/or Latin American publishers.

In many countries there are also wholesalers who will ship the books of all publishers of their country. But because of the long time for shipments, the lack of information about the books available, etc., they by no means cover all the needs of their retail customers. The position of these wholesale companies is also affected by the habit of many publishers, especially the foreign ones, of selling to booksellers directly on the same conditions as to the those wholesale firms.

It is the wholesaler who suffers more than publishers and booksellers from a custom in many Latin American countries (probably inherited from old Spanish commercial practices): the obligation to send for his bills to be paid. As wholesale companies, even more than general commerce in Latin America, are working with restricted capital, covering their operations mainly by the difference in trade terms between their suppliers and those given to their customers, the costs of all these money-collecting operations (unknown in this form in Europe and the United States) are a heavy burden to them. The extra checking of invoices to be presented personally to the customers at a certain date plus the collection and supervision, means hiring extra personnel and raises the general administration costs and the retail price of books higher than those of any other industrial product in the same countries.

Suppliers of Latin American companies should bear in mind this custom. Many of the claims about slow payments by Latin American distributors and booksellers can be explained not as reluctance to pay in time, but as a result of the administrative systems, which require the supplier to wait to present his invoices, which have to be checked before payment will be made, and to collect his money later personally. Even foreign accounts normally settled without this kind of reminder need extra handling time within the particular company, compared to payments to local publishers.

There is an interesting example of wholesale book distribution among the university presses in Latin America–mostly official organizations. Not only have they established collaboration in the co-production of scientific and textbooks, they als have (as for instance the group of Central American Universities) an interchange of their publications, which are distributed in each country by the local university publisher.

24 Retail Trade

Retail firms in Latin America have generally been founded in one of the following three ways: First, by private persons who during early colonial times, because of cultural ambitions and often to further their official position, were interested in the import of books from the European home countries, and were able to send for books for occasional re-sale to their friends. A small number of these "gentlemen booksellers" later founded bookstores, but nearly none of these has survived. Second, during the last two centuries there have been many immigrants who started bookstores, bringing with them the wide experience acquired in the book-trading countries of Europe. Most of them now run important bookshops in Latin America. A third group of stores is of particular importance in the book distribution of the region, even when they are restricted to connections to one or a small number of publishers' programmes and the interchange of books between only two countries: the retail sales outlets of internationally active Spanish, Portuguese and U.S. publishers (lately joined by branches of French and Italian enterprises) founded to remedy the lack of adequate retail distribution of the books of their particular mother company. These firms often have widened their activities to include books by other publishers and then changed over to become general bookshops.

There are also the bookshops of an official and semi-official character, i.e. bookstores of the universities, founded for the sale of the university presses' titles, or textbooks. In many cases they give a special discount to students at their university, and nearly all of them have also widened their activity to selling books by other publishers for their academic clientèle. Similar to them, there are bookstores owned or subsidized by official institutions.

Latin America

As a rule, in Latin America, however, bookshops are private ventures. Because they have a limited clientèle, rich enough or sufficiently educated to buy books, they suffer–most of all in the smaller countries–from a constant lack of capital, and it is difficult for this type of company to get credit facilities. Even with the growing number of readers and students in many Latin American countries, and with the support of tax exemption on book sales (→12), their situation is complicated by the necessity to have the major part of their stock in the form of imported books (→27). Another disadvantage is the lack of trained personnel, above all outside of the big cities of Latin America. So, the majority of bookshops in Latin America also have to sell stationery, photographic materials, toys, etc.

On the other hand, there are bookstore chains founded mainly for the distribution of books of one particular international publisher of books in Spanish, Portugese or even English, and big sales organizations for direct offers by door-to-door salesmen or by mail (→25).

Bibliography

M. DANIELS, *El comercio de libros en América.* (The commerce of books in America.) In: "Americas", vol. 9 no. 8, p. 40, August 1957. Washington, D.C., Panamerican Union 1957.

G. FUENTES PICHARDO, *Organización administrativa y contable de una empresa distribuidora de libros.* (Administrative and accounting organization of a distributing book company.) México, D.F., Escuela Nacional de Comercio y Administración, Universidad Nacional de Comercio y Administración, Universidad Nacional Autónoma de México (thesis) 1965. 135 pp.

P. S. JENNISON and WILLIAM H. KURTH, *El libro en América. Estudio de las principales barreras al comercio del libro en América.* (The book in America. Study of the principal barriers to the commerce of the book in America.) Washington, D.C., Panamerican Union 1960. XII, 172 pp.

J. POL ARROJO, *El libro y su comercialización.* (The book and its commercialization.) Madrid, Paraninfo 1970. 240 pp.

J. TORRE REVELLO, *Un catálogo impreso de libros para vender en las Indias Occidentales en el siglo XVII.* (A printed catalogue of books for sale in the West Indies in the 17th century.) Madrid, Beltrán 1930. 30 pp.

25 Mail-Order Bookselling

This type of book distribution must be mentioned together with the sale of books by representatives who visit customers in their homes and offices, generally offering credit sales. There are a number of really big organizations of this type, founded by U.S. and Spanish parent companies.

By way of their credit sales, these organizations have built up a "second book market" which, in Latin America, is nearly as big in its turnover as that of the traditional bookshops, bearing in mind that they concentrate on high-priced books and encyclopedias, and that the number of regular visitors to bookshops is smaller in Latin America than e.g. in Europe. The same factors have caused these direct-sales companies to widen their activities from sales by representatives, to entering the mail-order business.

Thus, this form of book-selling is important in covering the book needs of the subcontinent. By making their programmes available for monthly payment, credit sales and mail-order book organizations in Latin America have followed in a much more flexible way the needs of their clientèle. It must be said, however, that because of the high costs of operating, these companies (to which group also belong a number of small, often under-capitalized enterprises) add a relatively high interest rate. The traditional bookshops can of course sell the same titles more cheaply against cash payment.

Bibliography

G. Frigoleit Lerma, *Necesidad del control de cobranza por medios mecanizados en las empresas dedicadas a la distribución de libros a crédito.* (Necessity of control of money collecting by mechanization, in the companies engaged in the distribution of books on credit.) México, D.F., Escuela Nacional de Comercio y Administración, Universidad Nacional Autónoma de México (Thesis) 1965. 76 pp.

H. Lopez Lena Salinas, *Organización contable de una empresa dedicada a la edición, distribución y venta de libros en abonos.* (Account organization of a company engaged in the publication, distribution and sale of books in part payments.) México, D.F., Universidad Nacional Autónoma de México (Thesis) 1970. 133 pp.

26 Antiquarian Book Trade, Auctions

A small number of bookshops have antiquarian book departments, chiefly in the Argentina, Brazil and Venezuela, but only a few of them rely mainly on sales of antiquarian books. They usually send out catalogues: no book auctions take place.

Among the many outlets for the sale of second-hand books, even on public markets, the book collector can occasionally find rare books, but there is no way of placing special orders of particular titles or subjects unless with the antiquarian book departments of the few specialized companies.

27 Book Imports

Imported books constitute the main proportion of the titles in the national book markets of Latin America ($\rightarrow$2, 21). Because of the great need for books among the nearly 300 million Latin Americans (UNO sources give a population estimate of more than 650 million for the year 2000!), and bearing in mind the problems of local publishing ($\rightarrow$21), they are insufficient for these countries.

The Latin American governments have always understood this situation, and thus granted special tax facilities for the import of books and other cultural materials ($\rightarrow$12). There are attempts, however, to increase official support for local publishing by having special tax-reductions to aid the import of foreign books. Sometimes in competition, sometimes together with the leading publishing nations of Spanish-language books (and, much less, Portuguese books, in Brazil), the developing publishing nations in Latin America have tried to reduce the import of books in order to raise the sales of locally produced titles. Lately, in the form of a politics of "cultural defence of the language area", these ideas have found their way into some national "laws of the book" ($\rightarrow$12). They are expected to lower the influence of publishers from non-Spanish-speaking countries with their production of books in Spanish, or to cut down the import of Spanish-language books, especially from Spain. In any case, it is hard to find any bookseller in Latin America who does not sell imported books, which are either exported directly or distributed by branch offices of the large publishers who represent one or a number of lists for the local book trade of one or more neighbour countries.

Since comparative import statistics for the whole subcontinent are not reliable, the reader should consult the statistics given in the respective national chapters.

Bibliography

M. Daniels, *The contribution of the organization of American States to the exchange of publications in the Americas.* In: "Library Journal", vol. 13, no. 1, January 1958, pp. 45–55. New York, N.Y., R. R. Bowker 1958.

P. S. JENNISON and W. H. KURTH, *El libro en América. Estudio de las principales barreras al comercio del libro en América.* (The book in America. Study of the principal barriers to the commerce of books in America.) Washington, D.C., Panamerican Union 1960. XII, 172 pp.

H. KROPFINGER–VON KÜGELGEN, E. C. MORALES u. J. SPECKER, *Europäische Bücher in Neuspanien zu Ende des 16. Jahrhunderts.* (European books in New Spain at the end of the 16th century.) Wiesbaden, Franz Steiner 1973. VII, 145 pp.

S. TAUBERT, *Latein-Amerika als Absatzmarkt für deutsche Bücher.* (Latin America as a market for German books.) Frankfurt a. M., Börsenverein des Deutschen Buchhandels 1961. 182 pp. (Mimeographed).

28 Book Exports

Due to problems of high costs, small local markets, etc., Latin American publishers are achieving a rather low percentage of export sales as compared with leading international standards. But inside the region there exists an active exchange of books, giving many companies remarkable export figures into Spanish-speaking countries. This is particularly true for the few companies with branch offices in other Latin American countries and Spain or Portugal. They mostly receive wide support from their governments to expand these exports (→12, 27). In and outside Latin America, their books have to compete with a vast variety of books of higher printing quality and lower costs: the Latin American publisher cannot raise the generally low quantity of books printed (average editions of 3,000 copies) to compensate for the high costs and the lack of a local market. For these reasons, the conditions for the export of books vary from country to country in Latin America, and the international book-trade figures should be looked up individually. Statistics which give totals for Latin American book exports are deducted from a small number of these countries which publish these details. On the other hand, for the system of distribution in the language areas, even official figures include movements resulting from re-exports by internationally active wholesalers (→23).

Bibliography

M. DANIELS, *The contribution of the organization of American states to the exchange of publications in the Americas.* In: "Library Journal", vol. 13 no. 1, January 1958, pp. 45–55. New York, N.Y., R. R. Bowker 1958.

El Libro Argentino en América. (The Argentine Book in America.) Edited by the "Comisión Nacional Cooperativa Intelectual". Buenos Aires, Ministerio de Educación 1941. 219 pp.

29 Book Fairs

Actually, no book fair covers the whole Latin American subcontinent and its book trade as a whole in the same way as book fairs do in Europe and elsewhere (→BTW I, International Section 29). There is a need for such a venture, however, and it its hoped that the efforts of the *Centro Regional para el Fomento del Libro en América Latina* (Regional Centre for Book Development in Latin America, →4) to establish a book fair which could present to publishers and booksellers all the recent Latin American publications will succeed. Only local initiative could bring about the creation of a book fair in the geographically central city of Bogotá.

The regional exhibition which reached the most inter-American attention in Latin America is the

Bienal Internacional do Livro
(International Book Biennial)
Parque Ibirapuera
Caixa Postal–7832
BR São Paulo 2, S.P.
organized since 1970 by a special foundation sponsored by three Brazilian professional book organizations and two government institutions (the Brazilian Secretary of Sports, Culture and Tourism and the Municipality of São Paulo). It is to be held in the June of every other year. Within Central America, the
Expomundi-Exposición Mundial del Libro,
Prensa e Industrias Gráficas y Medios
Audiovisuales
(World Exhibition of the Book, Press,
Graphic Industries and Audiovisual Mediums)
Apartado 66
San Salvador, El Salvador
was founded in 1969 by the local booksellers' association in cooperation with the Ministry of Education. Held annually in October and November, the fair was attented by publishers from other Latin American countries, Spain and the United States in recent years, and thus gained influence all over the region.
Among the book exhibitions directed primarily at the reading public, a recent event in Mexico,
Feria Metropolitana del Libro
(Metropolitan Book Fair)
c/o Cámara Nacional de la Industria
Editorial
Vallarta 21–30
MX México–4, D.F.
has attracted attention, because of its size and the participation of distributors of Spanish and Argentine books residing in Mexico. Together with strong national participation, this has made the exhibition a nearly complete presentation of recent book production in the Spanish language. It was founded in 1972 by the Mexican Chamber of the Publishing Industry and is to be held annually in Spring.

Other book fairs of regional character exist in countries like Costa Rica and the Dominican Republic.
There are a number of public book exhibitions in the countries of Latin America, mostly organized by government institutions, but none of them has reached professional circles beyond the borders of the country in which they have been held.

Bibliography

Memorias relativas a la Primera Exposición de
Editores Centroamericanos. (Memories of the First Exhibition of Central American Publishers.) San José, Comité Feria del Libro 1964. IX, 270 pp.

32 Literary Prizes

The leading international literary prizes include many Latin America authors (→BTW I, International Section 32). Literary awards have grown in Latin America as elsewhere. One of the few with an international reputation is the *Premio Internacional de Novela "Romulo Gallegos"* (International Novel Prize "Romulo Gallegos"), established in 1965 by the Venezuelan "National Institute of Culture and Fine Arts" and first awarded in 1967. The competition is open to any Latin American, Spanish or Philippine writer who has written in Spanish and published in one of the countries of the Spanish-speaking area. This literary prize will be awarded every five years.
Another important literary prize is the *Premio "Casa de América"*, awarded annually by the Cuban cultural institution "Casa de América". It is divided into sections for novels, poetry, short stories, essays and literary testimonies, each of them with a money prize of US $ 1,000. The jury is always formed by writers and experts from all Spanish-speaking Latin American countries and from Spain and sometimes has a member from outside the area.

Latin America

Among the latest international prizes in Latin America, the *Premio Internacional de Novela "Mexico"*, offered by the Mexican Writers' Association jointly with a Mexican publishing house, has won certain attention in Latin American literary circles. It is awarded with an amount of US $ 10,000 and a guarantee to publish the selected manuscript. This prize is awarded annually.

Another literary prize which will certainly have a good effect on the subcontinent is the *Premio de Literatura das Americas*, granted by the organizers of the Bienal Internacional do Livro, São Paulo, which is to be awarded every two years during the international book fair in Brazil (→ 29). It was first given in 1970 to the famous Argentine poet Jorge Luis Borges.

In Spain and Portugal (→BTW I, respective chapters, 32) there are a number of prizes open to writers from Latin America which have added momentum to Latin America's literary life.

33 The Reviewing of Books

In recent years and maybe as a consequence of the "boom of Latin American literature" in Europe and the United States of America, the international magazines inside and outside of these countries which carry book critiques (→BTW I, International Section 33) have reviewed more and more books by Latin American authors. This is particularly true of literary periodicals published in Spain, Portugal and the United States.

In Latin America there are a number of magazines distributed all over the subcontinent which many publishers use for sales promotion, especially of scientific books reviewed in specialized periodicals which present an international view of the development in their particular subjects. When referring to the importance of the imported book in Latin America (→27), it was mentioned that Latin American reviews are often distributed all over the region. So, when looking for periodicals which reach a large audience in Latin America, one should always study the information given in the respective national chapters–at least those covering the leading book countries of the region.

Nevertheless, a small number of publishing companies use reviews as sales promotion, and very few magazines regularly carry reviews. Those that do, prefer to review all the books of their language area rather than just those produced in their own country.

Bibliography

D. DE ABREU, *O Livro e a industria do conhecimiento*. (The book and the knowledge industry.) Rio de Janeiro, Bibliotecnia 1968. 48 pp.

J. E. ENGELKIRK, *La literatura y la revista literaria en Hispano-América*. (The literature and the literary magazines in Spanish America.) In: "Revista Iberoamericana", no. 27, July–December 1961. Pittsburgh, Pa., University of Pittsburgh 1961.

F. FEUEREISEN and E. SCHMACKE, *Die Presse in Lateinamerika*. Ein Handbuch für Wirtschaft und Werbung. (The press in Latin America. A handbook for commerce and publicity.) 2nd. ed. München, Verlag Dokumentation 1972. 330 pp.

Presente. Revista de Arte y Literatura de Centro América. (Presence. Magazine for Art and Literature of Central America.) Tegucigalpa, Imprenta la Democracia 1965 ff. Bi-monthly.

J. TORRE REVELLO, *El libro, la imprenta y el periodismo en América durante la Dominación Española*. (The book, printing and periodicals in America during Spanish domination.) Buenos Aires, Peuser 1940.

34 Graphic Arts

The graphic arts industry in Latin America confronts the problem of book production jointly with its publishers (→21). To cover the most urgent needs, many printers have not yet begun to concentrate on the production of high-quality books, but tend to aim at quantity. Even this target is in many cases difficult for them to reach, as the majority of the countries depend on the import of machinery as well as raw materials for their printing.

The graphic industry in Latin America is conscious of these problems, and its regional organization, the

> Confederación Latinoamericana de Industrias Gráficas
> (Latin American Confederation of Graphic Industries)
> U Montevideo

is engaged in the training of highly qualified personnel, another problem which is also felt by the publishers. In collaboration with the Centro Regional para el Fomento del Libro en América Latina (Regional Centre for Book Development in Latin America, →4), it has recently begun to try to resolve this problem by organizing courses with international participation in the

> Colegio Industrial de Artes Gráficas
> (Industrial College of Graphic Art)
> RB São Paulo

the best-equipped training institution for executive printers in Latin America.

The international typographical organizations (→BTW I, International Section 34) in many cases have American member states which try to use their growing influence within these organizations to draw world-wide attention to the situation in Latin America.

Bibliography

Documentos para la Historia de la Tipografía en América. (Documents for the History of Typography in America.) México, D.F., Secretaría de Relaciones Exteriores 1936. IX, 361 pp.

G. Furlong Cardiff, *Orígenes del arte tipográfico en América, especialmente en la República Argentina.* (Origins of the typographical arts in America, especially in the Argentine Republic.) Buenos Aires, Huarpes 1947. 225 pp.

E. Llorens, *La industria gráfica en Argentina.* (The graphic industry in Argentina.) Buenos Aires, C.I.G.A. n.d.

J. W. Mata Lopez, *Breve estudio contable de una industria de artes gráficas.* (Short study of accounting in an industrial company of graphic arts.) México, D.F., Escuela Superior de Comercio y Administración, Instituto Politécnico Nacional (thesis) 1963, 82 pp.

I. Silva A., *La imprenta en la América Española.* (Printing in Spanish America.) Santiago de Chile, La Tracción 1930. 40 pp.

I. Thomas, *The history of printing in America, with a biography of printers, and an account of newspapers.* 2nd ed. 2 vols. Albany, N.Y., 1874.

J. Torre Revello, *Orígenes de la imprenta en España y su desarrollo en América Española.* (Origins of printing in Spain and its development in Spanish America.) Edited by the "Instituto Cultural Español". Buenos Aires, Araujo 1940. XIII, 384 pp.

F. de Ugarteche, *Pequeña historia de la imprenta en América.* (Short history of Printing in America.) Buenos Aires, Imprenta López 1943. 35 pp.

R. H. Valle, *Incunables del Imperio Español.* (Incunabula of the Spanish Imperium.) In: "America", vol. 1 no. 7, October 1949, p. 36. Washington, D.C., Panamerican Union 1949.

→2: Bibliography.

Argentina

1 General Information

Area Mainland 2,779,741 km², Antartic Zone 1,230,000 km², South Atlantic Islands 17,823 km²

Population 23,304 (8.3 per km²)

Capital Buenos Aires (2,972,453); Greater Buenos Aires has a population of 8,352,900

Largest towns Buenos Aires (2,972,453); Córdoba (799,000; Greater Córdoba: 870,000), Rosario (790,000; Greater Rosario: 948,000); La Plata (408,000; Greater La Plata: 506,000), Tucumán (325,000); Mar del Plata (317,000); Santa Fe (312,000); Mendoza (118,000; Greater Mendoza 440,000)

Government Federal Republic, presidential system; comprising 22 provinces with local governments; a Federal District; and a federally administered area (territorio nacional) that includes Tierra del Fuego, the Antarctic Zone and the South Atlantic Islands

Religion Roman Catholic 88.6%. Smaller religious groups include 450,000 Jews; 300,000 Protestants

National language Spanish

Leading foreign languages English, Italian, French

Weights, measures Metric system

Currency unit Argentine Peso (argent $) = 100 centavos

Education Compulsory up to 7th grade. Statistics for 1970: 3,638,050 students, 193,312 teachers at primary level; 974,826 students, 132,271 teachers at secondary level; 236,515 students, 16,004 professors at university level. 10 state universities; a number of private universities and other institutes of technical and advanced studies

Illiteracy 9% (estimated)

Paper consumption a) Newsprint 11 kg per inhabitant

b) Printing paper (other than newsprint) 0.66 kg per inhabitant

Membership UNESCO; IPA; CERLAL

2 Past and Present

The Jesuit missionaries Juan Bautista Neumann (an Austrian) and José Serrano (a Spaniard) established in 1700 the first printing press in what is today the province of Misiones. The next printing press was set up in 1764 in the university founded by the Jesuits in the province of Córdoba. In 1766 this press issued its first book, *Laudationes*. It was later transferred to the "Casa de los niños expósitos" (House of foundlings) in Buenos Aires, where, between 1781 and 1795, it issued 583 works. In 1826 there were 5 bookstores and 4 printing presses in Buenos Aires. In the last century the names of Casavalle, Coni, Kraft, Peuser, Estrada, Lajouane and Igón stand out as the main forerunners of the publishing business, which began to develop in the early years of this century. In 1901 the newspaper "La Nación" set up the "Biblioteca La Nación", a collection of books which reached a total of 850 titles and represents the first attempt at mass marketing in Argentina. At the same time, the textbook industry was growing. But the publishing business gained its main impulse from the Spanish Civil War, which produced a crisis in the Spanish-speaking publishing world, leading to the independent growth of the industry in Argentina. Today Argentina has approximately 160 publishing houses and 1,500 bookstores, a large proportion of which are in Buenos Aires.

Bibliography

D. BUONOCORE, *Libreros, editores e impresores de Buenos Aires.* (Buenos Aires booksellers, publishers and printers.) Buenos Aires, Editorial El Ateneo 1944. 300 pp.

G. FURLONG, *Orígines del arte tipográfico en América.* (The origins of the art of typography in America.) Buenos Aires, Ed. Huarpes 1947. 225 pp.
Bibliography on pp. 215–25. Early printing history of Argentina: pp. 125–209.

E. A. GARCIA. *Desarrollo de la industria editorial argentina.* (Development of the Argentine publishing industry.) Buenos Aires, Fundación Interamericana de Bibliotecología Franklin 1965. 186 pp. pp. 177–179: Bibliography.

J. T. MEDINA, *Historia de la imprenta en los antiguos dominios españoles de América y Oceanía.* (The history of printing in the ancient Spanish dominions of America and Oceania.) 2 vols. Santiago de Chile, Fondo Histórico y Bibliográfico José Toribio Medina 1958. CXLI, 542; XV, 540 pp.
vol. II, pp. 327–442: Argentina (Buenos Aires).

L. S. THOMPSON, *Printing in Colonial Spanish America.* Hamden Conn., Archon Books 1962. 108 pp.
pp. 56–65: Argentina.

3 Retail Prices

Retail prices are established by publishers, and usually respected by booksellers. However, there is no legislation or official regulations to enforce this, only an unwritten agreement. On several occasions the government has fixed maximum prices and frozen margins of profit, specially for textbooks.

There is currently no law governing publishers' discounts to booksellers. In general the discounts amount to approximately 15%–20% for textbooks and 30% to 40% for trade books. Various wholesalers enjoy an additional 10% discount.

4 Organization

In Argentina there are a number of professional associations, independent of each other. The oldest is the

Cámara Argentina del Libro
(Argentine Book Chamber)

Argentina

Paraguay 610, 7°
RA Buenos Aires
(→8).
The main Argentine publishing houses are represented in this association, as well as importers, wholesalers and booksellers. Other institutions are:
Cámara Argentina de Editores de Libros
(Argentine Chamber of Book Publishers)
Maipú 359, 2°, of. 31
RA Buenos Aires
and
Cámara Argentina de Publicaciones
(Argentine Chamber of Publications)
Florida 259, 2°, of. 224
RA Buenos Aires
This latter institution represents not only importers, wholesalers and booksellers, but also publishers and importers of magazines.
Cámara Española de Comercio–Sector Libros
(Spanish Chamber of Commerce–Book Section)
Av. Belgrano 863, 8°
RA Buenos Aires
which represents only importers of Spanish books.
Federación Argentina de Libreros
(Argentine Federation of Booksellers)
which represents many, but not all, Argentine booksellers.
All these institutions are strictly professional organizations, devoted to promoting the interests of their members. Their decisions are not legally binding. They publish only internal bulletins.

5 Trade Press

The monthly
Fichero Bibliográfico Hispanoamericano
(Hispano-American Bibliographical File)
Chile 1441, piso 1°, of. 3
RA Buenos Aires
includes articles, information, bibliographies and advertisements concerning Argentina (→Latin America 5).

The
Biblioteca Nacional
(National Library)
México 564
RA Buenos Aires
publishes a sporadic bulletin (→15).
One other publication devoted to the book trade is:
Los Libros
(Books)
Tucumán 1427, 2°, of. 207
RA Buenos Aires

6 Book-Trade Literature

N. MATIJEVIC, *Bibliografía bibliotecológica argentina.* Bahia Blanca, Universidad Nacional del Sur, Centro de Documentación Bibliotecológica 1969. XII, 354 pp. Lists 2,538 publications on librarianship, documentation and bibliographical theory and practice.
→2, 16, 21, 24.

7 Sources of Information, Address Services

The main sources of information are the professional associations (→4). General information can also be obtained from
Bowker Editores Argentina S.A.
Salta 596, P. 69
RA Buenos Aires
The addresses of all branches of the book trade are contained in
La Empresa del Libro en América Latina. (The Book in Latin America.) 2nd ed. Buenos Aires, Bowker Editores Argentina 1974. VIII, 306 pp.
pp. 1–86: Argentina.

8 International Membership

The *Cámara Argentina del Libro* (→4) belongs to the International Publishers' Association (IPA; →BTW I, International Section 4). Argentina is a member of UNESCO and of CERLAL (→Latin America 4).

9 Market Research

There is no organization specifically devoted to book-market research in Argentina. General information can be obtained from the professional associations (→4).
Centro Interamericano de Promoción
de Exportaciones
Apartado aereo 5609 CO Bogotá, Colombia
may also be consulted. The C.I.P.E. is an official dependency of the Organization of American States.

10 Books and Young People

The
Comité de Asesoramiento y Promoción para
la Literatura infantil y juvenil
(Advisory Committee for the Promotion of
Children's and Young People's Literature)
Yerbal 51
RA Buenos Aires
gives free advice on this subject and promotes the cause of good literature by means of lectures and exhibitions.

11 Training

Professional training for booksellers or publishers does not exist in Argentina.

12 Taxes

In Argentina books are exempt from import and export taxes. The book-export business enjoys a number of promotional benefits granted by the state.
The local book trade is subject to the normal taxation applied to all business.
Exports are granted a 30% refund on the F.O.B. value of the invoice, which is made effective when payment is made.

13 Clearing Houses

There is no general clearing house in Argentina. The *Cámara de Comercio Española*

–Sector Libros (→4) runs its own clearing house, exclusively for its members.

14 Copyright

Intellectual property in Argentina is protected by a copyright law (Law No. 11.723) passed in 1933 and later amended. It requires all works to be copyrighted and establishes contract terms and the relations between publishers and authors. Property rights remain in the hands of the author's heirs up to 50 years after his death.
Argentina subscribes to the Geneva Convention; the Berne Convention; the Montevideo Convention; the Buenos Aires Convention; the Washington Convention (→BTW I, International Section 14).

15 National Bibliography, National Library

The annual bulletin *Boletín Bibliográfico Nacional* is edited by the
Biblioteca Nacional
(National Library)
México 564
RA Buenos Aires
as a national bibliography. The volumes for the last years are still in course of preparation.

Bibliography

P. AVICENNE, *Bibliographical services throughout the world 1965–69.* Paris, UNESCO 1972. 310 pp.
pp. 43–48: Argentina.
I. ZIMMERMANN, *Current national bibliographies of Latin America.* Gainesville, Florida, University of Florida Press 1971. X, 139 pp.
pp. 18–24: Argentina.

16 Book Production

Total book production for the year 1971 amounted to 4,634 titles (of over 49 pages). The breakdown is as follows:

Argentina

Subject group	Titles
Philosophy and psychology	184
Physics, chemistry, mathematics	94
History, biography	245
Natural and biological sciences	37
Political science and law	370
Applied sciences and technology	346
Geography, cartography, travels	266
Dictionaries	139
Textbooks	408
General non-fiction	345
Religion and theology	123
Medicine and public health	147
Fiction	632
Children's books	115
Poetry, theatre, radio, TV (includes radio & TV drama)	893
Sociology	70
Art books and books on art	47
Education	175

These 4,634 titles were printed in 29,281,228 copies.

Bibliography

The most complete statistical information, up to 1968, appears in the booklet *Cifras estadísticas del libro* (Book statistics), issued by the *Cámara Argentina del Libro* (→4), which also puts out an important *Annual Report*.

17 Translations

UNESCO's "Statistical Yearbook" (1971 edition) shows the main tendencies in translation in Argentina for 1967 as follows: Literature: 40%; Social sciences: 46%; Pure and applied sciences: 14%.
According to the same source, translations amounted to 10.4% of Argentine book production for that year, the languages of origin being:

English	48%
Russian	2%
French	18%
German	13%
Other languages	19%

19 Paperbacks

Soft-cover books (including regular paperbacks as well as pocket books) are the rule, rather than the exception, in Argentina. A successful attempt has been made to sell books in news-stands as well as bookstores. Unfortunately no statistics are available for this activity.

20 Book Design

Until 1971 there was a yearly prize for the "best-made" books, awarded by the now extinct Franklin Interamerican Foundation of Bibliotecology. No prize for design exists at present.

21 Publishing

No complete record of publishing houses is available. Their number is estimated at 160. With very few exceptions they are all located in Buenos Aires. Estimated sales figures compiled by the *Cámara Argentina del Libro* (→4) for the year 1969 amount to 110,000,000 new pesos. According to another estimate of the same institution, the total number of people employed by the publishing business in 1961 was 12,633, dividing as follows
4,341 in publishing houses
1,540 in book import houses
240 in wholesale firms
6,510 in bookstores
Although no recent statistics are available, it can be reasonably estimated that these figures have gone up at least by 30% today.

Bibliography

The basic reference work is
E. A. GARCIA, *Desarrollo de la industria editorial argentina.* (Development of the Argentine publishing industry.) Buenos Aires, Fundación Interamericana de Bibliotecología Franklin 1965. 186 pp.

Another important source of information is R. H. BOTTARO, *La edición de libros en la Argentina*. (Book publishing in Argentina.) Buenos Aires, Editorial Troquel 1964. 103 pp.

22 Literary Agents

In general, literary agents in Argentina represent foreign book rights. Local authors normally either deal directly with foreign publishers, or are represented abroad by their local publishers.

23 Wholesale Trade

The wholesale trade is highly developed in Argentina. A widespread market, involving large distances, and the great number of imported books, favour the growth of big wholesalers centred in Buenos Aires. Most wholesalers represent a considerable number of local and foreign publishers. Many specialize in one particular branch of distribution, such as textbooks, technical works or foreign-language books.

24 Retail Trade

The main retailer is the bookseller. In recent years, however, news-stand sales have been on the increase. Bookstores are widespread all over the country, but the largest concentrations are to be found in cities with big universities.
The information to be gathered from "La empresa del libro en América Latina" (→7) indicates the following number of bookstores in the main cities of Argentina. However, an estimate advanced by professionals indicates at least double the number.
Some 200 bookstores are supposed to operate in the Province of Buenos Aires alone, in the sense of places where books are sold, though they are not necessarily specialized stores.

Buenos Aires	132
Prov. Buenos Aires	56
Catamarca	2
Córdoba	17
Corrientes	4
Chaco	3
Chubut	3
Entre Rios	7
Formosa	1
Jujuy	1
La Pampa	1
La Riojá	2
Mendoza	11
Misiones	5
Rio Negro	2
Salta	5
San Juan	3
San Luis	1
Santa Fe	20
Santa Cruz	1
Santiago del Estero	2
Tucumán	7

Bibliography

La Empresa del Libro en América Latina. Buenos Aires, Bowker Editores-Argentina (→7).
A. PUIGVERT: *Mercados del libro: Argentina.* (Book markets, Argentina.) Madrid, The Author 1967.

26 Antiquarian Book Trade, Auctions

Antiquarian booksellers in Argentina are grouped in the
Asociación de Libreros anticuarios de la Argentina (Antiquarian Booksellers of Argentina)
Defensa 1170
RA Buenos Aires
The "Asociación" has 25 members.
There is also the
Sociedad Argentina de Bibliófilos
Juncal 922, 10°
RA Buenos Aires
which, among other things, issues special editions for its members.
There are a number of *bouquinistes* and second-hand bookstores of little commercial importance.

Argentina

27 Book Imports

Book imports are not subject to duties. No import permit is required. There are two parallel exchange rates in Argentina, the "financial" exchange rate and the "commercial" exchange rate. Book imports come under the "financial" exchange rate, which quotes the peso higher (in relation to the dollar) than the commercial exchange rate. In 1970 books were imported worth 15 to 20 million US Dollars. The sources of imported books are mainly (1970):

Country	%
Spain	41.6
USA	25.5
Mexico	8.5
United Kingdom	4.9
France	3.9
Panama	3.1
Brazil	2.9
Italy	2.1

Periodical imports in 1970: US $ 1,676,839. Leading countries of origin:

Country	%
Spain	31.1
Italy	21.1
USA	15.2
Germany (F.R.)	12.8

Since November 1972 a special permit has to be obtained from the Ministry of Commerce, previous to any import.

28 Book Exports

In 1970, 19,354,414 books were exported, worth approximately US$ 12,455,300. The main buying markets were Chile, Spain, Uruguay, Mexico and Peru. Argentina's natural market, however, covers all of Latin America. The state promotes exports with various subsidies (→12).

According to the "Economic Report–Fourth Quarter of 1972", published by the Ministry of Finance (Buenos Aires, 96 pp.), book exports through customs during 1971 covered 14,647,135 copies, worth US$ 11,147,843. Besides that figure, it is estimated that another 5,634,000 copies were sent out of the country by registered mail. The same report for the previous year, 1970, gives the following figures: US $ 6,817,000.

Periodical exports were valued at US $ 2,310,435 in 1970. Leading countries of destination:

Country	%
Uruguay	46.0
Chile	12.2
Paraguay	8.6
Peru	8.3
Brazil	6.5
Bolivia	4.7
Mexico	4.1

29 Book Fairs

Occasionally book fairs and exhibits have been organized in Argentina. None, however, is held regularly.

30 Public Relations

There is no organization specifically devoted to promoting relations between the book trade and the public.

31 Bibliophily
→26.

32 Literary Prizes

There are a number of official prizes in Argentina. The best known are the *Premio Nacional de Literatura* (National Literary Prize) and the *Premio municipal de Literatura de la Ciudad de Buenos Aires* (Buenos Aires Municipal Literary Prize). Various publishers, magazines and newspapers have also on occasion established literary awards, mostly of short duration. At present the main ones are the *Premio Literario "La Nación"* (awarded by the newspaper "La Nación") and the *Premio Emecé* (awarded by the Emecé Publishing House).

The *Fondo Nacional de las Artes* (National Arts Foundation) also makes important awards to established authors and encouragement prizes to new authors. There is also the *Carlos Casavalle Award*, given biennially to the most outstanding publishers in the various fields of literature, science, etc.

33 The Reviewing of Books

Most Argentine magazines and newspapers include a literary section. The main literary sections in magazines and newspapers of national circulation are those of the newspapers "La Nación", "La Prensa", "La Opinión", and "El Clarín" and the magazines "Panorama", "Primera Plana", "Análisis" and "Confirmado".

34 Graphic Arts

The graphic societies of Argentina are grouped in the
> *Confederación de Industriales Gráficos*
> *de la Argentina*
> *(Confederation of the Graphic Industries*
> *of Argentina)*
> *Av. San Juan 1340*
> *RA Buenos Aires*

35 Miscellaneous

a) Authors
The most representative organization uniting Argentine authors is the
> *Sociedad Argentina de Escritores (SADE)*
> *(Argentine Society of Authors)*
> *México 524*
> *RA Buenos Aires*
There is also a chapter of the PEN Club International.

Bahama Islands

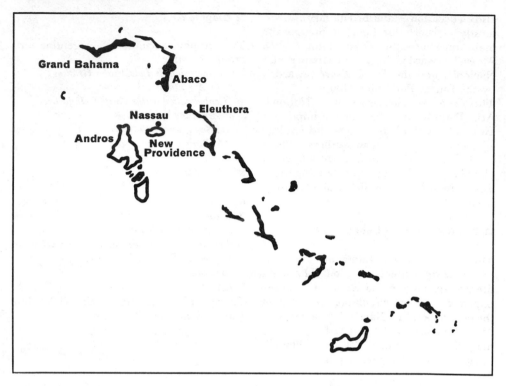

1 General Information

Area 9,149 km²

Population 190,000 (1974; 20.8 per km²)

Capital Nassau (on New Providence Island; 101,000); the main islands (700 islands all in all) are: New Providence (101,000); Grand Bahama (26,000); Eleuthera (9,500); Andros (9,000); Abaco (7,000)

Government The Islands are an independent member of the British Commonwealth. A bicameral Parliament has responsibility over the Cabinet

Religion The largest denominations are the Baptists, Roman Catholics and Anglicans

National language English

Weights, measures British Imperial System

Currency unit Bahamian dollar (B$) = 100 cents

Education 319 government schools with 41,668 pupils (1969); 70 private schools with 10,789 pupils (1969); 520 university students

Paper consumption a) Newsprint 5.4 kg per inhabitant (1971)
b) Printing paper (other than newsprint) 3.0 kg per inhabitant (1971)

2 Past and Present

The Bahamas, a chain of 700 islands, were discovered by Christopher Columbus in 1492, and became part of the Spanish Dominion. After British settlements in the second part of the 17th century Britain finally took the islands under the control of the Crown in 1717. Independence came in 1973.

Tourism accounts for 70% of gross national product and 50% of government revenue. Printing was introduced in 1783 by John Wells who came from Charleston, South Carolina and published *The Royal Bahama Gazette* in Nassau.

Bibliography

BR. F. SWAN, *The spread of printing, Western Hemisphere: The Caribbean area.* Amsterdam, Vangendt 1970. 47 pp.
   p. 26: Bahamas.

3 Retail Prices

Most of the books available in the Islands are imported. They are priced up according to the special overheads involved. School books are delivered at published prices.

5 Trade Press

Because of the close connections with the publishing and bookselling world of the United Kingdom, and lacking a national book-trade journal the
   Bookseller
   13 Bedford Square
   GB London W.C. I
is widely used, together with
   Publishers' Weekly
   1180 Avenue of the Americas
   USA New York, N.Y. 10036

6 Book-Trade Literature

→BTW I, United Kingdom 6; BTW II, USA 6.

7 Sources of Information, Address Services

Information may be obtained from
   Bahamas Chamber of Commerce
   P.O.B. N-665
   BS Nassau

21 Publishing

One publishing house (Etienne Dupuch Jr. Publications Ltd, P.O.B. N–7513, Nassau) is building up an educational book series.

27 Book Imports

In 1970 the Bahama Islands imported books and pamphlets at the value of US$ 1,130,000. Main suppliers were:

Country	US$
United Kingdom	644,000
USA	464,000

28 Book Exports

The export of "printed matter" reached the value of US$ 37,000 (1970) with US$ 29,000 for the United Kingdom.

Barbados

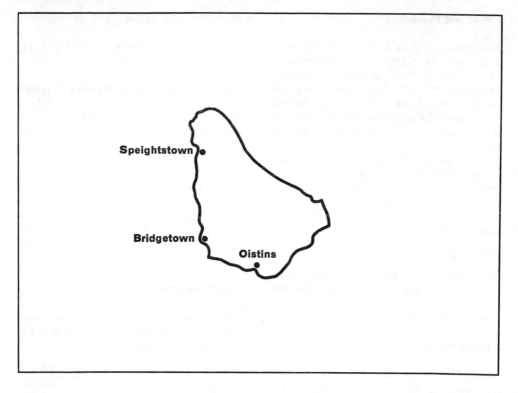

1 General Information

Area 424 km²
Population 240,000 (566 per km²)
Capital Bridgetown (12,000)
Largest towns Bridgetown (12,000), Speightstown (ca. 2,000); Oistins (ca. 2,000)
Government Independent nation since 1966 (formerly a British colony)
  Currently a member nation of the British Commonwealth with a Governor General representing the Queen of Great Britain; a bi-cameral legislature consisting of an elected body, the Senate
Religion Anglicans 134,000; Roman Catholics 6,500; Methodists, Moravians, Non-Conformists approx. 50,000
National language English
Leading foreign languages French and Spanish (but neither to any great extent; spoken only to accommodate the needs of the tourist trade)
Weights, measures British Imperial System: but

US measures are used at petrol stations. Proposals for conversion to the metric system are under discussion
Currency unit Barbados Dollar (BDS $) introduced in November 1973 has parity with U. K. sterling. $ 1.00 BDS equals approximately US 0.50 cents
Education Compulsory education is not statutory. However, school records show a very high percentage of the school-age population attending school regularly between ages 5 to 14 plus.– Free university is available to nationals at the Cave Hill Campus of the University of the West Indies–which in October 1973 had a registration of 660 full-time and 221 part-time students
Illiteracy Nil
Paper consumption a) Newsprint about 3.7 kg per inhabitant (1971)
  b) Printing paper (other than newsprint) 23.06 kg per inhabitant (1971)
Membership UNESCO

2 Past and Present

Barbados is believed to owe its discovery and its name to the Portuguese some time during the 16th century. The island was, however, claimed for England in 1625 and settled by the English in 1627. More than three hundred years under English rule elapsed until the island achieved nationhood on 30 November 1966. English life and customs prevailed, the entire social and industrial pattern being imitative of, or subservient to those current in Britain. David Harry, a printer from Philadelphia, is credited with the establishment of a printing press in Barbados round about 1730. The New York Public Library possesses Issue No. 120 of the *Barbados Gazette* 14–18 April 1733, which is considered to be the earliest extant piece of printing done in the island.

The vast majority of all local commercial publishing in fact comprised newspapers. The book trade as such has been nurtured and sustained on books and periodicals imported from Great Britain. The earliest firm in the business seems to have been Bowen & Sons, started in Bridgetown in 1837. The description of their bookstock –"books of every description and cheap paper-cover editions to volumes handsomely and strongly bound"–applies with equal force to the modern bookstores in Barbados. These are four in number, sited in the capital, Bridgetown (two have branch outlets in the smaller towns and in the suburbs). These book dealers import the substantial quantities of textbooks for schools and educational institutions, as well as the general publications for sale to libraries and the general public.

Bibliography

A. E. GROPP, *Guide to libraries and archives in Central America and the West Indies*. New Orleans, Middle American Institute, Tulane University of Louisiana 1941.

The Red Book of the West Indies. London, Collingridge 1922.

BR. F. SWAN, *The spread of printing, Western Hemisphere: The Caribbean area*. Amsterdam, Vangendt 1970. 47 pp. pp. 17–18: Barbados.

3 Retail Prices

Retail price in Barbados has always been governed by the fact that almost all the books come in from overseas. There is no retail-price agreement among booksellers in Barbados. Each bookseller tends to act independently, relating mark-up to the purchase price paid to suppliers in the metropolitan countries of the United Kingdom, the United States of America and Canada. Textbooks tend to be surcharged with a 25% mark-up on the publisher's price. On United Kingdom paperbacks, subject to discounts varying from 50% to 33% off the publisher's price, the mark-up to customers ranges from 10% to 16%. Sales to the Public Library services are normally at a discount of 10% off the net published price. Local government publications are sold at the published price.

4 Organization

No booksellers' association exists at present, an effort to form one some years ago having failed.

5 Trade Press   6 Book-Trade Literature

Specific material on these two topics (5 and 6) in so far as they concern Barbados certainly does not emanate from any local source. It is possible that an occasional article in a British or American magazine may treat the local book-trade scene. Otherwise the trade is entirely dependent on the British and American trade press for information in regard to their stock in trade.

Barbados

7 Sources of Information, Address Services

As indicated in →2 and other foregoing chapters, the Barbados book trade
is import-oriented; only government
publications and newspapers are produced
in substantial quantities in the country.
Sources of information concerning the
major section of the Barbados book trade
must be identical with those of the countries from which the books are imported,
viz. the UK, the USA, and Canada. With
regard to the trickle of sociological, historical and kindred works as well as the small
literary magazines recently issuing from
the University of the West Indies and
the territories of the English-speaking
Caribbean, information may be obtained
from:
> Cave Hill Campus
> University of the West Indies
> Cave Hill
> BDS St Michael

> Public Library
> Coleridge Street
> BDS Bridgetown 2

Questions concerning Barbados Government publications are best addressed to:
> Government Information Service
> Government Headquarters
> Bay Street
> BDS Bridgetown
Bookselling queries may be directed to:
> Cloister Bookstore
> Hincks Street
> BDS Bridgetown

8 International Membership

Barbados is a member of UNESCO. The
Ministry of Education is the coordinating
agent for the country's relations with this
international body and has set up as its
advisory arm the Barbados National
Commission for UNESCO.

9 Market Research

This aspect of the book trade has not so far
received formal attention.

10 Books and Young People

Librarians, teachers, and educationists
have throughout the history of Barbados
studiously discharged their responsibility
to the young
1. by selecting and providing appropriate
books for their information, education and
entertainment;
2. by furnishing suitable reading lists;
3. by frequent exhibitions of special
children's and young people's collections in
public libraries;
4. by the operation of special public
library services to children and young
people;
5. by the establishment of school libraries.

11 Training

The absence of formal training may be
attributed to the nature of the book trade
in Barbados. All the bookshops have been
family businesses; only in very recent years
has expansion begun to appear. Hitherto
training has taken the form of apprenticeship. No local facilities exist for theoretical
study of the book trade as a career.

12 Taxes

The book trade in Barbados is subject to
the usual taxes payable by other commercial and industrial enterprises. However,
there is no customs duties levied on imported printed material, and when one
bears in mind the fact that the bulk of the
stock-in-trade of booksellers is imported, it
is clear that some advantage accrues to the
trade as a result. Trade tax and income
tax would be the taxes payable.

13 Clearing Houses

No central agency exists. The individual book dealers make their separate arrangements for account settlement.

14 Copyright

Barbados has no copyright law of its own governing book authorship. There has been no formal accession to the Berne Convention or the International Copyright Convention (→ BTW I, International Section 14). It is assumed that the provisions of the Copyright Act of Great Britain applicable to Barbados prior to its independence in 1966 are still being honoured.
→ 15.

15 National Bibliography, National Library

As at the date of this statement, a national bibliography as a separate entity is not extant. However, throughout the past seven years, the Barbados Public Library (→ 7) has been issuing a quarterly accessions list of West Indian material catalogued in its Reference Department. These lists, entitled *West Indian Collection. Additions* contain all items of Barbadiana either received in compliance with the Copyright (Amendment) Act 1956 or acquired by purchase in the case of overseas publications. Full bibliographical details are recorded up to the point of collation. The Public Library in a joint enterprise with the Library Association of Barbados is currently taking steps to produce a national bibliography per se. The
Public Library
Coleridge Street
BDS Bridgetown 2
was established in 1847 by an act of the legislature. Two particular statutes, viz. the Registration of Newspapers Act 1900; and the Copyright (Amendment) Act 1956, invest the Public Library with the responsibility of preserving for posterity all newspapers and all other publications as defined in the Act. The onus for observing the legal deposit law lies with the editor/publisher of the newspaper or the author of the book, print or other publication, as the case may be.

The Public Library is a government department, falling within the portfolio of the Minister of Education, Youth Affairs, Community Development and Sport. It serves the nation by means of the main library in the capital; and a network of seven branch libraries and of centres in the main hospital, and in the prison and children's reform schools, as well as by means of mobile services to some twenty-five rural sites and some sixty primary schools. The Public Library is the instrument by which the national Government translates into reality its policy for library development within the nation, and the advisory body engaged in drafting proposals for the shaping of the aforesaid national library policy. The Public Library also furnishes the Ministry of Education with the data for dispatch to international organizations, such as UNESCO, in response to queries directed to the Government of Barbados on books and related matters.

Bibliography

P. AVICENNE, *Bibliographical services throughout the world 1965–69*. Paris, UNESCO 1972. 310 pp.
pp. 60–62: Barbados.

16 Book Production

Records available in the Public Library indicated that a total of 205 items were received during 1973. These represent publications deposited in compliance with the legal deposit requirements. According to UNESCO specifications, 20 of the items would classify as books, the remaining 185 as pamphlets. Government publications comprise by far the greater portion of this total production.

17 Translations

There is no record of translations having been produced.

18 Book Clubs

Book clubs in the normal connotation of the term are not a part of the book trade in Barbados. Owing to the very restricted publishing situation (→2) Barbadians have tended to make use (on an individual membership basis) of foreign-based clubs, such as the Book of the Month Club (USA).
Of particular significance to the history of public-library development in this country has been the contribution of two book clubs which flourished during the first decades of the 19th century. These were the Literary Society and the Library Association of Barbados, which, on the establishment of the Public Library in 1847, donated their book collections, thereby repairing the comission of the Public Library Act to make financial provision for acquiring book stock for the new library.

19 Paperbacks

These comprise a moderate proportion of the importation by the booksellers, and are available for purchase not only at bookshops proper, but also at supermarkets, pharmacies, and other retail outlets.

21 Publishing

As indicated (→2), only very limited publishing takes place in Barbados. The material produced consists almost entirely of the following items:
a) Newspapers (one daily and four weekly),
b) Periodicals,
c) Government publications, the vast majority being official gazettes and departmental reports,
d) Newsletters, reports, etc. issued by the private sector.
The publishing houses producing these items number eight; four concerned mainly with newspapers and one being the Government Printer. They are all situated in the capital, Bridgetown, or just on the outskirts.

22 Literary Agents

The occasion for the use of literary agents does not arise. Local authors of creative works of substance or other major works invariably have them published either in the UK or the USA and make their own direct arrangements with their publishers. Some scholarly publications are put out by the University of the West Indies.

23 Wholesale Trade

Instances of wholesale trade are confined to paperbacks only, which one or two established booksellers import for bulk sale to small retail outlets in pharmacies, supermarkets, hotel lobbies, boutiques, and the like.

24 Retail Trade

Four commercial bookshops serve the island community. One of the four also does some business with Montserrat. The University of the West Indies, Cave Hill Campus, is a source for some UWI publications. Government publications, which comprise a very significant portion of the local book output, are obtainable from the Government Information Office, sales booth.
A wide range of publications on a wide variety of subjects is stocked by the commercial bookshops, whose supplies are al-

most entirely imported. The table shows categories and value of the book imports handled by them during the year 1971. The source of information is the publication *Government of Barbados. Statistical Service. Overseas Trade.* Barbados, Government Printing Office 1973.

Category	BDS $
Printed books, pamphlets	999,396
Children's picture etc. books	3,504
Maps, charts, globes, etc.	22,946
Newspapers, periodicals	138,982

27 Book Imports

The story of the local book trade is virtually identical with that of book imports, since booksellers obtain almost all of their merchandise from overseas. Extracts from statistics for the year 1971 present a picture of predominant importation from the UK, with the USA and Canada featuring heavily, but very far behind the UK. Only in the case of newspapers and periodicals do we find one West Indian territory, viz. Trinidad and Tobago, heading the import table, and only in terms of items supplied, not of value.

Category	Country	Value (BDS $)	Percentage
Printed books, pamphlets	UK	655,419	65.6
	Canada	42,286	4.2
	USA	254,171	25.4
	Trinidad and Tobago	10,557	1.1
Newspapers, periodicals	UK	60,427	43.5
	Canada	5,292	3.8
	USA	24,179	17.4
	Trinidad and Tobago	44,294	31.9

In the case of printed books, the imports came from 28 countries. Twelve of these were English-speaking; the others showed a representation of the following languages: German, French, Spanish, Dutch, Italian, Japanese and the Scandinavian languages. Books are free of customs duty in keeping with government policy not to tax educational material.
→2, 3.

28 Book Exports

For 1971, exports of books and pamphlets were valued at 29,640 BDS $. 16.3 % of these went to the UK, Canada and the USA. The remaining 83.7 % was distributed among 15 Caribbean countries, with Antigua and the Netherlands Antilles taking 19.5 % and 18.9 % respectively. For the same calendar year, newspapers and periodicals exports brought in the sum of 39,095 BDS $. The vast majority of the trade was again regional; 96.3 % was divided among 9 countries, with Antigua 24.2 %, St Lucia 18.1 % and St Kitts 15.9 %. The extra-Caribbean countries receiving the total 3.7 % export were Canada and the USA.

29 Book Fairs

Book fairs do not constitute a feature of the book trade in Barbados. The closest approximation to these are the occasional exhibitions, designed to promote the reading habit, or to celebrate some special event. These are usually the work of the Public Library. The last major one was staged during International Book Year 1972, when successful efforts were made to mobilize librarians, booksellers and educationists into an enterprise on a national scale.

30 Public Relations

There is no organized activity in this field.

31 Bibliophily

No associations furthering the interest of book lovers exist.

Barbados

33 The Reviewing of Books

Three media, viz., the radio, the press and magazines, carry reviews of books from time to time. The Public Library (→7) formerly broadcast on radio a monthly programme of book reviews, or informal book talks. It is proposed to resume this exercise as soon as circumstances permit.

Of particular importance are the book reviews published in the twice-yearly literary magazine, BIM, which has played the role of mentor to all the West Indian writers who have achieved distinction from about 1940 onwards.

Belize (formerly British Honduras)

1 General Information

Area 229,963 km²

Population 140,000 (multiracial; 0.6 per km²)

Capital Belmopan (3,000)

Largest Towns Belize City (former capital and largest city, 42,000); El Cayo (16,484); Stann Creek (13,435)

Government A Colony with internal Self-Government through a two-chamber legislature with a ministerial system and cabinet responsibility

Religion Anglican, Baha'i, Baptist, Church of the Nazarene, Church of Scotland, Methodist, Roman Catholic, Salvation Army, Seventh Day Adventists

Language English

Leading foreign languages Spanish is spoken by 50 % of the population. A form of 'Creole' is spoken, the Mennonites speak German and Caribs and Mays Indians speak a number of dialects related to the Arawaks and Mayas

Weights measures British Imperial System. For petrol and paraffin the US gallon is used

Currency unit The monetary unit is the Belizean Dollar comprising 100 cents. The exchange rate is BH$4.00 to the £ Sterling

Education Elementary education is compulsory from 6–14. At 182 Elementary Schools (including one each for the physically and mentally handicapped) there are 33,000 pupils. At the 19 Secondary Schools there are 5,200 students. Provision also includes a Junior Secondary School, a Technical College with day, evening and part-time programmes, a Vocational Training Centre and a Teacher Training College. There are 3 Secondary schools offering courses for the General Certificate of Education Advanced Level examinations.

Illiteracy 5 %

51

Belize

2 Past und Present

Belize (formerly British Honduras) was once part of the Maya Empire although few Mayas or their descendants can now be traced. The multiracial population has been influenced by English and Scottish settlers (who became woodcutters) and by descendants of African slaves. Alternately owned by Spain and Britain, more recently the existing boundary has been contested by the neighbouring country of Guatemala. This has been finally rejected by Belizeans. The population is now predominantly Creole, Mestizos and of East Indian and African descent.

The former capital, Belize, is known today as Belize City and is the main port. The new capital, Belmopan, has been built (between 1967 and 1970), with British aid, 50 miles inland in the Cayo area. The old capital had been destroyed by hurricane in 1931 and severely damaged in 1961 by hurricane and resultant high floods.

In 1963 a National Economic Development Council was established as an advisory body to Government in the development and welfare of the country. It has been agreed that a policy of planned immigration is needed to provide more rapid population growth for the economic development of Belize.

To reduce the dependence of the economy on seasonal work or work requiring movement about the country:

a) development in plantation agriculture is being encouraged which will bring about more settled localities in rural areas

b) the Development Incentive Ordinance was created in 1960 with a view to encouraging the diversifying of industries and the manufacture of consumer items.

Tourism, with its supporting industries, is also being encouraged for the same purpose.

3 Retail Prices

Discounts are offered to libraries. Book prices are on the increase. No formal organization exists but booksellers keep in touch with each other.

7 Sources of Information, Address Services

The
Public Library
P.O. Box 287
Belize City
The Government Information Service established in 1962 prepares brochures and leaflets about the country and distributes a weekly newsletter. It also maintains a Photograph Collection and supplies photographs to newspapers and travel agencies.

10 Books and Young People

There are few local publications. The Library Services pay attention using imported books in Spanish and English.

11 Training

The Public Library (→4) conducts an annual course for library personnel which booksellers may attend.

12 Taxes

Duties are low; there is an entry tax only.

14 Copyright

The British Copyright Law is effective. Discussions on Copyright are now being held (→BTW I, International Section 14).

15 National Bibliography, National Library

The Central Library maintains a National Collection and prints a Bibliography of Belizean materials which is offered for sale.

24 Retail Trade

12 bookshops are reported.

29 Book Fairs

One book fair has been held.

30 Public Relations

Book promotional programmes have been arranged via the radio and by displays.

32 Literary Prizes

Awards have been made at annual National Day celebrations and on other occasions.

33 The Reviewing of Books

Book reviews are published in *National Studies, Journal of Belizean Affairs* and occasionally in the local press.

35 Miscellaneous

a) *Libraries*
The public library has seventy seven service points. There are private and school libraries. Libraries are well used. Belizeans are a reading population and the reading level is high.

b) *Radio*
Radio Belize broadcasts in Spanish and English.

c) *Newspapers and Magazines*
Belize Billboard
(P.O. Box 361 Belize City)
Belize Times
(P.O. Box 506 Belize City)
The Becon
(16 Church Street Belize City)
The Reporter
(63 Cemetery Road Belize City).

Bermuda

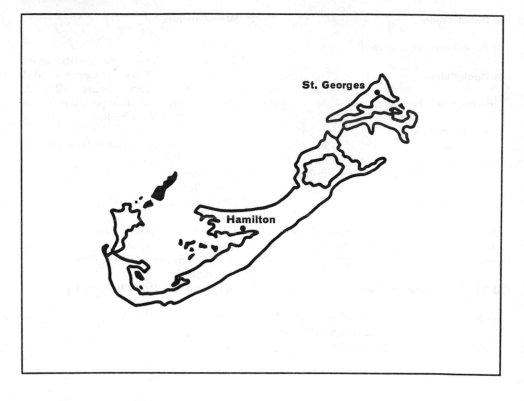

1 General Information

Area 53 km²
Population 52,000 (961 per km²)
Capital Hamilton (3,000)
Largest towns Hamilton (3,000), St. Georges (1,355)
Government British self-governing colony
Religion Anglicans 22,000; Methodists 6,000; Roman Catholics 5,500
National language English
Leading foreign languages French, Spanish
Weights, measures British (United States fluid measures are used)

Currency unit Bermuda Dollar ($ Bda) = 100 cents
Education Compulsory between 5 and 16 years. No university-level institutes (3,914 students–1966 –in 2nd-level schools)
Paper consumption a) Newsprint 13.7 kg per inhabitant (1967)
b) Printing paper (other than newsprint) 13.3 kg per inhabitant (1967)
Membership UNESCO

2 Past and Present

After the discovery of Bermuda by Juan de Bermudéz in 1522, this archipelago of about 360 small islands, about 950 km east of North Carolina, was settled up to 1612 by an offshoot of the Virgin Company. It became a British Crown Colony in 1684, receiving its first Prime Minister and a new constitution with almost full autonomy in 1968.

Book life began on Bermuda around 1783 with the arrival from Britain of printers who installed their small plants on the islands; it was only about a hundred years later, c. 1850, that independent bookselling started with the establishment of the first bookshop. However, in publishing as well as in book distribution, Bermuda islanders depended nearly exclusively on influences and shipments from the United Kingdom during early colonial times. Four publishers and five booksellers work on the islands, concentrated in Hamilton, the capital on the main island of the archipelago, Great Bermuda.

To day Bermuda traffics chiefly with the closer-by USA, and with Canada, the former the main supplier of books and magazines with nearly half of Bermuda's imports–while a fifth of the islands' international book trade is with the European homeland. Local publishing, on the other hand, is relatively small, so the trade still depends almost totally on the import of books. It is a book trade with high professional standards, serving a population with well-developed reading habits.

Bibliography

BR. F. SWAN, *The spread of printing, Western Hemisphere:* The Caribbean area. Amsterdam, Vangendt 1970. 47 pp. p. 26: Bermuda.

3 Retail Prices

Pricing policies on Bermuda are absolutely free, and only government publications have legally fixed prices. To calculate the sales price of imported books, the local bookshops follow international practice, charging a small percentage for the handling of imports and international accounts.

5 Trade Press

Professional reviews are nearly all of British origin (→BTW I, United Kingdom 5). Sometimes, articles about publishing and book matters on the Bermudas can be found in *"The Bermudian"*, a monthly magazine founded in 1930 and published by Bermudian Publishing Company Ltd, in Hamilton.

7 Sources of Information, Address Services

Information about the book trade can be obtained from British trade institutional sources (→BTW I, United Kingdom 4, 6, 7), and also from United States booktrade organizations (→USA, 4).

General book information on Bermuda may be obtained from the local

> *Bermuda Library*
> *Hamilton, Bermuda*

a general public library which is also the National Library (→15). There is also the

> *Bermuda Archives*
> *Woodside, Devonshire Parish*
> *Hamilton, Bermuda*

and, for inquiries of a commercial nature the

> *Trade Development Board*
> *50, Front Street*
> *Hamilton, Bermuda*

11 Training

Professional schools or training programmes do not exist for booksellers or pub-

Bermuda

lishers. Some advanced professionals attend courses in the United Kingdom or in the USA.

Local booksellers have introduced an apprenticeship scheme for their young employees, consisting of five years' training time in the bookshops.

12 Taxes

The book trade is free of taxes on the Bermuda islands, as are book imports and exports.

15 National Bibliography, National Library

Apart from occasional book lists compiled by the public library, and the publishers' catalogues, no bibliographies exist. Bermuda publications can be found only in international bibliographies listing English-language publications (→BTW I, United Kingdom 15; USA 15). An official National Library does not exist either. But the

Bermuda Library
Hamilton, Bermuda

a public library founded in 1839 with branches in St Georges and in Somerset, has stocks of about 90,000 volumes. From the year 1941 onwards this library was obliged by the local government to collect all Bermudan publications.

21 Publishing

There are four publishing companies, all situated in Hamilton. For their annual production no figures are available. Their catalogues mostly list textbooks, geographical, law, industrial and commercial books. Government institutions are also active in this field.

24 Retail Trade

Starting with a bookseller who came from Britain in 1850, the book trade in Bermuda now consists of five bookshops located in Hamilton. Apart from selling to the relatively literate local population, they find a fair number of customers among the international tourists coming to the islands (some 267,000 annually, 80% of them from the United States). Apart from the bookshops, there are a few newspaper stands, which began to sell paperbacks in 1939, and now handle paperbacks as well as hardcover books, up to 95% of them in English. All companies are founded and run by private individuals.

27 Book Imports

While in the past all books sold on the islands came from the United Kingdom, during the last decades the picture has changed to a more international distribution of Bermuda's book imports, and to some extent also to local production. Nevertheless, 95% of the books imported are in English, one half of them now coming from the United States, 20% from Great Britain and 6% from Canada. Local statistics for book imports are not available. British publishers' institutions, however, have published figures of their sales to Bermuda, which show that book imports as well as the buying of books on Bermuda has increased enormously during the last ten years:

Year	US $
1964	23,350
1965	41,150
1966	58,400
1967	70,750
1968	61,850
1969	121,500
1970	105,170

Keeping in mind the small population of the islands, and the fact that British book sales to Bermuda are estimated at 20% of total book imports, these figures are proof that the Bermuda islanders are keen book readers, but remembering that the islands are visited annually by tourists four times outnumbering the local population.

31 Bibliophily

A certain amount of book collecting does take place on the archipelago, forming part of the exhibitions, lectures, etc., put on by the

Bermuda Society of Arts,
Art Gallery, City Hall
Hamilton, Bermuda

Among the collection of the Society's library, mostly formed of books on art, there are a good number of bibliophile editions.

33 The Reviewing of Books

The local newspaper, "Mid-Ocean News", with an edition of 18,000 (1968), publishes weekly book reviews; similarly six local periodicals (total edition in 1969: 565,000 copies!) publish reviews. The two radio stations transmit book reviews weekly, received by 14,000 listeners. Television book programmes from near–by countries reach some 16,000 television sets. So, for local publications as well as for imported titles in the English language, there exists a large audience on the Bermuda islands.

34 Graphic Arts

The graphic arts in Bermuda can claim an international standard, influenced by British tradition and style. Twelve printers, three platemakers and a bookbinder serve the local publishers.

57

Bolivia

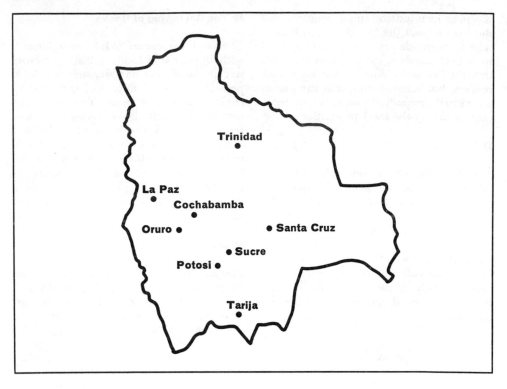

1 General Information

Area 1,098,581 km²
Population 4,773,000 (5 per km²)
Capital Sucre (legal capital 84,900); La Paz (government seat since 1900, 679,000)
Largest towns La Paz (679,000); Cochabamba (149,900); Santa Cruz (124,900); Oruro (119,700); Potosi (96,800); Sucre (84,900); Tarija (35,700); Trinidad (4,500)
Government Republic (last election 1966). De facto military government
Religion Roman Catholic, but complete freedom for all religions
National language Spanish; 60% speak native languages, among native languages: 50% Quechua, 35% Aymara, 15% Uru, Guarani

Leading foreign languages English, German, Portuguese
Weights, measures Metric system
Currency unit Peso Boliviano = $b. (= 100 Centavos)
Education Compulsory. 652,000 primary students; 136,000 college students; 10,950 university students
Illiteracy 64%
Paper consumption a) Newsprint 0.9 kg per inhabitant (1970)
b) Printing paper (other than newsprint) 0.5 kg per inhabitant (1965)
Membership UNESCO, CERLAL

2 Past and Present

The Inca civilization is not now thought to have had a written language, although an imperial accounting and recording system did exist. The system (Kipu) consists of cords with knotted strings in various colours, the configuration and colours serving to indicate amounts and probably events pertaining to the imperial administration. Even less is known of the well –developed civilizations that pre–dated the Incas, for example Tihuanacu, whose achievements are just now coming to light. The Inquisition with its severe censorship prohibited secular printing in peninsular America. Colonial intellectual life was originally centred on and regulated from Lima (seat of the Viceroy of Peru), 1542–1776. The first printing press was founded in Lima in 1584. From 1776 to the end of colonial rule intellectual life was dominated by the Viceroy of Rio de La Plata. Nevertheless the founding in 1623 of the University of San Francisco Xavier in Chuquisaca (now Sucre), gave the first impetus to autonomous intellectual development in Bolivia. (The University Library was founded in 1624.)

The first printing studio in Bolivia (which printed the famous Bertonio Aymara Dictionary) was founded in the town of Juli, in 1612, part of the Archbishopry of La Paz, but today Peruvian territory. During the struggle for independence the contending armies brought printing in the form of leaflets, introduced around 1820. The first known permanent printing office ("Imprenta del Ejercito Expedicionario del Sud") directed by Jose Rodriguez, was established in 1823 in La Paz. Subsequently printing was established in Potosi in 1824, in Sucre in 1830 and in Cochabamba in 1833. First Bolivian magazine: 1852 "Revista de Cochabamba". First known literary circles: "Sociedad Cortez", "Primera Asociacion de Escritores".

In 1857 the Frenchmen Pablo Gerard and Forgues established the first known commercial bookstore ("Librería Hispano Americana") in La Paz. Bolivia's seven leading towns all soon developed bookstores, since universities were founded in each of them. Most of these bookstores were originally run by Spaniards, and usually sold stationery and school utensils as well as books.

The first bookstores which dealt exclusively in books and printed matter were established in La Paz and Cochabamba during the Second World War (mainly by European refugees). Actually this kind of bookstore exists now in Santa Cruz, Oruro and Sucre as well.

Publishing developed from established bookstores. These bookstores also distributed many books, financed by associations and authors themselves (→21).

Bibliography

A. Costa de la Torre, *Catalogo de la Bibliografia Boliviana, libros y folletos 1900–1963.* (Catalogue of the Bolivian bibliography, books and brochures 1900–1963.) La Paz, Universidad de San Andrés 1969. 1,254 pp.

E. Finot, *Historia de la literatura Boliviana.* (History of Bolivian literature.) La Paz, E. Finot, Gisbert & Cia. 1964. 620 pp.

G. Furlong, *Orígines del arte tipográfico en América.* (The origins of the art of typography in America.) Buenos Aires, Ed. Huarpes 1947. 225 pp. Bibliography on pp. 215–225.–Early printing history of Bolivia: p. 83.

3 Retail Prices

As in most South American countries, the booksellers' organization *Cámara Boliviana del Libro* (→4) tried several times to establish fixed prices (30% over the official dollar exchange). However, the weak structure of this organization ended up with prices being fixed by government agencies, mainly by bureaucrats ignorant of the book trade, who regarded books like any other kind of merchandise. The first time any prices had been fixed and exchange control instituted, was during the 1934 Chaco War. Subsequently at various intervals foreign-exchange controls were reimposed and price controls reinstalled.

Today the prices for imported books are fixed by an agreement between the Ministry of Economics and "Cámara Boliviana del Libro". This agreement, signed on 3 December 1969 by the larger booksellers in La Paz, was chiefly because of pressure exerted by means of a long campaign, with threats of nationalization and intervention in case of noncompliance. These measures seriously threaten the further development and growth of book trading in Bolivia.

The salient points of the agreement are the following:

a) bookstores are obliged to have original publisher's catalogues of all books in stock available to the public, thus insuring the control of book prices

b) books not mentioned in catalogues (in other words, most recent publications, or very old ones) must have their price certified by special letters from the publishers or by commercial invoices

c) the maximum price for imported books is the official exchange rate plus 3%.

Distributors are "allowed ample freedom to sell under the aforesaid prices".

This enforced agreement seems to defy the Bolivian constitution, which clearly sets down the principle of free trade. In the near future greater exchange and price controls are expected. (→12).

4 Organization

The
Cámara Boliviana del Libro
(Bolivian Book Chamber)
Casilla 972
La Paz
was founded on 28 August 1946, with legal recognition granted by the government on 4 July 1947.

This organization, constitutionally, includes not only booksellers, but also authors and intellectuals. However, publishers were not explicitly included. In practice the 6–10 largest booksellers–and only those–are paying and are active members.

The organization started by publishing Bolivian authors, but failed after a total of two books. No other significant cultural activity resulted. Members only meet when threatened by governmental or other official pressures. All attempts to increase membership by including the numerous small booksellers throughout the country, and thus effectively organizing the *Cámara Boliviana del Libro*, has always failed due to the indifference of small merchants.

At the end of 1971 the Bolivian Book Chamber tried to make a new start, mostly because of a pending law case with the Mayor of La Paz. At present, only a few members come to the occasional sessions.

The bookstore-employees union
Sindicato de Empleados de Librerias
(Union of Bookstore Employees)
Casilla 2752, Plaza Murillo 519
La Paz
was founded on 20 October 1958. There are 80 members, all in La Paz.

The only recent attempt to provide Bolivia with a more effective booksellers' organization was recently proposed in issues of the magazine "Informativo Amigol Literario".

Printers' organizations:
Asociación de Industriales Gráficos
(Printers' Industrial Association)
c/o René Canelas
Imprenta Letras
Casilla de Correo 4346
Av. Illimani, entre Loayza y Bueno
La Paz
and
Federación de Gráficos
(Bolivian Typographical Union)
Indaburo No. 1184
La Paz

Bibliography

Informativo Amigol Literario. (Literary Information Amigol.) Cochabamba, Los Amigos del Libro.

5 Trade Press

A trade press, as such, does not exist, though literary magazines are occasionally published, mostly by universities and municipal organizations as well as by the Ministry of Education. Lately three Bolivian publishers have begun to produce house magazines. But the only magazine which mentions trade affairs is
Informativo Amigol Literario
Casilla 4415
La Paz

7 Sources of Information, Address Services

Normally information may be obtained from
Cámara Boliviana del Libro
(Bolivian Book Chamber)
Casilla 972
La Paz
However, at present this booksellers' organization is not functioning, so inquiries should be directed to:
Bibliografía Boliviana
Casilla 450
Cochabamba

Other information sources are the following:
Cámara Nacional de Industria
(National Chamber of Industry)
Casilla 611
La Paz

Cámara Nacional de Comercio
(National Chamber of Commerce)
Casilla 7
La Paz

Biblioteca Nacional de Bolivia
(National Library of Bolivia)
Sucre
and
Distribuidora Los Amigos del Libro
(Distributor Los Amigos del Libro)
Casilla 450
Cochabamba
The addresses of all branches of the book trade are contained in:
La Empresa del Libro en América Latina. (The Book in Latin America.) 2nd ed. Buenos Aires, Bowker Editores 1974. VIII, 307 pp.
pp. 89–94 pp.: Bolivia.
The following guides are published in more or less regular intervals:
Guía-Directorio de la Industria Boliviana, 1971. (Directory of Bolivian Industry.) La Paz, Cámara Nacional de Industria 1971. 124 pp.
Guía Profesional de Bolivia, 1971. (Professional Guide of Bolivia.) La Paz, Adolfo Sandoval Rodríguez 1971. 144 pp.
Guía Nacional de Bolivia, Comercial e Industrial, 1973. (Commercial and Industrial national Guide of Bolivia.) La Paz, Rolando Pommier Aguilar 1973. 300 pp.
Guía Nacional de Casillas Postales, 1971. (National Guide of Post Office Boxes.) La Paz 1971. 386 pp.
Guía General Clasificada de Bolivia, 1973. (Classified general Guide of Bolivia.) La Paz, Guillermo Reyes & Carlos Pacheco 1972. 685 pp.

Bolivia

8 International Membership

The Cámara Boliviana del Libro (→4), is a member of CERLAL (→Latin America 4).

9 Market Research

There does not exist anything that could be considered as market research.

The national efforts for a good statistical service are rudimentary, though Bolivia had very fine statistics during the last century, and individual efforts from some government agencies were and are made to have complete and reliable statistical data. Still, the discrepancy in statistical figures makes any general conclusions difficult.

10 Books and Young People

Bolivian youth are keen readers which is shown by their use of public libraries; for example: the Cochabamba Municipal Library (the best organized in the country) has up to 800 readers a day, during school term (90% schoolboys and -girls). The low national income makes a preocupation with textbooks and alphabetization so important that ordinary children's books are used only by a small (middle-class) minority.

Bolivian publishers, or individual authors who venture into the field of children's books, cannot compete with imported books. This is a pity, since Bolivia is rich in tales and legends which have rarely been adopted for textbooks, and which could be made available to the world through a proper children's book industry. There are three large Bolivian textbook publishers:

–a Catholic college has its own printing and wholesale organization

–two big booksellers specializing in printing and distributing textbooks.

Many textbooks apart from imported ones are published by authors and made available, not directly to schools, but through the book trade. The Bolivian government, through the Ministry of Education, started a big alphabetization campaign, organized with the help of the army, and using college boys getting their pre-military army training. But the complexity of this programme and lack of resources are hampering the work. The Ministry of Education, by decree, organized the *Banco del Libro* ("Book Bank"). Irregularly books and magazines are collected for these book centres, which are located mostly in densely populated districts. The idea behind this "Banco del Libro" is to educate the young in the use of books, to create reading habits and to care for new popular and school libraries, as well as helping the alphabetization programmes and educating adults. (Decree of 1 April 1970, No. 09177, creating the "Banco del Libro", and alphabetization campaign.)

Bibliography

W. GUTTENTAG, *Survey on the library situation in Bolivia*. Washington, Organization of American States 1973. 6 pp.

11 Training

There is no training for booksellers. The few good booksellers got their training empirically. Some attended courses outside the country. The "Union of Bookstore Employees" (→4) is just a place for dealing with union affairs and sporting events. There are two Librarians' Associations (Asociación de Bibliotecarios, La Paz, and Asociación de Bibliotecarios de Cochabamba, Cochabamba).

The San Andres University of La Paz is running a librarianship school in the Faculty of Philosophy and Literature. From time to time there are librarianship courses and seminars, organized by the "Patiño Foundation" in Cochabamba.

12 Taxes

Import taxes for books and magazines are 2% of the net value of the invoices plus freight.

There is no federal sales tax on books, but 5% on magazines.

Invoices must have 'free' seal from a Bolivian Consulate or a fine is imposed. Banks and custom-houses do not accept any invoice which is not free-sealed by a Bolivian Consulate.

Municipal taxes vary in every city, but are usually as follows:

2% sales tax, from which amount 20% goes to the local university.

The "Camara Boliviana del Libro" has been fighting the Municipality of La Paz in a High Court case which has been running for years now, over the 1927 law which established that books should be tax free, and which has never been revoked.

14 Copyright

Copyright used to be protected by the "Ley de Propiedad Intelectual" ("Law of Intellectual Property"), of 13 November 1909 completed 15 January and 30 October 1945, establishing 30 years hereditary rights for intellectual property.

"Ley de Imprenta" (Printing Law) of 19 January 1925 states clearly that any printed matter (book, magazine, newspaper, etc.) must bear the names of the publisher and the author; any publication without these is regarded illegal.

The "Decrete Supremo" (Supreme Decree) 5650, of 14 May 1957 establishes the obligation to send two copies of all printed publications to the National Library in Sucre.

The registration of intellectual property cannot be established without a receipt showing that these copies are registered in Sucre.

The "Decreto Supremo" 08617, of 8 January 1969, creates a National Registry (functioning under the order of the Ministry of Culture) and the obligation that the printer, before printing a book, has to request a number, which has to be printed in each book. Furthermore there is an obligation on the printer to send 4 copies of each edition to the Ministry of Culture (two to be payed for by the printer and two by the publisher or author); 2 copies are destined for the National Library in Sucre and 2 copies for the "Repositorio Nacional", which virtually constitutes a second National Library in La Paz.

At first the bookseller was held responsible for seeing that all Bolivian books sold in his bookstore had the registration number; later this decree was changed and the printer was made responsible for this. In each of the bigger cities a representative of the Ministry of Culture was responsible for enforcing the law.

By Decree No. 10367, 14 July 1972, the earlier decrees have been changed, and now three copies have to be given in La Paz to the Ministry of Education; one for the National Library in Sucre; one for the Library of Congress in La Paz, and one for a future library of the Ministry of Education. Furthermore, two copies have to be given to the "Banco del Libro" (Book Bank, →10); if not 50 copies many be confiscated. In practice, only the bigger publishers and printers are obliged to give away five copies. Nearly no official publications go through this legal channel. This changing pattern of decrees makes the building up of a real national depository and on official bibliography impossible.

Bibliography

P. LEWY, *Propiedad intelectual en Bolivia.* (Intellectual property in Bolivia.) Cochabamba, Ed. Los Amigos del Libro 1974. 377 pp.

Bolivia

15 National Bibliography, National Library

The National Library was founded in Sucre in 1825. Sporadically bulletins were published. Lack of funds and the non-enforcement of laws (→ 14) left the important National Library very incomplete.

Juan Siles Guevara published a pamphlet "Bibliografia de Bibliografias Bolivianas" (Bibliography of Bolivian bibliographies, 1969), which is an almost complete study of Bolivian bibliographical material.

Arturo Costa de la Torre published the first two volumes of a proposed three volume work: "Catálogo de la Bibliografía Boliviana" 1900–1963 (Catalogue of Bolivian bibliography, 1900–1963.) This book tries to continue the work of the great Bolivian bibliographer Gabriel Rene Moreno, whose bibliographical work covers all the republican years up to the beginning of this century.

Since 1962 Werner Guttentag T. has been publishing an annual "Bibliografía Boliviana" (Bolivian bibliography), which tries to take the place of an official National Bibliography. It contains bibliographical data concerning all books and brochures published in Bolivia. It further records all publications since 1962 which did not appear in a former volume, thus completing the "Bolivian Bibliography". These bibliographies also carry supplements listing books written about Bolivia and translations of Bolivian authors into other languages. Reviews on some important books are included.

Bibliography

P. Avicenne, *Bibliographical serivces throughout the world 1965–69*. Paris, Unesco, 1972. 310 pp.
pp. 70–71: Bolivia.
A. Costa de la Torre, *Catálogo de la bibliografía Boliviana, libros y folletos, 1900–1963*. (Catalogue of Bolivian bibliography, books and pamphlets, 1900 to 1963.) 3 vols. La Paz, Universidad San Francisco Xavier.
W. Guttentag T., *Bibliografía Boliviana*. (Bolivian bibliography.) Since 1963, for 1962; published annually. Cochabamba, Edit. Los Amigos del Libro.
J. Siles G., *Bibliografía de bibliografías Bolivianas*. (Bibliography of Bolivian bibliographies.) La Paz, Ed. Ministerio de Cultura, Información y Turismo 1969. 38 pp.
I. Zimmermann, *Current national bibliographies of Latin America*. Gainesville, Florida, University of Florida Press. X, 139 pp.
pp. 25–29: Bolivia.

16 Book Production

Bolivian book production during the past few years has been between 250 and 400 titles annually (including broschures).

Year	Titles
1962	260
1963	299
1964	343
1965	307
1966	296
1967	344
1968	331
1969	339
1970	361
1971	302
1972	292

Subject group (1972)	Titles
Art	7
Applied science	11
General works	6
History & geography	38
Linguistics	26
Literature	66
Philosophy	—
Pure sciences	8
Religion	18
Social sciences	58
Others	54

Bibliography

W. GUTTENTAG T., *Bibliografía Boliviana.*
($\rightarrow$ 15).

17 Translations

Besides translations from and into native
languages (mostly religious, by missionaries), very few translations are being published in Bolivia.
From 1962 to 1972 only 7 translations were
registered:
from: English   5
      Yiddish   1
      Russian   1
Translation of Bolivian authors into other
languages is also rare (1962–1972, 13
translations)
into   German   3
        Russian   2
        Czech   1
        Hungarian   1
        Hebrew   1
        English   3
        Portuguese   1
        Romanian   1

Bibliography

($\rightarrow$ 15)

18 Book Clubs

At present there are no book clubs in
Bolivia. In 1968 one bookshop in La Paz
tried to organize a book club with the help
of an Argentine publisher, but it did not
prosper.
Part of this failure is the constant political
and economic insecurity as well as distribution difficulties and difficulties in collecting money through the mail. Collecting
through the bank is too complicated and
expensive for this purpose.
On the other hand improved conditions
should make book clubs a success in
Bolivia, some day.

19 Paperbacks

Most books published in Bolivia are paper-
covered editions, and only a few books are
available in bound form. But this does not
mean that those are paperbacks in the
modern mass-production sense. The books
are just not case-bound because of economic reasons. Lately some publishers have
tried to publish popular collections, which
in size and intention could be considered
paperbacks, but their price, because of
small editions, is not as low as paperback
editions generally are.

20 Book Design

For many years, the Municipality of La
Paz has sponsored a prize in the form of:
–a Red Ribbon for the best publication
of the year
–a Garnet Ribbon for the best magazine.
Because of constant changes of authorities,
it is not known whether this tradition can
be maintained.
Bolivia has many artists, who design very
fine covers, and try to follow modern
trends. Even though printing conditions
are very poor, some excellent printing and
reproduction has been done.

21 Publishing

In Bolivia most publishing is carried out
by established booksellers. Some writers
(not counting textbook authors) publish
their and other authors' books themselves
and distribute them to the public. One
bookseller has a separate sales and distribution department for his publishing
work. Official agencies, such as universities,
learned societies, government agencies,
ministries and municipalities, also publish
books.
Commercial publishers exist in:

Bolivia

La Paz	7
Cochabamba	3
Oruro	1
Potosi	1 (semi-official)
Sucre	1

There are 11 official publishers throughout the country (not counting the ministries) with a fairly regular output of books.

1968 commercial publishers produced				42 titles
1969	"	"	"	54 "
1970	"	"	"	40 "
1971	"	"	"	59 "
1972	"	"	"	57 "

(not including textbooks)

→10.

Bibliography

M. MENESES and W. GUTTENTAG, *Book publishing in Bolivia*. St Louis, Miss., Washington University Libraries 1964. 34 pp.–9th Seminar on the Acquisition of Latin American Library Materials.– Mimeographed.

22 Literary Agents

There are no established literary agents in Bolivia. Most authors make their own arrangements for translations and re-publication abroad.
Only one publisher is acting as an agent for his and other publishers' authors:
Los Amigos del Libro
Casilla 450
Cochabamba

23 Wholesale Trade

Up to 1940 the book business and distribution was in the hands of two bookstores in La Paz. Some magazine distributors existed in Oruro and Cochabamba.
Today many foreign publishers have exclusive agents in Bolivia for promoting and wholesaling their books. There are also some major bookshops that distribute textbooks country-wide.
These distributing organizations (magazines included) are located in:

La Paz	5
Cochabamba	2

Some of these organizations exclusively distribute their books through their own branches and agents in Bolivia.
Sometimes official agencies (the Ministry of Education, University of Sucre) act as wholesale distributors to official organizations such as UNESCO, UNO, etc.)
In very few cases does the wholesale discount exceed 20% (→3). Sales are sometimes made freight paid for, and often on a sale-or-return basis.
For books published in Bolivia the discount oscillates between 20% and 30%. Most universities have official bookstores, with special privileges, which are able to offer lower prices, making survival of other booksellers, specially in smaller towns, almost impossible.

24 Retail Trade

There are very few stores in Bolivia selling only books. Most of them are stationery stores, which handle schoolbooks during the school season, and often books are a side-line only. There are 56 stationery stores in La Paz; 10 bookstores which also sell magazines, and sometimes records; 4 of these are modern establishments.

Place	Stationery stores	Bookstores
La Paz	56	10
Cochabamba	28	5
Oruro	15	2
Potosi	12	–
Sucre	10	1
Santa Cruz	14	3
Trinidad	3	–

In the rest of the country there are about 30 stationery stores which also sell books and magazines.

No turnover figures are available.

The fact is, no specialized bookstore can survive, because the market is too small. So the larger bookstores have all kinds of books, but few have well-organized book sections. In general the assortment of imported Spanish books is quite good, given the population, analphabetism and low income.

Few bookstores handle special orders. Only one, in Cochabamba, with branches in La Paz, Santa Cruz and Oruro, handles foreign-language material (English, German, French), with a branch at the International Airport in El Alto (La Paz). Because of poor postal conditions, scientific periodicals are handled only occasionally and reluctantly by bookstores (this is true of all kinds of subscription).

There are no special paperback-stores, and only one handles foreign paperbacks; many, however, sell Spanish paperbacks. Some stores sell games and cards as a side-line.

Most of the larger bookstores import their books directly, or, where exclusive distribution rights exist, buy from the corresponding agent. Even the smaller stationery stores frequently import books directly, in view of the discount structure in Bolivia ($\rightarrow$ 3, 23).

25 Mail-Order Bookselling

Because of postal conditions ($\rightarrow$ 18) there is no mail-order organization in Bolivia. But some bookstores, which regularly publish catalogues, or advertise in newspapers, send books to retail clients by mail or other transportation, such as plane and truck. Many parts of Bolivia are accessible only by plane or by truck, sometimes only on muleback.

One bookstore has a big medical section, and serves doctors throughout the country, sending regular catalogues, even to remote tropical places or icy high-altitude mining districts. But this and the difficulty of collecting money ($\rightarrow$ 18) make additional charges to the price of such books very high.

26 Antiquarian Book Trade, Auctions

In all larger towns, in the open markets, there are stands where old books are sold. In La Paz 24 such stands are concentrated. Some bookstores have a small section of older (out of print) Bolivian books. Because of the small editions, Bolivian books often become collectors' items quite soon. There is one bookstore in Cochabamba with an organized section of old Bolivian books; this firm mails catalogues to universities, other bookstores, etc.

27 Book Imports

Most books sold in Bolivia are imported ($\rightarrow$ 12).

Imports of printed matter in 1957:

Category	US $
Books	458,548
Periodicals	234,610
Newspapers	11,640

Books only (1967):

Country	US $
Spain	167,625
Mexico	92,158
Argentina	71,698
USA	76,840
Peru	20,684
Germany (F.R.)	5,791
France	5,023

Periodicals (1967):

Country	US $
Mexico	113,597
Argentina	54,993
USA	31,858
Chile	12,446
Spain	8,645
Germany (F.R.)	5,969

Bolivia

Bibliography

Anuario del Comercio Exterior. (Annual of foreign Commerce.) La Paz, Ministerio de Hacienda.

28 Book Exports

Bolivian books are exported principally to university libraries and institutions or to jobbers. With the growth of the small publishing industry in Bolivia, even if most books concern Bolivian affairs, a small export trade has begun to neighbouring countries (Chile, Peru, Argentina, Uruguay, Paraguay and Brazil). The estimated value of exports was in 1970: US$ 30,000. The participation of Bolivia at the Frankfurt Book Fair and other international events has helped the export of Bolivian books a little, and has furthered knowledge of Bolivian literature. High prices and small editions make the Bolivian productions not very competitive in the Hispano-American market.

29 Book Fairs

National book fairs are organized at irregular intervals by government or municipal authorities. The last big book fairs were organized by the Ministry of Education in Pa Paz, in 1964, and by the Municipality of Cochabamba, in 1968.
In Santa Cruz, during the International Industrial Fairs in 1969 and 1970, only one Bolivian publisher and one Argentine publisher participated.
In Oruro the municipality organized a National Book Fair during the Carnival festival in 1971. Five Bolivian publishers took part. Since Bolivia has begun to participate in some International Book Fairs, with the help of foreign governments or booksellers' organizations, the Bolivian Government and the public have become more conscious of the importance of such events,

and the Bolivian Foreign Ministry intends, to help organize Bolivian participation in as many countries as possible, as well as giving facilities for foreign book exhibitions. In Bolivia
  Werner Guttentag T.
  Casilla 450. Cochabamba
was authorized to make all contacts. Cochabamba is to organize a book event during its 400th anniversary.
A group of Bolivian writers prepared public fairs in La Paz and Oruro in 1973, where authors signed their books and sold them. Some Bolivian publishers participated with their own stands, exhibiting and selling the works of their authors.

30 Public Relations

The Cámara Boliviana del Libro (→4) has never been able to organize a public-relations department to publicize books.
Press and radio often have cultural programmes, where, sporadically, the idea of reading and the idea of the *Book* are propagated. By law, a National Book Week has been established, during which the Ministry of Education has to present a complete national programme, particularly through schools, to promote the idea of the book. But over the years, and with changing administrations, this decree (without any real legal authority) has merely forced booksellers to concede a 20% discount (→ "Banco del Libro", 10). Only individual bookstores and distributors make propaganda in newspapers, on the radio, television, and movie-houses, and also in some literary magazines (house magazines). But a real national programme does not exist.

32 Literary Prizes

The most important literary prize is the *Gran Premio Nacional de Literatura* (Great Literary National Prize), sponsored by the government through the Ministry of Education. It has only been awarded five times, the first in 1951 and the last in 1970.

There are several literary prizes, sponsored by municipal universities; but because of unstable conditions such events are irregular.

The Municipality of La Paz has the *Premio Franz Tamayo*, (Franz Tamayo Prize), named after the most important Bolivian author.

The University of Oruro is sponsoring an annual prize for poetry and short stories. The Municipality of Cochabamba awards an annual prize for several literary topics. But since the last revolution, in 1971, and a complete change of administration, nothing has been heard lately about these prizes. The publishing house Amigos del Libro (Book Friends), has since 1968 been sponsoring a national prize, *Erich Guttentag*, for the best Bolivian novel; the prize is awarded every 18 months. Because the works are judged by an international jury, Bolivian novelists are slowly becoming known outside the country. Manuscripts recommended by the jury have also been published.

33 The Reviewing of Books

Only La Paz's *Presencia* (the most widely read Catholic daily newspaper), has a regular Sunday literary supplement, which has been published for many years. Most other newspapers and radio stations try to carry literary pages and programmes.

In these literary supplements and programmes, books, mostly Bolivian, are reviewed, and seldom foreign books. There are a number of magazines, which, even though they do not appear very regularly make an important contribution to the furthering of Bolivian literature.

The most important magazines are:
Canata (Cultural Magazine) Municipalidad de Cochabamba; *Cultura Boliviana* (Bolivian Culture) published by the Universidad Técnica de Oruro (Technical University of Oruro); *Khana*–Revista Municipal de Artes y Letras (Municipal Magazine of Art and Culture) Municipalidad de La Paz; *Kollasuyo*–Revista de Estudios Bolivianos (Review of Bolivian Studies), La Paz; *Letras Bolivianas* (Bolivian Literature) published by the Universidad de San Simón (University of San Simón), Cochabamba; *Nova* (Cultural Magazine), La Paz; *Signo*. Cuadernos Bolivianos de Cultura (Notebook of Bolivian Culture), La Paz; *Temas Sociales* (Social Subjects) published by the Universidad de San Andrés (University of San Andrés), La Paz; and the following magazines from Bolivian publishers: *Carta Bibliográfica* (Bibliographical Letter), Empresa Editora Urquizo Ltda., La Paz; *Difusión*, Difusión Ltda., La Paz; *Informativo Amigol Literario* (Literary Information Amigol), Los Amigos del Libro Ltda., Cochabamba; *Nivel 4000*, Los Amigos del Libro Ltda., Cochabamba.

35 Miscellaneous

a) *Authors, Artists*
There are several authors' and artists' organizations in different parts of Bolivia. The most important are:
Sociedad de Escritores y Artistas
(Society of Writers and Artists)
Baptista No. 5617
Cochabamba

Fuego de Poesía
(Poetry's Fire)
La Paz

Unión de Poetas
(Poets' Union National Organization)
La Paz
and
Prisma
La Paz

Brazil

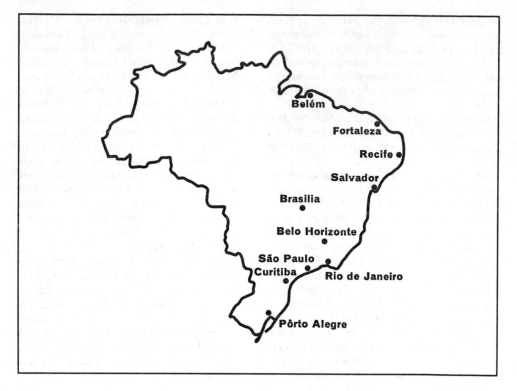

1 General Information

Area 8,511,965 km²
Population 95,305,000 (12 per km²)
Capital Brasília (440,000)
Largest towns São Paulo (6,339,000); Rio de Janeiro (4,394,000); Belo Horizonte (1,333,000); Recife (1,195,000); Pôrto Alegre (1,026,000); Salvador (975,000); Fortaleza (960,000); Curitiba (707,000); Belém (625,000)
Government Federative republic comprised under a representative regimen, by union of 22 states, 1 federal district, and 4 territories. The Union is responsible for setting and executing the national education plans, as well as for legislating over the directives and bases of the national education
Religion Mainly Roman Catholic
National language Portuguese
Leading foreign languages English, French, Spanish
Weights, measures Metric system

Currency unit Cruzeiro (Cr $) = 100 cents
Education Elementary course compulsory from 7 to 14 years. Free in official schools. Students at university level: 399,599 (1970) in 51 universities (887 superior schools)
Illiteracy About 35% national average: higher in the North-East, lower in the South
Paper consumption a) Newsprint 2.6 kg per inhabitant (1969)
b) Printing paper (other than newsprint) 1.2 kg per inhabitant (1969)
Membership UNESCO; IPA

70

2 Past and Present

Though discovered by the Portuguese in 1500, it was only during the 19th century that Brazil had its first printing press. The art of printing–amongst other activities– was the mother country's privilege that could not be overcome until the time when Portugal's Royal Family had to be transferred in a hurry from Lisbon to Rio, due to the siege imposed by Napoleon's armies.

This move started many great transformations in Brazil, such as the installation of the Royal Printers (1808) and the Royal Library (1810). Of great help for both events was the simultaneous shipping–with the Royal Family–of all the printing equipment recently bought from England and originally allotted to one of Portugal's State Offices, and also of a substantial collection of books that were intended to replace the ones destroyed together with the Ajuda Library during the Lisbon earthquake.

In spite of many problems, already before its independence from Portugal (1822) the country had at least five other printing offices in various places and some bookshops. The scarcity of books–generally illegally imported or under severe censorship–did not encourage commercialization. Through Empire and early Republic until more or less the first quarter of the 20th century, the number of publishers and booksellers (whose activities were practically undistinguishable) increased steadily, although the market was mainly supplied by Portugal and France.

The three decades that followed the beginning of the Second World War show the first attempts at specialization (some successful), and also of grouping around professional interests such as the foundation of the "Sindicato Nacional dos Editôres de Livros" ("National Syndicate of Book Publishers" →4), and of the "Câmara Brasileira do Livro" ("Brazilian Book Chamber" →4). This movement is probably the most relevant fact, historically, of the book trade in Brazil. Through better co-ordination between the trade and the government, the book business was able to organize itself and benefit from new favourable factors, such as the doubling of the country's population in the last 25 years, the social and economical changes which the country is undergoing, seriously devoted to industrialization and higher literacy, and from official and semi-official cultural development programmes. Today Brazil is beginning to export books.

Bibliography

G. Furlong, *Orígines del arte tipográfico en América.* (The origins of the art of typography in America.) Buenos Aires, Ed. Huarpes 1947. 225 pp.
Bibliography on pp. 215–25. Early printing history of Brazil: pp. 105–6.

Instituto Nacional do Livro. Abertas novas perspectivas. Entrevista com Maria Alice Barroso. (Opening of new perspectives. Interview with Maria Alice Barroso.) In: Revista do Livro. Rio de Janeiro, nr. 43, 1970. pp. 6–10.

C. Razzini, *O livro, o jornal e a tipografia no Brasil 1500–1822.* (The book, the periodical and typography in Brazil 1500–1822.) Rio de Janeiro, Kosmos Editora 1946. 445 pp.

Sindicato Nacional dos Editôres de Livros, Análise do Relatório Escarpit. (Analysis of the Escarpit Report.) In: Boletim Informativo, GEIL. Rio de Janeiro, nr. 17/18, Jan./Apr. 1970. pp. 5–8.

N. W. Sodre, *Historia da imprensa no Brasil.* (History of Brazilian printing.) Rio de Janeiro, Civilzação Brasileira 1966. 583 pp.

3 Retail Prices

Retail prices are set by the publishers; as a rule, books are sold at list prices. However, a 10% courtesy discount is often granted to regular clients.

Schools are granted a 20–30% discount on textbooks, and government agencies get from 20% to 40% on quantity purchases of text and trade books.

At present the Ministry of Education and some State Secretaries of Education have in their budgets allocations totalling over 5 million US $, and they want to get as many books as possible for their money.

4 Organization

The oldest professional association organized in Brazil (founded in 1941) is:

Sindicato Nacional dos Editôres de Livros
(National Syndicate of Book Publishers)
Avenida Rio Branco, 37–15° andar
RB 20000 Rio de Janeiro, GB

The Syndicate has two permanent technical councils with advisory functions, and is legally entitled to a seat on the following official agencies: "Grupo Executivo da Indústria do Livro–GEIL" ("Executive Group of the Book Industry"), and "Comissão do Livro Técnico e do Livro Didático–COLTED" ("Commission of the Technical and Educational Book"). It also maintains representatives at the "Associação Brasileira de Normas Técnicas–ABNT" ("Brazilian Bureau of Standards"); "Fundação Nacional do Livro Infantil e Juvenil–FNLIJ" ("National Foundation for Infants' and Juvenile Books"); and "Centro de Bibliotécnia" ("Centre of Library Techniques", supported by Franklin Book Programs, → USA 28).

A civil institution, founded in 1946, the

Câmara Brasileira do Livro (Brazilian Book Chamber) Avenida Ipiranga, 1267
RB São Paulo, SP

works closely with, and complements,

"Sindicato de Editôres". The majority of its members are publishers and booksellers from São Paulo, who in 1968 started yearly "Encontros de Editôres e Livreiros" ("Publishers' and Booksellers' Seminars"), in which guest foreign publishers deliver lectures and hold debates. Eight German publishers attended the 1971 "Encontro". Two Ministry of Education agencies, deserve special notice namely: "Instituto Nacional do Livro" ("National Book Institute"), founded in 1937, and "Grupo Executivo da Indústria do Livro–GEIL" ("Executive Group of the Book Industry") founded in 1965, both very active in the defence and promotion of book production.

Instituto Nacional do Livro
(National Book Institute)
Edifício Venâncio VI
RB Brasília, D. F.

Its main functions are: to stimulate reader, author and publisher through assistance to public libraries in the country, by granting literary prizes, and by sponsoring co-editions (→ 11).

Grupo Executivo da Indústria do Livro–
GEIL
(Executive Group of the Book Industry)
Palácio da Cultura, 11° andar
RB 20000 Rio de Janeiro, GB.

Founded to create incentives for industry, commercialization and book expansion, it has already coped with some of the most chronic publishing problems. The following representatives are its members on a Board of Directors: "Instituto Nacional do Livro"; "Banco Nacional do Desenvolvimento Econômico"; "Emprêsa Brasileira de Correios e Telégrafos"; "Academia Brasileira de Letras"; "Carteira de Câmbio do Banco Central"; "Carteira de Crédito Geral do Banco do Brasil"; "Câmara Brasileira do Livro"; "Sindicato Nacional dos Editôres de Livros"; "Sindicato das Indústrias Gráficas da Guanabara"; and "Sindicato das Indústrias Gráficas de São Paulo".

5 Trade Press

The aim of having a special journal for the professional organizations has not yet been realized. It is hoped, however, that, once the present consolidation period is complete, this deficiency will be rectified. Until then, the trade has to make do with isolated initiatives from private and official organizations closely related to it, such as:

Revista do Livro
(Book Magazine)
Palácio da Cultura, Ministério da Educação e Cultura, 9th floor
RB 20000 Rio de Janeiro, GB

published quarterly by the "Instituto Nacional do Livro" (→4) since 1956, which undoubtedly represents the most complete repository of book-trade matters in the country.

There is also the

GEIL–Boletim Informativo
(GEIL Informative Bulletin)
Palácio da Cultura, Ministério da Educação e Cultura, 11th floor
RB 20000 Rio de Janeiro, GB

issued at irregular intervals by a "Grupo Executivo da Indústria do Livro" (→4) since January 1967. Apart from the minutes of the Group's meetings, this bulletin contains matters of interest to the book trade, such as general news, legislation, projects in process, recommendations, reports, statistical data, etc.

Thanks to private initiative, one that deserves mention is

Correio do Livro
(Book Courier)
Rua Bahia, 988
RB São Paulo, SP

a monthly tabloid published during the past five years, and with a print order of more than 25,000 copies.

As a trade publication

O Editor
Av. Gomes Freire, 663–conj. 201
Caixa Postal 15.085
RB 20000 Rio de Janeiro

is devoted to new publishing, marketing and manufacturing techniques.

6 Book-Trade Literature

There is very little trade literature in Brazil, due in part to the fact that until recently the industry was by secondary importance within the overall picture. The most abundant literature flows from the professional meetings promoted, more frequently since 1948, by publishers and booksellers' associations in various cities.

Bibliography

D. DE ABREU, *A expansão da rêde de livrarias e a boa livraria.* (The expansion of the network of bookshops and the good bookshop.) Rio de Janeiro, A Casa do Livro 1970. 44 pp.

D. DE ABREU, *O livro e a indústria do conhecimento.* (The book and the knowledge industry.) Rio de Janeiro, Centro de Bibliotécnia 1968. 50 pp.

Primeiro Congresso de Editôres e Livreiros do Brasil. (First Congress of Publishers and Booksellers of Brazil), promoted by the "Câmara Brasileira do Livro". São Paulo, 22–26 Nov. 1948. São Paulo, Saraiva 1950. 115 pp.

Segundo Congresso de Editôres e Livreiros do Brasil. (Second Congress of Publishers and Booksellers of Brazil), promoted by "Câmara Brasileira do Livro". São Paulo, 18 to 23 Oct. 1954. São Paulo, Ed. Brasil Gráfico Ltda, n. d. 68 pp.

Terceiro Congresso de Editôres e Livreiros do Brasil. (Third Congress of Publishers and Booksellers of Brazil), promoted by the "Sindicato Nacional dos Editôres de Livros" and by "Câmara Brasileira do Livro", Rio de Janeiro, 5–9 Nov. 1956. Rio de Janeiro, Ministry of Education and Culture, Documentation Service 1959. 239 pp.

Brazil

E. R. GONDIM, *Vida e obra de Paula Brito.* (Life and work of Paula Brito.) Rio de Janeiro, Livraria Brasiliana Editôra 1965. 144 pp. Biography of Francisco de Paula Brito, (1809–61), typographer, editor and bookseller who exercised considerable influence in the development of the book business during the nineteenth century. With a bibliography.

A. HOUAISS, *Elementos de bibliologia.* (Elements of bibliology.) Rio de Janeiro, Instituto Nacional do Livro 1967. 2 vols.

R.B. DE MORAIS, *O bibliófilo aprendiz.* (The apprentice bibliophile.) São Paulo, Companhia Editôra Nacional 1965. 200 pp.

Relatório da Comissão Coordenadora do III encontro de Editôres e Livreiros, Rio de Janeiro, Sindicato Nacional dos Editôres de Livros 1970. 77 pp.

Sindicato Nacional dos Editôres de Livros (ed.), *Producão e comercializacão de livros na Região Rio-São Paulo.* (Production and marketing of books in the Rio–São Paulo Area.) Rio de Janeiro, Sindicato 1969. 40 pp.

7 Sources of Information, Address Services

Very little information is available at the time of writing. The board of directors of *Sindicato Nacional dos Editôres de Livros*
Av. Rio Branco, 37–15° andar
RB 20000 Rio de Janeiro, GB
has approved (in 1971) a project to publish a directory of publishers and booksellers (→4).
Special inquiries about libraries should be directed to
Instituto Nacional do Livro
Palácio da Cultura, 11° andar
RB 20000 Rio de Janeiro, GB
which has a complete file on all Brazilian libraries (→4).
On specialized libraries, the best source is:
Instituto Brasileiro de Bibliografia e Documentação

(Brazilian Institute of Bibliography and Documentation)
Avenida General Justo, 171
RB 20000 Rio de Janeiro, GB
which also supplies information and makes bibliographic surveys on request from interested parties, in the science and technology fields. On the other hand, its numerous publications, of which some are listed below, offer excellent reference material.
For statistical data specially referring to demographic and economical censuses, the best source is the IBGE Foundation (→9).

Bibliography

The addresses of all branches of the book trade are contained in
La Empresa del Libro en América Latina. (The Book in Latin America.) 2nd ed. Buenos Aires, Bowker Editores Argentina 1974. VIII, 307 pp.
pp. 95–127: Brasil.
and
O Mundo da Edição Luso-Brasileira. (The Luso-Brazilian book world.) Mem Martins, Publ. Europa–América 1969.
Contains the addresses of publishers, booksellers, libraries and other information.

IBGE Foundation. Instituto Brasileiro de Geographic e Estatística (Brazilian Institute of Geography and Statistics.) *Anuário estatístico do Brasil–1970.* (Brazilian Yearbook of Statistics.) Rio de Janeiro, Instituto 1970. 772 pp.

Instituto Nacional do Livro. Guia das bibliotecas Brasileiras. (Guide to Brazilian libraries.) 4th ed. Rio de Janeiro, Instituto 1969. 504 pp.

Instituto Brasileiro de Bibliografia e Documentação. Bibliotecas especializadas Brasileiras. (Specialized Brazilian libraries.) Rio de Janeiro, Instituto 1962. 375 pp.

Instituto Brasileiro de Bibliografia e Documentação. Periódicos Brasileiros de cultura. (Brazilian cultural periodicals.) Rio de

Janeiro, Instituto 1968. 280 pp.–Contains 2,049 titles of national periodical publications, organized in CDU classification, including essential data and address of publisher of each title.

8 International Membership

Brazilian publishers are members of IPA (→BTW I, International Section 4), now regularly attend the "Frankfurt Book Fair" and IPA meetings, and hold yearly "Encontros de Editôres" ("Publishers' Seminars" →4) in Brazil, where foreign guest publishers (1968, American publishers; 1969, French publishers; 1971, German publishers) deliver lectures and debate new techniques and exchange information with their Brazilian colleagues. The "National Syndicate of Book Publishers" (→4) has been very active advising the government on the revision of the Berne Convention. Brazil is a member of UNESCO.

9 Market Research

There is no institution in Brazil specifically devoted to book-market research. However, there are many reliable organizations conducting general market research. Cultural, scientific or commercial, according to their nature and purpose, these organizations, both public and private, have been helping the development of a process that started during the Second World War.

Although it is too early to speak of a tradition of regular surveying in the field of communications, something is already being accomplished. In the publishing and printing fields, there are three projects: one by the "Sindicatos das Indústrias Gráficas dos Estados da Guanabara e São Paulo"; and one by the "Grupo Executivo da Indústria do Livro" (→4). The first two, in 1967, partially cover the Brazilian market (Rio–São Paulo). The third attempts a global survey of the Brazilian publishing industry, in a joint venture with "Fundação Getúlio Vargas". The purpose of the survey is: to identify and analyse the capacity and structure of the publishing and printing industries; to analyse the cost structure and identify the factors which affect production costs of books; to evaluate the potential capacity of book production, now and in the future; to analyse the marketing of books and its influence in pricing; to identify factors that restrict the publishing capacity of the country; to evaluate qualified labour needs.

Fundação Getúlio Vargas
(Foundation Getúlio Vargas)
Praia de Botafogo, 190
RB 20000 Rio de Janeiro, GB

founded in 1944, is one of the Brazil's cultural institutions with a solid international reputation, specially after the creation of its "Instituto Brasileiro de Economia" (1951) ("Brazilian Institute of Economics"), which carries out studies and surveys on the Brazilian economy. It publishes nine specialized periodicals, "Conjuntura Econômica" being the most important. There is also the

Fundação Instituto Brasileiro de Geografia e Estatística (IGBE)
(Brazilian Institute of Geography and Statistics)
Av. Franklin Roosevelt, 194
RB 20000 Rio de Janeiro, GB

whose most important function is to collect and publish data referring to the General Census, broken down, in 1970, into the Demographic Census (some results are already known), and the Economic Census (Agricultural, Industrial, Commercial and Services).

Bibliography

Sindicato Nacional dos Editôres de Livros (ed.),
  *Produção e comercialização de livros na
  Região Rio-São Paulo.* (Production and
  marketing of books in the Rio–São

Brazil

Paulo Region.) Rio de Janeiro, Sindicato 1969. 40 pp.
J. M. Melo, *Comunicação social. Teoria e pesquisa.* (Social communication, theory and research.) Petrópolis, RJ, Editôra Vozes 1970. 320 pp.
Conjuntura Econômica. Rio de Janeiro, Fundação Getúlio Vargas, since 1947. Monthly.

10 Books and Young People

There is an excellent market in Brazil for juvenile books, and production is growing due mainly to the fact that the country's population is predominantly young.
Official data referring to the year of 1967 show:

Subject	Books (copies) First edition	Other editions
Juvenile books	26,437,822	3,705,263
Other	128,462,003	31,249,311
Totals	154,899,825	34,954,594

Subject	Booklets (copies) First edition	Other editions
Juvenile books	1,283,860	80,000
Other	29,395,534	6,886,864
Totals	30,679,394	6,966,864

The number of periodicals for adolescents and children in 1968 was 631, with a total print order of 9,648,172 copies per issue and a grand total of 267,372,675 for the year.
Important surveys in the adolescent book area have been made by:
Centro de Bibliotecnia
(Bibliotechnical Center)
Av. Rio Branco 156 sala 2732
RB 20000 Rio de Janeiro, GB
associated with Franklin Book Programs (→USA, 28), which since 1967 has been collecting, data about infantjuvenile literature.

The
Fundação Nacional do Livro Infanto-Juvenil
(National Infant-Juvenile Book Foundation)
Rua Voluntários da Pátria, 107
RB 20000 Rio de Janeiro, GB
is a member of the "International Board on Books for Young People" (→BTW I, International Section 10). Its main activities are promoting books, organizing libraries, fairs and contests for the infant-juvenile book market.

Bibliography

L. Arroyo, *Literatura infantil Brasileira.* Ensaio de preliminares para a sua história e suas fontes. (Brazilian children's literature. Some preliminary notes on its history and its sources.) São Paulo, Edições Melhoramentos 1968. 248 pp.
Bibliografia Brasileira de Livros Infantis. (Brazilian bibliography of juvenile books.) Compiled by the Bibliotechnical Center. Special Supplement of "Edições Brasileiras". Rio de Janeiro, Sindicato Nacional dos Editôres de Livros 1968. 160 pp.
Bibliografia Brasileira de Livros Infantis; Special Supplement of "Edições Brasileiras". Rio de Janeiro, Sindicato Nacional dos Editôres de Livros and Centro de Bibliotecnia 1970. 92 pp.
V. Cavalcanti, *Novas perspectivas para a literatura infantil.* As recomendações do Bureau Internacional Católico para a Infância. New perspectives for children's literature. Recommendations of the International Catholic Bureau for Childhood. In: Revista do Livro, Rio de Janeiro, n. 39, 1969. pp. 121–4.

11 Training

In 1969 the
Escola de Comunicação da Universidade Federal do Rio de Janeiro
(School of Communications of the Federal

University of Rio de Janeiro)
Praça da República
RB 20000 Rio de Janeiro, GB
started a "Course on Book Publishing".
The
SENAC–Serviço Nacional de
Aprendizagem Comercial
(National Commercial Training Service)
Avenida General Justo, 275A
RB 20000 Rio de Janeiro, GB
started, a few years ago, a training course
for bookshop personnel, which was dis-
continued; the "Instituto Nacional do
Livro" (→4) started a new course in 1970,
and plans to expand a training programme
for elementary teachers on the proper use
of textbooks.

Bibliography

MANUAL DA COLTED. (COLTED MANNUAL.)
*COLTED–Comissão do Livro Técnico
e Didâtico* (Commission for Technical
and Educational Books), which was set
up in 1967 by the Ministry of Education.
It was discontinued in 1971, and its activities have been transferred to "Instituto
Nacional do Livro" (→4), which has been
quite active in co-publishing textbooks
for the elementary level, and distributes
about 8 million copies per year to impo-
verished students.
P. A. DO N. SILVA, *A editoração na Universidade
Brasileira.* (Publishing in the Brazilian
University.) In: Revista de Cultura
Vozes. Petrópolis, Rio de Janeiro, no.
3, April 1971. pp. 45–50.

12 Taxes

The Constitution forbids any kind of tax
–except income tax–on the book trade.
Undoubtedly it is a protective measure of
great importance, meant to preserve from
the eventual actions of ordinary legislators
such an important instrument for the
country's progress.
This law was introduced in the Constitu-

tional text of 1967, suggested by the
"Sindicato Nacional dos Editôres de
Livros" (→4). The Government is also
studying more liberal regulations for stock
depreciation.

Bibliography

O. DE S. ANDRADE, *O livro Brasileiro –
progressos e problemas numa visão de conjunto.* (The Brazilian book – A general
picture of progress and problems.) In:
Revista do Livro. Rio de Janeiro, no. 37,
1969. pp. 11–54.
Constituição de Republica Federativa do Brasil.
Emenda no. 1 promulgada em 17 de
outubro de 1969. (Constitution of the
Brazilian Federal Republic. Amendment
no. 1 promulgated on 17 October 1969).
s.l. Departamento de Imprensa Nacional
1969. 96 pp.
R. A. A. VIEIRA, *Disponibilidade gráfico-
editorial da imprensa especializada.* (Gra-
phic-editorial availability of the specialized press.) Rio de Janeiro, Getúlio
Vargas Foundation 1969. 25 pp.

13 Clearing Houses

None exists at the moment. However, some
private banks are starting an accounts
payment service.

14 Copyright

Brazil has signed the "Inter-American
Convention on the Rights of the Author in
Literary, Scientific and Artistic Works"
(Washington, 1946); the "Berne Conven-
tion" (Brussels, 1948); and the "Universal
Copyright Convention" (Geneva, 1952)
(→BTW I, International Section 14).
Copyright is automatically granted when a
copy of a new book is delivered to the
"Biblioteca Nacional" ("National Library)
(→15). However, authorship is recognized,
in cases of lawsuits for piracy or plagiarism,
even when such deposit has not been made.

Brazil

Bibliography

H. DUVAL, *Violaçoes dos direitos autorais.* (Copyright violations.) Rio de Janeiro, Ed. Borsoi 1968. 567 pp.

W. MARTINS, *O livro contemporâneo – Os direitos autorais e outros problemas.* (The contemporaneous book – Copyright and other problems.) In: A Palavra Escrita de... (The Written Word.) Chapter XIV. São Paulo, Editora Anhembi 1957.

15 National Bibliography, National Library

Brazil's bibliographical survey was started over 160 years ago by
Biblioteca Nacional
(National Library)
Av. Rio Branco, 219–39
RB 20000 Rio de Janeiro, GB
This institution is part of the Education and Culture Ministry and, in spite of all its shortcomings, it has been able to keep up regular publication of the "Boletim Bibliográfico" ("Bibliographic Bulletin") since 1886.
Since November 1967 the "Instituto Nacional do Livro" ("National Book Institute", →4) has been publishing its "Bibliografia Brasileira Mensal" ("Monthly Brazilian Bibliography").
Also of great importance is the
Instituto Brasileiro de Bibliografia e
Documentacão (IBBD)
(Brazilian Bibliography and Documentation Institute)
Avenida General Justo, 171
RB 20000 Rio de Janeiro, GB
An organ of the *Conselho Nacional de Pesquisas* (National Research Council), its main task is to survey and publish the country's technical and scientific literature, using computerized equipment. It publishes a scientific Brazilian bibliography for nearly every field (Botany, Agricultural Sciences, Social Sciences, Law, Physics, Medicine, Technology), textbooks on library science and documen-

tation, and also a periodical specialized in scientific information. The Institute provides information and makes bibliographical surveys, on demand, for scientific and technological subjects; among other cultural functions, it keeps an updated file of all survey projects throughout the country and possesses a complete collection of bibliographical and information reference works. Worthy of mention also is the
Associação Brasileira de Normas Técnicas
(Brazilian Association for Technical Standards)
Avenida Almirante Barroso, 54–15°/
sala 1503–5
RB 20000 Rio de Janeiro, GB
a non-profit-making civil association founded in 1940. Its main objectives are the elaboration, adoption and diffusion of technical standards in the scientific, technical, industrial, commercial and agricultural fields and the incentive of the standardization movement in Brazil. It represents Brazil as the national standardization body and is a member of the ISO and the COPANT ("Comissão Pan-Americana de Normas Técnicas".)

Bibliography

Brazilian Association of Technical Standards. Normalização da documentação no Brasil. (Standardization of documentation in Brazil.) 2nd ed. Rio de Janeiro, IBBD 1964. pp. 93–116.

E. N. DA FONSECA, *Desenvolvimento da biblioteconomia e da bibliografia no Brasil.* (Development of biblioteconomy and bibliography in Brazil.) In: Revista do Livro, no. 5, Rio de Janeiro 1957. pp. 95–124.

Instituto Nacional do Livro. Bibliografia Brasileira Mensal. (Monthly Brazilian Bibliography.) Rio de Janeiro 1967.

Instituto Brasileiro de Bibliografia e Documentação. Bibliografia Brasileira de Medicina. vol. 11 (1967). (Brazilian Medicine Bibliography.) Rio de Janeiro 1970. 516 pp.

W. Martins, *A Biblioteca Nacional outras bibliotecas Brasileiras.* (The National Library–Brazilian libraries.) In: A Palavra Escrita (The Written Word). Chapter XIII. São Paulo, Ed. Anhembi 1957. pp. 403–23.

Ministry of Education and Culture, National Library of Rio de Janeiro. *Sesquicentenário 1810–1960: Guia da Biblioteca Nacional* (Sesquicentennial Anniversary 1810 – 1960; Guide to the National Library.) Rio de Janeiro. 1960, 72 pp.

Ministry of Education and Culture. National Library of Rio de Janeiro. *Boletim Bibliográfico* (Bibliographical Bulletin). Published at irregular intervals.

X. Placer, *A bibliografie e sua técnica.* (Bibliography and its techniques.) Rio de Janeiro, Ministry of Education and Culture, Documentation Service 1955. IV, 50 pp.

J. G. de Souza, *Referências bibliográficas sugestoes para um plano de normas de uniformização.* (Bibliographical references. Suggestions for a uniform standards plan.) In: Revista do Livro, Rio de Janeiro, no. 33, 1968. pp. 49–86.

I. Zimmermann, *Current national bibliographies of Latin America.* Gainesville, Florida, University of Florida Press 1971. X, 139 pp.
pp. 29–35: Brazil.

16 Book Production

The most recent official data confirm the growth of the Brazilian publishing industry in recent years. This expansion, however, is far from saturation point, inasmuch as the demographic explosion and the rising standard of living absorb its production.

Close to 80% of titles and 90% of copies are published (and printed) in Rio and São Paulo. These two cities also absorb a high proportion of copies sold.

Official statistics, issued by the Ministry of Education and culture for 1971, contain the following information:

Category	Titles
First editions (books of more than 48 pages)	5,219
New editions (books of more than 48 pages)	1,971
Total	7,190

The number of copies (both groups) reached 80 million, with 48 million for first editions. The leading subject groups were as follows (first editions):

Subject group	Titles
Literature	2,122
Law	419
School books	419
Education	355
Religion	292

17 Translations

Almost 100% of all elementary and secondary school textbooks are written by local authors.

A substantial percentage of juvenile books are either translated or adapted, mainly to take advantage of imported film positives, which permit an improved quality at a lower cost.

Many university and technical textbooks are translated and in some cases adapted.

Close to one third of new trade titles are translations, and those titles make nearly half of the total sales of trade books. As noted above, the available statistics are not very precise.

The official statistics for translations in 1971 refer to 1,371 titles, whereof 529 were of general character.

18 Book Clubs

There are no book clubs in Brazil in the modern sense of the word. Several attempts have been made in the past without great success, mainly because of poor mail services and galloping inflation, which has gradually been controlled since 1964.

The Brazilian Post Office was recently transformed into a Corporation and is being reorganized. With improved mail service, a stabilized economy and expanded printing capacity, Brazil will soon be ready for book clubs.

19 Paperbacks

Several attempts have been made in this field in the last 25 years, always with disappointing results, due to the following reasons:

a) In Brazil there are no separate rights for paperbacks, and therefore only second-rate or public-domain titles are available for pocket editions.

b) There are no separate marketing channels for paperbacks, except news-stands, which are not properly equipped to handle them. Most bookshops are not very keen on them.

c) As a consequence, savings from large press runs are seldom made; the cost reductions on paper and manufacturing are more than offset by reductions on the cover price.

The image of the paperback in Brazil has been mostly that of a second-class product. The "Instituto Nacional do Livro" (→4), however, is trying to change this image by sponsoring a low-priced line in educational and classics titles (close to 150 titles in 1970).

20 Book Design

In order to stimulate the publishing industry in the country, the "Instituto Nacional do Livro" (→4) started the *Santa Rosa Prize* in 1969 to be awarded for the best-produced book of the year. Taken into consideration are the cover, the design, the printing and other technical aspects. According to the rules, publishers and writer-publishers are allowed to enter as many books as they wish.

Bibliography

Revista do Livro. Rio de Janeiro, Instituto Nacional do Livro no. 41 1970. pp. 143–4.

21 Publishing

Until the First World War almost all Brazilian publishers were located in Rio. Many textbooks and general works were printed in Europe (→2). This was the so-called graphic bookseller period, from which the legitimate publisher was to develop half a century later. Up to the end of the First World War all publishing was done by booksellers and printers, as a subsidiary activity; the first publishing house without any connection to a bookshop or printing plant was founded in 1925 – its name is Cia. Editora Nacional, of São Paulo.

Since then, developing fast, São Paulo became the country's leading industrial state, in which is now concentrated over 50% of Brazil's book production. Rio accounts for close to 40%, and Pôrto Alegre, Belo Horizonte, Salvador and Recife are coming up and should soon have a bigger share of the market.

Bibliography

Ministry of Education and Culture. Education and Culture Statistics Service. *Emprêsas editôras e impressôras de livros e folhetos – 1967*. (Book and brochure publishing and printing houses.) Rio de Janeiro 1968. 31 mimeogr. pp.

Sindicato Nacional dos Editôres de Livros. Política de expansão editorial para o desenvolvimento. (Publishing expansion policy for development.) Suggestions ... to the Minister of Education on 28 November

1966. In: *Boletim Informativo do GEIL.* (GEIL Informative Bulletin.) Rio de Janeiro, no. 2, June 1967, p. 2.

Grupo Executivo da Industria do Livro. Situação da industria do livro. (Situation in the book industry.) Report ... to the Minister of Education and Culture, about the GEIL's activities in 1966 and plans for 1967, on 11 January 1967. In: Boletim Informativo do GEIL. Rio de Janeiro, no. 2, June 1967. pp. 3–4.

D. DE ABREU, *A expansão da rêde de livrarias e a boa livraria.* (The expansion of the network of bookshops and the good bookshop.) Rio de Janeiro, A Casa do Livro 1970. 44 pp.

22 Literary Agents

Brazilian authors make their contacts direct with their publishers. In most cases they also deal directly with foreign publishers or buyers of subsidiary rights.

The local publishers, on the other hand, deal directly with foreign publishers when buying educational rights, and with agents when trade titles are involved. Agents are becoming important.

23 Wholesale Trade

All large publishers have their own branches and/or agents in the six largest cities – São Paulo, Rio, Pôrto Alegre, Belo Horizonte, Recife and Salvador. Most of these agents maintain a good coverage of their territories, and this has led to a regional pattern of distribution rather than national wholesalers.

Some attempts have been made to create firms covering the whole country. "Disal" and "Catavento" in São Paulo, and "Distribuidora Record" (Rio and São Paulo) are the most active.

24 Retail Trade

The most frequently used book-marketing channel in Brazil is still the traditional bookshop. The insufficiency of outlets due to the low profitability of book retailing has stimulated, however, some attempts to create other points of sale in order to improve the sales flow of national and foreign book production. For example, there is a recent decree (1968) allowing pharmacies to sell books, benefiting from the same tax exemption as that granted to bookshops (→ 12). Another example is the selling through news-stands and department stores.

The Federal Government is studying other forms of support such as financing, through official banks, the purchase of bookshop sites and sponsoring professional improvement courses for bookshop personnel.

Altogether, there are about 500 bookshops in the country; another 500 shops (mainly stationery and variety shops) also sell books, mainly textbooks when classes open, and juveniles in December.

Supermarkets and pharmacies are also experimenting with books, displaying wire racks with about 100 assorted titles.

Bibliography

D. DE ABREU, *O livro e a indústria do conhecimento.* (The book and the knowledge industry.) Rio de Janeiro, Centro de Bibliotécnica 1968. 50 pp.

D. DE ABREU, *A expansão da rêde de livrarias e a boa livraria.* (The expansion of the network of bookshops and the good bookshop.) Rio de Janeiro, A Casa do Livro 1970. pp. 11–43.

H. CARO, *Balcão de livraria.* (Bookshop counter.) Rio de Janeiro, Ministry of Education and Culture, Documentation Centre 1960. 101 pp.

Brazil

25 Mail-Order Bookselling

Few firms at present make sales through the mail. Poor postal services ($\rightarrow$ 18) hindered this technique in the past and a recent steep increase in postal rates has further disouraged some of the remaining operators.

But this postage increase should, in due course, make things easier, since it will improve the service. One of the negative factors for mail order was the limitation of home delivery to the metropolitan area, saddling the best potential customer (the dweller of medium and small interior cities, whose normal response is 40 % better) with the annoyance of having to visit the local post office to pick up–and pay for–his book.

Bibliography

O aumento das tarifas postais para o livro. (The increase of postal rates for the book.) *Observaçoes a respeito dos preços de franquiamento para os livros.* (Remarks about postage rates for books.) GEIL, Inf. Bulletin no. 2

Remessa de livros para o exterior por via postal. (Sending books abroad by mail.) GEIL, Inf. Bulletin no. 1

A tarifa postal e o livro. (Postal rates and the book.) GEIL, Inf. Bulletin no. 4

Sugestoes para a reestruturação do reembôlso postal. (Suggestions for remodelling Postal C.O.D.) GEIL, Inf. Bulletin no. 6/7

26 Antiquarian Book Trade, Auctions

Of an active second-hand book trade which flourished up to the early forties only a few antiquarian booksellers remain. And most of these sell new books as a side or main activity.

"Livraria Kosmos" is the outstanding house in this field. "Livraria São José", with a huge inventory of out-of-print books, is the meeting place of writers, and is the last survivor in a street where two dozen "sêbos" (second-hand bookshops) lived peacefully during the first war years. A true picture of the market is given by the failure of

Associação Brasileira de Livreiros-Antiquários
(Brazilian Association of Antiquarian Booksellers)
s/o Livraria Kosmos
Rua do Rosario, 137
RB 20000 Rio de Janeiro, GB

in getting more than 4 members. Book auctions are rarely held.

A recent decree issued by Congress (1968) forbids the export of books and other printed material published before the 19th century as well as collections of periodicals over 10 years old. Special permits are required for exhibits abroad.

Bibliography

R. B. DE MORAIS, *O bibliófilo aprendiz.* (The apprentice bibliophile.) São Paulo, Companhia Editora Nacional 1965. 200 pp.

O. DE S. ANDRADE, *O livro Brasileiro – progressos e problemas numa visão de conjunto.* (The Brazilian book – progresses and problems in a general picture.) In: Revisto do Livro. Rio de Janeiro, no. 37 1969. pp. 11–54.

27 Book Imports

As has already been mentioned ($\rightarrow$ 12), conditions for imports granted by the Constitution are very favourable. The figures below also reflect the devaluation of the cruzeiro.

Years	Quantity (t)	Cr$ 1.000
1961	1,363	916
1966	1,507	13,488
1967	2,089	23,620
1968	1,817	21,928
1969	2,383	32,429

Main suppliers are the USA, with a 50% share of the market:

Country	1968 Cr$ 1,000	Percentage
USA	11,273,897	51.4
Portugal	2,750,864	12.5
Spain	2,384,014	10.8
France	1,210,807	5.5
Argentina	918,013	4.1
United Kingdom	797,541	3.6
Germany (F.R.)	615,529	2.8
Mexico	569,854	2.6

Bibliography

Fundação Instituto Brasileiro de Geografia e Estatística. Anuário Estatístico do Brasil. (Statistical Yearbook.)–1970. Rio de Janeiro 1970. 333 pp.

Grupo Executivo da Industria do Livro. Boletim Informativo. (Informative Bulletin.) Rio de Janeiro, no. 4, Sept./Oct. 1967. pp. 6–7; no. 15/16, Sept./Dec. 1969, p. 2; no. 17/18, Jan./Apr. 1970. 6 pp.

O. DE S. ANDRADE, *O livro Brasileiro; progressos e problemas numa visão de conjunto.* (The Brazilian book; progresses and problems in a general picture.) In: Revista do Livro. Rio de Janeiro, Instituto Nacional do Livro, no. 37 1969. pp. 35–39.

M. ABRAMO, *O livro no Brazil. Alguns dados sôbre a sua história e sua evolução.* (The book in Brazil. Some data about its history and its evolution.) In: Revista de Cultura Vozes. Petrópolis, RJ, v. 65, no 3, April 1971. 17 pp.

28 Book Exports

The Brazilian book is a victim of the language barrier, Portuguese being spoken only in Portugal and its former African territories besides Brazil. Red tape, deficiencies in trade publications and lack of aggressiveness of booksellers and publishers have further reduced the international market penetration by the Brazilian book. "A Casa do Livro" has set up an Export Department which can handle orders from booksellers and libraries.

Lately a reaction to this situation is noticeable: there is more frequent participation in international fairs and exhibitions, and the reformulation of export procedures in an attempt to simplify and speed up formalities.

Official figures are not reliable, for they include periodicals, and exclude exports of less than US$ 100.00. An educated guess would put Brazilian exports to close to US$ 500,000.00, mainly to Portugal.

29 Book Fairs

In 1970 the first "International Book Biennial" was held in São Paulo, sponsored by the "Fundação Bienal de São Paulo" ("São Paulo Biennial Foundation"), "Instituto Nacional do Livro" ("National Book Institute", →4), and "Sindicato Nacional dos Editôres de Livros" ("National Syndicate of Book Publishers" →4). Twenty-three countries participated, and the sponsors experienced an even more expressive international representation for the following fairs.

The most popular fair is the one held annually in Rio de Janeiro since 1955, with over 100 publishers and booksellers taking part, and which lasts one month. A 20% discount is granted.

Bibliography

I Bienal Internacional do Livro 1970. (Ist International Biennial of the Book 1970.) Catalog. São Paulo, Secretaria da Fundação Bienal de São Paulo 1970. 164 pp.

30 Public Relations

Little was done in this area in the past. Today the following measures are under way:

Brazil

1. Industry-wide contacts with government agencies, aiming at
a) An official book policy
b) More libraries
c) Adequate supply of elementary textbooks for students with no purchasing power
d) Better postal service
e) Financing from official banks and other sources of credit
f) Expansion of facilities and training of personnel.
2. The government has sponsored some events such as the "National Book Campaign" (1960), "National Book Day" (1967), and "Culture and Sciences Day" (1970) with debates, courses, lectures, exhibitions, contests about books and their use.
3. Individual publishers and their trade associations have been active promoting
a) Professional seminars (publishers' and booksellers' meetings) with guest foreign publishers
b) Participation in international activities (IPA, Frankfurt Book Fair, Ibero-American Book Trade Association, etc.)
c) Better contact with mass media promoting discussions and debates on books
d) Advertising of books
e) Promotion of autograph parties, etc.

Bibliography

J. FERREIRA, *O livro como forma de comunicação e conhecimento.* (The book as a means of communication and knowledge.) In: Revista do Livro. Rio de Janeiro, no. 43, 1970. pp. 18–22.

G. FREYRE, *O problema do livro.* (The problem of the book.) In: Revista do Livro. Rio de Janeiro, no. 37, 1969. 165–6 pp.

III Encontro de Editôres e Livreiros. (Third Meeting of Publishers and Booksellers.) (Serra Negra, São Paulo, Brazil.) August 1970. Report of the Coordinating Committee. s.l., Brazilian Book Chamber and National Syndicate of Book Publishers 1971. pp. 15–6 and 58–61.

31 Bibliophily

The
Sociedade dos Cem Bibliófilos
(One Hundred Bibliophiles Society)
c/o Fundação Castro Maya
Rua Murtinho Nobre, 93
RB 20000 Rio de Janeiro
was founded, with the double purpose of encouraging and developing the activity of book lovers and to publish illustrated limited editions of Brazilian books for its members.
Several fine editions have been published by the Society. At the time of writing it is dormant.

Bibliography

E. FRIEIRO, *O verdadeiro bibliófilo.* (The true bibliophile.) In: Revista do Livro. Rio de Janeiro, no. 5, 1957. pp. 183–6.

E. N. DA FONSECA, *Oliveira Lima, bibliófilo e bibliógrafo.* (Oliveira Lima, bibliophile and bibliographer.) In: Revista do Livro. Rio de Janeiro, no. 32, 1968. pp. 149–51.

R. B. DE MORAIS, *O bibliófilo aprendiz.* (The apprentice bibliophile.) São Paulo, Companhia Editoria Nacional 1965. 200 pp.

J. LEITE, *Sôbre a Sociedade de Bibliophilos Brasileiros.* (On the Society of Brazilian Bibliophiles.) In: Estudos Brasileiros. Rio de Janeiro, no. 1 1938. pp. 100.

32 Literary Prizes

The awarding of literary prizes is a common practice, though relatively recent. Sponsored by official, semi-official and private institutions, the prizes–varying in purpose, style and value–have been awarded to new authors and known ones. It was the "Academia Brasileira de Letras" ("Brazilian Academy of Letters") who, in 1909, initiated the practice of awarding prizes in Brazil. Its most important prize is the *Machado de Assis*, in honour of its patron, bestowed upon the writer of the best book published in the previous year. Recently created, the *Prêmio Nacional Walmap* (Walmap National Prize) is today the most important in Brazil and–for unpublished novels–one of the biggest in the world: its total value is US $ 10,000. It is organized by the literary section of a leading newspaper (O Globo) and sponsored by a banker.

Other annual prizes: *Fernando Chinaglia Prize*, by the "União Brasileira de Escritores" (Brazilian Writers' Union); *Jabuti Prize* by "Câmara Brasileira do Livro" (Brazilian Book Chamber); *Esso-Jornal de Letras Prize* for university students; *Brasilia Literature Prize* to the value of US $ 4,000, intended for a set of works by a national author, granted by "Fundação Cultural, Distrito Federal", together with 8 minor prizes.

Created by law in 1967, the *National Literary Prizes* distributed by the "Instituto Nacional do Livro" (National Book Institute), include six prizes for published works (Novel, Poetry, Short Story, Short Novel, Brazilian Essay, Brazilian History and Literary and Linguistics Essays). The INL also awards the *Viriato Corrêa Prize* for juvenile literature, created in 1968. Apart from other minor prizes of a transitory character, created by the INL, one worth mentioning is the *Santa Rosa Prize* for the best-produced book of the year, created in 1969. "Sindicato Nacional dos Editôres" and "Câmara Brasileira do Livro" (→4) have decided to award a prize to the best elementary/secondary textbook published each year.

Bibliography

Academia Brasileira de Letras (ed.), *Anuário 1965–1969. (1965–1969 Yearbook.)* Rio de Janeiro pp. 237–60.

Almanaque de Seleçoes 1971. (1971 Almanac.) Rio de Janeiro, Seleções do Reader's Digest 1971. pp. 344–6.

A. OLINTO, *O IV Premio Nacional Walmap.* (The fourth National Walmap Prize.) In: O Globo, Rio de Janeiro 22 April 1971. p. 6.

Revista do Livro. Rio de Janeiro, INL (National Book Institute), no. 33–43, 1968 to 70.

33 The Reviewing of Books

Practically all Brazilian magazines and newspapers carry a book review section. The same applies to radio and TV stations. The most important newspapers are *O Globo, O Jornal* and *Jornal do Brasil* in Rio de Janeiro, *O Estado de São Paulo* in São Paulo; magazines: *O Cruzeiro, A Cigarra, Visão, Veja,* and many others; newspapers specializing in literature: *Jornal de Letras, Correio do Livro* and *O Jornal do Escritor.*

Bibliography

Instituto Brasileiro de Bibliografia e Documentação. Periódicos Brasileiros de cultura. (Brazilian cultural periodicals). Rio de Janeiro, 1968. 280 pp.

A. BASTOS, *Coluna literária vende livros?* (Do literary columns sell books?) BBB-Revista dos Editôres. Rio de Janeiro, vol. 8, no. 5, June 1960.

V. CAVALCANTI, *Literatura 1968.* (1968 literature.) In: Revista de Livro. Rio de Janeiro no. 36, 1969. pp. 175–90.

L. BELTRAO, *Comunicação moderna e literatura.* (Modern communication and literature.) In: Revista do Livro. Rio de Janeiro, no. 38 1969. pp. 39–49.

O. M. CARPEAUX, *Pequena bibliografia crítica da literatura Brasileira.* (Small critical bibliography on Brazilian literature.) 3rd. ed. Rio de Janeiro, Editôra Letras e Artes 1964. 340 pp.

A. COUTINHO, *Crítica e críticos.* (Criticism and critics.) Rio de Janeiro, Organização Simões Editôra 1969. 248 pp.

Brazil

A. COUTINHO, *A crítica literária no Brasil.* (Literary criticism in Brazil.) In: *Crítica e Poética.* Rio de Janeiro, Livraria Acadêmica 1968. pp. 115–57. With bibliography.

34 Graphic Arts

The two more important trade associations are:

Sindicato das Indústrias Gráficas de São Paulo
(Syndicate of the Graphic Industries of São Paulo)
Rua Marquez de Itu, 70–12° andar
RB São Paulo, S.P.

and

Sindicato das Industrias Gráficas de Guanabara
(Syndicate of the Graphic Industries of Guanabara)
Rua Miguel Couto, 131
RB 20000 Rio de Janeiro

Bibliography

J. B. C. DE M. SERPA, *Resoliçoes do I Congresso Latino-Americano de Indústria Gráfica.* (Resolutions of the Ist Latin-American Congress of the Graphic Industry.) Report by the GEIL representative. GEIL Informative Bulletin. Rio de Janeiro, no. 5 Jan./Feb. 1968, p. 3.

35 Miscellaneous

a) Authors
Except for the colonial period Brazil has always had several "belles lettres" associations. None of them, however, have proved to be very professional in their defence and protection of the author's interests. The *Academia Brasileira de Letras*, the *União Brasileira de Escritores*, the *Pen Club* and other civil associations have been of little use–due to their own statutory and legal limitations–in helping writers to obtain legal professional recognition, including social-security benefits. At present steps for the creation of the first Writers' Union in Rio de Janeiro are being taken, including official recognition by the Labour Ministry. Similar initiatives are being taken in other States.

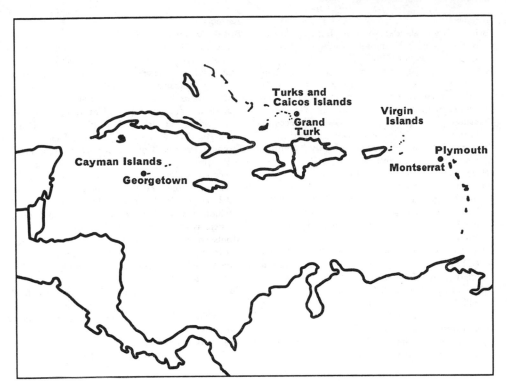

1 General Information

Area, Population, Capital, Largest towns

a) British Virgin Islands (Leewaard Islands) comprising, Tortola, Virgin Gorda, Anegada and Jost Van Dyke
147 km²; population, 10,848; capital: Grand Town (2,183)

b) Cayman Islands, comprising Grand Cayman, Cayman Brac and Little Cayman
260 km²; population: 10,652; capital: George-town (3,975)

c) Montserrat (Leeward Islands)
101 km²; population: 13,000; capital Plymouth (the only town) (3,500)

d) Turks and Caicos Islands, comprising Grand Turk, Salt Cay 6 Cays and Rocks, South Caicos, East Caicos, Grand (Middlc) Caicos, North Caicos, Providenciales and West Caicos
430 km²; population: 6,600; capital: Grand Turk (2,330)

Government British Virgin Islands: Partial internal self-government with a Ministerial System. There is an Administrator as the Queen's Representative, and Legislative and Executive Councils. Government has been traditionally stable

Cayman Islands: A British Colony with Executive and Legislative Councils

Montserrat: A British Colony with representative Government. It has a Ministerial System, an Administrator and Legislative and Executive Councils. Montserrat elected, in 1966, to retain constitution and not to move to Self-Government status

Turks and Caicos Islands: British Colony. State Council with Legislative and Executive powers Governor of Bahamas is Governor of Turks and Caicos Islands

British West Indies

Religion

British Virgin Islands: Anglican, Baptist, Church of God, Jehova Witnesses, Methodist, Roman Catholic, Seventh Day Adventists

Cayman Islands: Anglican, Baptist, Church of Christ, Church of God, Latter Day Saints, Pilgrim Holiness, Presbyterian, Roman Catholic, Seventh Day Adventists

Montserrat: Anglican, Methodist, Pentecostal, Roman Catholic, Seventh Day Adventists

Turks and Caicos Islands: Seventh Day Adventists

National language English

Weights, measures Imperial system

Currency unit The monetary units are:

British Virgin Islands: The United States Dollar is the sole currency in use owing to the proximity to the US Virgin Islands and Puerto Rico

Cayman Islands: The Cayman Island Dollar (CI $) which comprises 100 cents. It has a fixed parity of CI $2.40 to the £ Sterling

Montserrat: The Eastern Caribbean Dollar (EC $) which comprises 100 cents. Exchange rate is EC $4.80 to the £ Sterling

Turks and Caicos Islands: The Jamaica Dollar (J $) which comprises 100 cents. Exchange rate is J $2.40 to the £ Sterling

Education

British Virgin Islands: Compulsory. Free. 14 primary schools. One secondary school. Students may go up to Certificate of Education at Advanced Level. One Education Institute and University of the West Indies (UWI) Extra-Mural Classes. For higher education students often go to UWI at three campuses (Jamaica, Trinidad, Barbados), the USA, Puerto Rico and the US Virgin Islands

Cayman Islands: Compulsory from 5–15. Free. 19 primary schools. One junior high, 3 secondary and 1 comprehensive Schools. There is one Further Education Institute, 2 US type High School. The territory contributes to the University of the West Indies. There is also one Secretarial College

Montserrat: Compulsory. There are 8 pre-primary, 14 primary or elementary, 1 secondary (with technical wing) and 1 junior secondary schools

Turks and Caicos Islands: Primary education is free and compulsory for ages $4^1/_2$–15. 16 primary schools. There are 2 secondary schools

Illiteracy British Virgin Is. and Cayman Is.: low; Montserrat: 25 %; Turks and Caicos Is.: nil

2 Past and Present

The book trade in these islands cannot be fairly described in sophisticated terms. Factors which affect reading and therefore the retail trade include the concentration of facilities, utilities and bookshops in the capitals. In most parts of this Region there is an oral tradition. In most of the territories the majority of young people on leaving school migrate in search of job/ vocation opportunities or go to study abroad. After qualifying professionals frequently elect to stay abroad or take up attractive offers in the larger Caribbean countries.

British Virgin Islands: The people are predominantly of African extraction with a trace of Indian and Amerindian blood. Unlike other areas, the Islands are underpopulated. Recently, there has been an increase in West Indian immigration. Arrangements for technical aid and expertise are made with other Caribbean countries. This link, in the case of Trinidad & Tobago, has resulted in some business with bookshops and printing firms.

Cayman Islands: The majority of the population is described as "mixed". 20% are of African descent and 20% of European. Turtle fishing, a traditional pursuit, has declined considerably. The Islands have become an important trans-shipment centre for lobsters. The sea and 'marine' life attract young Caymanians as a means of livelihood.

Montserrat: was named in 1493 by Columbus after a famous mountain in Spain. Twice in its history for brief periods the Island was French. Its cultural influences have been African and Irish. Means of livelihood has been until recently, mainly agricultural. Development, especially in tourism, has influenced the rapid growth of construction and service industries. While the book situation in the Island cannot be described as a "trade", demands of the new industries for reading materials and information and increased training in these areas should lead to an increased demand for books.

Turks and Caicos Islands: At least 90% of the population is of African descent. The rest includes United States Service and civilian personnel. Salt, previously the most important industry and principal export, has been replaced by the frozen crawfish and conch industry. Tourism is, however, rapidly becoming the major industry.

Bibliography

BR. F. SWAN, *The spread of printing, Western Hemisphere: The Caribbean area.* Amsterdam, Vangendt 1970. 47 pp. pp. 29–30: Montserrat.

3 Retail Prices

In general practice there is a mark-up on the landed cost of books. Libraries may receive special rates either as discounts or a mark-up on the published price of books. Discount rates for fiction and general non-fiction vary and special rates apply for school texts. No specific figures were made available. The worldwide increase in prices of books is of course applicable and this is further aggravated by increased shipping and postal rates.

7 Source of Information, Address Services

In these islands with their usually close knit communities, sources of information are often personal. The local press, as well as the press of larger Caribbean countries, are useful sources. The Libraries are often important sources of information:

Public Library
Road Town
Tortola

Public Library
Georgetown
Grand Cayman
or
Public Library
Plymouth
Montserrat
and
Public Library
Grand Turk
Turks and Caicos Islands

10 Books and Young People

Special collections may be maintained in children/teenage sections of Public Libraries (e.g. British Virgin Islands), and in the School (Primary and Secondary) Libraries (e.g. British Virgin Islands and Montserrat). Bookshops (British Virgin Islands and Montserrat) may emphasize their children books. The collections are mainly imported books from English-speaking countries but may and often do include some provision for books produced in the Region.

12 Taxes

In the British Virgin Islands, printed material is allowed in duty free but there is a wharfage charge of 1%. In Montserrat books are duty free.

13 Clearing Institutions

British Virgin Islands report a clearing house for Penguin Books only.

14 Copyright

Laws are based on the British 1911 Act. In the British Virgin Islands an amendment applied in 1973 to provide for acceptance of the International Copyright Convention. Montserrat is influenced by the International Conventions (→BTW I, International Section 14).

15 National Bibliography, National Library

British Virgin Islands and Montserrat report that some of the functions of a National Library are carried out by the Public Library (→7). In Montserrat, the University Centre Library shares the responsibility. British Virgin Islands has published a bibliography of the library's holding of Br. V.I. materials, a Br. V.I. chronology, and is compiling a Union Catalogue of Government Reports. No bibliography activity is reported in the other territories.

Bibliography

I. ZIMMERMANN, *Current national bibliographies of Latin America*. Gainesville, Florida, University of Florida Press 1971. X. 139 pp.
pp. 88–102: West Indies, The Caribbean.

22 Literary Agents

In the British Virgin Islands the Public Library via its publication *Literary World Bulletin* acts as a local literary agent.

24 Retail Trade

A total of six bookshops are reported, four in the British Virgin Islands, one in the Cayman Islands and one in Montserrat. Books are imported mainly from the USA and the United Kingdom from publishers, book agents or booksellers. There are some imports from regional booksellers of internationally and regionally published material.

27 Book Imports

The British Virgin Islands report for 1973, an amount of US$ 12,868 spent in books imported. Montserrat records an average of 400 books and 10 periodicals imported per annum.
Turks and Caicos Islands book imports from the United Kingdom

Year	£
1964	33.00
1965	108.00
1966	9.00
1967	187.00
1968	135.00
1969	60.00
1970	4,622.00

30 Public Relations

British Virgin Islands: There is some promotion of books and reading in this country through book groups, reading clubs, appropriate radio programmes, children's library programmes, annotated booklists and the Government News Release Channels. In International Book Year a Book Jacket Competition promoted books, reading and art.

32 Literary Prizes

British Virgin Islands Children's Short Story Competitions have been sponsored by the Public Library.

33 The Reviewing of Books

The following periodicals carry reviews of books by local persons:
British Virgin Is.: *Island Sun* and the *British Virgin Is. Magazine*
Montserrat: *Montserrat Mirror*

35 Miscellaneous

a) *Radio*
British Virgin Islands: There is a commercial broadcasting station.
Montserrat: There is one Government owned broadcasting station with programmes (in English) reaching the Eastern Caribbean. The commercial station, Radio Antilles, broadcasts in English, French and Spanish. Television transmissions are received from Antigua.
b) *Newspapers*
There is one weekly newspaper in each of the countries:
British Virgin Is.–Island Sun
  (P.O. Box 21, Road Town)
Cayman Is.–Caymanian
  (P.O. Box 167, Grand Cay)
Montserrat–Montserrat Mirror
  (P.O. Box 200, Plymouth)
Turks and Caicos Is.–Conch News
  (Grand Turk)
c) *Cinemas*
Two cinemas and one Drive-In Cinema are reported in the Cayman Island.
d) *Tourism*
Within recent years considerable promotion in tourism has been the trend in all these countries. They have been "discovered" by resort developers and this has influenced increased activity in the construction and service industries. An increased demand for books is an expected result.
e) *Other Influences*
The Cayman Islands have no direct taxation and, due to tax haven facilities, have become an international financial centre. At least 10 Trust Corporations have been established as well as an "Investment Dollar" market. An overall population increase has been created by the resultant immigration. In the Turks and Caicos Islands no taxes are levied on land, property or income.

British West Indies

f) *Library Facilities*
British Virgin Islands
Established in 1943, the British Virgin Islands Library operates from the main library in Road Town, serves Tortola by a mobile library service and the other islands by deposit stations. The Service is administered by a qualified librarian.

Cayman Islands
There is a government public library service centred in Georgetown and expanding to other areas.

Montserrat
There is one small public library, one secondary school library and a reference library at the University of the West Indies Extra-Mural Department. These all serve chiefly the residents of Plymouth. There is a village sponsored library in Salem.

Turks and Caicos Islands
The small Library Service is based in Grand Turk. Some of the schools have small libraries.

Canada

1 General Information

Area 9,973,546 km²

Population 21,984,000 (14.5 per km²) (1971)

Capital Ottawa (602,510)

Largest towns Montréal (2,743,208); Toronto (2,628,043); Vancouver (1,082,352); Ottawa (602,510); Edmonton (495,702); Hamilton (498,523); Winnipeg (540,262); Québec (480,502)

Government Independent federation within the British Commonwealth. Comprises ten provinces and two territories, which are administered by the federal government

Religion Roman Catholic 48%
United Church of Canada (Protestant) 20%
Anglican Church of Canada 13.2%
Smaller religious groups and dissidents 18.8%

Official national languages English and French (60.2% have English as their maternal language, 26.9% French, and 13.0% other languages)

Weights and measures British Imperial System

Currency unit Canadian dollar ($) equals 100 cents (c)

Education Compulsory. 5.6 m. pupils enrolled in 15,841 primary and secondary schools (1972–73). Higher education enrolment: 1,651 per 100,000 inhabitants in 246 universities, colleges and technical institutions of academic standard (1972–73). Education is a provincial jurisdiction

Illiteracy 0–3%

Paper consumption a) Newsprint 30 kg per inhabitant (1970)
b) Printing paper (other than newsprint) 27 kg per inhabitant (1970)

Membership UNESCO, IPA, ICBA, ILAB, UIELF

93

Canada

2 Past and Present

The Canadian book trade has developed along two distinct patterns, one for each of the two official-language communities. Within each segment, recent years have witnessed dramatic changes amidst controversies that are yet to be resolved.

The beginnings of the book trade in Canada are linked to its printers, as they have been in other countries. The first establishment was located in Halifax (1751), where the colonists would first touch before continuing inland. Soon presses were operating in Montréal and Québec City, and before the turn of the century in Upper Canada (Ontario). They survived on weekly newspapers, some general books of interest to pioneering settlers, government printing contracts and, particularly in Québec, religious books which included schoolbooks. But the trade lacked organization, with the result that the distribution system became increasingly complicated.

By 1850, Toronto had begun to establish itself as the publishing centre of English Canada. But Canadian publishers faced severe handicaps, chief of which was perhaps the Colonial Copyright Act (known commonly as the Foreign Reprints Act) which was passed in England in 1847. This Act permitted the importation into Canada of cheap reprints, and while American publishers were thus able to flood the Canadian market, the Canadians themselves were prevented from doing so. In addition, the Act gave little if any protection to Canadian authors, who were thereby encouraged to seek publishers in London or New York. Only in 1875 was royal assent given to a Canadian copyright law which stipulated Canadian "domicile" for authors and local manufacture of books. While this led to a period of Canadian publishers pirating popular American authors' works and flooding the U.S. market, primarily through direct-mail sales, it eventually also regulated import publishing by awarding exclusive agencies for British and American books to Canadian publishers. This important development tended to encourage publishers' wholesale operations, and as they concentrated attention on their agency activities, their original publishing programme suffered and they divested themselves of their retail outlets.

Even the system of schoolbook publishing, which continued largely unchanged until World War II, tended to stimulate production rather than publishing skills–with some notable exceptions. Texts were commissioned by the ministries of education and tendered for publication. Prior to World War I, this system was made more rigid by prescribing single texts for most subjects, which prescriptions would remain in force for at least seven but normally 15 or even 20 years.

But the turn of the century had also seen the establishment of a new generation of Canadian publishers who had been trained in Canada and who were concerned with publishing original works. They all financed their indigenous programmes through their agency business and schoolbook printing-contracts. With the branches of some large British houses that also became active in Canada at about that time, these publishers to a very large extent developed and sustained a Canadian literary culture. Surviving the depression years and stimulated by the removal of restrictions following the war years, Canadian publishing developed largely through widening markets created by a rapid population growth. But the increasingly heavier reliance on agency publishing was reinforced when U.S. publishers discovered the Canadian markets and established their own branches in Toronto. Although bookstores had traditionally supplied local schools with their textbooks, the rapid development of Canada and the increasing competitiveness of agency publishers had damped the growth of the retail system as institutional administrators, whether in schools, colleges or public libraries, preferred to deal directly with the agents, and eventually also the jobbers.

As a highly developed nation with close historical and geographic ties to the United Kingdom and the United States, Canada enjoys the advantages but also suffers the disadvantages of being in the common market of the English language. A very large proportion of the nearly 100,000 English-language titles produced annually in the U.K., the U.S. and elsewhere are more or less readily available to Canadian readers since Canadian agents are unique in holding stocks of a very large number of titles. But the maintenance of an efficient, competitive agency operation frequently tends to stifle original Canadian publishing. On the other hand, the publisher has become locked into the system if the availability of foreign books is to be maintained at this high level, since it is rare for him to obtain co-publication rights which include the British or American markets; the relatively small market of Canada is normally a prerogative of the U.K. or U.S. publisher when authors or publishers in those countries assign copyrights. Having thus evolved as a highly complex structure dependent on external conditions while serving (if indeed it did not develop) highly sophisticated customer groups, the Canadian English-language book trade is perhaps more sensitive than those in other countries to the current cycle of social change. Although the French-language book trade in Canada also developed in its early phases on the traditional base of the printer, the dominant influence on the Québec publishing industry has been the involvement of the Catholic religious communities which established themselves in the 1850's and, in order to meet the increasing needs of the school system which they controlled, decided to write and publish their own books. The need for secular books was therefore left to the bookseller-publishers to satisfy.

This dualism continued until World War II, when enterprising individuals moved in to satisfy the needs of Québec readers whose supply of French books had been cut off by the war. Unlike the established secular publishers who could not survive without their bookselling activities, the new publishing houses existed by reprinting and distributing French titles. Although they did not survive long after the end of the war, they did set a precedent which demonstrated that such operations were feasible.

The determining factors which established the Québec book trade in its current pattern took place in the late 1950s. After more than 200 years of domination by the church, an increasingly secularized society in Québec finally loosened the controls on education exerted by the religious communities. With the establishment of an education department during the early years of the "Quiet Revolution", coupled with the Québec government's decision to remove the tax exemption on the publishing revenues derived by religious communities, the foothold gained by the commercial publishers was confirmed.

With the implementation of some recommendations made by the Bouchard Commission ($\rightarrow$ 3), the distinctiveness of the Québec book trade in the North American system appears to be assured.

Bibliography

Brief to the Ontario Royal Commission on Book Publishing. Toronto, Publishers Council 1971. 57 pp. + appendices.

Ontario Royal Commission on Book Publishing: Background Papers. Toronto, The Queen's Printer and Publisher, Province of Ontario 1972: F.L. BARRETT, *Textbook selection in the other Canadian Provinces,* pp. 331–343.

95

Canada

V. E. P. Day, *The authorization of textbooks for the schools of Ontario from 1846 to the present*, pp. 311–330.

H. P. Gundy, *The development of trade book publishing in Canada*, pp. 1–37.

G. Laberge and A. Vachon, *Book publishing in Québec*, pp. 374–395.

3 Retail Prices

The historical development of the English-language publishing industry in Canada conformed closely to the general pattern that now distinguishes the North American book trade from that operating in Europe. As a result, the institutional market–both library and schoolbook–is served directly by the publisher and, to an increasing degree, the jobber rather than the bookseller. Prices are therefore determined by the publisher in terms of his own costing requirements.

Although legislation prohibits industry-wide price fixing, generally accepted norms are in existence despite divergences. The bookseller, serving primarily the general reading public, is free to set his own prices or to indulge in price wars with his competitors. Indeed, the Anti-Resale Price Maintenance Bill, which was enacted at the end of 1951, requires the manufacturer to sell his products to any legally constituted retail outlet, and permits the retailer to establish prices below the list price. Despite this freedom, bookstores generally follow the publisher's suggested retail price and recognize the folly of conducting price wars, accepting the fact that book buyers normally do not "comparison shop". Even if booksellers still offer special discounts to special customers, and small bargain stores as well as large chain store "special offers" are available to the public, the trade retail-price system is fairly normalized and no longer disruptive. The usual maximum average publisher's discount is 40%, but there is little uniformity possible where volume discount practices also apply.

Neither local nor provincial variations appear to have much effect on the public attitude towards book prices. British Columbia, the only province to have a sales tax on books, still has a very high per capita book consumption.

Concern about prices is expressed in Canada mainly in regard to imported books. This is so because Canadians have a constant and virtually comprehensive awareness of the original prices listed in the various media used by the publishers in the U.K. and the U.S. Since individual titles and lines are priced in accordance with the varying discounts received by the agents in Canada, the normal higher prices of imports into a small-market country such as Canada are questioned by buyers who are aware of the prices of the same books in the two larger originating countries.

The 40% discount is also an average accorded to libraries, while jobbers require at least 46%. The latter case is causing concern among publishers in that there appears to be an increasing trend for large bookstore operations to establish their own wholesale systems and thus to take advantage of the larger discount rates.

Schoolbooks are generally referred to as "short discount" books and have a basic discount of only 20%. The institutional market–departments of education, school boards and agencies such as provincial schoolbook bureaus–are supplied traditionally directly by the publishers, but with increasing difficulty and frustration. In Canada, education is a matter of provincial jurisdiction, with the result that there are eleven distinct requirements for marketing schoolbooks, further complicated by increasingly decentralized administrative controls coupled with a changing educational philosophy which is causing a proliferation of the titles a publisher must produce or carry in order to service these markets. More recently established educational publishers of primarily non-book or non-print materials required as complements or supplements for books, operate with "net" prices since they deal almost exclusively with institutional buyers.

We have seen (→2) that the Québec book trade had a unique development though more closely related to the European system than the North American. In 1962 the Québec government set up a commission to investigate charges of price fixing, and in response to a request by the Conseil Supérieur du Livre (→4) to study the problems facing the bookselling trade in Québec. The report of the Bouchard Commission (December 1963) made three main recommendations: that the sale of French-language books be regulated by a board, that publicly subsidized institutions be required to purchase their books from provincially accredited bookstores, and that the government set up a wholesale centre to supply Québec booksellers with books written in French.

In 1965, Québec enacted the recommendation for bookseller accreditation, but attempts in 1967 and 1969 to establish a wholesale centre were successfully defeated by the Québec Booksellers' Association with the support of the CSL. During this period the influx of foreign publishers and distributors was increasing. They dealt directly with the institutional buyers, thereby disrupting the distribution based on the network of bookstores. In addition, commission agents from France, specializing in the distribution of exported books, were able to make further inroads in the traditional network by using export incentives offered by the French government to increase the discounts they offered Québec institutional buyers.

The Québec government came to the rescue of booksellers–and publishers–in 1971 with the publication of three orders-in-council, followed by a series of amendments, which spell out the ownership requirements for those houses which seek government assistance in publishing, regulate the operations of accredited bookstores (those wishing to service the institutional markets), and compel provincially subsidized institutions to purchase all but specifically named categories of books in French and English from accredited retailers. Officially stated as being a method permitting the government to control the expenditure of public funds, these regulations do not affect the price of books sold to private institutions or individuals. However, the price of books purchased by public funds is governed both in terms of copyright ownership and the publisher's discount to the bookseller. Books with a Canadian copyright, or for which exclusive distribution is held by a single agent, are priced in accordance with the publisher's list price and his discount to the retailer. For instance, if the bookseller receives a discount of 38%–40%, he must pass on a 15% discount to the institutional buyer; similarly, for government- approved schoolbooks where the publisher's basic discount is normally 20%, the institution will receive an 8% discount; where the bookseller buys a "net" priced book, receiving no discount from the publisher, he is entitled to add 15% to the listed price when he sells that book to an institution. Finally, for French- and English-language books from France, Belgium, Switzerland, Great Britain and the USA that are not distributed by exclusive agents in Canada, the government has provided currency conversion rates, again fixed in terms of the discount obtained by the bookseller from the foreign publisher.

Bibliography

M. Bouchard and Cl. Saint-Germain, *Rapport de la Commission d'enquête sur le commerce du livre dans la province de Québec.*

Canada

(Report of the Commission of Inquiry into the book trade in the province of Québec.) Montréal, Government of Québec 1963. 259 pp.

G. LABERGE AND A. VACHON, *Book publishing in Québec. Ontario Royal Commission on Book Publishing: Background Papers.* Toronto, The Queen's Printer and Publisher, Province of Ontario 1972, pp. 374–395.

This article contains as appendix the text of Orders-in-Council 352-72, 353-72 and 354-72, published in February 1972, respecting book publishing and distribution in the Province of Québec.

4 Organization

The English-language book trade in Canada does not have a central association. The senior book- publishing organization is the

Canadian Book Publishers' Council (CBPC)
45 Charles Street East, Suite 701
CDN Toronto, Ontario M4Y 1S2

which came into existence in 1910, assuming its present name as an autonomous, non-profit organization in 1960. Its membership has always included the major book-publishing firms which until recent years have been located in and around Toronto. As new firms have been established across the country, the Council's membership has begun to reflect this increasing decentralization. The CBPC has some 50 members, representing over 80% of the book-publishing activity in English Canada.

The Council exists primarily to serve the interests of its members, facilitating business relations with the important customer groups, assisting in the development of business standards, organizing and administrating an exhibits programme, developing industry statistics and information, promoting professional development, establishing and maintaining contacts with related book-trade organizations and insti-

tutions in Canada and other countries. The Council publishes a *Newsletter*; an annual detailed *Directory* of its member firms, listing their staff and publishing programs; *Foreign Rights Handbook*, which lists yearly the rights information pertaining to member houses; and other publications such as *Planning a Book Exhibit* and *Selecting Learning Materials*. In addition to the chairmen of its six standing committees (Bookseller Relations; Exhibits; Exports; Information & Statistics; Library Relations; Programme & Professional Development) who with the executive officers comprise an Executive Committee, the Council also has two divisions acting on behalf of specialized publishers: *Canadian Educational Publishers' Group*, and *University & College Publishers' Group*; their presidents are members of the Executive Committee. The latter Group has a Medical and Health Sciences Committee. The Council also has ad hoc committees dealing with photocopying, children's books and metric conversion. The members of the Executive Committee are elected by the membership as a whole, with the exception of the group presidents who with their boards of directors are elected by their respective memberships. The secretariat includes an executive director and his assistant, an accounting officer, exhibits co-ordinator and a research assistant, and houses a reference library on the Canadian book trade.

In 1971, an

Independent Publishers' Association
35 Britain Street
CDN Toronto, Ontario M5A IR7

was formed to look after specific problems related to Canadian-owned, English-language book-publishing firms. It has now an embryonic administrative organization, which enables it to become more formally involved in book-trade activities on behalf of its members. With the exception of seven of their members who also belong to the Council, the other twenty-odd houses are mainly small and young, demonstrating editorial vigour but lacking fully developed marketing facilities.

1972 saw the foundation of the

Association of Canadian University Presses/
Association des Presses universitaires
canadiennes
227 Laurier Avenue
Room 211
CDN Ottawa, Ontario

With its 11 founding members, this bilingual association aims to serve the special professional needs of university-based scholarly publishing programmes.

Canada also has an organization for publishers of encyclopedias and related materials, the

Educational Reference
Book Publishers' Association
200 University Avenue
Third floor
CDN Toronto, Ontario

founded in 1953. Their eight members have been concerned primarily with problems relating to the various methods of marketing multi-volume reference sets.

The French-language book industry in Canada functions mainly through a federation established in 1961:

Conseil Supérieur du Livre
(CSL)
436 est, rue Sherbrooke
CDN Montréal 132, Québec

Three affiliated organizations are grouped under the CSL, each of them electing a vice-president and councillor to sit on the Executive Committee, which also includes the president, a secretary and treasurer as well as the director general. The secretariat includes, in addition to the director general, an administrative secretary, accountant and "agent de promotion culturelle". The CSL has nearly 50 publisher members.

The aims and activities of the Conseil are similar to those of the Canadian Book Publishers' Council, and the two bodies continue to co-operate on concerns that are national or international in scope, while respecting the differences of the trade in each language group.

The Conseil has six standing committees: exhibits-exports, catalogues and technical problems, literary agency and copyright, information and publicity, and professional development. Like the CBPC, it also has a joint committee with librarians–"Association des Bibliothécaires de langue française".

The senior member organization of the Conseil is the

Association des Éditeurs Canadiens
436 est, rue Sherbrooke
CDN Montréal 132, Québec

founded in 1943, and incorporated shortly after its reorganization in 1961. The AEC represents trade publishers through an annually elected executive whose president is a vice-president of the Conseil Supérieur du Livre.

Unlike the Canadian Book Publishers' Council whose traditionally accepted basic criteria for membership stipulate professionalism and legal incorporation in Canada, the Association des Éditeurs Canadiens requires Canadian citizenship and residence in Québec as well as at least 80% Canadian ownership of the member firm's shares.

Representing schoolbook publishers within the Conseil is the

Société des Éditeurs de manuels scolaires du
Québec
436 est, rue Sherbrooke
CDN Montréal 132, Québec

which was founded in 1960. It also has an annually elected executive committee whose president sits on the executive of the Conseil as vice-president. Its membership requirements are similar to those of the AEC.

Since the establishment of the Conseil Supérieur du Livre, the Québec university presses had belonged normally to both of the above-mentioned associations, but in late 1972 they resigned these memberships in order to organize the

Association des Presses Universitaires du Québec
(Association of Québec University Presses)
436 est, rue Sherbrooke
CDN Montréal 132, Québec

which intends to seek institutional membership in the Conseil in order to seek a stronger representation of their specialized interests within the Québec book industry. These presses have also joined the ranks of the newly founded Association of Canadian University Presses.

The second major part of the Canadian book trade is represented by

Canadian Booksellers' Association (CBA)
2 Bloor Street East, Suite 31
CDN Toronto, Ontario M4W 1A8

and the

Association des Libraires du Québec (ALQ)
436 est, rue Sherbrooke
CDN Montréal 132, Québec

The Canadian Booksellers' Association, founded in 1952, serves the interests of its approximately 200 members, English-language booksellers across Canada. It has two divisions–Commercial Stores and College Stores–each with its own chairman and directors. Since each division has approximately the same number of members, this factor is reflected in the CBA's Board of Directors, as is the geographic distribution of the membership across Canada's vast territory. The elected officers of the CBA include president, past-president and secretary-treasurer. The ongoing administrative work of the Association is handled by a part-time executive tecretary.

There are a number of standing committees concerned with activities of interest to all CBA members such as publisher relations, relations with federal and provincial governments, and transportation. In addition, the CBA has a separate joint-action committee with the Canadian Book Publishers' Council to promote and develop common projects and programmes.

The interests of Québec booksellers, selling primarily French-language books, are represented through the Conseil Supérieur du Livre by the Association des Libraires du Québec, which was founded in 1960 as La Société des Libraires canadiens. Like the two constituent publishing bodies of the CSL, the booksellers have an annually elected executive committee whose president is a vice-president of the Conseil. The ALQ has some 45 members.

Most ALQ members have received accreditation by the government; indeed, membership criteria reflect the terms spelled out in the regulations governing la politique du livre described earlier (→3). The Association has participated in the formulation of these regulations, and its activities as conducted through standing and ad hoc committees reflect their continuing concerns with dissemination trade information, standardization and professional development.

Bibliography

Brief to the Ontario Royal Commission on Book Publishing. Toronto, Canadian Book Publishers' Council 1971. 57 pp. + appendices.
Aside from a detailed description of the Council, this document also summarizes the main issues of Canadian English-language book publishing.
Canadian Publishers & Canadian Publishing. Toronto, The Queen's Printer and Publisher, Province of Ontario 1973. 371 pp.
CBPC Directory is produced annually by the Canadian Book Publishers' Council.
CSL Annuaire, published annually by the Conseil Supérieur du Livre, gives a detailed description of the book-trade organization and activities in Québec, and includes information about copy-

right, literary awards and book-related trade periodicals.

Ontario Royal Commission on Book Publishing: Background Papers. Toronto, The Queen's Printer and Publisher, Province of Ontario 1972. xi, 395 pp.

5 Trade Press

The journal of the English-language book trade in Canada is
Quill & Quire
56 The Esplanade
CDN Toronto,
Ontario M5E 1A8
It is independent of any element in the Canadian book trade, and has continued over the years to gain the acceptance of both the trade and the major customer groups as the medium through which official announcements and industry news are communicated monthly. In recent years Quill & Quire has adopted a policy of preparing special issues which, in addition to regular features and news, deal more comprehensively with selected aspects of the Canadian book community. Quill & Quire now also publishes independent, signed reviews of Canadian books under the following categories: fiction, juvenile, non-fiction and textbooks. The journal compiles spring and autumn announcements listing Canadian titles being published during each half-year.
Another monthly journal serving the Canadian book community is
Books in Canada
Canadian Review of Books Ltd
6 Charles Street East
CDN Toronto, Ontario M4Y 1T2
Founded in 1971 as a result of a study of trade book promotion in Canada (→ 33), this independent magazine is devoted primarily to independent reviews of Canadian books, but carries also commentary and surveys dealing with the book trade in Canada. It receives wide circulation through subscription and gratis distribution in bookshops across Canada.
Canadian Printer and Publisher
481 University Avenue
CDN Toronto, Ontario M5W 1A7
is a monthly journal largely concerned with the Canadian graphic arts industries but also contains important news and developments relating to book publishing. The journal of the French-language book trade is
Vient de Paraître
436 est, rue Sherbrooke
CDN Montréal 132, Québec
It is published quarterly by a standing committee of the Conseil Supérieur du Livre (→ 4) and comprises editorials, commentary and trade news as well as a listing of recently published books prepared by the Bibliothèque Nationale du Québec (→ 15). Although its editorial policy is international rather than Canadian, an outstanding journal for its specialized market is
Scholarly Publishing
University of Toronto Press
CDN Toronto, Ontario M5S 1A6
originated and published quarterly since 1969 by the University of Toronto Press.

6 Book-Trade Literature

Comprehensive works dealing with the Canadian book trade are few in number, and most of the important ones have been the result of government-commissioned studies. Other works, more directly related to specific subjects, are listed with each section.

a) Bibliography

Canadiana. Ottawa, National Library of Canada. A monthly catalogue of new books and pamphlets relating to Canada compiled and published by the National Library.
H. Bohne (ed.), *Canadian books in print/ Catalogue des livres canadiens en librairie.*

Toronto, University of Toronto Press. Published annually since 1967 (→15).

b) General Surveys

P. DE BELLEFEUILLE, A. PONTAUT et al., *La bataille du livre au Québec: Oui à la culture française, non au colonialisme culturel.* (The book battle in Québec: Yes to French culture, No to cultural colonialism.) Montréal, Editions Leméac 1972. 137 pp.

M. BOUCHARD AND CL. SAINT-GERMAIN, *Rapport de la Commission d'enquête sur le commerce du livre dans la province de Québec.* (Report of the Commission of inquiry into the book trade in the province of Québec.) Montréal, Government of Québec 1963. 259 pp.

Canadian Publishers & Canadian Publishing. Toronto, The Queen's Printer and Publisher, Province of Ontario 1973. 371 pp.
This is the final report of the Ontario Royal Commission on Book Publishing, and comprises the most comprehensive study made of the book trade in Canada.

ERNST & ERNST MANAGEMENT CONSULTING SERVICES, *The book publishing and manufacturing industry in Canada.* Ottawa, Department of Industry, Trade and Commerce 1970. iii, 172 pp. (Also published simultaneously in French as *L'industrie de l'édition et de la production du livre au Canada,* iii, 172 pp.)
This survey report remains the primary source of statistics on the Canadian book industry, despite the fact that much of the data was estimated rather than definitive, and some of its conclusions were controversial.

W. J. HOWARD (ed.), *Editor, author, and publisher.* Toronto, University of Toronto Press 1969.

Ontario Royal Commission on Book Publishing: Background Papers. Toronto, The Queen's Printer and Publisher, Province of Ontario 1972. xi, 395 pp.
A collection of 18 studies on the Cana-

dian book trade commissioned by the Royal Commission.

c) Handbooks

H. BOHNE AND H. VAN IERSSEL, *Publishing: the creative business.* Toronto, University of Toronto Press 1973. 92 pp.
This introductory handbook to the book-publishing industry's business practices covers all the major administrative functions except sales and order fulfilment. Appendices illustrate standard business and agreement forms. Though designed for Canadian publishers, it conforms with international practice.

P. M. WILLIAMS, *A guide to scholarly publishing in Canada.* Ottawa, Humanities Research Council of Canada and the Social Science Research Council of Canada 1971. 111 pp.

7 Sources of Information, Address Services

Information about the English-language book trade may be obtained from the Canadian Book Publishers' Council (→4), and the Canadian Booksellers' Association (→4). For French-language trade information, the Conseil Supérieur du Livre (→4) may be contacted.

The most comprehensive lists of publishers' and wholesalers' addresses is contained in "Canadian Publishers' Directory", published annually by *Quill & Quire* (→5), or in the index of *Canadian Books in Print/ Catalogue des Livres Canadiens en Librairie* (→15). The Directory also lists foreign publishers and their Canadian representatives.

Trade addresses and information about libraries in Canada may be obtained from:
Canadian Library Association
151 Sparks Street
CDN Ottawa, Ontario K1P 5E3
or
Association canadienne des bibliothécaires de langue française

8515, boulevard Saint-Laurent
CDN Montréal 351, Québec
Bibliographic information is available from the National Library of Canada (→15) and Bibliothèque Nationale du Québec (→15).

8 International Membership

The Canadian Book Publishers' Council (→4) and the Association des Éditeurs Canadiens (→4) are members of the "International Publishers' Association"; (→BTW I, International Section 4) in addition, the AEC and the Société des Éditeurs de manuels scolaires du Québec (→4) are members of "l'Union Internationale des Éditeurs de langue française" (→BTW I, International Section 4).
The Canadian Booksellers' Association (→4) and the Association des Libraires du Québec (→4) are members of the "International Community of Booksellers' Associations" (→BTW I, International Section 4).
The Antiquarian Booksellers' Association of Canada (→26) is a member of the "International League of Antiquarian Booksellers" (→BTW I, International Section 26).
Canada is a member of UNESCO (→BTW I, International Section 4).

9 Market Research

In a country where book-industry statistics have been virtually non-existent until recent times, it is perhaps not surprising that trade-wide market research is at best sporadic.
Although the educational group of the Canadian Book Publishers' Council (→4) has attempted to develop an annual market research program, their efforts have failed to produce satisfactory comprehensive analyses for two main reasons. The first is the lack of uniform standards or bases in data reporting by the provincially legislated educational systems. This problem is being compounded as each province gives increasing administrative autonomy to its regional or county school boards. The second reason is the publishers' own competitive defensiveness which sometimes renders them reluctant to divulge information; some important houses have a firm policy which prohibits the release of market data even in confidence.
The result is that in the absence of nationwide and mandatory filing of returns, the Canadian book industry operates without comprehensive national market data. This means that individual companies conduct their own research and compile their own data, relying principally on the reporting of their trade, college and educational representatives. It is obvious, therefore, that only the larger publishing houses which do have representatives are able to produce any meaningful marketing information for their operations.
Data pertaining to the bookselling trade is even more difficult to obtain. In 1965, the federal statistics bureau (now called Statistics Canada) produced a first survey on independent book and stationery store operations, but did not segregate the figures for each category. In 1969, the federal Department of Industry, Trade and Commerce commissioned a study of the Canadian book industry which was released in late autumn 1970. The resultant statistical and economic analysis of the Canadian book-publishing and manufacturing industry confirmed the need to establish a regular book-trade statistics programme–although the majority of publishers were willing to participate, many of them could not supply the requested data. Such a programme should be comprehensive, involving all elements of the trade, and being based on nation-wide and mandatory filing of returns. Another benefit of such a programme would be the establishment of

Canada

a statistical "framework" that would facilitate the development of much-needed
national market research.
At this point in time, there is hope that the
book trade will be able to negotiate
successfully with the federal government
and "Statistics Canada" for the establishment of a comprehensive, annual statistics
programme.

Bibliography

ERNST & ERNST MANAGEMENT CONSULTING
SERVICES, *The book publishing and manufacturing industry in Canada.* Ottawa, Department of Industry, Trade and Commerce 1970. iii, 172 pp.
See also (→6 *Bibliography*) for French
edition.

10 Books and Young People

Publishing for young people in Canada is
one of the most difficult endeavours in the
Canadian book trade, yet it is one that
needs to be improved most urgently.
The stiff competition from foreign children's books in a small market which requires relatively high unit costs (particularly in comparison with the readily available U.K. and U.S. books), has kept the
demand for Canadian books at a low level.
So low in fact that even such imaginative
stimulants as the "Writing for Young
Canada" programme run by W.J. Gage
Ltd for six years failed to gain the support
of even the institutional market. The attempt to help create a stable of accomplished writers for young people was therefore largely frustrated. Recent annual book
production in this category has fluctuated
between thirty and sixty titles, usually
remaining at the lower end of the scale.
Not until 1972 did the Canadian Book
Publishers' Council (→4) set up an ad hoc
committee on Canadian children's book
publishing, although it had for many
years been involved in the Children's

Recreational Reading Council, an advisory and publicity body of professionals
concerned about books which, owing to
lack of wide-spread support, has functioned
sporadically.
One of the more active promotional programmes for children's books–Young Canada's Book Week/La Semaine du Livre
pour la Jeunesse Canadienne, held every
November–is operated by the Canadian
Association of Children's Librarians of the
Canadian Library Association (→7) with
the support of the Canadian Booksellers'
Association (→4) and the Canadian Book
Publishers' Council (→4). During this
week-long celebration, posters, book marks,
book lists and other promotional giveaways
are distributed widely in conjunction with
library book exhibits and special displays
in bookshops. The CACL also makes
annual awards for the best children's
books.
Although it reaches primarily librarians,
the most important review periodical is
    In Review: Canadian Books for Children
published quarterly by the Ontario Provincial Library Service. The general public is,
however, poorly served. *Books in Canada*
(→5) does have one or two special issues
yearly devoted largely to reviews of Canadian children's books. Some of the larger
newspapers also publish one or two pages
of such reviews, normally during Young
Canada's Book Week, which coincides with
the Christmas sales period.
In Québec, where the crisis in children's
book publishing may be even more severe
than in English-speaking Canada (between 1960 and 1970, the annual output in
this category dropped from 49 to seven), a
recently formed organization gives hope
for improvement:
    Communication-Jeunesse
    Case postale 682
    Station Outremont
    CDN Montréal 154, Québec
This association of authors, designers,

librarians, booksellers and publishers concerns itself not only with books but all the media through which ideas are communicated to children. It organizes conferences, undertakes studies and produces documentation in all relevant areas. In addition, it publishes a series of booklets containing collections of biographies and bibliographies of French-language children's authors in Canada–*Auteurs canadiens pour la jeunesse*.

Bibliography

SH. EGOFF, *The republic of childhood. A critical guide to Canadian children's literature in English*. Toronto, Oxford University Press 1967.

SH. EGOFF, *The writing and publishing of Canadian children's books in English*. In: *Ontario Royal Commission on Book Publishing: Background Papers*. Toronto, The Queen's Printer and Publisher, Province of Ontario 1972, pp. 245–269.

SH. EGOFF AND A. BELISLE, *Notable Canadian children's books/Un choix de livres Canadiens pour la jeunesse*. Ottawa, National Library of Canada 1973. x, 91 pp.
This annotated catalogue also gives an account of the history of children's books in both languages.

11 Training

Although the events that engulfed the Canadian book trade since the mid-1960's have generated a new awareness of training needs, as will be described later, in general booksellers and publishers have been largely amateur in their approach. Neither element of the trade has minimum standards or qualifications that are controlled by a central organization. Obviously many booksellers and publishers have highly efficient operations owing to their own in-house training programs, augmented by participation in seminars and courses abroad, particularly in the United States.

Foreign-owned subsidiary publishing houses especially are able to reinforce their own training programmes by having direct access to the expertise developed by their parent houses.

The one notable exception is the standards, and subsequent training programme, established in 1965 by the Québec provincial government in co-operation with the Association des Libraires du Québec ($\rightarrow$ 4) for the accreditation of Québec booksellers. The regulations governing accreditation as set out in the Booksellers Accreditation Act (*Québec Revised Statutes 1965*, Loi de l'accréditation des libraires), were revised in terms of *la politique du livre* by Order in Council 353–72 (*Québec Official Gazette*, February 26, 1972); see also ($\rightarrow$ 3). The annual training programme, known as *Séminaire du Livre*, is organized by a standing committee of the Association des Libraires du Québec, and runs for two weeks every summer, covering a three-year programme. Some 40 candidates follow the courses, which are run with the assistance of grants from the Québec Cultural Affairs Department and the government of France.

For the remainder, the Canadian Booksellers' Association ($\rightarrow$ 4) and the Canadian Book Publishers' Council ($\rightarrow$ 4) organize both separate and joint technical and training seminars covering the most important aspects of the trade. The CBPC has since 1969 also sponsored a ten-week general survey course on book publishing through the University of Toronto Extension Department, but plans to change this to an in-depth course of similar length on the editorial aspects of publishing. Various seminars are also organized for its members by the Conseil Supérieur du Livre ($\rightarrow$ 4). In 1970, the Conseil organized the first professional French-language book publishing course in Canada with the co-operation of l'Université de Montréal. Two Toronto-based, trade-related organizations–the Book Promotion and Editorial Club (→20), and the Canadian Association of Publishers' Educational Representatives–have a lively programme of seminars for their members. There is also expectation that a one-year diploma course for booksellers will be inaugurated by a Toronto-area community college.

Bibliography

Vient de Paraître, Séminaire sur la librairie, March 1973, p. 23.

12 Taxes

All Canadian provinces, with the exception of British Columbia, which maintains a 5% sales tax, exempt books from taxes. Nor is there a federal sales tax on books.

For the importation of books into Canada, however, there is a certain amount of confusion. Under the British Preferential Tariff, all books from the U.K. enter Canada duty-free. But unless books from the U.S. receive certification that they are purchased for "educational purposes" by the importing agent, they are subject to a 10% customs duty. Aside from the duties levied on the many non-book components such as records, tapes, film strips and cards, that increasingly form an integral part of various materials of instruction produced by book publishers, the importing agents during the past two years have encountered an increasing number of problems relating to the certified "free and exempt" categories of educational books. The difficulties occur because the individual customs clearing points are authorized to interpret and apply the regulations locally, with the result that frequently the "letter of the law" rather than the "spirit of the law" is applied.

Canada does not have a value added tax.

13 Clearing Houses

There is no central clearing house in Canada, although an attempt was made in 1953 when a group of publishers formed the Co-operative Book Centre of Canada Ltd. The primary purpose of this operation was to keep library business in Canada, in the face of the increasing practice of "buying around" the authorized agent. The Co-op had the potential of becoming a clearing house, but owing to many difficulties it failed after 17 years. When its assets were acquired by a single firm, it became merely another wholesale customer for the publishers.

Some 25 publishers have formed an industry group in

Creditel of Canada Ltd
931 Yonge Street
CDN Toronto, Ontario M4W 2H6

so as to improve their company's credit controls. Beyond exchanging actual ledger experience, the participants may also purchase additional services such as follow-up of unpaid accounts.

With the formation of the Association for the Export of Canadian Books (→28) and the establishment of Canadian book centres abroad, clearing house services will be provided for Canadian publishers' foreign markets. Through the Export Credit Insurance Corporation, a federal government agency set up in 1944, publishers may obtain reasonably priced coverage for protection against non-payment by foreign purchasers; this coverage does not include accounts handled by commission sales agencies.

14 Copyright

The current Canadian Copyright Act became law on 1 January 1924. Because there have been only minor amendments since that time, the Act has been creating increasing problems for the Canadian author and publisher, partly because its definition of copyright is ambiguous and partly because it does not take into account the new technologies which affect the ownership of materials under its jurisdiction.

The Act applies only to "every original literary, dramatic, musical and artistic work", and provides protection for the lifetime of the author and a period of fifty years thereafter. Anyone may reproduce a work, however, twenty-five years after the author's death, following agreement from and the paying of royalties to the copyright owner. Original posthumously published works are protected for fifty years from first publication. Being signatory to the Universal Copyright Convention (10 August 1962), Canadian copyright protection is extended to all countries that are party to the UCC. Registration is not necessary in Canada in order to secure copyright protection.

Canada has also been a longstanding member of the other large international copyright treaty–the Berne Union–having ratified the Rome revision of 1928.

There exist in Canada two important organizations concerned with questions of copyright:

Canadian Copyright Institute
112 King Street West, Suite 401
CDN Toronto, Ontario M5H 1H8
and
La Société Canadienne-française
de Protection du Droit d'auteur
136 est, rue Sherbrooke
CDN Montréal 132, Québec

Bibliography

Canadian Publishers & Canadian Publishing. Toronto, The Queen's Printer and Publisher, Province of Ontario 1973. Chapter 3: Copyright and book publishing, (pp. 79–121 and appendix) is important for a full understanding of the current situation in Canada.

H. G. Fox, *Canadian law of copyright and industrial designs*. Toronto, The Carswell Company Ltd. 1967.

R. C. Sharp, *Some copyright concerns of Canadian authors and publishers*. In: *Ontario Royal Commission on Book Publishing: Background Papers*. Toronto, The Queen's Printer and Publisher, Province of Ontario 1972. pp. 111–134.

15 National Bibliography, National Library

In 1967, the major book associations–Canadian Book Publishers' Council (→4), Canadian Booksellers' Association (→4), Canadian Library Association (→7), Conseil Supérieur du Livre (→4)–formed a committee which produced the first edition of *Canadian Books in Print/Catalogue des Livres Canadiens en Librairie*
University of Toronto Press
CDN Toronto, Ontario M5S 1A6
This edition appeared in two volumes, one containing author and publisher lists, the other listing something over ten thousand separate titles. In subsequent years the two volumes were combined but the sixth edition, for 1972, appeared again with a second volume comprising a subject index. This improvement was made possible with a grant from the Federal Government in commemoration of International Book Year. In the 1972 edition 19,397 entries are recorded, of which 13,059 are English-language and 6,338 French-language.

Canadian Books in Print was inspired by the *Catalogue de l'Édition au Canada français* published by the Conseil Supérieur du Livre. Its seventh edition listing active titles as at 30 June 1972, has been renamed *Répertoire de l'Édition au Québec* and reflects a joint data-bank agreement between the Conseil and France-Expansion (Paris). In addition to the *Répertoire*, Canadian French-language books will now also be listed in the *Répertoire des Livres disponibles de la Francophonie* published by France-Expansion. Updating will be provided with the assistance of a monthly listing based on legal deposit:

Bibliographie du Québec
Bibliothèque Nationale du Québec
1700, rue Saint-Denis
CDN Montréal 130, Québec

Legislation enacted by the Government of Québec in January 1968 requires all publishers located in that province to deposit within 30 days of publication two copies of each title they publish. Similar federal legislation in January 1963 permitted the establishment of

Canadiana
National Library of Canada
395 Wellington Street
CDN Ottawa, Ontario K1A 0N4

a monthly catalogue which lists publications of Canadian origin or interest noted by the National Library. It includes quarterly, semi-annual and annual accumulations as well as an annual index.

Nationally available library services for scientific and technical books are provided by

National Science Library
National Research Council of Canada
100 Sussex Drive
CDN Ottawa, Ontario

Bibliography

D. E. RYDER (ed.), *Canadian reference sources. A selective guide.* Ottawa, Canadian Library Association 1973. 185 pp.
It contains over 1,200 items divided under the general headings of general reference works; history and allied subjects; humanities; science; and social science. An extensive index is included, together with appendices.

16 Book Production

Canada has long been a highly literate country with a literature of its own, in each official language, but a real surge in Canadian book production has occurred within the last decade. The centenary of Confederation undoubtedly played an important role in this development and probably gave rise to the increasingly more widely spread feelings of nationalism and of national awareness. This period also saw the birth of a significant number of publishing houses, most of which publish trade books and especially belles–lettres.

The 1972 edition of *Canadian Books in Print/Catalogues des Livres Canadiens en Librairie* records 19,397 active titles, of which 13,059 are in English and 6,338 in French. The only annual book-production statistics available in Canada are those compiled by the National Library ($\rightarrow$ 15) for UNESCO; separate but comparable figures for Québec are produced by the Bibliothèque Nationale du Québec ($\rightarrow$ 15). Both sets of figures use the UNESCO definition of a book and subject groups.

The number of books published in Canada in 1970 was 2,434, comprising 2,110 new titles and 324 new editions. By 1972, Canadian production had increased to 4,224 titles, including 3,967 new titles and 257 new editions. The following table shows the number of titles published in 1972 in the principal classifications in both English and French, as shown in the National Library statistics:

Subject group	Titles	Percentage of total production
Fiction and poetry	551	13.0
School textbooks	489	11.5
Education	411	9.7
Political science and economy	367	8.7
History, biography	347	8.2
Law, public administration	268	6.3
Religion, theology	248	5.8
Sociology	203	4.8
Arts	199	4.7
Technology	177	4.2
Geography	169	4.0
Literary history and criticism	163	3.8

17 Translations

Neither the traditional orientation of the Canadian book-publishing industry nor the size of its national market has particularly encouraged any significant translations activity in Canada, and this despite, or perhaps because of, the fact that Canada has two official languages which are widely used throughout the world–English and French. What Canadian authors themselves could not produce was already readily available from the United Kingdom, the United States and France. It is true that some of the major literary and historical works in each language have been translated into the other, but their number is disappointingly small.

Although no statistics are readily available to illustrate the point, the educational reformation of the early 1960s, brought about during the so-called "Quiet Revolution" in Québec which had the effect of removing the control of education as well as of textbook publishing from the religious orders, generated a period of considerable activity in translating Canadian and U.S. English-language books into French. As indigenous secular French-language textbook publishing developed in Québec, so the number of translations decreased. There is still some translation and adaptation of senior-level and advanced textbooks published in English in North America, in preference to importing them from France, owing to cultural and educational similarities.

The implementation of a federal policy of bilingualism, following the exhaustive studies of the Royal Commission on Bilingualism and Biculturalism, has had the fortunate effect of increasing co-publishing ventures of contemporary Canadian authors in both official languages. To encourage this trend and to make possible the translation of earlier Canadian works, the federal government's interim book policy announced in early 1972 includes the designation of $ 215,000 annually to assist translation. Eligible translators must be Canadian citizens and their translations must be published by Canadian-owned houses.

Canada has also declared itself officially as a multi-cultural society, thereby making available financial assistance to encourage publication in the minority languages. Recent work indicates that some of these may also appear in one or both of the majority languages.

18 Book Clubs

The first book club in Canada was set up in 1928 when a large department store offered its customers "a selective literary service". Although the club survived for only four years, it reached a membership of over 5,000 and demonstrated the validity of this type of direct-mail book merchandizing in a country such as Canada. While there is only one club offering exclusively Canadian selections (founded in 1959 and having a membership that has begun to increase rapidly since 1971), the growing number of book clubs and club members in Canada indicates their effectiveness in overcoming the country's vast territorial expanse to reach readers in even the most remote and inaccessible of communities.

Some booksellers have expressed concern over this increasing competition, especially from the large communications corporations who use their own media to advertise on a large scale the clubs they have set up for their subscribers and readers. Generally, publishers find that bookclub selections give prestige and publicity which increase sales in retail outlets. Clubs also tend to keep reference books and other important works in circulation longer than bookstores can afford to do with their concern for meeting the readers' current interest needs.

Since virtually all clubs handle only hard-cover editions, this can represent an important addition to the publishers' revenue profile. For Canada's relatively restricted market, clubs buy copies from the publisher or, preferably, attach themselves to the initial print-run; one large club, however, follows its parent company's policy, and re-sets and prints even its Canadian selections to be consistent with a standard-size format. For an author, selection of one of his works may add between 2,000 and 10,000 copies sold through book clubs.

It is estimated that in 1969, book-club and other mail-order sales accounted for $ 17,6 million (8%) of the total $ 222 million book consumption in Canada. Most of these sales are of foreign (and particularly U.S.) books, reflecting not only the fact that U.S. clubs have Canadian operations or direct access through other means to readers in Canada, but that Canadian clubs, whether general or specialist, emphasize foreign books. In recent years, however, many of the major clubs have begun to include, and highlight, Canadian selections available to their Canadian members.

There are no regulations to govern book-club operations in Canada as there are in the United Kingdom, for example. Advertised discounts to members may range as high as 60% or 70%, and there are no restrictions on bonuses, dividends or other premiums offered by the clubs.

Bibliography

Quill & Quire, January 1973.

19 Paperbacks

Canadian paperback publishing is to a very large degree restrictred to "quality" paperbacks. Although a couple of Canadian firms do produce original and reprint mass-market editions (characterized by lower price levels, uniform formats and distinct distribution channels), it is fair to say that Canada is a virtually homogeneous part of the North American market of U.S. firms specializing in that kind of publishing activity.

As a result, the marketing system used for such editions, being similar to that developed for most periodicals on this continent, is also linked to the U.S. It was owned and controlled increasingly by U.S. distributors until the Ontario government took rapid action on interim recommendations from its Royal Commission on Book Publishing by passing legislation to stop this process in the province (*The Paperback and Periodical Distributors Act, 1971*).

Despite earlier attempts that failed and current efforts that may have some limited success, it appears unlikely that Canada will develop a significant mass-market paperback industry of its own. Original Canadian titles must continue to seek mass-market publication through the highly competitive U.S. trade.

An increasing number of Canadian publishers, including those who specialize in educational materials, are issuing "quality" paperback editions where they would only have produced hardcover editions earlier.

Depending on the subject and intended markets, the trend is towards simultaneous publication for a variety of reasons, including efforts to reach a wider university and school-student market with cheaper editions; the blurring of the distinction between trade and text publishing; and the increasing practice of libraries purchasing duplicate copies in paperback editions or, in the case of school libraries particularly, considering certain titles as "consumables" (that is, the topicality of the subject treatment will have been exhausted within the one to three-year life expectancy of a paperback).

Technological developments in the book-manufacturing industry have given paperback publishing a new stature, making it feasible for Canadian publishers to produce short-run reprints to meet needs in the increasingly fragmented educational markets, for instance.

Another area where technology and paperback publishing is beginning to develop in Canada is in "Canadiana reprints". A heightened awareness of Canada generated by sentiments of nationalism has awakened interest in Canada's past, both for her long out-of-print literature and the wide range of historical documents. Several publishers have established their own series of such titles.

No useful statistics on the volume or the bibliography of Canadian paperback publishing exists at the moment.

Bibliography

Canadian Publishers & Canadian Publishing. Toronto, The Queen's Printer and Publisher), Province of Ontario 1973. 371 pp.

20 Book Design

Perhaps the most significant development in encouraging and fostering book design and production in Canada occurred in 1972 when the Canadian Book Publishers' Council (→4) obtained a federal grant under the International Book Year programme to plan a national competition. This initiative was received with enthusiasm by all elements of the book industry, and representatives of concerned organizations formed, in early 1973, a Canadian Book Design Committee whose administrative work is handled at this stage by the Canadian Book Publishers' Council.

Approval was expected for plans to launch the first competition in 1974. It would conform to the standards of the Design Canada programme, and would be supported by a substantial grant from the federal Department of Industry, Trade and Commerce under whose jurisdiction Design Canada operates with the co-operation of the National Design Council.

The annual Look of Books competition established in 1969 by the Book Promotion and Editorial Club, an unofficial body of Toronto-based publishers' promotion, editorial and design personnel, will be merged with the national competition. This imaginative project failed unfortunately to gain national support, particularly from the Québec book community. During International Book Year in 1972, the collection of award-winning titles received widespread attention through a promotion and exhibit programme organized by the Canadian Book Publishers' Council for Canadian schools, colleges and libraries. The collection was also shown abroad, notably at the Frankfurt Book Fair and the International Book Production Exhibition held in London.

The high standards of book design in Canadian English-language publishing are best typified by the University of Toronto Press, whose consistently impressive and frequently award-winning designs are directed by Allan Fleming. In 1970, the Press' *Economic Atlas of Ontario* won the international competition at Leipzig as "The Most Beautiful Book in the World".

Bibliography

C. DAIR, *Design with type*. Toronto, University of Toronto Press 1968.

C. J. EUSTACE, *Developments in Canadian book production and design*. In: *Ontario Royal Commission on Book Publishing: Background Papers*. Toronto, The Queen's Printer and Publisher Province of Ontario 1972, pp. 38–60.

21 Publishing

In Canada, publishing developed in the populated centres, moving westward with the colonists, who settled as far inland as Upper Canada (Ontario). While Québec and Montréal were the original centres for publishing in both languages, by the 1850s Toronto had become, and was to remain, Canada's English-language publishing centre. Important publishers are still located in some of the major cities east of Toronto, and new houses have come into existence during the past decade in the Prairie provinces and British Columbia, frequently as university presses or based in the local academic community. Montréal is the centre of French-language publishing, with Québec City continuing as an important secondary centre.

Of 62 houses which reported fifty or more Canadian titles in print in 1972, Toronto was the base for 31 of them, Montréal for 19 (three of them English-language firms). That year *Canadian Books in Print* (→15) listed nearly 950 firms and organizations which publish books, but it would be safe to estimate that the organized segment of the trade (the some 125 houses with association memberships) account for about 95% of the entire publishing activity in Canada.

While there are no statistics available to permit a comparative analysis of the size or profitability of Canadian publishing houses, a 1969 survey produced for the Department of Industry, Trade and Commerce showed that about 65% of the French-language publishers had annual sales of less than $1 million as compared to 55% in the English-language segment. The largest French firm reported sales of less than $4 million, while in the other language the highest sales report was in excess of $10 million. The majority of the largest companies in the English-language segment were foreign-owned subsidiaries. The same report estimated total book consumption in Canada at $222 million in 1969, of which some $191 million was English, $27 million French and $3 million other languages. Of the total, $77 million or nearly 35% were sales of books

produced in Canada. It was pointed out that this represented 0.06% of the gross national product (GNP), comparing it to figures ranging from 0.21% to 0.26% in other countries with active publishing industries. In addition, Canadian publishers sold an estimated $84 million worth of imported books (→27). Sales of school books represented 50% of the total, with trade books 27% and reference books 19%.

Bibliography

H. BOHNE (ed.), *Canadian books in print/ Catalogue des livres Canadiens en librairie*. Toronto, University of Toronto Press 1972. 1,092 pp.

Canadian Publishers & Canadian Publishing. Toronto, The Queen's Printer and Publishers, Province of Ontario 1973. 371 pp.

ERNST & ERNST MANAGEMENT CONSULTING SERVICES, *The Book publishing and manufacturing industry in Canada*. Ottawa, Department of Industry, Trade and Commerce 1970. iii, 172 pp. (See also →6 *Bibliography* for French edition.)

22 Literary Agents

Although there is a small number of literary agents in Canada, most writers act in their own behalf when seeking publication through Canadian houses. Established authors are normally represented by their publishers in seeking international markets or in selling subsidiary rights.

When the three Canadian book centres abroad (→28) are fully established, participating publishers will be able to procure specified services from each centre, acting as agents on their behalf. Member publishers of the Conseil Supérieur du Livre (→4) have organized a literary agency, l'Agence littéraire des Editeurs canadiens-français, to give all Québec publishers better access to international markets, through the sale or purchase of rights and through export sales development.

Since foreign-owned subsidiaries have been actively involved in original Canadian publishing for a long time, these firms have an added dimension in getting their Canadian authors into the international market through their parent and sister companies. But no standard arrangements govern these channels.

Bibliography

H. S. MARSHALL AND I. MONTAGNES, *International publishing*. In: *Ontario Royal Commission on Book Publishing: Background Papers*. Toronto, The Queen's Printer and Publisher, Province of Ontario 1972, pp. 154–172.

23 Wholesale Trade

Canada is in the curious position of having its book-publishing industry develop historically from roots that are based in large measure on wholesaling and agency publishing. As has been discussed earlier ($\rightarrow$ 2), many Canadian publishing houses established their own publishing programme on revenues derived from their retailing and wholesaling operations; for many, these revenues are still vital to permit the continued publishing of Canadian books. Wholesale bookselling as a distinct activity in Canada is fraught with many problems because of major incursions from abroad, which operations are not integrated into the highly complicated book trade in Canada.

The problems manifest themselves in terms of the book imports from the U.K. and the U.S., and have become known as "buying around". Where Canadian wholesalers, and foreign companies operating out of Canada, respect the authorized and exclusive Canadian agents by buying from them whenever possible,

they form an important element in the distribution chain. However, when this distribution system is disrupted, by foreign wholesalers by-passing the authorized agent and selling the books directly to the client, the entire system is in danger of breaking down because the U.S. wholesaler, especially, is able to offer what are essentially non-competitive prices since they are based upon his ability to obtain prices given on quantities that supply the entire North American market and, increasingly, those of some European countries. No acceptable method has yet been developed to ensure that all Canadian markets are supplied from a distribution system that involves the authorized Canadian agent.

The school and public-library markets are most vulnerable to "buying around", since they feel they must seek lowest prices–and their acquisitions budgets are usually the first to be cut whenever public purse strings are tightened. However, their justification for buying around the Canadian agent–that the foreign wholesaler offers lower prices and better services–involves what is essentially a "chicken and egg" argument.

Further complications have been added to wholesaling in Canada with the implementation by the government of Québec of its *politique du livre* ($\rightarrow$ 3) and with the apparent wholesaling operations established by booksellers with chains of bookshops.

Bibliography

Canadian Publishers Directory. Published annually by Quill & Quire.

24 Retail Trade

Although it is an important element in the book-distribution network in Canada, the retail bookselling trade is underdeveloped both in terms of numbers and ability to service a population which is so widely and, outside the urban regions, sparsely scattered across a very large landmass. The Canadian Booksellers' Association (→4) has determined that it is economically unfeasible for a comprehensive bookshop to survive in a city with a population of less than 50,000 inhabitants. Some of the problems facing booksellers operating outside Québec have been described earlier (→3).

While the Government of Québec regulated the book trade in the province of Québec through Orders-in-Council (→3) published in 1971, and revised three times since then, the *politique du livre* is too recent to evaluate usefully. However, Québec librarians have been vociferous in describing the damaging effects that the requirement to purchase directly from retail bookstores with government-regulated prices has had on their acquisitions programmes.

Owing to the increased awareness of Canadian books and authors that developed in the extensive public debate on Canadian nationalism since 1970, a number of venturesome booksellers established specialist shops for exclusively Canadian books. Although other stores segregated their Canadian books into Canadiana sections, this did not always meet with the approval of the other parties concerned, many of whom felt that Canadian works should be able to make their own way among all other books; this debate is not yet finished. It is evident, however, that Canadian booksellers are selling far greater numbers of Canadian books than they have ever done before.

There are no useful statistics available on the retail trade in Canada.

25 Mail-Order Bookselling

The variety and number of operations involved in direct selling by mail promotion has increased dramatically in Canada over the past few years. The applications of this technique have gone well beyond those relating to highly specialized and expensive books. Direct mail promotion and selling is particularly suited to a country as geographically large as Canada with a retail trade that is nowhere near as extensive or well developed as that found in most European countries.

26 Antiquarian Book Trade, Auctions

Although the antiquarian book trade in Canada is a matter of controversy at this time insofar as determining the period when the market was established in Canada, it is probably safe to say that the trade in Canadiana has over the years been consistent with the productivity of Canadian book publishers. While Canada has always had a number of rare-book dealers, most of the sales have been handled by the rare-book dealers of London, Paris and New York.

During Canada's centennial year in 1967, two important developments took place. One was the establishment of *Montréal Book Auctions Limited*, which has since become very active and has drawn international attention to its auctions. The second was the formation of

The Antiquarian Booksellers' Association of Canada
1022 Sherbrooke Street West, Room 6
CDN Montréal 110, Québec

With a membership that has now surpassed 30, the ABAC is becoming an active trade association which will undoubtedly ensure the establishment of a rare-book market in Canada. Since most of the Canadian book trade, both new and antiquarian, is located in Québec and Ontario, antiquarian book fairs are generally organized for Montréal and Toronto.

The journal of the Canadian antiquarian book trade is *Abacus*, published irregularly by the ABAC; the first issue appeared in July 1967.

Apart from the antiquarian, or rare-book-dealers there are also second-hand booksellers in Canada. Such bookstores usually deal in university and other textbooks, or publishers' remainders which they then sell at bargain prices. Information about second-hand booksellers may be obtained from the Canadian Booksellers' Association (→4).

27 Book Imports

As has been discussed variously in earlier sections, Canada is unique in its historical and geographical relations with the two largest English-language countries in the world–the U.K. and the UA–being both the beneficiary and the victim of their great wealth in terms of books. In their study of the Canadian book-publishing industry, the Ontario Royal Commission on Book Publishing discovered that in 1971, 57 publishers in Canada claimed to be the exclusive Canadian agent for 543 foreign publishers; this revealed that the same number of exclusive Canadian agents had lost over 120 foreign agencies since 1961. Although statistics are not readily available, estimates for 1969 showed that the imported book represented 65% of total Canadian book consumtion ($ 144.8 million of a total $ 222 million). The import figure can be further broken down as:

Source and type of supplier	Publishers' sales value (Million $)	%
Foreign-made books imported and marketed by Canadian publishers	83.7	37.8
Foreign-made books imported by Canadian distributors who are not publishers	30.0	13.5
Foreign-made books imported by Canadian end users	31.1	14.0
Total	144.8	65.3

A breakdown of these import figures by country of origin is not available.

Bibliography

ERNST & ERNST MANAGEMENT CONSULTING SERVICES, *The book publishing and manufacturing industry in Canada*. Ottawa, Department of Industry, Trade and Commerce 1970. iii, 172 pp.

28 Book Exports

With a few notable exceptions, Canadian publishers have until very recently tended to concentrate their efforts on domestic rather than export markets. As outlined earlier (→2), the evolution of the Canadian book trade was determined very largely by its political, cultural and geographic links with the United Kingdom, France and the United States.

Being geared to market imported books, and producing original titles that normally tended to be of interest to Canadian readers only since they were intended to meet needs not satisfied by the foreign books, it is understandable why the export market was of minor concern to Canadian publishers. The exceptions are, of course, the scholarly presses whose production must be marketed internationally, and those houses with established contacts which permitted edition or territorial rights of some books to be sold abroad. In the latter group belong also the foreign-owned subsidiaries with direct access to non-Canadian markets through their head office and the other branches.

The only available sales figures, compiled by Ernst & Ernst Management Consulting Services for the Federal Department of Industry, Trade and Commerce, reveal that book exports were valued at an estimated $ 5.5 million in 1969. Of this figure, it is estimated that the combined total of original English- and French-language Canadian books was 73%. A survey of

21 member firms of the Canadian Book Publishers' Council (→4) showed that their gross revenues from exports (including books, parts of books, and materials for book manufacture such as film and plates) increased from $2.5 million in 1970 to nearly $4 million in 1971.

The Ernst & Ernst study estimated that in 1969 only 1% of the estimated $15 million revenues of Canadian French-language publishers were derived from exports.

In February 1972, the Federal Government announced in its six-point interim policy on book publishing the objective "to quadruple the number of books exported over the next five years". To this end, an annual budget of $500,000 was allocated for export development over the next three years, of which $100,000 would go towards increasing the government's assistance for Canadian displays at selected international fairs and other foreign book exhibits. The remaining $400,000 was allocated for "the establishment and effective operations" of Canadian book centres in the United States, the United Kingdom and continental Europe.

To plan the establishment and eventually to control the operations of the first three Canadian book centres abroad, the

Association for the Export of Canadian Books/
Association pour l'exportation du livre canadien
112 Kent Street
CDN Ottawa, Ontario K1A OH5

was formed and legally constituted in November 1972. The Association's board of directors comprises two government-appointed directors in addition to two from each of the five major book publishing associations in Canada (→4): Canadian Book Publisher's Council, Independent Publishers' Association, Association of Canadian University Presses, Association des Éditeurs Canadiens, and Société des Éditeurs de Manuels Scolaires du Québec.

Centres were opened in 1973 at the following addresses:

Books Canada Ltd
Suite 600, 17 Cockspur Street
GB London, S.W. 1Y 5BP

Livres du Canada S.A.
1 quai Conti
F Paris 75006

and

Books Canada Inc.
35 East 67th Street
USA New York, N.Y. 10021

Each centre is legally constituted in the host country as a consortium of publishers. Eligible publishers may participate through one of three membership classes to benefit from the marketing activities of each centre.

With adaptations to meet local conditions, each centre has a manager and staff to handle promotion, selling, warehousing, distribution and related accounting services.

Since 1964, Canadian French-language books have been distributed through trade and text-book centres (Centres de Diffusion du Livre canadien-français) organized by the Conseil Supérieur du Livre in France. Similar centres were established in 1970 in Belgium.

Bibliography

ERNST & ERNST MANAGEMENT CONSULTING SERVICES, *The book publishing and manufacturing industry in Canada*. Ottawa, Department of Industry, Trade and Commerce 1970. iii, 172 pp. See also (→6 *Bibliography*) for French edition.

H. S. MARSHALL AND I. MONTAGNES, *International publishing*. In: *Ontario Royal Commission on Book Publishing: Background Papers*. Toronto, The Queen's Printer and Publisher, Province of Ontario 1972, pp. 154–172.

29 Book Fairs

During International Book Year in 1972, the first Québec International Book Salon was launched in Québec City. Much like the Brussels International Book Fair, this first international fair in Canada is designed primarily to display books to the general public rather than to the trade. Exhibitors are encouraged to sell their books during the Salon through accredited Québec booksellers in order to reach the institutional market as well (→3). The Salon is to be held yearly in mid-May. In 1972, some 600 publishers from ten countries displayed over 80,000 titles; paid attendance exceeded 50,000. Numerous regional salons are also held annually in the major urban centres in Québec.

North America's first international, *professional* book fair was held in Montréal on May 15–19, 1975. Modelled on the Frankfurt Book Fair, it is designed to complement and supplement the world's largest fair by enabling publishers to complete negotiations initiated at Frankfurt or vice versa.

While bringing more Canadian publishers into closer contact with the international publishing scene, the

Foire internationale du livre de Montréal (FILM)
Montréal International Book Fair
436 est, rue Sherbrooke
CDN Montréal 132, Québec

also hopes to encourage greater participation by South American publishing firms. Conceived originally by the Conseil Supérieur du Livre (→4) and operating under its auspices, FILM has received the full support of the other Canadian publishing associations, who are also involved actively in the planning.

In English-language Canada, the Canadian Book Publishers' Council (→4) has for many years operated an active and efficient exhibits program for its members designed

to meet specialized needs of specialist markets.

The Council also provided interim planning and co-ordinating services for the entire English-language participation in foreign and international exhibits where the Canadian presence is sponsored by the federal Department of Industry, Trade and Commerce as part of its export development programme. This function is now handled by the Association for the Export of Canadian Books (→28).

The most important of these fairs is the Frankfurt Book Fair, which Canadian publishers have attended since the 1950's. Since about 1965, this participation has become more formalized and greater in scope through the assistance provided by various government departments and agencies. In addition to several individual company stands, the collective national stand provides a representative and fairly comprehensive idea of Canadian book production in both languages. A special collection of award-winning titles is also displayed in the book-design section.

Bibliography

Planning a Book Exhibit. 2nd revised ed. Toronto, Canadian Book Publishers' Council 1972.

30 Public Relations

Much of the work carried out by most of the book-trade organizations (→4) is obviously designed with public relations in mind, whether this involves the preparation of press releases or participation in such undertakings as Young Canada's Book Week (→10). Plans are realized to launch a wider and more ambitious publicity campaign to make Canadians more aware of Canadian authors and their books. To be known as "Canada Book Week", it is was launched in autumn 1974. Aside from a number of formal, organized celebrations, it would rely on local community groups across Canada developing activities that would highlight Canadian books in the remote and less accessible areas of the country.

The Conseil Supérieur du Livre (→4) in 1972 engaged an *agent de promotion culturelle* to promote Canadian French-language books throughout the province of Québec. Supported by a grant from the Canada Council, the *agent* makes periodic visits to bookstores, libraries, public institutions and cultural groups, thereby coming into direct contact with various customer groups as well as the general reader. His activities involve the organization of publicity campaigns and book exhibits.

31 Bibliophily

Although there are numerous local literary circles in Canada that have continued in existence despite periods of inactivity, all are informal. There is no national body to unite the interests and activities of Canadian bibliophiles except in so far as they relate to bibliographic research and publication.

Founded in 1946, the Bibliographical Society of Canada/La Société Bibliographique du Canada has as its general aim "to co-ordinate bibliographical activity and to set standards ... and to encourage the preservation and extend the knowledge of printed works and manuscripts, particularly those relating to Canada; and to facilitate the exchange of information concerning such rare items". The Society has reprint and monograph series as well as *Papers Cahiers* published since 1962.

Inquiries may be addressed to:

The Secretary-Treasurer
Bibliographical Society of Canada
32 Lowther Avenue
CDN Toronto, Ontario M5R 1C6

32 Literary Prizes

Aside from a number of minor literary prizes awarded by private organizations or publishers, there are some awards that have significant importance for the literary community in Canada.

Perhaps the most important–and controversial–are the *Governor General's Literary Awards* made by the Canada Council each year. Worth $ 2,500 to the winner, a prize is awarded in each official language in each of three categories–poetry, fiction and non-fiction. Attention has been drawn to these awards in recent years when winners have refused to accept their prize on political grounds.

The Canada Council also awards the *Prix Molson*, founded in 1963, for outstanding contributions to the artistic and cultural life of Canada. Three $ 15,000 prizes are given annually.

The Government of Québec has the annual *Prix David* (carrying a $ 5,000 prize), awarded to Québec authors, either French or English speaking, who have published at least three works.

The Greater Montréal Council of Arts offers an annual $ 3,000 prize *(Grand Prix Littéraire de la Ville de Montréal)* to the author of a literary work published in the city. On the jury's recommendation, the Council will also pay for its translation into the other official language.

Other prizes include:

Canada-Belgium Literary Prize, co-sponsored by the two governments, awarded in alternate years to a French-language Belgian or Canadian writer on the basis of the writer's complete works.

Book of the Year Award (Canadian Association of Children's Librarians).

Prix Jeunesse (Association canadienne des éducateurs de langue française).

Concours Littéraires du Québec (biennial literary competitions sponsored by the provincial Cultural Affairs Department, with

$ 2,500 prizes awarded in six categories plus an award for works in the English language by Québec authors).

Stephen Leacock Medal for Humour (established in 1946 by Stephen Leacock Associates).

Royal Society of Canada Awards (comprising three biennially awarded medals for achievements in or contributions to imaginative or critical literature, humanities, historical works).

Amelia Howard-Gibbon Award (Canadian Association of Children's Librarians medal for outstanding illustrations of children's books published in Canada; established in 1971).

33 The Reviewing of Books

The need to establish a Canadian literary periodical that would provide regular and consistent information about books being written and published in Canada while also developing reviewers and reviewing, has been debated for a long time. Although Canada does have competent reviewers and a reasonable number of outlets, which during the past two or three years have increased both in terms of numbers and in attention focused on Canadian books, there are problems that are unique to Canada.

In a study of "the state of book-reviewing and literary criticism in English Canada", Val Clery noted the particular dilemma faced by Canadian reviewers and readers. Being at the hinge of two great cultures that express themselves in the English language, Canada has access to an immense wealth of new books published every year in the United Kingdom and the United States. In an age of almost instantaneous international communications, Canadians also read the reviews of these books almost as soon as they are available in the originating country. The result is that the scarce space provided for book reviews in the Canadian print media is to a very

considerable extent taken up by evaluations of foreign books from a Canadian viewpoint, satisfying appetites whetted by promotion from abroad.

In the context of comparative book production, this may seem only justifiable, but viewed in the perspective of a developing national literature, it is not surprising that Canadian writers and publishers feel their work does not receive the full support of the media. Clery's study revealed that two important Toronto daily newspapers–the *Star*, claiming Canada's largest circulation, and the *Globe and Mail*, styling itself "Canada's National Newspaper"–each with one or two-page weekend book sections which contain consistently competent reviews, had in 1969–70 devoted only 22% and 19% respectively, of their reviews to Canadian books. In the study, this was further related to the fact that each paper was therefore able to review only 5.8% and 2.9% respectively of all Canadian titles published.

Given Canada's vast geographic dimensions, these newspapers cannot be expected to extend their Ontario-centred urban influence across the country. The implication is that other Canadian readers have even less information about Canadian books. However, some large urban centres have newspapers with useful weekend book sections that deserve mention:

The Montreal Star
The Ottawa Journal
The Winnipeg Free Press
The Calgary Herald Tribune
The Vancouver Sun

Since 1971, *Books in Canada* (→5) has attempted to reach a wide general public through, primarily, gratis distribution in bookstores. With a circulation of almost 35,000 copies, this independent monthly journal is devoted to reviewing Canadian books. Unfortunately it has not yet received sufficient support from the trade to permit its existence on advertising revenue alone, and must therefore remain at the mercy of government grants for its publication.

In Québec, the reviewing of French-language books in the past decade has improved considerably owing to the concerted efforts made by the trade and the sympathetic response from the media. The three major daily newspapers, each with large weekend book sections and frequent special articles on French-language books and writers, are:

Le Devoir (Montréal)
La Presse (Montréal)
Le Soleil (Québec)

Bibliography

V. CLERY, *Promotion and response. Report on the Media Response Survey of trade book Publishing.* Toronto, Canadian Book Publishers' Council 1971. 59 pp. Stapled.
Matthews' List. Meaford, Ontario.
A directory of the communications industry, published annually with three revisions included in the subscription.

34 Graphic Arts

There has been a real proliferation of graphic arts societies in Canada in recent years, indicative of the serious concern and dedication to the development of design that has made Canada one of the most highly regarded countries in this context. None of these societies has yet achieved national scope, although they all play an important role locally, organizing competitions and holding exhibits.

For book designers, the Book Promotion and Editorial Club (→ 20) attempted to run a national design competition–the Look of Books–but its basically local Toronto membership did not have resources sufficient to promote it for Canada-wide acceptance. As a result, the Canadian Book Publishers' Council (→ 4) initiated, during International Book Year in 1972,

the formation of the Canadian Book Design Committee, a group bringing together interested people from all concerned segments involved in the book-production process. Their aim is to plan and promote a national book design competition, through which attention is focused on the book and the importance of the design elements in it. The first competition took place in 1974.

Inquiries concerning the graphic arts in Canada or Québec may be addressed directly to:

Society of Graphic Designers of Canada/
Société des Graphistes du Canada
1465 Yonge Street, Suite 6
CDN Toronto, Ontario M4T 1Z2
and
Société des Graphistes du Québec
Case postale 202
Succursale Youville
CDN Montréal 351, Québec

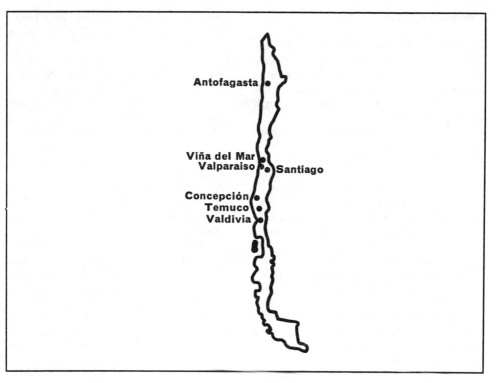

1 General Information

Area 741,767 km²*
Population 9,566,000 (1970)
Capital Santiago (2,437,000)
Largest towns Santiago (2,437,000); Valparaíso (257,800); Viña del Mar (126,400); Concepción (211,900); Temuco (173,200); Valdivia (178,200); Antofagasta (108,325)
Government Centralized republic. There are three central powers: Executive, Legislative, and Judicial. The Legislative power is composed of a two-chamber Congress, and the Executive power is headed by the President of the Republic.
National language Spanish
Leading foreign languages English, French

Religion Roman Catholic 89%; Protestant 6%; Other religious groups 5%
Weights, measures Metric system
Currency unit Escudo (E°) = 100 cents
Education 73,035 students in 8 universities and other establishment of higher learning (1966)
Illiteracy 11,5% (1970)
Paper consumption a) Newsprint 5.1 kg per inhabitant (1970)
  b) Printing paper (other than newsprint) 5.3 kg per inhabitant (1970)
Membership UNESCO

* This area corresponds to the Chilean territory on the American Continent; 1,250,000 km² on the Antarctic Continent are to be added.

Chile

2 Past and Present

Throughout the period prior to Chile's independence (1810), intellectual activity was extremely precarious. There existed practically no circulation of books, except among the clergy. The first printing press was installed by the Jesuits in 1748.

In the nineteenth century, once the country had been freed from Spanish colonial rule, events gradually took place that contituted the nation's cultural awakening. Some of the successive landmarks were:

1811 The first newspaper, *La Aurora de Chile* (Chile's Dawn) comes into life.

1813 Foundation of the National Library.

1827 *El Mercurio* starts being published in Valparaíso.

1840 Inauguration of the first bookshop.

All of this culminated in 1842 in the foundation of the Chile University and the blooming of a powerful intellectual movement which to a large extent left its imprint on the country's subsequent cultural evolution.

In the twentieth century the country already has the appearance of a nation with a developing culture of its own: universities, magazines, publishing houses, a significant literary output. During the thirties the publishing business experienced a conspicuous growth, Chile ranking ahead of all Latin American nations in the field. This growth declines late in the forties, when countries like the Argentina and Mexico, in turn, begin to excel as great book-publishing centres.

Chile at present possesses a steady and important publishing business, a network of big bookshop covering its whole territory, and a noteworthy rate of book consumption per capita.

Bibliography

D. AMUNATEGUI, *La primera imprenta de Chile la trajeron los jesuitas.* (The first printing press in Chile was brought by the Jesuits.) In: Revista Chilena de Historia y Geografía No 78, pp. 82–87. Santiago 1933.

G. FELIU, *Bibliografía histórica de la imprenta en Santiago de Chile.* (Historical bibliography on the printing press in Santiago, Chile.) Santiago, Editorial Nascimento 1964. 163 pp.

G. FURLONG, *Orígenes del arte tipográfico en América.* (The origins of the art of typography in America.) Buenos Aires, Ed. Huarpes 1947. 225 pp. Bibliography on pp. 215–25.–Early printing history of Chile: pp. 107–110.

J. G. GUERRA, *Sarmiento, su vida y sus obras.* (Sarmiento, his life and works.) Santiago, Editorial Elzeviriana 1901. 360 pp.

R. LATCHAM, *Antología, crónica de varia invención.* (Chronicle, anthology from various sources.) Santiago, Editorial Zig-Zag, 1965. 356 pp.

J. T. MEDINA, *Historia de la imprenta en los antiguos dominios españoles de América y Oceanía.* (The history of printing in the ancient Spanish dominions of America and Oceania.) 2 vols. Santiago de Chile, Fondo Histórico y Bibliográfico José Toribio Medina 1958. CXLI, 542; XV, 540 pp. v. II, pp. 297–326: Chile (Santiago de Chile).

These two volumes offer all the classical contributions of the great Chilean scholar J. T. Medina about Latin America's printing history.–Reprints of the bibliographical works of J. T. Medina have recently been published by N. Israel, Amsterdam.

As to the unsurpassed contributions of J. T. Medina in many fields of book history, cf.:

M. A. BROMSEN (ed.), *José Toribio Medina. Humanist of the Americas.* An appraisal. Washington D. C., Pan American Union 1960. LIV, 295 pp.

H. NEIRA, *Cartas de un librero a un escritor joven.* (Letters from a book dealer to a young writer.) Santiago. Librería Neira 1948. 133 ps.

R. Silva, *Panorama literario de Chile.*
(Chile's literary panorama.) Santiago,
Editorial Universitaria 1961. 570 pp.

L. S. Thompson, *Printing in Colonial
Spanish America.* Hamden Conn., Archon
Books 1962. 108 pp.
pp. 87–93: Chile.

S. Tornero, *Reminiscencias de un viejo
editor.* (Remembrances of an old publisher.) Santiago, Imprenta El Mercurio
1889. 231 pp.

3 Retail Prices

Retail price conditions are basically
the same prevailing in all other Latin
American countries and have, generally
speaking, been inherited from the Spanish
book trade. The retailer sells Chilean
books at the price fixed by the publishing
house, and imported books at the price
fixed by the distributor. In the latter case,
however, considerable trouble can arise,
because importers do not apply a uniform
standard when fixing the price of foreign
books. Particularly sharp, for instance, are
the differences in price between the wholesale importer and the importer who sells
directly to the public through his own
shops.
There exists no legislation intended to regulate this aspect in the book trade. The
"Chilean Book Chamber" (→4) has been
trying for many years to set up standards
that would avoid anarchy in the retail
prices of foreign books. But it has had scant
success.
An additional handicap is that book publishing and imports are concentrated in the
capital, Santiago, and to a very narrow
extent in Valparaíso. As a result, in most
provincial localities–especially in those
more than 500 km away from Santiago
(over 2,000 km, in the extreme cases of
Arica and Punta Arenas)–retail prices
will be substantially increased due to
packing and freight expenses.

Special discounts are granted to public
libraries (from 10% up to 25%, depending
on whether the books are imported or
printed locally) and to college students
(10%, 15% and 20%). In the latter case,
the top discounts are granted by the bookshops belonging to the universities.

4 Organization

There is only one organization:
*Cámara Chilena del Libro
(Chilean Book Chamber)
Ahumada 312
RCH Santiago*
grouping publishers as well as wholesale
distributors and booksellers, although not
all of them are affiliated to this institution.
The Chamber's basic purposes are: to
represent its members before the national
authorities; to help outline a national
policy on books; to combat all obstacles
against the free circulation of printed material; to promote the habit of reading
among the people; etc.
Although at times the Chamber has made
serious efforts to develop an active policy
beneficial to its aims, in general its per-
formance is feeble and ineffectual. It cannot do any better owing to the character of
its members, sometimes contradictory and
even antagonistic.
Within the Chilean Book Chamber is the
*Cámara Chilena de Editores
(Chilean Chamber of Publishers)
Ahumada 312
RCH Santiago*
which is not independent and not very
prominent.
The Book Chamber has no publications of
its own.

6 Book-Trade Literature

Material on this subject is practically non-
existent. The only items worth mentioning
are the 28-page pamphlet *El libro y el*

Chile

problema editorial en Chile (The Book and the publishing problem in Chile) by J. Almendros (Santiago 1958), and the article *El problema editorial en Chile* (The publishing problem in Chile) by L. Osorio (Revista Aurora No 5–6, Santiago, January 1956.)

7 Sources of Information, Address Services

Information on the marketing of books may be obtained from
> Cámara Chilena del Libro
> (Chilean Book Chamber)
> Ahumada 312
> RCH Santiago

Basic information on Chilean book production may be obtained from the
> Biblioteca Nacional
> (National Library)
> Alameda esq. Mac Iver
> RCH Santiago

Bibliography

The addresses of all branches of the book trade are contained in
La Empresa del Libro en América Latina. (The Book in Latin America.) 2nd ed. Buenos Aires, Bowker Editores Argentina 1974. VIII, 307 pp.
pp. 147–157: Chile.

8 International Membership

UNESCO

10 Books and Young People

No significant action is taken in Chile in this field. Suffice it to quote UNESCO's data on Chilean publishing in 1968. During that year, only nine books for children were published.

12 Taxes

Theoretically, there is no tax. Nevertheless, some kinds of regulation prevail which lead, directly or indirectly, to higher costs for the import of books. One is the requirement of a previous registration of the import, and the compulsory coverage of the respective value through the Central Bank. Furthermore, the Chilean Customs House charges a certain amount on every package of books imported.

14 Copyright

In 1955 Chile ratified the "Interamerican Convention", as well as the "Universal Copyright Convention". ($\rightarrow$BTW I, International Section 14.)
In general, the norms set up by the Universal Copyright Convention are applied. National regulations are summed up in Law No. 17, 336 issued in April, 1971.

Some provisions contained in the Chilean Law on Intellectual Copyright:
–The copyright comprises those patrimonial and moral rights protecting use, property and preservation of the work.
–Foreign authors residing abroad will enjoy the protection granted them by the international conventions which Chile has signed and ratified.
–The law covers books, pamphlets, articles and papers; encyclopedias, guides, dictionaries, selections and compilations of all kinds; radio or TV scripts adapted from any literary work; any adaptions, translations or other transformed texts, as approved by the author.
–The law protects and defines the following types of works: individual, co-produced, collective, anonymous, pseudonymous, unpublished, posthumous, original, and derived.
–The copyright lasts for the author's lifetime plus 30 years after his death. Should it by assigned to the surviving spouse, protection will apply during the latter's lifetime. Once these terms have lapsed, the work becomes common cultural property.
–As exclusive depositary of the moral right, the author has throughout his life the faculty to claim paternity on same, to associate it to his name or known pseudonym, and to reject any deformation, shortening or other amendment done without

124

his previous, declared consent. This right is transferable to the surviving spouse.

–The patrimonial right entitles the author to personally use his work, to make total or partial cession of his rights on it, and to authorize use of same by other parties.

–The licence towards publication of a work shall be worded in any contractual form, specifying the rights granted the licensee, the licence term, fees and payment terms, minimal, maximal or indefinite number of copies authorized, territorial coverage, etc. The licence fee shall be not less than 10% on the retail sales price per copy, if a share on the produce of sales is applied. The author reserves for himself the exclusive right on translation, public display, and cinema, record or TV adaptation.

Bibliography

R. ESPINOZA, *De los derechos intelectuales sobre las obras artísticas.* (On intellectual copyright protecting artistic works.) Santiago 1959.

M. I. MARTINEZ, *La propiedad intelectual.* (Intellectual copyright.) Santiago 1963.

S. YÁNEZ, *La naturaleza jurídica del derecho de autor.* (The juridical nature of copyright.) Santiago 1956.

15 National Bibliography, National Library

Entrusted with preservation of the country's entire printed heritage is the

Biblioteca Nacional
(National Library)
Alameda esq. Mac Iver
RCH Santiago

founded in 1813.

The Compulsory Deposit obliging all printers to deliver copies of the books, magazines, journals or leaflets they publish has been in force since 1925.

Although inscription is provided of every book and pamphlet in a periodical bibliographical bulletin, fulfilment of this provision is sporadic. The bibliographical list was published for some years in the *Anales de la Universidad de Chile* (Annals of the Chile University); and from 1960

through 1968 in the magazine *Mapocho*, published directly by the National Library. The bibliographical catalogues were deficient and confused, and were issued with considerable delay in respect to the dates of publication. Yet they constituted the only source of information available. *Mapocho* having ceased publication, this information can only be obtained now by approaching the *Sección Chilena* (Chilean Division) of the "National Library".

Bibliography

P. AVICENNE, *Bibliographical services throughout the world 1965–69*. Paris, UNESCO 1972. 310 pp.
pp. 89–90: Chile.

I. ZIMMERMANN, *Current national bibliographies of Latin America*. Gainesville, Florida, University of Florida Press 1971. X, 139 pp.
pp. 35–39: Chile.

16 Book Production

In 1970, a total of 1,370 titles were issued, as per following breakdown:

Subject group	Titles
General	23
Philosophy	20
Religion	55
Social studics	651
Philology	81
Theoretical sciences	83
Applied sciences	130
Arts	33
Literature	147
Geography, history	147

(UNESCO *Statistical Yearbook* 1971. Paris, UNESCO 1972).

17 Translations

38 Translations were published in 1969 (22 from English, 6 from French, 6 from German, 3 from Italian, and 1 from another foreign language), the subjects

being: philosophy: 6; religion: 1; social studies: 1; literature: 30.

A factor impairing the development of this important publishing activity is the heavy tax on the transfer of funds abroad in payment of copyrights.

18 Book Clubs

At present book clubs do not exist in the country. In the fifties, there were attempts to organize some clubs, as an initiative on the part of local and foreign publishing houses; but they had short life, due to defective planning.

19 Paperbacks

Paperbacks are new in Chile. During the forties, there was the *Biblioteca Zig-Zag* (Zig-Zag Series) which, though close to the modern concept of paperbacks, restricted its subjects to school reading of Chilean and Spanish literature and, since it did not try distribution channels other than the conventional one through bookseller's shops, in the end the experiment failed and was discontinued.

In 1967 the *Cormorán* series got started, modern in design and overtly universal as to its subjects. However, its editions are still smaller than paperbacks elsewhere. The series *Quimantú para todos* (Quimantú for Everybody) appeared in 1971, with a minimum of 30,000 copies distributed through bookseller's shops and newspaper stands. Its success, quite considerable, induced the publishers to further enlarge their production by issuing a new pocket-book series called *Minilibros*, appearing every week in editions of not fewer than 50,000 copies.

21 Publishing

It is no easy task to determine the exact number of Chilean publishing houses, be-cause many of them, though called such, only issue books now and then. In any case, at present they total no more than twenty, over two thirds being located in Santiago, the capital of the country.

Most of the titles appearing every year are published by the authors themselves, by public organizations, educational institutions, etc.

23 Wholesale Trade

No figures are available on the volume of sales reached in the wholesale trade. There is evidence, however, that the highest percentage is controlled by distributors dealing in imported books; there are about 50 in the country, most of them with headquarters in Santiago.

Quite a number of these distributors are local branches of important foreign publishing houses, mainly Spanish, Argentinian, and Mexican.

Chilean publishing houses operate through their own wholesale divisions, characterized above all by their still precarious development. They advertise modestly, and lack suitable outlets throughout the country, their work being basically centred in Santiago and four or five of the principal provincial capitals.

24 Retail Trade

Out of the approximately 250 bookshops existing in the country, some 200 operate in Santiago, Valparaíso, Concepción, Viña del Mar, and the two or three towns following in importance. Three quarters of the latter are located in the provincial capitals.

In the above-mentioned cities there are some excellent bookshops, well organized and offering the public an efficient service. There are also bookshops specializing in French, English, and German material.

Yet, from one end of the country to the

other the total of bookshops proper–i.e. of establishments devoted exclusively to selling books and magazines–does not exceed 100. There are still–particularly in the provincial towns–the "stationery", a shop selling copybooks and other writing materials and school utensils, for whom the sale of books is just a small part.

In the last few years a significant role in the retailing of books has been played by the so-called "sale by instalments" method, salesmen visiting prospective customers in their homes or at work.

Over the last year or two the sale of paperbacks by magazine and newspaper stands has been promoted.

26 Antiquarian Book Trade, Auctions

Some twenty bookshops are engaged in this trade, the development of which has no special importance in the country.

27 Book Imports

Even if Chile is bound by UNESCO's Convention with regard to free circulation of books, there have actually been for over two decades, rather severe regulations on book imports, owing to the country's chronic shortage of foreign currency. Despite this, Chile has a good import standard and is, in Latin America, among the countries showing one of the highest per capita rates in foreign books' consumption.

Unfortunately the figures supplied by the Chile Central Bank do not reflect separately the values corresponding to books and magazines. The data given, therefore, cover both items. Yet, it may be estimated that more than two thirds of the totals indicated correspond to books.

In 1971, imports amounted to US $ 13,799,000; the main supplying countries were:

Country	Value US $	Percentage of Total
Argentina	3,198,000	23.1
Spain	3,167,000	22.9
Mexico	1,607,000	11.6
USA	1,142,000	8.2
Germany (F.R.)	307,000	2.2
France	241,000	1.7
Italy	112,000	0.8
Colombia	75,000	0.5
United Kingdom	69,000	0.5

28 Book Exports

In 1971, books and magazines were exported for a total value of US $ 1,473,000, to the following chief countries:

Country	Value US $	Percentage of total
Argentina	460,000	31.2
Colombia	369,000	25.0
Peru	220,000	14.9
Bolivia	120,000	8.1
USA	57,000	3.9
Mexico	54,000	3.6

29 Book Fairs

Just one contest takes place every year, as a result of the initiative of the Chilean Book Chamber: the *Chilean Book Fair*, which had real significance and impact in the forties, but is now an ineffectual routine acticity.

32 Literary Prizes

The most important literary prize is the *Premio Nacional de Literatura*, awarded annually to an author–poet or prose writer–for his lifetime work. This was first granted in 1941, and has been won by the most prominent Chilean writers, Gabriela Mistral and Pablo Neruda among them.

Of lesser significance are: the *Premio Municipal*, awarded by the Santiago

Municipality for the best novel, story, volume of poems, essay, and play published during the respective year; the *Premio Gabriela Mistral*, also yearly, rewarding unpublished works; the *Premio Alerce* (Larch), destined by the Chilean Writers' Association for authors who are just starting; etc.

33 The Reviewing of Books

In their Sunday issues, the local newspapers devote a great deal of space to the reviewing of books particularly *El Mercurio* in Santiago, which has not only columns with literary comments, but also a fixed page devoted to scientific and technical publications. *La Nación* and *El Siglo*, both in Santiago, deal mainly with works of a literary nature, as does *El Sur* in Concepción. Extensive sections on this subject are included in: *Anales de la Universidad de Chile* (Annals of the Chile University); *Atenea*, a review issued by the Concepción University; and *Revista de Literatura Chilena* (Chilean Literature Journal), published by the Spanish Department at Chile University.

Colombia

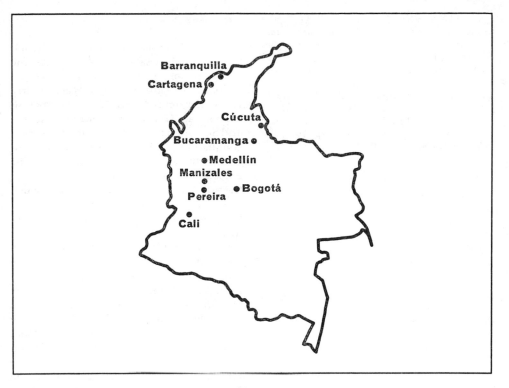

1 General Information

Area 1,138,914 km²

Population 20,141,670 (17.7 per km²). The country's population comprises various ethnic groups, as follows:
Indians 2.2%, Negroes 6.0%, Mestizos (mixed Indian and White) 47.0%, Mulattos (mixed Negro and White) 24.0%, White 20.0%

Capital Bogotá (2,400,640)

Largest towns Bogotá (2,400,640); Medellín (990,480); Cali (846,250); Barranquilla (643,310); Cartagena (308,620); Bucaramanga (284,020); Manizales (276,900); Pereira (231,360); Cúcuta (212,760)

Government Centralist republic (article1 of Colombia's Constitution). For administrative purposes the country is divided into 22 departments, 4 intendancies and 4 commissaryships. Presidential system. The president is elected by direct popular vote for a period of 4 years.

Parliament (Congress) is formed by the Chamber of Representatives (210 members) and the Senate (118 members). Each member is elected by direct popular vote for a period of 4 years. Uppermost in the Judiciary is the Supreme Court of Justice, whose members are appointed by the corporation itself. Magistrates of the High Tribunals are also appointed by the Supreme Court, and these magistrates in turn appoint the judges at the lower levels

National language Spanish

Leading foreign languages English, French

Religion 98% Catholic. The remaining 2% belong to other religious denominations

Weights, measures Metric system

Currency unit Col. Peso (col. $) = 100 centavos

Education Number of students enrolled in elementary schools (1969): 2,933,432. Number of students enrolled in secondary schools (1969):

129

614,147. Number of students enrolled in higher institutions (1969): 85,608. There are a total of 46 universities and institutions of higher learning

Illiteracy Illiterate population over ten years of age: 32%

Paper consumption a) Newsprint 2.4 kg per inhabitant (1970)

b) Printing paper (other than newsprint) 1.8 kg (1970)

Membership UNESCO, CERLAL

2 Past and Present

The first European conquerors to reach Colombian shores did so fifty years after the advent of Johannes Gutenberg's invention of printing with movable type. Thirty years later, on 6 August 1538, two Spanish conquerors, Gonzalo Jiménez de Quesada and Sebastián de Belalcázar, and a German conqueror, Nicolás Federmann, met together by chance on a plateau on the Andean mountains and resolved to found there the city of Santa Fe de Bogotá, which was to become the future capital.

One of these conquerors–Gonzalo Jiménez de Quesada (1506–79)–was also a writer. Upon his return to Nueva Granada (the name given to the country in those days) from later journeys to Spain, he brought with him the first books to come into the country. Along with his activities as explorer and conqueror, Jiménez de Quesada found time to write the first books to be written in this territory: "Relación de la conquista del Nuevo Reino de Granada" (Story of the conquest of the New Kingdom of Granada), 1538 or 1539; "Compendio historial de las conquistas del Nuevo Reino" (Historical outline of the conquest of the New Kingdom), 1569 (?); "Los ratos de Suesca" (Leisurely hours in Suesca), etc.

Spain's policy in regard to cultural affairs in her American domains has been largely distorted by so-called black legend. It is a fact that as early as 1548, and by Royal Decree of Emperor Charles V, the tax-exemption law on books, which had been in force in Castilla since 1480, was made to apply to the New World. Such exemption remained in effect until 1720. In that year a 2% tax was imposed on books from Spain, while books from other lands were taxed by 4%. These taxes, however, were abolished in 1721. It was not until 1766 that taxes on books from foreign nations were re-established.

Nevertheless, book circulation was often restricted in Spanish possessions. In 1506 King Ferdinand prohibited the circulation of "anti-religious, frivolous or scandalous" books. In 1502 it became a requirement, both in Spain and in Spanish America, to obtain a licence before a book could be printed. Moreover, starting from 1558, censorship became the rule during colonial days. Between the years 1770 and 1804 orders were made on various occasions to stop circulation of all books contrary to the Spanish Monarchy and those advocating the principles of Diderot's and d'Alembert's "Encyclopedia" and the French Revolution.

Nueva Granada proclaimed its independence in 1810 (actual independence was obtained in 1819) and, from that year on, both the freedom of the press and freedom of circulation of printed matter have been respected except during brief periods of restraint. However, penalties have been established against abuse, defamation and slander. Book imports, particularly from Europe, have been steadily increasing since the beginning of the nineteenth century. Moreover, since the last century, and particularly in Bogotá, numerous bookstores have started business.

The most reliable historical records show that the first printing press that came into the country went into operation for the first time in October 1737, under the supervision of members of the Jesuit Order. It is also known that the first book to be published was the "Septenario al Corazón Doloroso de María Santísim" (Septenary to Holy Mary's sorrowful heart). That printing press worked continuously until 1767, except for a few periods of inactivity. In that year King Charles III ordered the Jesuits out of the country. Later, in 1777, the Royal Printing Office was established. It was property of the Viceroyship and its first director was Antonio Espinosa de los Monteros. In 1793 the "Imprenta pa-triótica" (Patriotic Press) was founded by the forerunner of Colombian independence, Antonio Nariño. In his shop Nariño printed a Spanish version of the rights of men and citizens (August 1794), which had a tremendous impact on the course of the struggle for the independence of Nueva Granada. At about the same time several printing presses went to work in some of the major cities.

Bibliography

DEPARTAMENTO NACIONAL DE ESTADISTICA (DANE), *Anuario general de estadística.* (General yearbook of statistics.) 1967 to 1968. Bogotá, Dane 1969.

L. GONZAGA, *Efemérides colombianas.* (Colombian ephemera.) Bogotá, Procuraduría de los hermanos cristianos 1920.

J. M. HENAO Y G. ARRUBLA, *Historia de Colombia.* (History of Colombia.) 8th ed. Bogotá, Librería Voluntad 1967.

Incunables Bogotanos, siglo XVIII. (Incunables of Bogota, 18th century.) Bogota, Banco de la Republica 1959. 240 pp. Bibliography and historical description covering many fields of early printing in Colombia.

INSTITUTO GEOGRAFICO AGUSTIN CODAZZI, *Atlas básico de Colombia.* (Basic atlas of Colombia.) Bogotá, Editorial Andes, 1970.

J. ORTEGA-TORRES, *Constitución política de colombia.* (Colombian political constitution.) Bogotá, Edit. Temis 1970.

J. J. ORTEGA-TORRES, *Historia de la literatura colombiana.* (History of Colombian literature.) 2nd. ed. Bogotá, Edit. Cromos 1935.

G. FURLONG, *Orígines del arte tipográfico en América.* (The origins of the art of typography in America.) Buenos Aires, Ed. Huarpes, 1947. 225 pp. Bibliography on pp. 215–25.–Early printing history of Colombia: pp. 99–103.

A. CACUA-PRADA, *Don Manuel del Socorro Rodríguez.* Bogotá, Banco de la República 1966.

Colombia

T. Higuera, B., *La imprenta en Colombia*. (The printing press in Colombia.) Bogotá, Imprenta Nacional 1970.

J. T. Medina, *Historia de la imprenta en los antiguos dominios españoles de América y Oceanía*. (The history of printing in the ancient Spanish dominions of America and Oceania.) 2 vols. Santiago de Chile, Fondo Histórico y Bibliográfico José Toribio Medina 1958. CXLI, 542; XV, 540 pp.
II, pp. 237–251: Colombia (Bogotá).

L. S. Thompson, *Printing in Colonial Spanish America*. Hamden Conn., Archon Books 1962. 108 pp.
pp. 76: Colombia.

3 Retail Prices

No agreement has been made, either in the past or in the present century, among booksellers and distributors about retail sales prices. Neither has any settlement been negotiated on conditions of sale from publishers to booksellers. The first agreement on liquidity of foreign currency for the purpose of determining prices for sales to the public was reached in 1951 at the "Colombian Chamber of Book Trade" (→4). Such an agreement was renewed several times until 1959. In that year Congress gave its approval to the first article of law 155, by which guilds were forbidden to set prices by private agreement without previous government study and approval. This law was later broadened and rules and regulations for it were established by decrees 3307 of 1963, 1802 of 1964 and 2562 of 1968.

Bibliography

Libros colombianos (Colombian Books), Nos. 1–6, magazine of the Colombian Chamber of Book Trade (→4).

Ministerio de Gobierno, *Leyes de 1959*. (Laws of 1959). Bogotá, Imprenta Nacional 1960.

J. Ortega-Torres, *Código de comercio*. (Commercial code), Bogotá, Edit. Temis 1972.

4 Organization

The most important association concerned with the promotion of book business and production is the
Cámara Colombiana de la Industria Editorial (CCIE)
(Colombian Chamber of Publishing Industry)
Apartado aéreo 89–98
Calle 15 No. 9-30. Oficina 206.
CO Bogotá
This organization resulted from the merging of the "Cámara Colombiana del Libro" ("Colombian Chamber of Book Trade"), an association founded in 1951, and the "Asociación Colombiana de Editores" ("Colombian Association of Publishers"), founded in 1966. Fusion of these two organizations was formally agreed in December, 1970.

The objectives of the "Colombian Chamber of Publishing Industry" are to promote book industry and trade; to act as intermediary between the guild and public authorities, and also between the guild and similar organizations abroad, particularly those in Spanish-speaking countries; to organize book fairs and exhibitions; to grant prizes for science and literature; to popularize Colombian books; and to make requests or suggestions to public authorities on matters concerning the development of the book.

The
Comité Sectorial de la Industria Editorial (Special Committee for the Publishing Industry)
Carrera 13 No. 27–00, piso 10
CO Bogotá
has been at work since March 1970, as part of the Ministry of Economic Development. It is made up of representatives from both government and private industry. The

purpose of the Committee is to study the problems relating to book production and trade.
→ 11 (CERLAL).

Bibliography

CAMARA COLOMBIANA DEL LIBRO, *Estatutos*. Bogotá 1951.
ASOCIACION COLOMBIANA DE EDITORES, *Estatutos*. Bogotá 1967.
Libros (Books), magazine of the Colombian Chamber of Publishing Industry, 1971 (→ 5).

5 Trade Press

The most important publication dealing with bookselling and publishing is the magazine
Libros
(Books)
Apartado aéreo 89-98
CO Bogotá
which is published by the Colombian Chamber of Publishing Industry (→ 4). This magazine first appeared in 1966, was discontinued in 1968, and re-appeared in 1971.
Moreover, the
Instituto Caro y Cuervo
Calle 24 No. 5-60, Oficina 203
CO Bogotá
a government-supported institution engaged mainly in philological research, has since 1958 been publishing the *Anuario Bibliográfico Colombiano* (Colombian Bibliographic Yearbook). This yearbook provides a record of all books published in Colombia.
Books are listed in their proper order according to the Dewey system of classification and following the rules of the American Library Association and the Library of Congress. The country's leading newspapers publish book reviews and commentaries, either weekly or every other week.

6 Book-Trade Literature

→ 2, 3, 4, 5.

7 Sources of Information, Address Services

General information about book production and the trade may be obtained from the "Colombian Chamber of Publishing Industry" (→ 4) and also from its magazine "Libros" (→ 5).
As regards bibliographic research, queries may be addressed to
Biblioteca Luis Angel Arango
Calle 11 No. 4-14
CO Bogotá
or to
Instituto Caro y Cuervo
Calle 24 No. 5-60, Oficina 203
CO Bogotá
The addresses of all branches of the book trade are contained in
La Empresa del Libro en América Latina. (The Book in Latin America.) 2nd ed. Buenos Aires, Bowker Editores Argentina 1974. VIII, 307 pp.
pp. 129-140: Colombia.

8 International Membership

The „Colombian Chamber of Publishing Industry" is not affiliated to any international association of booksellers or publishers. It keeps in close contact, however, with similar associations throughout Latin America. The Republic of Colombia is a member of UNESCO.
→ 11 (CERLAL).

11 Training

There is no school in Colombia for training members of the book trade. They receive on-the-job training, often relying on their own initiative and personal effort.
In May 1971 the Colombian Government with UNESCO assistance, founded, the

Colombia

Centro Regional par el Fomento del Libro en América Latina (CERLAL)
(Regional Centre for Book Development in Latin America)
Calle 70, No. 9–52
Ap. Aéreo 17438
CO Bogotá
(→ Latin America 4). All Spanish-speaking countries are expected to participate. One of the purposes of the Centre is to organize a training school for members of the trade and to give special courses on all aspects and levels in the publishing industry.
The
Escuela Interamericana de Bibliotecología
(Interamerican School of Library Science)
CO Medellín
is an institution for training personnel in library administration.
Both the "Pontificia Universidad Javeriana", founded by the Society of Jesus, and the "Universidad de La Salle", founded by the Christian Brothers in Bogotá, have been offering courses in Library Science since 1973.

12 Taxes

Publishers and booksellers pay taxes on the same basis as industry and business in general. Thus they pay income tax, with rates increasing according to profits; industrial and commercial municipal tax, which averages about 1% of total sales value; national stamp duties, which must be paid on bills of exchange and sale contracts; and sales tax, which amounts to 4% of the retail price except for textbooks and technical or scientific books.
Consular fees amounting to 1%, and also a special tax of 3% destined to the promotion of exports and the coffee industry, must be paid on all imported books according to article 229 of ordinance 444 of 1967 and article 20 of ordinance 688 of 1967. The importer has to meet an addi-

tional expense of about US $ 10 for the application forms used in the procedure for legalizing imports.

Bibliography

J. I. Bonilla-Suarez, *Los impuestos de renta, complementarios, especiales y recargos.* (Income, complementary and special taxes and overcharges) 5th ed. Bogotá, Editional Andes 1969.
Salvador Linares, *Impuesto a las ventas.* (Sales tax.) Bogotá, Edit. Temis 1967.

14 Copyright

According to article 35 of Colombia's Constitution, artistic and literary property is protected "throughout the author's lifetime and for a period of eighty years after his death under the provisions of the law". Some benefits are granted to owners of "works published in any Spanish-speaking country–without special international agreement–as long as that nation honours the principle of reciprocity in its legislation".
Copyright is regulated by articles 670 and 671 of the Civil Code, by law 86 of 1946, and by decree 1258 of 1949. Publishing contracts, when the publisher is a private citizen, must abide by these legal texts, but when the publisher is a business firm, they must adhere to the provisions given in title XV, book IV, articles 1354–1376 of the Commercial Code which went into effect on 1 January 1972. The Ministry of Government has appointed a special Commission (27 June 1973) which is now working on a revision of the law on Copyright (law 86 of 1946).
By law 6 of 1970, Colombia joined the Washington Interamerican Convention on Copyright. This convention was signed in Washington on 22 June 1946. However, it was not until December 1970 that it was ratified by Colombia. This country has not adhered so far either to the Berne Con-

vention, or to the Universal Copyright Convention.

Colombia has subscribed to and ratified the following international agreements on artistic and literary property:
a) The agreement on artistic and literary property approved during the Fourth Interamerican Conference of Buenos Aires, 11 August 1910, and ratified in Colombia by law 7 of 1936. It applies to relations between Colombia and Argentina, Bolivia, Brazil, Costa Rica, Chile, Ecuador, the United States of America, Guatemala, Haiti, Honduras, Nicaragua, Panama, Paraguay, Peru, the Dominican Republic and Uruguay;
b) The agreement on artistic and literary property subscribed in the Bolivarian Congress of Caracas, 17 July 1911, and approved in Colombia by law 65 of 1913;
c) The international Convention on restrictions to the circulation and traffic of obscene material signed in Geneva on 12 September 1923 and ratified in Colombia by law 47 of 1933.

Colombia has further subscribed and ratified the following bilateral agreements:
a) The agreement with Spain on warranty on artistic and literary property, signed in Bogotá on 28 November 1885, and approved in Colombia by law 31 of 1886;
b) The Trade and Friendship Treaty between Colombia and Switzerland, signed in Paris on 14 March 1908, and ratified in Colombia by law 15 of 19 August 1908. Article 11 of this Treaty is the only one which refers to copyright;
c) The commercial treaty with Sweden subscribed on 9 March 1928;
d) The joint declaration signed by Colombia and Italy on 27 October 1892;
e) The convention on protection of literary and artistic works subscribed by Colombia and France on 28 April 1953 and approved by law 12 of 1959;
f) The convention on protection of scientific, literary and artistic works signed jointly with the Federal Republic of Germany on 9 October 1963, and approved by law 24 of 1964.

Bibliography

J. ORTEGA-TORRES, *Código civil.* (Civil code.) 7th ed. Bogotá, Edit. Temis 1970.
E. SANTA, *Régimen de propiedad intelectual y de prensa.* (Regulations on press and copyright.) Bogotá, Imprenta Nacional 1962.

15 National Bibliography, National Library

The National Library
Biblioteca Nacional
CO Bogotá
was founded on 7 January 1777 by Viceroy Manuel Antonio Flórez and was originally called the Royal Library. Today it operates as a branch of the Ministry of National Education. Part of its duties are to care for and arrange the National Historical Archives, and also to make collections of periodical publications and books published in Colombia. As specified by article 76 of law 86 of 1946, the publisher of a book is expected to send a copy to the National Library, another to the library of the National University, and a third copy to the Caro and Cuervo Institute (→ 5) before he can make the required legal deposit at the Ministry of Government.

Apart from the *Anuario bibliográfico colombiano* (Colombian Bibliographic Yearbook), which was first published in 1958 containing a bibliographic registry from 1951 through 1956, there is no periodical publication concerned with Colombian bibliography. This yearbook is published by the Caro and Cuervo Institute.

Bibliography

General works
P. AVICENNE, *Bibliographical services throughout the world 1965–69.* Paris,

Colombia

UNESCO 1972. 310 pp.
p. 94: Colombia.
I. ZIMMERMANN, *Current national bibliographies of Latin America*. A state of the art study. Gainesville, Florida, University of Florida Press 1971. X, 139 pp.
pp. 39–44: Colombia.

Special works

G. GIRALDO-JARAMILLO, *Bibliografía de bibliografías colombianas* (Bibliography of Colombian bibliographies), 2nd. ed., revised and put up to date by RUBEN PEREZ-ORTIZ, Bogotá, Publicaciones del Instituto Caro y Cuervo 1960. XVI, 204 pp. 2 h.
I. LAVERDE-AMAYA, *Bibliografía colombiana* (Colombian bibliography), 2nd. ed., Bogotá, Imprenta y Librería de Medardo Rivas 1895. 296 pp.
FLOREN LOZANO, *Obras de referencia y general de la bibliografía colombiana*. (Reference and general works of Colombian bibliography.) Medellín (Colombia), Escuela Interamericana de Bibliotecología 1968. 226 + 2 pp.
An annotated list of 1,188 reference works, mostly published in Colombia since 1900.
E. POSADA, *Bibliografía bogotana* (Bogotan bibliography), Bogotá, Imprenta de Arboleda y Valencia; Imprenta Nacional, 1925–1927. 2 v., XXII, 506 pp.; XII, 596 pp.

16 Book Production

Colombian book production has been rather small for many years. Books printed abroad have been in widespread use. However, in the last 25 years, the publishing industry has advanced somewhat, especially in the field of textbooks for the elementary and secondary school levels. Books in current use at the higher educational levels come, for the most part, from Spain, Mexico, and Argentina. Books in English published in the United States are also frequently used in universities.

A certain number of books on literature, economics, legislation and jurisprudence are being published in Colombia. However, publication in these areas is still scanty.
According to the information provided by the National Department of Statistics (DANE), book production was as follows:

Year	Titles	Copies
1967	684	7,240,395
1968	718	8,549,017
1969	705	8,217,415
1970	745	8,635,804
1971	728	8,764,512

Production of periodical publications, particularly journals, is far greater. Newspapers, such as "El Tiempo" (The Times) and "El Espectador" (The Spectator) of Bogotá, reach a daily circulation of 300,000.

Periodic Publications: 1968

Category	Number of publications	Circulation
Daily	33	3,854,136
Weekly	64	730,880
Fortnightly	27	59,082
Monthly	94	372,758

Bibliography

DEPARTAMENTO NACIONAL DE ESTADÍSTICA (DANE), *Anuario general de estadística*. (General yearbook of statistics), 1967 to 1968. Bogotá. Id., *Industria manufacturera* 1969. Bogotá.

17 Translations

Not many books originally written in foreign languages are being translated and published. The exception to this, however, is textbooks for the elementary and secondary schools. On the other hand, a number of books on the social, political and juridical sciences are being translated and published yearly. Translations are most frequently made from English, Russian, French and Italian. Statistical data for two recent years are shown below:

Language	1970	1971
English	54	69
French	12	10
German	5	9
Russian	28	21
Italian	9	8
Total	108	117

21 Publishing

According to data supplied by the "Special Committee for the Publishing Industry", Colombia has a total of eighteen publishing firms, with headquarters in Bogotá, Medellín and Cali. Every publishing house assumes responsibility for the distribution of its books.

Some Spanish, Mexican and Argentine publishing firms have branch offices in Colombia. They keep a permanent stock of books and take care of their distribution throughout the country. Twelve of these subsidiaries of foreign publishing firms are in Bogotá, four in Medellín, and two in Cali.

23 Wholesale Trade

The wholesale trade started to develop barely ten years ago and is primarily concerned with the distribution of Spanish, Mexican and Argentine books. Leading distributors of Spanish books in Bogotá are "Editoras Unidas Colombianas, Ltda" (carrera 13 # 16–07); "Aguilar, S.A., de Ediciones" (calle 13 # 7–40); "Ediciones Labor, Ltda" (carrera 9a. A, # 18–08); "Editorial Ramón Sopena Colombiana, S.A." (carrera 24 # 11–42); "Editora Gustavo Gili Ltda", (calle 22 # 6–28); "Colombiana de Editores Reunidos" (Avenida de las Américas, # 25N–96, Cali).

Chief distributors of Mexican books are "Editorial Roble" (calle 19 # 5–51, piso 50); "Comex Ltda" (calle 20 # 7–17, of. 708); "Editorial González Porto" (carrera 8a # 21–39) and "Interamericana de Colombia, S.A." (calle 19 # 12–76, piso 30.); all of Bogotá.

The main distributors of Argentine books are "Ediciones Cruz del Sur" (calle 22 # 6–32, Bogotá) and "Editorial Losada Ltda" (calle 18A # 7–17, Bogotá).

Distribution of Colombian books is by the publishers themselves, as no particular firm undertakes it. Recently, however, the "Librería Mundial" (carrera 7a. # 16–74) has been getting into this line of work.

24 Retail Trade

In the retail trade the traditional bookstore system is of major importance. However, door-to-door salesmen are also employed. Nowadays there are more than sixty large bookstores in the country, distributed as follows: 25 in Bogotá; 12 in Medellín; 8 in Cali; 5 in Barranquilla; 3 in Manizales; and several others in other cities.

Further information about bookstores in Colombia may be obtained upon request from the "Colombian Chamber of Publishing Industry" (→4).

27 Book Imports

Book imports are increasing steadily. Main providers are Spain, Mexico, the United States and Argentina. During 1970, 40% of all book imports came from Spain, 20% from Mexico, 20% from the United States, 8% from Argentina and 12% from other countries. Gross figures, including books and magazines, are as follows:

Year	US $
1966	8,625,217
1967	6,452,986
1968	8,249,187
1969	12,401,860
1970	14,274,363
1971	11,764,549
1972	16,732,305

Book imports are controlled by the Institute of Foreign Trade (Instituto de Comercio Exterior–INCOMEX). Applications for importation, made either by public or private enterprises, must be submitted to INCOMEX for their approval. Import regulations are specified in ordinances 444, 688, and 1165 of 1967. This last ordinance refers to imports under $ 40.

All imported books, except those from nations within the area of the Latin American Association for Free Trade–ALALC– are taxed 1 ½% according to article 229 of ordinance 444, and an additional 1 ½% according to article 20 of ordinance 688. All applications for importation are charged 1% of the gross amount for consular fees, $ 5 for national stamp duties, and $ 4.50 for the blank forms. In order to get through the nationalization procedure, the importer must pay a 4% sales tax on all reading material except on textbooks and scientific books, which are non-taxable according to ordinance 435 of 1971, article 13. The supplier from abroad must send an invoice and a price catalogue so that the importer may apply for the permit.

Bibliography

A. CASTILLO, *Legislación aduanera colombiana.* (Colombian customs legislation.) 2nd ed. Bogotá, Edit. Temis 1971.

28 Book Exports

Because of the scantiness of book production in the past, exports have necessarily remained at a low level. However, book exports have risen considerably in the last few years. Main customers are other Latin American countries and the United States. Figures for the last five years are given below:

Year	US $
1966	577,630
1967	729,575
1968	2,688,351
1969	1,801,180
1970	1,844,477
1971	3,081,627
1972	3,513,007

Both books and magazines are included in these figures. Exports are regulated according to ordinances 444 and 688 of 1967. Books and magazines are classified as "minor exports". This type of export is granted a financial stimulus equivalent to 15% of the gross amount. This kind of subsidy is given in the form of certificates which are accepted as payments on income tax. Such certificates may be obtained upon surrendering to the Bank of the Republic all U.S. currency derived from the export transaction.

35 Miscellaneous

a) *Authors*

The

Asociación de Escritores y Artistas Colombianos (Association of Colombian Writers and Artists)
Calle 24 No. 5–60
CO Bogotá
was founded in 1954.

This is a private guild to which all kinds of writers belong. Its purpose is to protect copyright and deal with matters of common interest to writers vis-à-vis Government and private enterprise. Further, the association is concerned with the promotion of writing as a profession.

Another guild is the
Asociación Nacional de Autores Colombianos de obras didácticas (AUCOLDI)
(National Association of Colombian Authors of Educational Books)
Calle 14 No. 12–50, 10 piso
CO Bogotá
This association was founded in 1969. Members are authors of textbooks for the elementary and secondary school levels. Its main purpose is to protect the interests of Colombian authors of textbooks who must face foreign competition in this field.

b) *Graphic arts*

The
Asociación Colombiana de la Industria Gráfica (ACOGRAFICA)
(Colombian Association of Graphic Industry)
Carrera 6a., No. 14–74, Of. 604
CO Bogotá
was founded in 1969.
This association has taken the place of the Asociación Nacional de Impresores (National Association of Printers)–ANADIM–which was founded on 9 January 1959. All branches of the graphic industry (typography, lithography, photoengraving, composition, bookbinding, etc.) are represented in ACOGRAFICA. This association welcomes inquiries. ACOGRAFICA has a branch which operates under the name of Industriales Gráficos Asociados de Anadim, Ltda (Industrial Printers Associated to Anadim, Ltd), which supplies materials to members of ACOGRAFICA as well as to its own members.

Bibliography

Asociacion Colombiana de Escritores y Artistas Colombianos, *Estatutos* (Statutes). CO Bogotá 1954.

Asociacion Nacional de Autores Colombianos de Obras Didacticas, *Estatutos*. (Statutes.) CO Bogotá 1969.

Asociacion Nacional de Impresores (anadim), *Estatutos*. (Statutes.) CO Bogotá, Edit. Andes 1965.

Asociacion Nacional de Impresores, (anadim), *Estatutos de Industriales Gráficos Asociados de Anadim* (Statutes.) Bogotá 1964.

Costa Rica

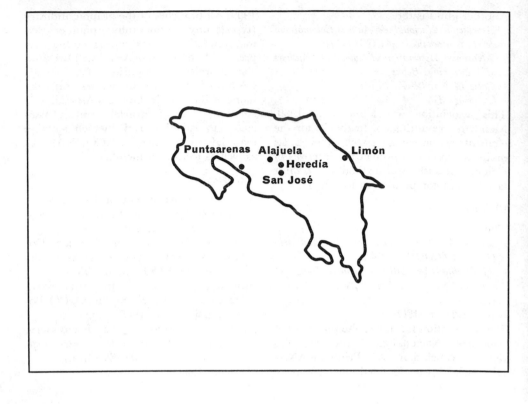

1 General Information

Area 50,000 km²

Population 1,640,000 (33 per km²; White and Mestizo 97.6%, Negro 1.9%, Indian 0.4%, Asiatic 0.1% = 1950)

Capital San José (192,145)

Largest towns San José (192,145); Alajuela (27,305); Puntaarenas (22,547); Heredía (22,345); Limón (21,997)

Government Presidential democracy. The President and the one-house legislative assembly of 57 members are elected for terms of four years

Religion Roman Catholic 95%, Protestant 3%

National language Spanish

Leading foreign languages English, German

Weights, measures Metric system, also old Spanish measures

Currency unit Colón (C) = 100 centavos (c.). Also Central American Peso (C.A. $) for commercial operations within the Central American Common Market (equal to US$ 1)

Education Compulsory and free between 7 and 14 years. 7,502 students at 5 universities and colleges of academic standard

Illiteracy 15.6%

Paper consumption a) Newsprint 4 kg per inhabitant (1959)
b) Printing paper (other than newsprint) 1.6 kg per inhabitant (1970)

Membership UNESCO

2 Past and Present

After its discovery in 1502 by Christopher Columbus, and the Spanish settlement in 1563, Costa Rica was governed from Spain–mainly by way of Guatemala and Panama. And especially from the latter, influences can be felt to our own days. After the time of independence (in 1821) from Spanish colonial domination, however, the Republic became the most advanced Central American country as regards education and culture, mainly because of its majority of European descendants. This was helped by a political stability which enabled governments to concentrate their efforts on the cultural and educational development of the country's inhabitants. Moreover, Costa Rica has no military force to maintain and finance. The results can be felt by the relatively high *niveau* of libraries and bookshops, universities and schools.

The first printer and publisher began to work in Costa Rica in 1830, by official initiative. Similarly indiviudal bookselling started in 1870, when the provisional president of the Republic himself, Bruno Carranza, imported books on special demand for his friends. The first bookshop was opened by a Spanish immigrant in 1885 bearing the name of "Librería Española" (Spanish Bookshop), and the following ten years brought a number of Spanish and German booksellers to Costa Rica whose activities have given the country a highly profcssional book trade.

Today, some 20 publishers and about double the number of bookshops are active, five of the former and about 15 of the latter being private firms of importance in all fields of the profession. They generally work with colleagues in Spain, the USA, Mexico and Panama (the Central American economic centre), and from these countries business information and samples as well as the majority of books are introduced. While all bookstores are private ventures, government and semi-official firms have won a good position in publishing.

Bibliography

A. BLEN, *Ligeros apuntes sobre la bibliografía de Costa Rica 1830–1912.* (Some notes on the bibliography of Costa Rica.) 7 vols. San José, Biblioteca Nacional 1944.

M. B. MacDONALD and D. R. McLAUGHLYN, *Viad y obras de autores de Costa Rica.* (Life and work of the authors of Costa Rica.) La Habana, Alfa 1941. 94 pp.

J. MALDONER Y SALVADOR, *Revista de Costa Rica.* Notas bibligraficas. (Review of Costa Rica. Bibliographical notes.) Madrid, Maroto 1890. 19 pp.

These three publications, mainly bibliographical, contain a number of notes on the history of printing, publishing and the book in Costa Rica after its independence.

3 Retail Prices

Publishers' prices are respected in the case of locally published books, while imported books and periodicals are calculated freely by every importer. A special discount of 10% is granted to students.

4 Organization

The profcssional organization of the Costarican book trade, located in the centre of book activity, the capital of San José, is the

Cámara del Libro de Costa Rica
(Book Chamber of Costa Rica)
Apartado 5203
CR San José

It was founded in July 1970 and comprises 25 members, who represent about 500 sales outlets. The majority of thc members, however, ar mass sales organizations and credit-sale companies; some of the most important bookstores are not associated.

The Costarican book trade, apart from this situation, plays an important role in the first efforts to unite the Central American trade–as for instance, in the field of university publishing by the *Council of Central American Universities*, located in San José. An example of this role was the organization of the *First Booksellers' Seminar of Central America* in 1968 and the *Superior Council of the Central American Universities*, the latter being an example of the Central American cooperation in education and culture.

5 Trade Press

The relatively new Cámara del Libro de Costa Rica (Book Chamber of Costa Rica, →4) is the publisher of the only Central American trade periodical,

Anaqueles
Revista de la Cámara del Libro de
Costa Rica
(Bookstands. Review of the Book Chamber
of Costa Rica)
Apartado 5203
CR San José

which has been published irregularly since 1970. It carries mainly business information and articles about the sale of books and periodicals.

There are two more periodicals in the book field which publish news on the most important events in the Costarican and Latin American book trade with varying frequency,

Asociación Costaricense de
Bibliotecarios–Boletin
(Bulletin of the Association of
Costarican Librarians)
Apartado 3308
CR San José

published irregularly since 1955, and the

Hipocampo
Revista Literaria

Apartado 5670
CR San José

mainly a literary, bi-monthly publication.

6 Book-Trade Literature

Bibliography

N. KOPPER, *The book-trade in Costa Rica, the present state of Costa Rican bibliography, the state of exchange in Costa Rica.* Washington, D.C., Pan American Union 1965. 13 pp. Working paper No. 14, 10th Seminar on the Acquisition of Latin American Library Materials.

7 Sources of Information, Address Services

Costa Rica so far is the only Central American country where a professional institution, able to contact a number of cultural institutions and scientific libraries, can offer special information about the book and the book industry–although there are special address services (general publication and promotion agencies, especially one which is used often by the "Book Chamber", is sometimes able to give addresses).

Professional information can be obtained from the

Cámara del Libro de Costa Rica
(Book Chamber of Costa Rica)
Apartado 5203
CR San José

In similar cases, too, the Promotion Office of the Spanish publishers in Central America, established in Costa Rica in the sixties, is helpful:

Instituto Nacional del Libro Español
–Delegación para Centro America–
(Central American Delegation of the
Spanish National Book Institute)
Apartado 2490
CR San José

This institute gives data about the Latin American book market, and principally organizes book exhibitions all over the continent, working as an information office for members in Spain.

Bibliography

A. C. GROPP, *Libraries and archives of Costa Rica*, with private libraries, bookbinders, booksellers and printers. New Orleans, Middle American Research Institute, Tulane University, 1941. 38 pp.

The addresses of all branches of the book trade are contained in

La Empresa del Libro en Américan Latina. (The Book in Latin America.) 2nd ed. Buenos Aires, Bowker Editores Argentina 1974. VIII, 307 pp.

pp. 141–145: Costa Rica.

15 National Bibliography, National Library

While an official bibliography exists in Costa Rica since 1946, there are a number of private publications giving bibliographic information back to colonial times. The annual bibliography, started in 1946 by the National Library, was continued in 1958 as

Anuario Bibliográfico Costaricense
(Costarican Bibliographical Annual)
Asociación Costaricense de Bibliotecarios
Apartado 3308
CR San José

under the editorship of the National Association of Librarians. On the other hand, the National Library is continuing to publish an irregular bibliographical publication, the

Boletin Bibliográfico
(Bibliographical Bulletin)
Biblioteca Nacional
Calle 15/Avenida 5
CR San José

which was also started in 1946. In addition to these official and general bibliographies, a number of special bibliographies are published by different institutions (→2: Bibliography), among them an annual list of theses presented in Costa Rica, published by the National University

The National Library of Costa Rica,
Biblioteca Nacional
Calle 15 y Avenida 5
CR San José

was founded officially in 1887 by law. Its collection contains 200,000 volumes, thus constituting the biggest library in the country. By a later law (which also established the publishing company of the Ministry of Education) issued in 1957, its obligation to collect all books and periodicals published in the country was legally confirmed. Its excellent, modern filing system of its special collections give it a unique position in Central America.

Costa Rica can boast a number of important libraries, special and scientific, a good part of them governmental institutions. Outside the capital, the library of the *Interamerican Institute of Agricultural Sciences* (Commemorative Orton, Turrialba) deserves special note, being the biggest agricultural library in Latin America.

Bibliography

P. AVICENNE, *Bibliographical services throughout the world 1965–69.* Paris, UNESCO 1972. 310 pp.
pp. 94–5: Costa Rica.

I. ZIMMERMANN, *Current national bibliographies of Latin America.* Gainesville, Florida, University of Florida Press 1971. X, 139 pp.
pp. 74–76: Costa Rica.

16 Book Production

Costa Rican bibliographies list 294 titles in 1968, and 284 in 1969. However, there are a good many titles published by printers or by the authors directly, which never show in statistics. This custom could, according to experts' estimates, nearly double the annual title production in the country with an average edition of 2,500

143

copies per title. Half of the titles listed in the bibliographies are scientific, mainly sociological, books.

19 Paperbacks

In accord with the economical situation of the majority of book-buyers, paperback titles play an important role in the book trade. They are sold in bookshops as well as at news-stands. Many of the books published in the country are paper-covered while a half of the paperbacks sold are imported–mainly from Spain. So only about 20% of imported paperbacks are in foreign languages (English, German and French, in that order).

21 Publishing

About 50 firms are active in publishing. Some of them are founded by foreign booksellers working in the country for more than 100 years, with a number of titles of national importance in their catalogues. There are also a number of government publishers, responsible for nearly 30% of the country's book production. The biggest of them is the publishing company of the Ministry of Education, whose activity is mostly literary and educational, having published a good porportion of the books of local authors. This publisher, founded by law in 1957, is also in charge of certifying educational textbooks for all types of schools in Costa Rica. By this system, applied also to imported textbooks, the government has established a policy which obliges educational publishers in or selling into Costa Rica, to publish works of a quality acceptable to the Ministry.

Another publishing house worthy of mention is that of the *Association of Central American Universities*, which publishes most of the books written by professors and scientists working in any of the national universities of the six Central American Republics. Thus, this company fulfils an important function in Latin American scientific publishing in general. Another government institution, publishing all official publications as well as important titles on national history and culture, is the *Imprenta Nacional* (National Printing Office).

As in most Latin American countries, printers and authors who occasionally publish books have an important place in local publishing. Because of the reduced possibilities of the market, most local and literary titles are published in this manner.

Bibliography

Informe de la Dirección de la Imprenta Nacional 1889. (Report of the Directory of the National Printers 1889.) In: Dirección de Estátistica y Censos, Reporte. San José, Imprenta Nacional 1890. 9 pp.

Relamento de la Imprenta Nacional. (Regulations for the National Printing Company.) In: Costa Rica, Leyes, Decretos. San José, Tipografía Nacional 1956. 17 pp.

24 Retail Trade

Costa Rica, particularly the capital, has a fair number of well-stocked bookshops. As at the beginning, more than 100 years ago, foreign booksellers, who introduced and observed the European professional tradition, are still among the most active companies.

A special position is held by a number of credit-sales organizations, some of them branches of United States and European companies. In San José there are also two antiquarian bookshops.

27 Book Imports

As in the neighbour countries, the majority of books sold in Costa Rica (according to experts 89%) are imported. The statistics give an amount of US $ 241,641 for 1970 for the import of books.

Main suppliers are Spain, the United States and Mexico–Spanish publishers have recorded an annual import of 0.35 US-cents per capita from Spain.

28 Book Exports

For the same year, 1970, statistics give a figure of US $ 442,178 for book exports. Apart from Spain, other Central American countries buy books from Costa Rica. So Costa Rica seems to be the only Latin American country with a positive balance in international book trading. Studies of trade relations within Central America, however, suggest that a good part of the sales to those countries are re-exports of imported books, Costa Rica being the site of distributors representing international publishers all over the region. This is true of books published in the country by the *Publishing Company of the Central American Universities*, reinforcing Costarican book exports on one side, but representing all Central American literary and scientific labour on the other.

29 Book Fairs

A number of regular book fairs are held in Costa Rica. They are mostly meant for the general public. However, the "Feria del Libro", sponsored by the government, is also of importance to the book professionals of the Central American and Spanish-speaking countries. This fair, held annually since 1968 for eight days in the National Park in San José, enjoys the participation of publishers from Spain, Mexico and Argentina, the three most important countries of this language area.

Furthermore, local booksellers organize four other exhibitions of a national character. Many smaller book exhibitions in different cities of the interior complete this activity.

Bibliography

Memorias Relativas a la Primera Exposicion de Editores Centroamericanos 1964. (Memoirs of the first exhibition of the Central American publishers.) San José, Feria del Libro 1964. IX, 270 pp.

Primera Feria Nacional del Libro. 24 a 30 de Agosto de 1954. (First National Book Fair.) San José, Imprenta Universal 1954. 70 pp.

33 The Reviewing of Books

Newspapers, periodicals and radio stations in Costa Rica are very active in the discussion of books, both national and foreign. Five newspapers with a total edition of 95,000 copies have regular book reviews, while the 35 radio stations as well as the 4 TV-channels have at least one weekly transmission devoted to books.

Cuba

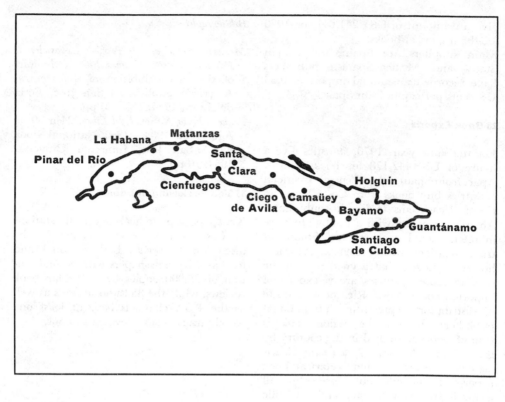

1 General Information

Area 110,921 km²
Population 8,553,395 (77 per km²)
Capital La Habana (1,745,360)
Largest towns La Habana (1,745,360); Santiago de Cuba (275,970); Camaüey (196,854); Holguín (131,508); Santa Clara (131,504); Guantánamo (130,061); Matanzas (85,376); Cienfuegos (85,248); Pinar del Río (73,206); Bayamo (71,660); Ciego de Avila (60,910)
Government Republic. The legislative and executive powers are vested in the Council of Ministers of the Revolutionary Government, in accordance with the Constitutional Law of the Republic which was promulgated on February 1959. President of the Republic: Dr Osvaldo Dorticós Torrado; Prime Minister: Dr Fidel Castro Ruz. Political administrative division: six provinces (Pinar del Río, La Habana, Matanzas, Las Villas, Camagüey, and Oriente).

The Communist Party of Cuba is the governing party
Religion Entire separation between State and Churches. The State respects the religious beliefs and practices as the individual right of every citizen
National language Spanish
Leading foreign English, French and Russian
Weights and measures Metric system
Monetary unit Peso (= 100 centavos)
Education Compulsory up to intermediate level. 37,000 students of university level are enrolled at the three universities of the country (Havana, Santa Clara, and Santiago de Cuba). There are 257,919 students at intermediate level; elementary education is attended by 1,759,167 pupils; 29,188 students are engaged in professional technology, and there are 26,921 students training to be teachers. In addition there are 185

2 Past and Present

The origins of printing in Cuba date back to 1720. This relatively slow development of printing in Cuba is explained by the fact that during the first decades of Spanish colonization very little attention was paid to the island by the ruling powers.

In the year 1723 a general price-list was produced in the printing shop of the Andalusian, Carlos Habré. Apart from being the first printed document in Cuba that we know of, it also boasted, as a special feature, an illustration on the front cover.

From then on, the evolution of printing in Cuba was extremely slow. The arrival of the Governor, Don Luis de las Casas, however, which provoked a veritable and significant cultural awakening in the colony, initiated an era of rapid development in printing, beginning in the last decade of the 18th century.

In spite of this not very bright general situation, one branch of the graphic arts–lithography–spread rapidly and shared a remarkable development in the country. Later on, new techniques in graphic reproduction limited lithography in Cuba almost exclusively to artistic printing for the tobacco industry, in which lithographic tradition has maintained its strong position well into our own day.

During the centuries of Spanish colonization censorship proved to be a formidable obstacle to the development of the Cuban book. Along with the development of a national culture, many authors appeared in the country who contributed valuable works; in the field of thought or art, however, the Cuban writer was constantly subjected to material and cultural limitations which inevitably made it almost impossible for him to get his works published during this period.

Many excellent works were published abroad or in clandestine printing shops;

specialized schools functioning at present and there is a wide-spread movement for adult education: 354,128 students. The total number of students and pupils in the country is 2,405,604 (figures for the school year 1971–72)

Illiteracy Eliminated during a national campaign which was carried out in 1961 and which reduced illiteracy from 23.6% to a mere 3.6%

Paper consumption a) Newsprint 2.7 kg per inhabitant

b) Printing paper (other than newsprint) 3.5 kg per inhabitant (figures for 1970).

Membership UNESCO

others fell into oblivion and remained forgotten for many years.

Apart from this situation, around the end of the 19th century 75% of the island's population were still illiterate, largely due to the fact that slavery had been maintained as long as possible.

From the very beginning, the production and diffusion of books had to be limited to about 200 copiers per title because of the small number of educated people. These copies were distributed at a very high cost on subscription in advance. In the beginning distribution was restricted to Havana and Matanzas; during the second half of the 19th century it was extended to other provincial capitals.

In 1898, North American intervention restricted the possibility of a free development of the literary and scientific movement, which had just begun to show signs of awakening at the end of the 19th century, under the provisions of the Republic.

From 1902, the year in which the Republic established itself, until the triumphal Revolution in 1959, the most prominent feature of the country's publishing activities is the almost complete absence of genuine publishing houses.

Of the few works which were dedicated to the subject of printing and publishing generally a few thousand textbooks were printed. These were sold at inflated prices to students at private schools, institutes, and universities, or were exported to other Latin American countries.

The scientific book and the literary book were definitely not business in a country where, after 50 years of Republican life, of 6.15 million inhabitants more than one million were still illiterate.

The Cuban narrator Onelio Jorge Cardoso has described the situation of writers as follows: "I never had publishers and could not publish my books. There were writers who made great efforts to obtain money in order to be able to publish their book. Of course, all the copies of the edition had do be given away to friends as presents, because there was no one who was interested in the Cuban author. There were cases in which the writer appealed to some rich politician and tried to get him to pay for the edition or to defray at least part of its costs. Surely this attitude was wrong; in my opinion it resulted from the total lack of interest on the part of the State towards the Cuban author."

Meanwhile, the novels by Corin Tellado, the Comics that were drawn in the United States and translated in Mexico, the North American magazines that were published in Spanish, e. g. "Life", selections of "Reader's Digest" and the "Times" among others (the latter two were printed in Cuba and distributed all over the Spanish-speaking world), pornography, and the stultifying venom of the yellow press aggravated the publishing scene in Cuba during this period.

Superman had always been more popular in Cuba than Alejo Carpentier or Nicolás Guillén. The intellectual life of the country, even in its best moments, always found the enormous number of illiterates or semi-illiterates a stumbling block.

The Revolutionaries resolved to change the chaotic cultural panorama of Cuba within a short period—but where were they to begin?

The first organization to be in charge of the reproduction of books was established 15 March 1960, fifteen months after the revolutionary seizure of power. The characteristic features of this organization, the *Imprenta Nacional de Cuba* ("National Printers of Cuba") were mass editions unprecedented in the country, and the low prices of its books. The great transformation of the book in Cuba had begun.

In 1961, during the stupendous campaign proposed to eliminate illiteracy, the publishing industry lent its assistance by printing more than a million primers for use in elementary education.

The enormous results of this campaign, which radically reduced the index of illiteracy in the country, as well as the subsequent organization of special educational programmes for adults created to guarantee the uninterrupted, continued education of the people who had just learned to read and write, were the first decisive steps towards the creation of a vigorous publishing movement in Cuba. Another measure of vital importance was the nationalization of education which on one hand–because it was free–allowed a more efficient attack to be made on the lack of education, and on the other, facilitated a more rational and uniform policy in the compiling of textbooks.

The *Imprenta Nacional* operated until May 1962. Its industrial equipment became the foundation stone for the *Empresa Consolidada de Artes Gráficas* ("Consolidated Enterprise of Graphic Arts"), which is a part of the Ministry of Industries.

This measure made way for the gradual merging and cooperation among smaller printing works and the integration of technical equipment in medium and large-sized printing works.

Parallel to that, the *Editorial Nacional de Cuba* ("National Publishers of Cuba") was founded, under the Council of Ministers.

The publishing system was completed by the appearance of publishing houses like the *Editora Universitaria*, the *Editora Pedagógica*, the *Editora Juvenil* and the *Editora Política*. The quality of books was considerably improved during this period.

In the field of graphic design a movement was initiated which has won a great deal of praise since then, and which in former times had been practically non-existent.

At the end of 1965 a special project, the *Edición Revolucionaria*, came on to the scene. This was established to find a way to cover the urgent need for textbooks at university level, which until then could not be produced in Cuba because of the restrictions that international conventions had imposed on intellectual property. It was necessary to make a decision, and this decision was to create the *Edición Revolucionaria*.

The first achievements of the *Edición Revolucionaria*, whose publications were given away free to university students, showed that the moment had arrived to develop a new publishing policy in the country. This resulted in the concept of an organization that would have the same dynamic and progressive spirit as the *Edición Revolucionaria* and that would stimulate a complex and ambitious programme in the field of publishing.

This institution was the *Instituto Cubano del Libro* ("The Cuban Book Institute"), which was founded in 1967 ($\rightarrow$4).

This organization unites in a single structure all the national factors that play a part in Cuban book affairs, starting from the actual editorial work right up to the distribution to the public, including industrial production, the necessary public relations, and the international book trade. The objective of the institute's work is to cover the growing national needs for books and other publications. After the recent National Congress of Education and Culture the main tasks of the Institute since its creation were outlined in even more explicit terms: to contribute in a decisive way to the gigantic educational effort, which can at present be seen in the country; by the development of the following principal targets listed in the following order of importance: textbooks, complementary educational publications, literature for children and youth, and publications of an ideological and political character. This strategical definition does not mean that other targets are being neglected.

Cuba

In 1959 the nation's production of books reached the figure of almost one million copies. The Cuban Book Institute produced 21 million copies in 1972. The optimal utilization of the means at hand may be seen in the following figures: In the first year of its existence the Institute produced little more than 8 million copies. With the same industrial installations this number was doubled in only three years.

Bibliography

G. Furlong, *Orígines del arte tipográfico en América.* (The origins of the art of typography in America.) Buenos Aires, Ed. Huarpes (1947). pp. 95–98: Cuba.

J. T. Medina, *Historia de la imprenta en los antiguos dominios españoles de América y Oceania.* (The history of printing in the ancient Spanish dominions of America and Oceania.) Vol. 2. Santiago de Chile, Fondo Histórico y Bibliográfico José Toribio Medina 1958. pp. 211–230: La imprenta en La Habana.

L. Otero, *Cultural policy in Cuba.* Paris. Unesco, 1972. 55 pp. (pp. 45–53: Instituto Cubano del Libro).

Br. F. Swan, *The spread of printing, Western Hemisphere: The Caribbean area.* Amsterdam, Vangendt 1970. 47 pp.

L. S. Thompson, *Printing in colonial Spanish America.* Hamden, Conn. 1962. pp. 94 ff: The beginning of printing in the Spanish Antilles.

3 Retail Prices

Until the Revolution in 1959 books could be obtained only in the more important cities of the country. Since the majority of the books were imported their prices were far too high to make them available to the masses. The acquisition of educational texts was always a problem, even for the nation's middle-class families. This situation contrasted sharply with the fact that there were large stocks of shoddy novels and books at very low prices which represented the only literature available to the majority of the people.

At the time of the Revolution the distribution of the book ceased to be ruled by the laws of the market and was transformed in a rational proportion which is focused on the raising of the cultural and political level of the people. The first book by the revolutionary publishers, "Don Quixote", had an edition of 100,000 copies and sold at 25 centavos per copy, thus inaugurating a policy which was to be maintained up to the present: mass editions and low prices. In the educational system of Cuba textbooks are given away free to all pupils and students.

On the other hand, the price of the book does not, nor could it in the future, present an obstacle which prevents someone who needs it professionally or who reads it for recreational purposes, from buying it, because the objective which is pursued with the sale of the book is not dominated by a commercial interest; that is to say, prices are adjusted to the social function of the book.

4 Organization

Instituto Cubano del Libro (ICL)
(Cuban Book Institute)
Belascoaín # 864 esq. a Desagüe
C La Habana

The sphere of influence of the ICL comprises all the formative elements of a policy which directs its efforts exclusively towards the book in Cuba. The national and international commercialization of the book represents only one among the numerous aspects of the whole complex of the processes involved in the printing, publishing and distributing of books and in the maintenance of international relations.

Inquiries regarding foreign book trade, importation as well as exportation, may be addressed to:

Instituto Cubano del Libro (ICL)
(Cuban Book Institute,
Dirección de Comercio Internacional
(Directorate of International Trade)
Obispo # 461 e/Villegas y Aguacate
Box number 6540
C La Habana 1
The body which is in charge of the national distribution of books is the:
Dirección Nacional de Distribución
(Directorate of National Distribution)
O'Reilly 407
C La Habana

5 Trade Press

The *Departamento de Divulgación de la Dirección Editorial* ("Department of Information of the Publishing Directorate") of the Cuban Book Institute (→4) publishes a fortnightly bulletin, *Boletín*, which reviews the editorial activities and the publication of significant works in Cuba and other countries. The address is:
Boletín
Instituto Cubano del Libro
Belascoaín # 864, esq. a Desagüe
C La Habana
At present in its final stages of preparation is a review which is going to be published every three months and whose sections will include articles on the book trade. →7.

7 Sources of Information, Address Services

Anyone interested in general or specific information on the Cuban book trade may direct inquiries to the following addresses (→4):
Instituto Cubano del Libro (ICL)
(Cuban Book Institute)
Belascoaín # 864, esq. a Desagüe
C La Habana
and
Instituto Cubano del Libro (ICL)
Dirección de Comercio Internacional
(Directorate of International Trade)
Obispo # 461 e/Villegas y Aguacate
Box number 6540
C La Habana 1
The *Dirección de Comercio Internacional* sponsors the *Departamento de Información* ("Department of Information"), which is in charge of the organization and diffusion of information concerning the foreign book.
Exhibition Centre: Its objective is to exhibit new book titles received from different countries of the world.
The documentation centres of the organizations receive information about books received. They are exhibited in the hall by means of bulletins which are compiled and dispatched. In this way their delegates can visit the hall and review the titles in order to find out whether they are really useful for them and thus include them in their purchasing plans.
Catalogue Section: Its aim is to keep the various organs of the home economy up to date with the latest titles published by foreign publishers. This is done by means of catalogues.
Visitors' Service Area: Here the organizations are provided with the latest catalogues that have come in and receive information and instruction on how to use the lists and catalogues.
Bibliographical Section: This section compiles bibliographies on different subjects and in various languages, with the objective of assisting the *Dirección de Importación* ("Directorate of Importation") in the exercise of its function, namely the importation of books. It gathers information on the book from all over the world and extrapolates the factors and circumstances that play an important part in the selection of works which are needed and which can be acquired in the usual way.
It also helps to save time in the task of selecting, and is specially concerned with the diffusion of technical, economic and social information.

151

The activities of the bibliographical section consist principally in information retrieval and documentation. Its task is to analyse titles in different languages which are considered to be of value in their subject field.

Bulletins: The monthly bulletin of the *Dirección de Distribución Nacional* (→5) is compiled by the "Publishing Directorate". In this bulletin authors are listed in alphabetical order.

The bulletin is distributed among the national organizations and lists all new titles received during the past month. The contents of the monthly bulletin of the *Centro de Importación* are grouped according to different subjects and within each of these subjects authors are listed in alphabetical order. Apart from the non-illustrated titles, 20 illustrated works are chosen. Also listed in the bulletin are the latest catalogues that have come in and a bibliography that has been compiled by the respective department. 75–100 titles are entered into the section of *Novedades Extranjeras* ("Foreign Novelties"), a selection of all those that have been classified during the month. This bulletin is also distributed among the national organizations; its circulation is 2,000 copies per month.

Services to Foreign Countries: Catalogues, leaflets and guides are compiled to meet requests for information that come in from different countries of the world (→15).

9 Market Research

The growing demand for books and especially the exigencies of the new educational schemes necessitate a "policy of priority"; that means, the prior knowledge of the actual needs is an imperative requirement for the preparation of the publishing programmes for printing and distributing.

The compiling of programmes for the thorough publication and importation o books is based on studies by the competent departments of the ICL (→4) and of the interested organizations. The distribution and commercialization of books is nothing but the result of these activities.

In the market research for national book exportation attention is directed towards the needs of individual nations. Statistical information on the market is procured and analysed to enable the distribution of books in a way that is most effective and profitable for the majority of the people.

Import activities are based on the principle that they serve only as a subsidiary to national production, that is to say, the production of those titles that cannot be absorbed because of technical and publishing limitations, above all regarding textbooks, reference books, books on technology and literature for children. The study of potential markets and the prior determination of supply and demand are operations which can be resolved only by the development of information systems, analysis, and computation.

> *Instituto Cubano del Libro (ICL)*
> *(Cuban Book Institute)*
> *Dirección de Comercio Internacional*
> *(Directorate of International Trade)*
> *Obispo # 461 e/ Villegas y Aguacate*
> *Box number 6540*
> *C La Habana 1*

This Directorate is responsible for the execution of all operations pertaining to the importation and exportation of publications, books, brochures and magazines. Its functions are split between two subdivisions: the *Centro de Importación* and the *Centro de Exportación* (→27, 28).

At present national commercial bureaux are being opened and agents and representatives of the ICL are being appointed in various countries of the world. (Current information regarding this process may be obtained from the *Dirección de Comercio Internacional*, →4).

10 Books and Young People

Apart from the fact that Cuba has brought forth one of the most famous writers of children's literature in the Spanish language, José Marti, this type of literature did not figure in the scarce publishing output before the Revolution. The importation of comics and other forms of literature for children did not even at its best adapt itself to the cultural and social characteristics of Cuban children and juvenils unless they were simply agents of corruption.

At present the promotion of a literature for children, which is adapted to Cuba's historical circumstances, has been the object of attention for the Congress of Education and Culture. The following organizations are responsible for the advancement of children's literature in the country: *Ministerio de Educación* ("Ministry of Education"), *Instituto de la Infancia* ("Institute of Infancy"), *Unión de Pioneros de Cuba* ("Union of Cuban Pioneers"), *Sala Infantil de la Biblioteca Nacional* ("Children's Room of the National Library"), *Seminario Infantil 'Pionero'* ("'Pionero' Children's Seminar"), and the *Editorial 'Gente Nueva'* ("New People"), the publishing department of children's literature of the Cuban Book Institute (→4, 21). Various intellectuals, artists and institutions of the country have lent their support to the promotion of children's literature. Literary competitions, visual arts exhibitions, seminars, congresses and other events are organized. The universities offer their support with the study of the psychological and evolutionary characteristics of the child.

Books for children constitute one of the most important fields for imports and co-editions.

In spite of the limited number of colour-printing presses, whose capacities are principally employed in the production of textbooks for students, 2.5 million copies of books for children and youth were produced in 1972.
→17.

11 Training

Before the victorious revolution, the few booksellers of the country were limited to the role of simply sellers. Neither cultural nor technical instructions were given to them. Today this group includes about a thousand workers, for the most part women with a low level of education.

Up to now the main efforts in the educational field were aimed at a higher percentage of school enrolment. Within the scope of the adult educational programme set up on a large scale in the whole country, most of the capable workers participate in continuation training courses at the Faculty for Workers and Peasants, in university courses for the employed, and in language courses. In the province La Habana, for instance, 70% of all employees are taking such courses. Education is not only a right of which every worker can make use, but also a social duty for which everybody makes great efforts.

The same is true of the area around the Instituto Cubano del Libro (→4) as well as of similar institutions in the country. During the past years various working groups, seminaries and lectures on certain subjects have repeatedly been organized. Furthermore, special literature dealing with different aspects of the book, such as the production, the graphic techniques and literary criticism, was distributed.

At the end of the sixties the National Library arranged courses for the booksellers of the capital. Since 1972 these courses have been taken up again under the direction of the Department for Education of the Instituto Cubano del Libro (→4). In the last three months of 1972 a Booksellers' House was opened in the province of La Habana, in which 30 employees took part. With the experience gained from these courses, those organized for early 1973 were expanded to increase their capacity, and new booksellers' courses were started in different provinces of the country.

As in other industries in the country the courses take place within working hours, they are free of charge and the participants get their usual salary.

The demands for specialization are constantly increasing. The aim is no longer simply to sell a book, but to assist the interested person in such a way that he receives the book that corresponds to his individual needs. The potential reader is to be motivated, just as the bookshop is to be led to its natural, cultural and social tasks. It is planned to achieve this without neglecting the language studies that are considered essential for this occupation.

In addition, there are courses for the advancement of management personnel that are aimed at raising the cultural, technical and political level and to teach management techniques. The continued training of management personnel as well as potential executive personnel is one of the most important tasks of this adult-education programme.

14 Copyright

→ 21; BTW I, International Section 14.

15 National Bibliography, National Library

Since 1959 the *Biblioteca Nacional José Martí* ("José Martí National Library") has been compiling the *Bibliografía Nacional Cubana* ("National Cuban Bibliography"), which before the Revolution was generally the concern of private bibliographers.

Up to now these efforts have resulted in the compilation of the volumes that encompass the bibliography of the years from 1959 to 1962 and from 1963 to 1964, as well as annual volumes since 1965.

However, additional efforts are being made to bridge the bibliographical gap between 1917 and 1936. The volumes which cover the years 1917–1920 and 1921–1924 have been completed, and data for the following years is being collated. Understandably the *Biblioteca Nacional José Martí* can compile the Cuban Bibliography only from well-organized sources which supply the books and periodical publications that have appeared in Cuba since the date of the printing of the first book in 1723.

The labour of accumulation and investigation of Cuban lore is extended even to illustrations, records, musical scores, maps, slides, reproductions of paintings, exhibition catalogues, concert programmes, cigar and cigarette box-labels, photographs, manuscripts, outstanding personalities of Cuban culture and history, etc.

The National Library compiles numerous bibliographies or indexes of periodical publications and does research on subjects pertaining to national culture and history which is principally based on their own resources.

The *Revista de la Biblioteca Nacional José Martí* ("The José Martí National Library Review") surveys part of this research, and in the *Anuario Martiano* ("Martí Almanac") works are published or reviewed which are related to the life and achievements of this great Cuban patriot. This Almanac is prepared in the Martí Room of the National Library, but it assembles any notable essays by authors from different parts of the world who are doing research on José Martí.

The National Library also functions as a public library. In its Music Department one can listen to recordings of the most celebrated musical compositions; in the Visual Arts Department reproductions of famous paintings can be hired and taken home, while in the Youth Department, in addition to the usual library services, children and adolescents are encouraged to take part in different activities, such as the narration of stories (adapted from the classics of world literature or from national, Latin American or African folklore), discussions on movies, reading circles, competitions, and so on.

In the Science and Technology Information Department, which keeps a collective catalogue of the scientific and technological publications that have been received in Cuban libraries, quick information on these subjects can be obtained by research centres, industrial enterprises and educational establishments.

To recapitulate, the National Library does not just fulfil its functions as a library, it is also a cultural centre of the Nation, frequented by poets, narrators, critics, historians, musicians, painters, scientists, and others who want to make contact with the public. It is a centre where various activities that reflect the living culture of the nation are promoted and where the works of its most illustrious past are revealed.

Bibliographical information is obtainable from the

> *Instituto Cubano del Libro*
> *(Cuban Book Institute)*
> *Belascoaín 864, esq. a. Desagüe*
> *C La Habana*

and the

> *Biblioteca Nacional José Martí*
> *(National Library José Martí)*
> *Plaza de la Revolucion*
> *C La Habana*

16 Book Production

At the time of the victory of the Cuban Revolution about 200 titles and little more than one million copies were published, including telephone directories and other printed matter. In 1972, 764 book titles and 21 million copies were issued.

As for the five years from 1967 to 1972 which have elapsed since the foundation of the Cuban Book Institute (→4), the production of books amounts to 3,911 titles and 88.1 million copies.

These quantities are distributed as shown below:

Books		Million
Year	Titles	copies
1967	500	8.5
1968	686	13.2
1969	685	15.8
1970	647	16.3
1971	629	13.3
1972	764	21.0

Brochures		
Year	Titles	Copies
1970	193	6,919,339
1971	254	6,610,692
1972	178	5,774,055

Magazines		
Year	Titles	Copies
1970	494	5,627,833
1971	477	6,402,050
1972	477	5,268,396

17 Translations

Within the framework of the various publishing houses of the Cuban Book Institute (→4) translations of foreign book titles play an important part. For the publishers of Social Sciences, Art, and Literature, for instance, works are translated which deal with the Humanities and the Literary Arts, and works of different authors, classical as well as contemporary. This activity extends to the translation of articles that have appeared in various foreign publications. Most of these translations are from the French, English, Russian, Italian, Portuguese, and German. There are scores of such translations every year.

Cuba

The *Editorial 'Gente Nueva'* ("'New People' Publishers") commissions the translation from Russian, English and French of tales for children by classical and contemporary authors. Information, which deals with the world of the child and which is of great interest to the above mentioned publishers is also translated.

19 Paperbacks

With the Revolution, the paperback has achieved a success which is unprecedented in the history of the country. The first book title published by the Revolutionary Government, "Don Quixote", was issued in four volumes whose overall edition totalled 400,000 copies. It was printed on newsprint on the presses of the newly nationalized reactionary newspapers, stapled together with wire and bound in carton. It was sold at 25 centavos per volume.

Part of Cuban books are manufactured with modest means, for instance, with cardboard and paper made from bagasse and printed on rotary presses. The ink which is used is alo manufactured in the country. Only a solution of this nature has made possible editions of tens and hundreds of thousands of copies for an underdeveloped country like Cuba, which in the middle of a revolutionary process is anxious to satisfy the daily growing demand for reading matter.

The press on which the "Selections of Reader's Digest" were printed before was now used to print the titles of the collection *Cuadernos Populares*. This collection had been compiled specifically for those who had just learned to read and write, with the intention to supply adequate reading matter for this incipient reading public.

Our most popular publishing house, *Huracán* ("Hurricane"), has concentrated on the publication of paperbacks. In November 1972 the hundredth *Huracán*

volume was imprinted with the stamp *Año Internacional del Libro* ("International Book Year"). In four years of work 100 volumes were published, comprising 82 titles and 70 authors; the total number of copies was over six million.

For the other publishing houses too the publication of paperbacks has proved to be the basic way of satisfying the ever-growing demands for mass publications.

20 Book Design

If publishing and the printing industry involved in the production of books received their impetus from the Revolution, the design and front covers of Cuban books rely on the cooperation of Cuban painters, on the experience gained in the graphic work of the mass media, on modern conceptions of design and colour, and on the excellence of national paintings. This excellence has now become a symbol of the Cuban book, whose typographical layout satisfies not only a referential but also a decorative demand.

Some of the cover designs and illustrations of the Cuban Book Institute (→4) have been displayed at national art exhibitions. At international fairs and exhibitions the design and illustrations of Cuban books have won attention and recognition.

21 Publishing

Publishing constitutes the basic and principal function of the whole complex of the Cuban Book Institute's activities (→4). The Institute is the body which is in charge of the realization in material form of the educational, scientific, technological, artistic, and cultural policy of the country. For this reason it draws up a programme of publications which both reflects editorial policy and tries to harmonize the educational priorities–an essential component of the editorial programme–with the needs of the people; that means, the publishing departments of the Cuban Book Institute are responsible for the control of the editorial apparatus of the country in regard to non-periodical publications.

To recapitulate, the preparation of originals which are geared towards industry determines the work of the Institute, and the fixing and orientation of editorial policy is the essence of this activity. An editorial movement dedicated to the Cuban book did not exist before the victory of the Socialist Revolution.

The first steps towards the realization of these objectives were taken immediately after the masses had risen to power, that is, with the creation of the *Imprenta Nacional* ("National Printers of Cuba"), which later became the *Editorial Nacional de Cuba* ("National Publishers of Cuba")

Today the publishing houses are united within this structure. As a result of the country's development new specialized publishing centres have sprung up. These are intended to cover not only the general cultural needs, but also the needs of the more specialized groups and sectors formed by the Revolution, which demand constant development and advancement of their scientific and artistic standards. An example of this is the creation of the *Edición Revolucianaria*, the "Revolutionary Publishers", who, sustaining one of the principles of the Cuban Revolution, refuse to acknowledge the international institution of copyrights and proclaim the need of all developing countries to have recourse to any of the world's cultural achievements that might in one way or another be of help to their own technical and economic progress. This is also a principle with all other Cuban publishing houses.

The other Cuban publishing houses are: *Editorial Pueblo y Educación* ("Publishers for People and Education") who specialize in educational textbooks; *Edición Revolucio-naria; Editorial de 'Ciencias Sociales'* ("Publishers of Social Sciences"); *Editorial 'Gente Nueva'* ("'New People' Publishers"); *Ediciones Deportivas* ("Sport Publications"); *Editorial Organismos* ("Organizations' Publishing House"), whose function is to facilitate the publication of specialized materials required by technicians for all national institutions and which are necessary for their development plans; *Editorial Arte y Literatura* ("Publishers of Art and Literature"); and the *Ediciones Huracán* ("Hurricane Publications"), with their paperback editions of more than 70,000 copies (in only four years almost seven million copies comprising over a hundred titles and ninety authors have been published by *Huracán*). The rest of the publishing houses, with the exception of *Pueblo y Educación*, have editions which vary between 5,000 and 50,000 copies per title.

Parallel to these publishing houses and dependent bodies of other national organizations are the publications of the *Unión Nacional de Escritores y Artistas de Cuba* (UNEAC) ("National Union of Cuban Writers and Artists"), and the *Casa de las Americas* ("House of the Americas"), whose objective is the dissemination of Latin American literature.

Pueblo y Educación: In coordination with MINED (Ministry of Education) this organization works on the planning of textbooks, and its staff prepare the originals of textbooks for various educational levels: primary, secondary and pre-university; for the training of teachers and for adult education. The planning of requirements, the compiling of originals, and the distribution of the books is carried out by MINED. The Cuban Book Institute undertakes the preparation of these originals for the department concerned, and their printing and later delivery to MINED for distribution.

At the same time they publish textbooks at

a higher level for the universities. The programme is determined by requests made by university schools and departments, who indicate the titles they need for their teaching. The majority of the books produced are given away gratis to students; smaller quantities are intended to cover the needs of other organizations. These publications are issued under the following names: *Edición Revolucionaria* (ER), *Cuadernos H*, or *Pueblo y Educación*.

Gente Nueva: publishes books for children and youth.

Part of each edition is distributed through the commercial network of the bookstores, but the majority are produced for student libraries which are affiliated to MINED, and national organizations active on behalf of children.

Huracán: Mass editions of novels, reports, travel and adventure books catering for all tastes.

Ciencias Sociales: publishes series of books on politics, history, sociology, philosophy, and general social subjects. The major objective of these works is the ideological and political education of the masses and the supply of information on classical and contemporary social thought for the professional training sectors.

Ediciones Deportivas: publishes books which deal with the manifold aspects of sports.

Organismos: These publishers produce material on request from different organizations in the country, for instance material for the information and further development of these organizations, etc.

Ambito: has recently begun to publish works in Spanish, English, French, and other languages, which are principally intended for foreign countries and aimed at a wide reading public. They are large-format books, profusely illustrated, and reflecting different aspects of Cuban culture, the visual arts, museums, natural environment, politics, etc.

Casa de las Americas: publishes literary works, essays, sociological and historical works on Latin America. It is an official institution which promotes cultural relations with the intellectuals of Latin America and which sponsors the annual competitions known as *Casa de las Americas.*

Unión Nacional de Escritores y Artistas de Cuba (UNEAC): Association of Cuban Writers and Artists. One of the tasks of this organization is the selection and preparation for publication of works by Cuban authors.

22 Literary Agents

In Cuba there are no literary agents to mediate between publisher and author. The determining factors for the publication of a literary work are its quality and its message, which is supposed to pave the way for the development of new social structures and the new man.

Cuban writers no longer finance their own works, nor are these distributed among just a small circle of friends. The Cuban publishers and their printing works, the whole complex of the Cuban Book Institue, are all engaged in the diffusion of the works of Cuban writers without the mediation of literary agents.

23 Wholesale Trade

The task of wholesale distribution is the delivery of publications which were issued on request of the various national organizations, for the National System of Education (Ministry of Education and universities) as well as for other, complementary educational and cultural activities and institutions: for professional and technical training, for libraries, for the compiling of reference works and works of general information, etc. The further distribution of the works according to their specific character is carried out by the organizations themselves.

24 Retail Trade

Retail Distribution: Is through the network of ICL libraries (→4) and the Provincial Commissions of the Institute.

Books for Commercial Circulation: Once the distribution of the publications which the ICL has given priority to has taken place, the distribution of the remaining quantities is undertaken.

Distribution Network: The national distribution network is divided into seven districts (one for each province), including the island of Pinos, a small island adjacent to Cuba which is a part of the national territory, and the region of the province of Havana. Since the distribution of books is of both economic and political importance, and since this activity was completely neglected during the time of the Republic, it is now organized by the provinces.

The province of Oriente is divided into two regions: north and south.

This network comprises the 185 bookstores and the 782 retail shops in the country.

Hall of Exchange: The *Salas de Intercambio* ("Halls of Exchange") is an institution which resulted from the urgent search for new possibilities for the utilization of publications whose supply is insufficient to meet ever-growing demands.

Above all, they fulfil a social purpose: they enable the working classes to count on a service which enables them to exchange one book for another, thus widening their sphere of circulation. The transitory character of this mechanism is determined by time and goes hand in hand with the development and enlargement of the country's productive capacities.

Specialized Services–Vietnam Libraries: These are bookstores which have established themselves in all provinces and which are dedicated to the sale of publications. Their service consists in enabling skilled workers and technicians to gain access to impor- ted publications, books and magazines (subscriptions) by means of catalogues.

25 Mail-Order Bookselling

Within the country a book mail-order service exists only for medical doctors, but there is a general mail-order service for magazines. Foreign subscriptions are attended to by the Directorate of International Trade (→4) if accompanied by a cheque which is cashed in Canadian Dollars–except in those banks whose main office is in the United States.

26 Antiquarian Book Trade, Auctions

Whereas before the Revolution there were small establishments which bought and sold second-hand books for commercial gain, bookstores dedicated to this activity are now operating in Havana whose chief aim is the recovery of valuable works which are required by bibliophiles and which enrich the libraries.

27 Book Imports

The Centre of Importation of the ICL Directorate of International Trade (→4) fulfils the country's needs for foreign books whether for use by organizations or for publication, especially in regard to the educational programmes. Seen from this angle, it fulfils a most important function, because it is the only department of a national organization which is dedicated to this activity; it monopolizes the importation of books into Cuba.
→7,9.

28 Book Exports

The activities of the Centre of Exportation (→4) have been rather limited since the Revolution due to the pressing educational demands at home.

Cuba

In spite of the obstacles which prevent a wider circulation of publications mainly printed in Spanish–a few in English and French–Cuban editions of books and magazines are in relatively high demand all over the world as a result of the revolutionary process.

The Institute has done everything in its power to establish the Cuban book in international spheres, not chiefly for commercial reasons, though only a small number of publications could be set aside from pressing home demand. Special emphasis is placed on the exportation of works concerning the history of Cuba, national literature, historical works dealing with the Revolution, Marxist literature, Latin American literature from the Third World, a wide range of books on Vietnam, and a whole series of literary, technological magazines and others of general interest.

The publishing departments of the ICL and especially the *Editorial Ambito* manufacture books principally intended for exportation. At present the depots of the Directorate of International Trade dispose of quantities of publications which can be exported. For Cuba the possibility of trading books–both import and export– has been limited because of the policy of isolation, boycott, and blockade that the country has been subjected to by the United States.

This situation has greatly infringed the free international traffic of publications and has kept the exchange figures low, except for short periods during which this policy lapsed.
→ 7,9.

29 Book Fairs

The explosive growth of the book in Cuba after the victory of the Revolution has justified the participation of Cuban publishers in events of this nature–a thing which the small publishing houses that existed before 1959 could not hope to achieve. The increase in the volume of editions, the improvement in quality, etc., now allow Cuba to participate in these events.

Of the book fairs and exhibitions that the Cuban Book Institute has participated in during the last few years we need only mention a few: the Frankfurt Book Fair, Federal Republic of Germany; the International Sofia Book Fair, the People's Republic of Bulgaria; the International Warsaw Fair, the People's Republic of Poland; the International Book Fair in Leipzig, German Democratic Republic, etc. (→BTW I, International Section, 29).

On its own account and in collaboration with publishing organizations of several countries the ICL has organized further exhibitions of Cuban Books in those countries, for example, the exhibitions which took place in Leningrad (July 1971) and Moscow (July 1972) in the Soviet Union; Sofía (March 1972) in the People's Republic of Bulgaria; Algiers (May 1972) in the Democratic and Popular Republic of Algeria; Santiago de Chile (October 1972) in the Republic of Chile; and others.

30 Public Relations

In Cuba the public relations of the ICL (→4) are promoted by the *Departamento de Divulgación* ("Department of Information") and abroad by the *Departamento de Relaciones Internacionales* ("Department of International Relations"), both of which are affiliated to the Cuban Book Institute (→4).

The principal objectives of these departments are:

1. To diffuse information with the aid of all communications media that provide the populace with a better knowledge of the ICL.

2. To contribute to the creation of a culti-

160

vated literary taste and to the creation of critical readers.

3. To assist in the promotion of literary production and scientific research in the country.

4. To guarantee all social and cultural organizations a continuous flow of information, of a general as well as of a political character, in which technical and specialized information has priority because of its extensive use in all fields of work.

→7.

32 Literary Prizes

The principal literary awards established in Cuba are:

Premio Casa de las Americas.

This award was established with the object of giving an opportunity to Latin American writers. The work for which the prize is awarded is diffused by the *Casa de las Americas* ("House of the Americas") saving the author all expenses. His name and his work are honoured by critical appreciation. For the annual awarding of the prize, the *Casa de las Americas* summons several representatives of Latin American literature as members of the jury. In this way mutual contacts are established which have led to an active and reciprocal relationship between writers of Latin American culture who previously had no knowledge of each other. In some cases, writers and critics who are not of Latin American provenance are invited to join the jury, but they must be able to speak Spanish and their intellectual and literary activities must link them in some way to Latin American culture. The integrity of these judges is one of the principal contributing factors towards the universal prestige of this award.

Literary Competitions organized by the *Unión de Escritores y Artistas de Cuba (UNEAC) ("Union of Cuban Writers and Artists").*

At present, the UNEAC sponsors two annual literary competitions of a national character: the *Premios UNEAC*, established in 1965, and the *Premios David*, established in 1967:

Premios UNEAC. These comprise six literary genres: Novel *(Premio "Cirilo Villaverde");* Poetry *(Premio "Julián del Casal");* Narration *(Premio "Luis Felipe Rodríguez");* Theatre *(Premio "José Antonio Ramos");* Essay *(Premio "Enrique José Varona");* and Biography *(Premio "Enrique Piñeyro").* The latter two competitions are held every ten years.

The *Premios UNEAC* are regulated by the following rules: Only Cuban writers can participate, be they members of UNEAC or not. Part of their works may have been published. A jury consisting of three persons of acknowledged intellectual prestige is designated for each competition. The sole prize for each competition consists in the publication of the work and a journey to one of the socialist countries which have cultural agreements with UNEAC. The verdicts are irrevocable. According to their own judgement the members of the jury can also bestow honourable mentions; these, however, do not imply that UNEAC is going to publish the work.

Premios David. These comprise three competitions: Poetry, Narration, and the Theatre.

The rules governing this competition are: Only Cuban writers who have not previously published any book are allowed to participate. The work may be published only in part. The jury for each competition consists of three writers. Their verdicts are irrevocable. The prize for each of the three competitions consists in the publication of the work. The members of the jury may bestow honourable mentions according to their own judgement.

Premio "26 de Julio". This award comprises various genres: Novel, Poetry, Narration, Testimony, Essay, etc.

Cuba

33 The Reviewing of Books

Cuban magazines of general interest include sections of literary criticism of books published by the Cuban Book Institute ($\rightarrow$4).

Almost simultaneously with the publication of an important work, a wide movement aimed at the popularization of the title, and articles on the author and the era, literary criticisms, linguistical analyses, etc. are published.

Radio and television arrange special programmes to help diffusion and popularization of the work, such as round-table discussions, adaptations and commentaries. There is very close collaboration between the Cuban Book Institute and the mass media of communication, which permits the use of these media as suitable vehicles to promote reading and at the same time stimulate critical judgement and a literary and political analysis of the work.

There is a long list of magazines and newspapers which include book reviews. Among these are:

Revista Bohemia
Avenida Independencia y
San Pedro
C La Habana

Revista Mujeres
San Miguel 260
C La Habana

Revista Romances
Ermita 107
C La Habana

Revista Union
17 No. 351, Vedado
C La Habana

Verde Olivo
Avenida Independenca y
San Pedro
C La Habana

Revista Cuba
Avenida de Simón Bolivar No. 552
C La Habana

Islas
Universidad de Las Villas
Departamento de Lengua Espanola
de La Escuela de Letras
C Las Villas

Revista de la Biblioteca Nacional
Plaza de la Revolución
C La Habana

Caiman Barbudo
Calzado y 8, Vedado
C La Habana

34 Graphic Arts

Part of the Cuban Book Institute ($\rightarrow$4), the *Dirección Industrial* ("Industrial Management") is the body responsible for the administration and organization of the industrial processes involved in the production of books, brochures, and magazines, whilst ensuring their good quality and the most efficient employment of human and material resources. The *Dirección Industrial* is subdivided into two branches of management:

The *Sub-Dirección de Producción Industrial* ("Subdivision of the Management of Industrial Production") is responsible for the programming and exploiting of the resources available, the procuring of the necessary materials, and the maintenance of the technical equipment and industrial installations. Its activities are based on annual, four-monthly, and monthly working plans.

The *Sub-Dirección Tecnica* ("Subdivision of Technological Management") is responsible for the establishment of processing techniques and useful employment of equipment; the investigation of new graphical techniques and their application in our departments. To this end it collects information on equipment, techniques, potential suppliers, and the experience of other countries ($\rightarrow$16).

Dominican Republic

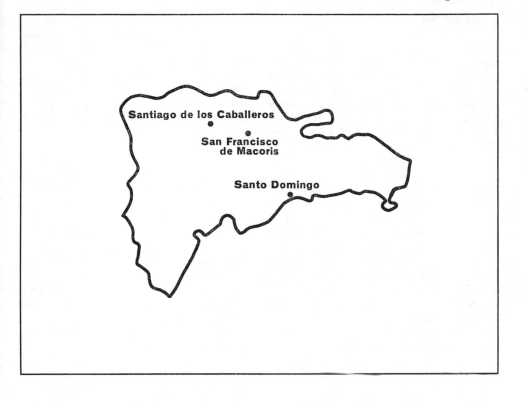

1 General Information

Area 48,734 km²

Population 4,325,000 (89 per km² – Mestizos and Mulattos 60%, White 28%, Negro 12% in 1970)

Capital Santo Domingo de Guzman (577,370 in 1967, called Ciudad Trujillo between 1936 and 1961)

Largest towns Santo Domingo (557,370), Santiago de los Caballeros (329,000), San Francisco de Macoris (33,785)

Government Presidential democracy

Religion Roman Catholic 95% (state religion)

National language Spanish

Leading foreign languages Creole French, English

Weights, measures Metric system (since 1913); British and Spanish measures still in commercial use

Currency unit Dominican Republic Peso (RD$) = 100 centimos (cts). At par with the US-$

Education Compulsory, from 7th to 14th year (where possible). 9,963 students at three universities (1968) and five colleges of academic standard

Illiteracy 35.5% (1960)

Paper consumption a) Newsprint 0.7 kg per inhabitant (1970)

b) Printing paper (other than newsprint) 0.5 kg per inhabitant (1970)

Membership UNESCO, CERLAL

Dominican Republic

2 Past and Present

The Dominican Republic, as part of the former island of "La Hispaniola", is the point where the Spanish first put foot on American soil. The country thus has a rich history which includes outstanding events for the American continent, especially for Latin America. The diary of Christopher Columbus was partly written on the island. The foundation of the university in 1538 (the first one in the Americas) helped to lessen depredations of cultural and literary life during colonial times compared with other countries in the continent. The first library was formed by a companion of Columbus', Diego Méndez y Segura, and in 1509 it was enriched by books brought on behalf of the Viceroy. For its cultural attraction in America, the island of "La Hispaniola" was at that time called the "Athens of America".

The first printer settled in 1750, but it was only after independence from Spain that the Dominican Republic slowly began to develop publishing. However, only in the last ten or twelve years did the small number of books published increase, in titles as well as in copies printed–including, first in importance, books by national authors. It is remarkable that two of these national authors became presidents in this century.

Today there are about twenty publishers and nearly as many bookshops in the Dominican Republic–seven of the latter are wholesalers too. Half a dozen of the publishers, some of them founded at the same time as bookshops, contribute to the nation's output with books of national and international origin, among them those of the Academy of History and the National and the Catholic University. All firms are concentrated in the capital. The main problem is the agricultural character of the national product (exports are mostly sugar and bananas), more than 50% of the working people earning their income by this monocultural agriculture, with a total Gross National Product per capita of US $ 295. As regards book publishing and selling, it must be borne in mind that there is still a high rate of illiteracy, and that more than half of the Dominican Republic's population consists of people under 20 years of age.

Bibliography

G. FURLONG, *Orígines del arte tipográfico en América*. (The origins of the art of typography in America.) Buenos Aires, Ed. Huarpes 1947. 225 pp. Bibliography on pp. 215–25.–Early printing history of San Domingo: p. 117.

La imprenta y los primeros periódicos de Santo Domingo. (Printing and the first periodicals in Santo Domingo). Ciudad Trujillo (Santo Domingo), Imprenta San Francisco 1944. 257 pp.

Br. F. SWAN, *The spread of printing, Western Hemisphere: The Caribbean area*. Amsterdam, Vangendt 1970. 47 pp.

J. TORRE REVELLO, *El libro, la imprenta y el periodismo en América durante la dominación española*. (The book, printing and journalism in America during Spanish domination.) Buenos Aires, Casa Jacobo Peuser 1940.

J. TORRE REVELLO, *Un catálogo impreso de libros para vender en las Indias Occidentales en el Siglo XVII*. (A printed catalogue of books sold in the West Indies in the XVII century.) Madrid, Beltrán 1930. 30 pp.

4 Organization

The only professional association of the book trade is that of the booksellers,
Cámara del Libro Dominicano
(Chamber of the Dominican Book)
Apartado Postal 656
Mercures 49
DOM Santo Domingo
It was founded chiefly to defend the inter-

ests of booksellers and publishers, and secondly for the promotion of national books on the local and export markets. The chamber, also working under the name of *"Asociación Dominicana de Libreros"* (Dominican Association of Booksellers), prepares a programme for the better training of bookshop employees, hitherto given only inside the firms, which will include volunteer studies in Spain, Argentina and Mexico.

7 Sources of Information, Address Services

The main source of information on book questions in the Dominican Republic is the
Asociación Dominicana de Libreros
(Dominican Association of Booksellers)
Apartado Postal 656
Mercures 49
DOM Santo Domingo
General, commercial information on the country can be obtained from the
Cámara de Comercio, Agricultura y Industria
del Distrito Nacional
(Chamber of Commerce, Agriculture and
Industry of the National District)
Arzobispo Nouel 52-Altos
DOM Santo Domingo
The chamber maintains a special library of 8,000 volumes.
Although some of the eight publicity agencies in Santo Domingo have among their material addresses relating to the book trade, there is no special agency for this type of information. Addresses of publishers and booksellers can be found, however, in the International and Latin American directories.

Bibliography

The addresses of all branches of the book trade are contained in:
La Empresa del Libro en América Latina. (The Book in Latin America.) 2nd ed. Buenos Aires, Bowker Editores Argentina 1974.

VIII, 307 pp.–pp. 243–245: Republica Dominicana.
The West Indian and Caribbean Yearbook. London, Thomas Skinner 1958 ff. Annual.

10 Books and Young People

Efforts at promoting reading among children and young people in the Dominican Republic are part of an extended programme of "Campañas de Alfabetización", i.e. of teaching the majority of children and adults to read. While the rate of illiteracy, according to the 1960 census, was 35.5% among the general population, thanks to the government's efforts, this has decreased to 27% for people aged 15–49 years.
The government introduced obligatory reading of one hour per day in the primary schools, and two hours of reading and discussion of general or Latin American literature in the secondary schools. Furthermore, the Ministry of Education has commissioned its "Department for Exchange and Cultural Promotion" to buy the textbooks for schools.

14 Copyright

In 1947 the Dominican Republic joined the Inter-American Convention of 1946 for the protection of Copyright (→BTW I, International Section 14). But not being member of the Universal Copyright Convention (→BTW I, International Section 14) and, on the other hand, many Latin American countries not yet having ratified the Panamerican one, there were recently some cases of pirate editions printed in the Dominican Republic, mostly of Latin American bestselling novels. Publicity in the local press against these practices, and even legal steps, have not had the desired result, as in many cases the affected author's countries had not signed any copyright conventions.

Dominican Republic

Serious publishers have together with the government fought against piracy, the government is at present pressing the reform of copyright law on national scale, and offers foreign authors official protection which will enable them to take legal steps against incursions of their rights.

15 National Bibliography, National Library

On the occasion of the international book fair held in Santo Domingo in 1970 (→29) the Dominican government announced the creation of a National Library, which will be legally obliged to collect every title published in the country, and to actualize the national bibliography. This new National Library starts with three important private collections of national books, bought by the government for this purpose. Furthermore, it will be able to collaborate with a number of traditional and fairly complete libraries, such as that of the National University, founded in 1538, and those of the Secretary of State of the Interior and of the General Department of Statistics, both of which already receive, by legal deposit, copies of books printed in the republic.

The library of the National Autonomous University has frequently fulfilled the functions that are normally those of a National Library in other countries; thus it has, for instance, a fairly complete collection of works by national authors and on the country, and has also contributed to the publication of bibliographies and books for the library profession (→Bibliography). When announcing the formation of a National Library, the government foresaw that from the year 1974 onwards national book production will be presented in an official bibliography, based on registration in the new institution. There has been, for ten years, a

Grupo Bibliográfico Nacional de la
República Dominicana

(National Bibliographic Group)
Calle Chiclana de la Frontera
DOM Santo Domingo

In total, the country has 18 libraries, two of which are university libraries and two school libraries.

Bibliography

Anuario Bibliográfico Dominicano 1946 (Dominican Bibliographic Annual 1946). Santo Domingo, Oficina de Canje y Difusión Cultural 1947.

P. AVICENNE, *Bibliographical services throughout the world 1965–1969*. Paris, UNESCO 1972. 310 pp.
pp. 108–109 have information about Dominican bibliographical sources.

Biblio-Notas. (Biblio-Notes). Santo Domingo, Biblioteca de la Universidad Nacional "Pedro Henríquez Ureña" 1971 ff. Mimeographed.
List of publications received, including national books and periodicals.

L. FLOREN LOZANO, *Bibliografía de la bibliografía Dominicana*. (Bibliography of the Dominican bibliography.) Santo Domingo, Roques Román 1948. 66 pp.

J. V. POSTIGO, *Libros Dominicanos*. (Dominican books.) Santo Domingo, Librería Hispaniola 1970. 92 pp.
Published on the occasion of the International Book Fair 1950. The author previously published a similar catalogue in 1955.

J. ZIMMERMANN, *Current national bibliographies of Latin America*. Gainesville, Fla., University of Florida Press 1971. 10, 139 pp.
pp. 107–110 on Dominican bibliographies.

16 Book Production

No figures are available. Though there has been an increase during the last ten years in the number of titles and of copies printed, Dominican book production still is relatively small. Most of the titles are paperbound. The catalogue presented in 1970 on the occasion of the International Book Fair (→15, Bibliography) lists more than 500 titles as Dominican books available, about 5% of them published outside the country.

21 Publishing

Among the twenty publishing companies listed in the Dominican Republic, all of them working in the capital, nine firms are publishers of books only. Among them are some booksellers who publish series of national authors and books on national history. Official and semi-official institutions also do publishing, among them the University of Santo Domingo and the Catholic University "Madre y Maestra". Production by these publishers is relatively small. Most editions are in paperback covers. There is a notable lack of children's books, with the exception of some titles for the early reader. The are also very few translations of internationally known novels. In recent years, however, by increasing the size of editions per title, and thanks to government support by exemption from taxes for raw material, the publishers' position has slowly improved. Nevertheless, when compared with other Latin American countries, the almost complete lack of book promotion is surprising.

24 Retail Trade

Of the 15 bookshops registered in the national and international directories, only two are located outside the capital, in the city of Santiago de los Caballeros. They are all private firms, a number of them traditional companies also active in publishing and the wholesale trade for foreign books; the latter activity is reported by seven bookshops.

These firms mostly handle imported books and periodicals. One of their tasks

is the training of employees–a professional career is not known in the republic–within their association (→4). The booksellers also take part in the national and international book exhibitions (→29), and the catalogues of the major ones are the only existing sources for Dominican literarure.

27 Book Imports

Nearly all books sold in the bookshops of the country are of foreign origin. The imported book has an important role in the cultural development of the population. Accepting this, the government has relieved the import and distribution of foreign books and periodicals of all duty, taxes and any other limitation.

The figures given by the National Statistical Office for 1968 and 1969, although for "books and other printing-matter", give a wide distribution of supplying countries, listing 53. Among them, the USA, Puerto Rico and Spain are the most important. The following table gives countries selling books for more than US $ 5,000 to the Dominican Republic in any of the two years mentioned:

Country	1968 US$	1969 US$
USA	418,904	521,962
Puerto Rico	66,732	195,272
Spain	138,765	164,655
Argentina	31,408	45,048
Venezuela	22,294	35,357
France	5,447	24,518
Mexico	25,641	22,143
Germany (Federal Rep.)	8,901	16,749
Italy	12,190	12,584
Japan	5,911	9,182
Colombia	9,572	8,524
Panama	12,146	7,128
United Kingdom	15,538	4,093
Canada	12,661	3,649
Total	801,776	1,082,473

167

Dominican Republic

This total amount, compared to the imports of other goods, is nearly half the value of the country's import of agricultural machinery and equipment, and double that of cattle and other livestock.

The country's geography poses a number of problems for the Dominican book importer. Only in a few cases can he avoid the disadvantage of being far from the major book-production centres of Latin America. With Argentina, Venezuela and Colombia, agreements have been signed for a special air-freight tariff on books. In other cases for even the most active book suppliers, book imports by air are too expensive. This method of supply is used when big quantities of textbooks are imported. Other transport facilities are very slow and sometimes irregular.

Another difficulty lies in obtaining foreign exchange for payments of book imports. By way of the Central Bank, it takes about eight months to get a payment finally settled. There is an easier way, with a banker's cheque, which takes only one month, but this is possible only with amounts below US $ 200. But as the Dominican importer can count his currency at par with the US $, the exchange currency used in the region of nearly all his main suppliers, he avoids losses on foreign imports and exports. The Central Bank will also let the importer deposit a letter of credit for book imports, without previous deposit, which makes it possible for him to enjoy credit terms. Furthermore, there are contracts with Venezuela and Colombia for a reciprocal credit on bank drafts in US $.This, in the opinion of some, has enormously boosted the import of books over the last decade.

28 Book Exports

Reduced national book production is not conducive to good sales figures to other countries. The statistics of the National Statistical Office (→27) show that in 1968 and 1969 the seven most important customers for books and printed brochures–followed only by minor shipments in 1969 to the Central American countries for ten dollars each–were:

Country	1968 US$	1969 US$
Puerto Rico	15,746	14,565
USA	5,770	5,761
Spain	—	5,001
Colombia	—	3,802
Venezuela	20	800
Germany (Federal Rep.)	1,041	—
France	55	—
Total	22,637	29,989

The same sources mentions for periodicals:

Country	1968 US$	1969 US$
Puerto Rico	8,202	12,891
USA	24,917	11,112
Venezuela	—	1,204
Netherlands Antilles	1,071	104
Peru	32	—
Total	34,222	25,311

29 Book Fairs

Having held only one national book exhibition in more than ten years, Dominican booksellers and publishers won the cooperation of their government to organize the first international book fair in the Republic in 1970. The *"Primera Exposición Mundial del Libro y Festival Internacional de la Cultura"* (First World Exhibition of the Book and International Festival of the Culture) was held from 11 November to 11 December 1970. It was attended by 200 publishers from 26 countries in America, Europe and Asia, exhibiting a total of 30,000 volumes. This event will be repeated.

168

Bibliography

J. D. Postigo, *Libros Dominicanos*. (Dominican books.) Santo Domingo, Librería Hispaniola 1971. 92 pp.
A catalogue published on the occasion of the First World Book Exhibition in Santo Domingo. Shows more than 500 titles. A similar one was published by the author in 1955.

33 The Reviewing of Books

Just as great as the lack of an efficient bibliographical service is the dearth of reviews of new general and professional books. Book reviews of local and important international books is confined almost exclusively to periodicals.

The country has six newspapers with a total edition of 33,000 copies, and 17 magazines with a total edition of 48,000 (1969). The 21 radio stations also regularly transmit book news.

Bibliography

Ahora. Santo Domingo. 1962 ff. 36 issues annually.
The leading cultural review of the country.

La imprenta y los primeros periódicos de Santo Domingo. (Printing and the first periodicals in Santo Domingo.) Ciudad Trujillo (Santo Domingo), Imprenta San Francisco 1944. 257 pp.

Ecuador

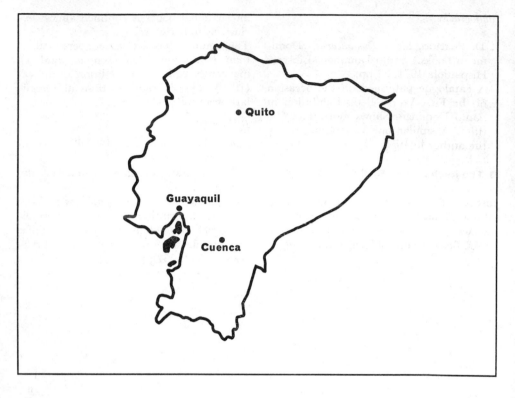

1 General Information

Area 281,341 km²
Population 6,598,300 (23.4 per km²)
Capital Quito (575,116)
Largest towns Guayaquil (main port; 879,000); Quito (575,116); Cuenca (80,956)
Government Ecuador is an independent, sovereign, democratic and unitarian state which is governed by the principles of liberty, justice, equality and labour. The national territory is divided into 20 provinces, including the insular province of Galápagos
Religion The majority of the inhabitants practise Roman Catholicism. There are small groups of different Evangelical Churches. The State guarantees religious freedom
National language Spanish
Other language Quechua (a language which is spoken by the natives living in the Andean

region). The State recognizes Quechua as an element of the national culture
Leading foreign language English (taught in all the national establishments of secondary education)
Weights and measures Metric system (the yard and the pound are also popularly used)
Currency unit Sucre (= 100 centavos)
Education 6 years of compulsory elementary education (929,000 pupils). Secondary: 3 years of basic curriculum and 3 years of diversified curriculum (174,000 pupils). Higher education: 16 universities, polytechnics and other institutes of higher education (23,000 students)
Illiteracy 30%
Membership UNESCO, CERLAL

2 Past and Present

In 1754 the first printing press arrived in the territory which today constitutes Ecuador and which was called *Presidencia de Quito* at that time. It was installed in the small town of Ambato and transferred to Quito four years later. In this printing shop the first Ecuadorian newspaper, *Primicias de la Cultura de Quito* ("Beginnings of Quito's Culture"), was edited, the contents of which were written almost exclusively by Eugenio Espejo. Unfortunately only seven numbers of this newspaper could be published; the first one appeared on 5 of January 1795, and the last one on 25 March of the same year. The lack of printing offices in the Presidency of Quito was, however, made up for by a great abundance of manuscript texts that were used by university professors to dictate their subjects. No less than 408 manuscripts have remained of the University of San Gregorio. Today nearly all of these are to be found in the *Biblioteca Nacional* (National Library, → 15), except for a small number housed in the library of the *Instituto Superior de Humanidades Clásicas* (Higher Institute of Classical Humanities).

The literary and philosophical-theological output of the colonial era was fertile, but the books were printed in Madrid, Barcelona, Lyon, Rome, Valencia, Lima, and elsewhere.

In 1886, when Ecuador was already an independent state, a decisive step was taken by setting up the printing press of Quito University, which was to publish works of a cultural nature. This press has produced valuable scientific and literary works. Nowadays, the *Editorial Universitaria* ("University Publishers") is an important centre of book production in the country.

In 1944 the *Casa de la Cultura Ecuatoriana* ("House of Ecuadorian Culture") was founded. Its mission was to sponsor and to support scientific research as well as literary and artistic creativity. It is an autonomous institution situated in Quito and which has set up numerous centres in the main provincial capitals.

Several of these centres have their own presses for the publication of works by national and foreign authors. The *Editorial de la Casa de la Cultura Ecuatoriana* ("Publishers of the House of Ecuadorian Culture") deserves a special mention, as do the publishing departments of the centres that have been set up in Guayaquil and Cuenca.

The "Law of National Culture", passed by the Government only recently, has done a great deal to facilitate a better organization of the "House of Ecuadorian Culture".

Among the decisive steps that were taken during the historical evolution of publishing in Ecuador the juridical and historical publications of the *Corporación de Estudios y Publicaciones* ("Corporation of Studies and Publications") should be mentioned. This is a private, non-profit-making organization which has stimulated the publication of important collections of lawbooks and valuable historical works. Another milestone is the publication of *Populibros* (paperbacks for mass consumption) that has been undertaken by the *Publicaciones Educativas Ariel* ("Ariel Educational Publications"). About one hundred small volumes that make up an excellent collection of works by Ecuadorian authors, past and present, have been placed within easy reach of the public by means of these low-priced editions, thus considerably stimulating the reading habit and expanding the general culture of the people.

At present efforts are being made for the setting up of publishing houses throughout the country which, backed by national and international funds, are to produce

Ecuador

books for the consumption of all the countries belonging to the Andean region.

Bibliographie

G. Furlong, *Orígines del arte tipográfico en América*. (The origins of the art of typography in America.) Buenos Aires, Ed. Huarpes 1947. 225 pp.
Bibliography on pp. 215–25. Early printing history of Ecuador: pp. 113–16.

J. T. Medina, *Historia de la imprenta en los antiguos dominios españoles de América y Oceanía*. (The history of printing in the ancient Spanish dominions of America and Oceania.) 2 vols. Santiago de Chile, Fondo Histórico y Bibliográfico José Toribio Medina 1958. CXLI, 542; XV, 540 pp.
v. II, pp. 257–262: Ecuador (Quito).

L. S. Thompson, *Printing in Colonial Spanish America*. Hamden, Conn., Archon Books 1962. 108 pp.
pp. 80–84: Ecuador.

Fr. J. M. Vargas, *Historia de la cultura Ecuatoriana*. (Cultural history of Ecuador). 3 vols. Guayaquil, Publicaciones Educativas Ariel 1972.

3 Retail Prices

Since a considerable percentage of the books purchased in the country are imported, it is necessary to divide this chapter into two parts: (a) prices of books which are produced in the country, and (b) prices of imported books:

a) *Books that are published in the country:* There is no definite rule for the fixing of the prices. In general the price is fixed by the publisher, who is often his own author.

The government has not set up any price controls and does not interfere with the regulating of prices. However, the *Superintendencia de Precios* ("Supervision of Prices") may intervene at any moment, in accordance with the legal provisions that have been established recently and that authorize this organization to regulate not only the prices of books but of all consumer goods.

b) *Imported books:* The *Sociedad de Libreros del Ecuador* ("Society of Booksellers of Ecuador", →4) is constantly making efforts to regulate and unify the prices of imported books. In the majority of cases positive results have been obtained. A general rule that has established itself within this Society says that the price of the imported book should be the equivalent of the price on the cover in dollars or in the currency of the country of origin plus an extra 20% added to cover freight, packing, insurance and other expenses.

4 Organization

The most important organization for the Ecuadorian book trade is the
Sociedad de Libreros del Ecuador
(Society of Booksellers of Ecuador)
P. O. Box 3329
EC Quito
The "Society of Booksellers" is constituted by all the principal enterprises that are involved in the trade in books, magazines and other printed matter. It was founded on 18 April 1955, and was approved on 7 May by Decree No. 2738 of the Ministry of Social Welfare.

The founder and first President of the society was the distinguished writer, Jorge Icaza.

Among the principal objectives of the Society are the following:

To unite all those who participate in the book trade and to represent them to defend their interests.

To support the spirit of solidarity with the objective of developing the book trade in a way that enhances its prestige.

To study, to recommend, to negotiate and to petition in favour of the book trade and to collaborate in the study of all legal projects or dispositions that are directly or indirectly linked with the book.

To sponsor exhibitions and book fairs.

To keep up relations with similar institutions in other countries.

The legal representative of the society is the President.

The society has developed a great activity in defence of the free circulation of the book and its exemption from taxes and duties.

Bibliography

Estatutos de la Sociedad de Libreros del Ecuador (Statutes of the Society of Booksellers of Ecuador.) Quito 1955.

7 Sources of Information, Address Services

Information on the book market, bookstores and importers of books can be obtained from:

Sociedad de Libreros del Ecuador
(Society of Booksellers of Ecuador)
P. O. Box 3329
EC Quito

Addresses of bookstores and booksellers in Quito can also be obtained from:

Cámara de Comercio de Quito
(The Quito Board of Trade)
Calle Guayaquil 1242
EC Quito

Addresses of bookstores and booksellers in Guayaquil can be obtained from:

Cámara de Comercio de Guayaquil
(The Guayaquil Board of Trade)
AV. Olmedo 414
EC Guayaquil

Bibliography

The addresses of all branches of the book trade of are contained in

La Empresa del Libro en América Latina. (The Book in Latin America.) 2nd ed. Buenos Aires, Bowker Editores Argentina 1974. VIII, 307 pp.
pp. 159–161: Ecuador.

8 International Membership

Ecuador is a member of UNESCO. The National Commission of UNESCO has its seat in Quito; its President is the Minister of Education.

10 Books and Young People

Up to the present day national production of literature for children has been scarce; at the moment, however, a special interest for this form of literature has begun to develop. There is reason to hope that in the near future there will be an increase in the national production of such works.

Recently the publication of a collection of works for young people, which were taken or extracted from famous works by national and foreign authors, has been initiated. This collection has met with great approval by the public.

12 Taxes

In accordance with the Common Law which imposes taxes on both capital and labour income, the book industry and book trade have to pay income tax like any other enterprise; on the other hand, the marketing of the book does not undergo the usual 4% tax on commercial transactions, thereby receiving a preferential treatment against other products and services that are generally charged with this impost.

The importation and exportation of books is equally exempt from customs duties.

After the arrival of a consignment, imported either by postal package, ordinary mail or sea freight, a fee of 0.25% on the fob-value of the books has to be paid for every two weeks of storage. In addition a fee of $6^0/_{00}$ on the cif-value, the so-called "statistic control fee", is deducted.

Should the books arrive by air, import duty forms have to be filled in on which stamps to an approximate value of 56.00 sucre are attached.

The exportation of books is also charged with the "statistic control fee" ($\rightarrow$ 27, 28).

14 Copyright

Copyright for writers and artists is regulated by the following laws:

Ley de Propiedad Intelectual (Law of Intellectual Property; Official Registry No. 435 of 11 February 1958).

Reglamento de Aplicación de la Ley de Propiedad Intelectual (Regulation of the Application of the Law of Intellectual Property; Official Registry No. 605 of 2 September 1958).

Codificación de la Ley de la Propiedad Intelectual (Codification of the Law of Intellectual Property), passed by the Permanent Legislative Commission on 25 November 1959, and together with other laws published in a book entitled *Constitución y Leyes de Ecuador* (Constitution and Laws of Ecuador), which is a supplement to the Official Registry No. 1202 of 20 August 1960.

Ley Nacional de la Cultura (National Law of Culture; Official Registry No. 257 of 10 March 1973.)

The Law of Intellectual Property protects all intellectual, philosophical, scientific, literary or artistic creations, no matter in what form they may be. Consequently this law encompasses writing, illustrations, musical compositions, paintings, sculpture, photographs, cartographical works, motion pictures, radio, television, translations, adaptations, musical arrangements, instrumentation, dramatizations; in general, all productions and transformations of literary, artistic or scientific works.

The Law permits the reproduction of short fragments or small selections of works in the form of anthologies, criticisms, or books on the history of literature.

Unless there is a definite prohibition, the Law permits the reproduction of articles or graphic material taken from magazines and newspapers.

The registration and recording of intellectual or artistic creations takes place at the *Registro General de Propiedad Intelectual* (Official Registry of Intellectual Property), which is a department of the Ministry of Education. The registration is free of charge, but three copies of each printed work are required to be handed in; if the work which is to be registered has not yet been published, it is sufficient to send a copy of the original to the Registry.

Works that have been published must be registered within six months after the date of the first edition.

Should his rights have been violated, the author is entitled to demand:

a) the cessation of any acts that violate such rights;

b) the confiscation of the frauds that remain in the offender's possession, and the restitution of the value of the copies that have been sold;

c) a commensurate indemnification for damages.

Persons who are guilty of an infringement of these rights can be fined from 500 to 6,000 sucres, confiscation of the works and payment of damages.

The respective lawsuits are negotiated in front of the Provincial Court (Civil Court) and become prescriptive after two years.

The Law of National Culture establishes that one of the objectives of the "House of Ecuadorian Culture" is to "watch over the protection of copyright".

A disposition of Article 33 of the same Law states that the period after which copyright becomes prescriptive is 25 years. Once this period has elapsed, the copyright becomes the property of the House of Culture.

Ecuador has been a member of the Universal Copyright Convention since 5 June 1957 ($\rightarrow$ BTW I, International Section 14).

15 National Bibliography, National Library

In Quito there is a so-called "National Library", but in reality this is not a library of national works. It is, rather, a general library, a collection of all kinds of works, a considerable number of which are foreign. There are very few modern works, the majority dating back to past decades.

One of the most complete libraries of Ecuadorian works is the *Biblioteca Ecuatoriana Aurelio Espinoza Polit* (Cotocollao). This library was founded by the Jesuit priest and notable humanist, Aurelio Espinoza Polit, in 1828. Initially it was intended to collect only the works of Ecuadorian authors, but later on the library expanded its repertoire with the accumulation of all kinds of national works.

Today an estimated 70,000 volumes are housed in this library. It includes books, brochures, magazines and newspapers that have been published in Ecuador or written by Ecuadorian authors since the eighteenth century.

There is another library in Guayaquil, the *Biblioteca Rolando*, which was founded by Carlos A. Rolando, a citizen of Guayaquil, on 24 May 1913. This library has valuable documents on the nation's history and also claims a well-furnished collection of works by Ecuadorian authors. It comprises 24,000, volumes including newspapers published from 1830 to the present day.

A complete national bibliography has not yet been compiled. There are, however, two bibliographical works, one entitled *Bibliografía Científica del Ecuador* (Scientific Bibliography of Ecuador) and written by Carlos Manuel Larrea, and the other *Bibliografía Jurídica del Ecuador* (Juridical Bibliography of Ecuador), written by Juan Larrea Holguín. Information on these works can be obtained from the:

Corporación de Estudios y Publicaciones

(Corporation of Studies and Publications)
P. O. Box 1287
EC Quito

Bibliography

P. Avicenne, *Bibliographical services throughout the world 1965–69*. Paris, Unesco 1972. 310 pp.–p. 109: Ecuador

I. Zimmermann, *Current national bibliographies of Latin America*. Gainesville, Florida, University of Florida Press 1971. X, 139 pp.–pp. 45–50: Ecuador.

16 Book Production

In 1969 the overall volume of the production of books, newspapers and magazines amounted to:

Category	Copies	Value (Sucres)
Books	97,159	2,254,621
Paperbacks	4,000	340,000
Newspapers	67,398,292	49,724,249
Magazines	1,227,000	8,861,645

The majority of the books produced are used as textbooks for elementary and secondary education. The above figures have notably increased during recent years because of a considerable increase in the production of paperbacks and magazines.

21 Publishing

The book market principally consists of imported books. Except for the textbooks for elementary or secondary education, national production is not very voluminous. There are very few publishing houses, the most important of them being the publishing departments of the centres of the House of Culture and the different university publishers (→2).

There are two private publishing houses worthy of mention: one of them specializes in legal and historical works and the other in popular works and paperbacks.

It is also interesting to note that recently there has been a vigorous growth in the field of magazine publishing.

It frequently happens that the author of a book is also his own publisher and even does his own distributing by delivering his work to the bookstores. Similarly, textbooks may be published and distributed by their own authors.

The Ministry of Education publishes textbooks for the elementary level, the majority of which are destined for the students of the National Schools who are lent the books for their own use during the academic year. (→2).

23 Wholesale Trade

Ecuador has hardly any wholesale dealers in the true sense of the world.

24 Retail Trade

The bookstores generally import books and sell them directly to the public. Occasionally these bookstores also distribute works of foreign publishing houses. In this case books are imported at wholesale prices and sold to other stores at a cut rate.

Some foreign publishers have their own branches in the country, but these are principally dedicated to the sale of their own books by instalments.

At the time when lectures and schools start (October in the Inter-Andean region and May in the coastal region) the bookstores, which have imported large quantities of textbooks, sell them at a cut-rate price to numerous private educational establisments.

There are distributors of magazines who import paperbacks at a wholesale price and deliver them to supermarkets, small bookshops and newsagents.

Without taking into account small bookshops and stationers selling books on a limited scale there are 45 enterprises in the country engaged in the book trade: bookstores, distributing houses, and organizations which sell books by instalment payment; 22 of these operate in Quito, 15 in Guayaquil, and 8 in the rest of the country.

27 Book Imports

In Ecuador the importation of books and magazines is free and tax-exempt. It is not necessary to obtain a permit for importation, nor are any other transactions required. The foreign currency for the payment of the imported books is acquired on the free market, at a price which is more or less equivalent to the official exchange rate. Only the importation of books that violate public morals and good manners is prohibited. The controlling is carried out when the books arrive in the country or when they are delivered to the importer. There are no official statistical data on the importation of books, but it is estimated that the total volume of book imports amounts to approximately one million US $ annually.

The majority of these books are imported from the Argentina, Mexico and Spain, followed by Colombia and the United States, listed in this order according to their importance as supplying countries for Ecuador. (→12).

28 Book Exports

The exportation of books is very limited, but also exempt from taxes or customs duties. There are no statistical data about the exportation of books. (→12).

29 Book Fairs

Occasionally the "Society of Booksellers" and the "House of Culture" as well as other institutions have organized book fairs. There is, however, no regularity nor a special date for these events.

Ecuador participated several times at the Frankfurt Book Fair (→BTW I, International Section 29).

32 Literary Prizes

The most important national prize is the *Premio Tobar* ("Tobar Prize"), which is awarded by the Municipal Council of Quito every year on 6 December. The prize goes to the Ecuadorian author of what is considered to be the best book published in Quito for the first time during the preceding year (the year being reckoned from 6 December).

The award, which was established by means of a Municipal Decree on 28 October 1932, is based on a testamentary provision made by Mrs. Isabel Tobar, who in her will dedicated a certain sum of money to this purpose. This fund has been deposited at interest; the interest constitutes the annual prize.

The Decree provides that dissertations of a scientific nature will receive preferential treatment in the bestowal of the award. If several works of this character are presented, those that deal with typical Ecuadorian matters will have priority.

The "Jurado Calificador", the Jury that examines the works, is composed of three members chosen by the Municipality of Quito. When passing judgement on the presented works the members of the jury must concentrate on the following criteria: the book which wins the award–be it short or long–must have a high intellectual value, its doctrine should be clearly defined and methodically arranged, and it should be an original expression in the respective field of study.

In addition to the "Tobar Prize" occasional competitions are organized and prizes for literary and scientific works are awarded, but these are irregular events, which are not of the same importance as the "Tobar Prize".

33 The Reviewing of Books

Book reviews are a part of newspapers, magazines, and television programmes.

Nearly all newspapers have a daily literary and cultural section and many of them publish special weekly supplements dedicated to literature and book reviews.

The most important newspapers to place a certain emphasis on the reviewing of books are the following: *El Comercio* and *El Tiempo* in Quito, *El Universo* and *El Telégrafo* in Guayaquil, and *El Mercurio* in Cuenca.

Two large-circulation magazines which frequently publish book reviews are *Vistazo* and *Nueva*.

There are also periodicals and other publications which specialize in the subject. The most important representative of these is *Letras del Ecuador*, a magazine on literature and art, published in Quito by the *Núcleo Central de la Casa de la Cultura Ecuatoriana* (Main Centre of the House of Ecuadorian Culture).

In the provinces other magazines are published, as, for instance, *El Guacamayo y la Serpiente* ("The Macaw and the Snake"), which is published by the *Núcleo del Azuay de la Casa de la Cultura*, Cuenca; and *Cuadernos del Guayas*, published by the *Núcleo de Guayaquil de la Casa de la Cultura* Guayaquil.

34 Graphic Arts

Ecuador's graphic industry is represented by the

Federación de Industriales Gráficos del Ecuador (Federation of Graphic Industries of Ecuador) P.O. Box 3282. EC Quito

This institution can supply information on the graphic arts and industry in the country.

El Salvador

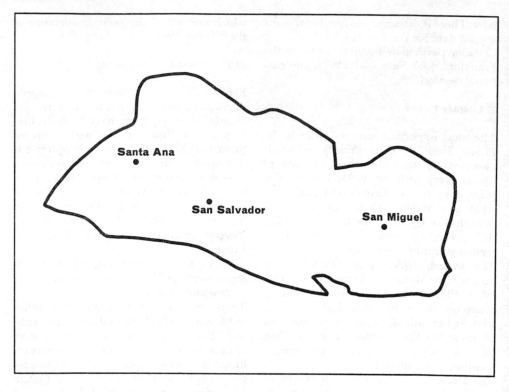

1 General Information

Area 21,393 km²
Population 3,266,000 (153 per km² in 1968)
Capital San Salvador (436,841 in 1968)
Largest towns San Salvador (436,841), Santa Ana (152,346), San Miguel (82,977)
Government Presidential Republic
Religion Roman Catholic 88%
National language Spanish
Leading foreign language English
Weights, measures Metric system; also old Spanish measures still in use
Currency unit Colón (C.) = 100 centavos (c.)
Education Compulsory for 7 years (where possible). 6,748 students (1967) in 2 universities and 3 colleges
Illiteracy 52% (1967)

Paper consumption a) Newsprint 3.2 kg per capita (1968)
b) Printing paper (other than newsprint) 0.6 kg per capita (1968)
Membership UNESCO, CERLAL

2 Past and Present

Since El Salvador was conquered by the Spanish, who came from Mexico in 1525, it formed part of the Spanish colonies directed by the "Capitanía General" in Guatemala. During that time, as in all Central American countries, literary life and the printing and selling of books was strictly controlled by the Spanish crown, and developed only a little in the Christian missions. Under these circumstances, there might have been printed, on a home-made press, by a Franciscan in the Salvadoranean province of Santa Ana, a little treatise on indigo, *El Puntero apuntado con Apuntes breves*. Experts are still at variance as to whether it was printed in 1641 (thus being the first print in Central America, twenty years before the introduction of printing in Guatemala), or some time after 1746. Long after the declaration of independence from Spain in 1821, and the forming of an independent republic at the dissolution of the Central American Republic (whose capital was in San Salvador), the country, after 1841, began to develop a small printing and bookselling industry. In the following years, too, booksellers came to settle, immigrants from Spain and from neighbour countries; and today about 80 publishers (fewer than 10% of them publishing books) and 35 bookshops are active in the country. Nearly all of them are in the capital, with only a few in Santa Ana and San Miguel. Their main contacts are with suppliers in Spain, Mexico, Argentina and the United States. In general commerce, dependence on the United States is strong, even though the latter is only one of the main customers and suppliers of the country (27% of El Salvador's exports and 31% of her imports). But West Germany and Japan, apart from some neighbour countries, are increasing their commercial contacts with El Salvador. Though she is the smallest country of Central America, El Salvador is the most intensively cultivated. There has been considerable industrial development recently, but agriculture is still the main source producing chiefly coffee.

Bibliography

J. C. Escobar, *La importancia del libro.* Exposición Salvadoreña en Tegucigalpa. (The importance of the book. Salvadoranean exhibition in Tegucigalpa.) San Salvador, Imprenta Nacional 1943. 17 pp.

A. Guerra Triguemos, *El libro, el hombre y la cultura.* Discurso de clausura de la exposición del libro americano Abril 1948 (Book, man and culture.) San Salvador, Ministerio de Cultura 1948. 33 pp.

3 Retail Prices

Publishers' catalogue prices, although legally not binding, are widely respected by Salvadoranean booksellers. Similarly, prices of imported books are subject to an exchange rate unified by custom and arrangement. Students get a 10% discount in all bookshops.

4 Organization

By general law, every industrial or commercial company has to belong to the
Asociación Salvadoreña de Empresas Industriales
(Salvadoranean Association of Industrial Enterprises)
27 Calle, Poniente No. 1041
San Salvador
Apart from contact among themselves within this corporation, the most important booksellers form the
Asociación de Libreros –
Comité Feria Internacional del Libro
(Booksellers' Association –

El Salvador

Committee of the International Book Fair)
Apartado Postal 66
San Salvador
This was founded in 1968 to organize the annual international book exhibition in San Salvador (→29), but also took over joint presentation with the government in any legal or parliamentary problem (→24) and the discussion of common arrangments for pricing, discounts, etc.

7 Sources of Information, Address Services

For book-trade queries, the most complete information could be obtained from the booksellers' association,
Asociación de Libreros
Comité Feria Internacional del Libro
(Booksellers' Association – Committee of
the International Book Fair)
Apartado Postal 66
San Salvador
Its special library on the country and the monthly bulletin of the
Cámara de Comercio e Industria de El
Salvador
(Chamber of Commerce and Industry)
Edificio Dueñas
San Salvador
are useful for inquiries of an economic nature. On the literature of the country, dates and figures can be found in the National Library,
Biblioteca Nacional
(National Library)
8a. Avenida Norte 228
San Salvador
There are no special address services in the country, but the *Associación de Libreros* (→4) has information on bookshops, while the Chamber of Commerce and Industry would be ready to give the addresses of their publisher and bookseller members.

Bibliography

The addresses of the book trade are contained in:

La Empresa del Libro en América Latina. (The Book in Latin America.) 2nd ed. Buenos Aires, Bowker Editores Argentina 1974. VIII, 307 pp.
pp. 163–164: El Salvador.
Economía Salvadoreña. (Salvadoranean economy.) San Salvador, Instituto de Estudios Económicos, Universidad de El Salvador 1952 ff. Semestral.

10 Books and Young People

Under the direction of the National Library, special events, lectures and invitations to visit the public libraries are organized from time to time.
During the *Feria Internacional del Libro* in October and November, one day is dedicated to children, a Sunday, on which children attending the fair are given a small book present and there are lectures on children's books, etc. (→29).

12 Taxes

Books are free of taxes in El Salvador. This applies to the sale and the production of books as well as imports.

15 National Bibliography, National Library

El Salvador's National Library was founded in 1870 and in 1970 stocked nearly 90,000 volumes:
Biblioteca Nacional
(National Library)
8a. Avenida Norte 228
San Salvador
Here there is an almost complete collection of books for the national book depository. The National Library is also the centre of the Librarians' Association,
Asociación Salvadoreña de Bibliotecarios
y Amigos de la Biblioteca
(Salvadoranean Association of Librarians
and Friends of the Library)
c/o Biblioteca Nacional

8a. Avenida Norte 228
San Salvador
The national network of libraries is formed by the National Library, 9 university and 191 school libraries, 54 special and 42 public libraries, a relatively large number for the smallest Central American country. Among them are the excellent library of the Organization of Central American States
Biblioteca Centroamericana,
Paseo Escalón
San Salvador
and the central library of the National University
Biblioteca Central de la Universidad de El Salvador,
7a. Avenida Sur 124
San Salvador
with 95,000 volumes–the biggest in the country.
National book production has only recently acquired an annual national bibliography, *Anuario Bibliográfico Salvadoreño,* started in 1970. Former titles can be found only from time to time, in the few monographs published on early Salvadoranean or Central American printing.

Bibliography

Anuario Bibliográfico Salvadoreño. (Salvadoranean Bibliographical Annual.) San Salvador, Biblioteca Nacional 1970 ff.
H. H. Orjuela, *Bibliografía Salvadoreña.* (Salvadoranean bibliography.) San Salvador, Dirección General de Publicaciones del Ministerio de Educación 1962. 60 pp.

16 Book Production

National book production, due to the limited number of publishers, is relatively small. Furthermore, as many authors publish at their own expense through small printing companies, the figures occasionally registered are not complete.

There are no continuous statistics; 27 first editions (16 of them general literature) are listed for 1967.

19 Paperbacks

Paperback series are widely distributed in the country, all of them of foreign origin. Their proportion of national book sales is estimated at between 60% and 70%.
Bookshops being the main sales outlets to the public, paperbacks are also sold in hotels, drugstores, supermarkets, etc.

21 Publishing

There are about 80 publishing companies in the country, many of them small firms combined with a printing plant and / or a newspaper. Only 10% of these firms, however, are publishers of books, and the government is very active in this field. There are, for instance, the publishing company of the Ministry of Education, with between 60 and 80 titles in its catalogue, the National Printers, and the publishing department of the University of El Salvador. Experts estimate the government's participation in national book production to amount to as much as 80%. But even including official publishers, the main field of publishing is literature.

23 Wholesale Trade

There are three wholesale companies working in El Salvador, mainly as distributors of books for big foreign publishers from Spain, the United States, Mexico and the Argentina. For booksellers they also order any book published in and outside the country, and export Salvadoranean books.

24 Retail Trade

There are 35 bookshops in the country, most of them also selling stationery, drawing materials, toys, etc. Books, above all paperbacks and magazines, are also sold in supermarkets, drugstores and hotels. The majority of them are in San Salvador, and a few in Santa Ana and San Miguel.

There is a tendency, among many traditional bookshops, however, to concentrate on their stationery departments, leaving out books. This is due to recent and continous parliamentary efforts to limit the booksellers' gross income on books in order to lower the price of books. This government initiative has so far been opposed with some success by booksellers (1970), who object on grounds of high costs for imported books and the need to hold large stocks to meet the requirements of a small book-buying public.

27 Book Imports

Because imported books constitute the largest part of local bookshops' business (90%), import figures provided quite useful information on the capacity of the national market. The sources, however, give different dates. Thus the national statistics for 1967 give a net value of 558,000 Colones (US $22,286), mainly from other Central American countries and the United States, but the annual of the Organization of Central American States has US $553,000 for the year 1968. This was divided up as follows:

Country	US$
Mexico	111,000
USA	67,000
Panama	58,000
Venezuela	45,000
Argentina	39,000
Others	233,000
Total	553,000

For Spain, still of traditional importance in the book trade, El Salvador ranks among the minor clients in Latin America. However, as in other cases, imports from Panama, Mexico and possibly Venezuela contain a good number of re-exports of Spanish books.

28 Book Exports

Due to the modest size of the national publishing industry, book exports are small. National sources give a value of 517,000 Colones for 1967 (US $20,680). The main customers have been the United States and the Central American neighbour countries.

29 Book Fairs

El Salvador has a tradition for organizing book exhibitions for the local public as well for those in neighbour countries. With 15 years' experience in national book exhibitions, the local booksellers together with the Ministry of Education founded an international book fair in 1969, where books are sold in a public park every October and November, and "national authors' day" and a "childrens' day" are held. More than 20,000 titles are exhibited, and during the third fair (1970) books worth US $21,500 were sold to 90,000 visitors. This fair is the biggest of its type in Central America and enjoys the participation of publishers from other Latin American countries, Spain and the United States.

Bibliography

J. C. ESCOBAR, *La importancia del libro*. Exposición Salvadoreña en Tegucigalpa. (The importance of the book. Salvadoranean exhibition in Tegucigalpa.) San Salvador, Imprenta Nacional 1943. 17 pp.

A. GUERRA TRIGUEMOS, *El libro, el hombre y la cultura*. Discuros de clausura de la exposición del libro americano Abril 1948. (Book, man and culture.) San Sal-

vador, Ministerio de Cultura 1948.
33 pp.

33 The Reviewing of Books

Apart from its eight newspapers with a total edition of 62,000 (1967) copies, El Salvador has 24 periodicals. A good number of the latter regularly publish book news and literary criticism. The total number of book reviews published annually is estimated to be 50 in newspapers (chiefly in *Prensa Gráfica*) and 100 in periodicals.

The three radio stations and the two TV-channels also, from time to time, report on books and have literary features.

Bibliography

Anaqueles. (Bookshelves.) San Salvador. Biblioteca Nacional. Irregular.

Cultura. (Culture.) San Salvador, Dirección General de Publicaciones del Ministerio de Educación 1955 ff. Quarterly.

ECA Estudios Centro Americanos. (Central American Studies.) San Salvador, Universidad José Simeón Cañas 1946 ff. Monthly.

Guión Literario. (Literary Guide.) San Salvador, Dirección General de Publicaciones 1956 ff. Monthly.

I. LOPEZ VELLECILOS, *El periodismo en El Salvador.* (Periodism in the El Salvador.) San Salvador, Editorial Universitaria 1964 ff. 480 pp.

French Guiana

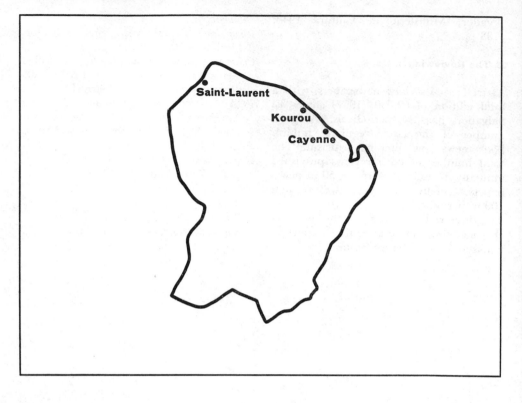

1 General Information

Area 91,000 km²
Population 44,392 (0.5 per km²–Negroes, Creoles, Asians, 3,000 tribal Indians)
Capital Cayenne (24,581)
Largest towns Cayenne (24,581), Saint-Laurent (6,000), Kourou (5,570)
Government Overseas Department within the French Community
Religion Predominantly Roman Catholic
National language French, also "Creole Patois"
Leading foreign languages Spanish, English
Weights, measures Metric system
Currency unit Franc Français (CFA) = 100 centimes (c)
Education Compulsory and free for 10 years; 2,334 pupils of 2nd degree enrolled (1967)
Illiteracy 28% (1950)

Paper consumption a) Newsprint 1.5 kg per capita (1968)
b) Printing paper (other than newsprint) 0.2 kg per capita (1967)
Membership UNESCO → (BTW I, France 8)

2 Past and Present

The coast of Guiana was discovered by the Spanish in 1499. In those days, it was thought of as the mysterious El Dorado. French Guiana, lying north of Brazil and east of Surinam, was first settled in 1604, when the French founded Cayenne. Penal settlements which gave the area its image for a long time were founded in 1852 around the mouth of the River Maroni and the Iles du Salut–which includes Devil's Island–and demolished in 1958.

General imports are: 73.5% from France, to 4.5% from the U.S.A. Exports of shrimps, timber and agricultural products go to France, the United States, Canada and the United Kingdom.

7 Sources of Information, Address Services

Bibliothèque Franconie
(Library Franconie)
Cayenne

15 National Bibliography, National Library

The only public library is the
Bibliothèque Franconie
(Library Franconie)
Cayenne
with 120,000 visitors in 1966. There are also two school libraries.

Bibliography

A. ABONNEL, J. HERAULT, R. SABAN, *Bibliographie de la Guayane française.* (Bibliography of French Guiana.) 2 vols. Paris 1947.

24 Retail Trade

There are four bookshops in Cayenne:
Librairie-Papeterie MM. Beaufort
16 rue du Lieutenant-Brassé
Cayenne

La Boutique Bleue R. Tillet
Av. Pasteur/Boîte Postale 243
Cayenne

Librairie-Papeterie Emilio Gratien
25, av. du Général de Gaulle
Cayenne
and
Librairie-Papeterie Universelle
Mme. Laguerre
26, rue Lallouette
Cayenne

27 Book Imports

Of the total imports 75% are from France, nearly 5% from the USA

French Guiana's book imports from France
1966 40,000 FF
1970 589,000 FF

31 Bibliophily

Association Les Amis du Livre
(Association Friends of the Book)
c/o Bibliothèque Franconie
Cayenne

33 The Reviewing of Books

1 daily Newspaper, 2,000 copies (1967).
8 periodicals = 40,000 copies (1967).
4,200 radio receivers, 1,300 TV sets.

Grenada and the Grenadines

1 General Information

Area 344 km²

Population 105,000 (305 per km²)

Capital St. George's (8,644); *largest islands:*
Grenadines (Carriacou, 8,179);
Petit Martinique

Largest towns St. George's (8,644); Grenville
(1,900); Gouyave (or Charlotte Town) (1,760)

Government An independent country, within the
Commonwealth, since February 7, 1974

Religion Anglican (25%), Methodist, Plymouth
Brethren, Roman Catholics (63%), Salvation
Army and Seventh Day Adventists

National language English

Leading foreign language French Patois is still used
by older people but is on the decline

Weights, measures British Imperial System

Currency unit The Eastern Caribbean Dollar,
(EC$) comprising 100 cents. Exchange rate is
EC$4.80 to £1 Sterling.

Education Primary education is free and compulsory but is not enforced. 57 Primary schools
have a population of 30,321 pupils. There are
11 Secondary Schools with a population of
3,039 students. A Technical Centre serves the
Government schools and offers day and evening
classes for adults. Domestic and commercial
art classes–day and evening–are offered at an
Institute. There are 26 housecraft and handi-
craft centres and departments

Illiteracy Rate is low

2 Past and Present

The early British settlers were harassed by the Caribs of whom there is little trace today. Originally colonized by the French, Grenada changed hands between the British and French until it was restored to Great Britain by the Treaty of Versailles in 1783. Later a rebellion against British rule in 1796 had be suppressed. It was a member of the defunct W.I. Federation from 1958–1962. In 1967 it became an Associated State in voluntary association with Great Britain. In 1974, under the ruling Government and despite the opposition of the other parties, it achieved its independence.
The population is predominantly of African descent; there are some East Indians and in the 1960 census nine Caribs were noted.
Despite Government's encouragement to pioneer industries, there is little activity other than in the secondary processing of local produce. There are a few consumer industries. Efforts are concentrated on developing the tourist industry which is on the upward trend. Grenada is the base of the largest number and greatest variety of charter yachts in the region. Between 1965 and 1970, stay-over visitors more than doubled; cruise liners increased from 38 to 125, and yachts calling from 345 to 1,150. Apart from the construction of hotels to support the tourist industry, personal land investment by overseas owners is encouraged. Very modern houses are being built by persons who spend part of the year– usually the winter months–in the Island.

Bibliography

BR. F. SWAN, *The spread of printing, Western Hemisphere: The Caribbean area.* Amsterdam, Vangendt 1970. 47 pp.
pp. 26–29: Grenada.

7 Sources of Information, Address Services

The
Public Library
St. George's.

15 National Bibliography, National Library

Limited library facilities are reported and no functions of a National Library or listing of local publications are undertaken.

21 Publishing

Government Reports and other official publications are printed by the Government Printer. Printers in Trinidad & Tobago list Grenada clients in their books.

27 Book Imports

No details are available. Books are imported from the United Kingdom mainly and also the United States of America and the larger regional countries.

35 Micellaneous

a) *Newspapers, Magazines*
   There is one "daily" newspaper published five days each week; there are two weeklies. There is a keen market for Trinidad & Tobago daily and weekly newspapers.
b) *Radio*
   The Government owned and operated West Indian Broadcasting Station (WIBS) network links Grenada, St Lucia, St Vincent and Dominica. Programmes are non-commercial. The need for financial support by wholly or partly sponsored programmes from commercial advertising is being discussed.

Guadeloupe

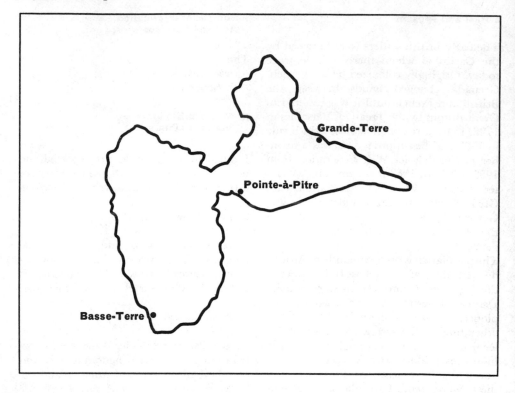

1 General Information

Area 1,779 km²
Population 318,000 (179 per km²)
Capital Basse Terre, Island of Basse Terre (15,732)
Largest towns Pointe-à-Pitre, GrandeTerre(29,522);
  Basse-Terre (15,732)
Government Overseas Department of the French
  Community
Religion Predominantly Roman-Catholic
National language French and Creole "patois"
Leading foreign languages English, Spanish
Weights, measures Metric system
Currency unit Franc Français (*CFA*) = 100 centimes
Education Compulsory for eight years. 174 students
  in a technical college (1969)
Illiteracy 35%

Paper consumption a) Newsprint 1.1 kg per inhabitant
  b) Printing paper (other than
  newsprint) 1.1 kg per inhabitant
Membership UNESCO (→BTW I, France 8)

2 Past and Present

Guadeloupe, lying in the centre of the Leeward Islands about 800 km south-east of Puerto Rico in the West Indies, was discovered by Columbus in 1493. European colonization began 1635 with the arrival of French *flibustiers*, and the islands formally became a French Colony in 1674. In September 1956 Guadeloupe voted in favour of the new constitution of the Fifth French Republic and remained an Overseas Department within the new French Community.

In early colonial times, people on Guadeloupe depended on direct shipments from European France for merchandise, first among them books and periodicals.

Nearly no commercial connections existed to its neighbour islands and to the South American continent. The exception was and still is her relations with Martinique, the smaller but somewhat more important French overseas department with nearly the same number of inhabitants. Martinique, the north-eastern of the Lesser Islands, separated from Guadeloupe only by the British island of Dominica, is important for Guadeloupe as a transfer point for a number of goods.

When printers and booksellers settled on Martinique during the first half of the 18th century, they soon directed a good part of their activities to the inhabitants of Guadeloupe. Similarly today, while a local newspaper and 13 booksellers exist in Guadeloupe, a few of the latter are branches of Martinique firms, so that some books and newspapers coming to Guadeloupe arrive via the neighbouring island. France, however, is still the most important supplier to the island, and the main sources of professional information for the Guadeloupan book trade are in Paris. Only a small percentage of its contact is to publishers in the USA.

Pointe-à-Pitre, the biggest city, became the centre of the book trade, with two thirds of the local trade, the rest being situated in the capital, Basse-Terre. Booksellers on Guadeloupe are suffering the same problems as many colleagues in Latin America: the distances from their main suppliers in Europe. However, Guadeloupe booksellers –because of lack of local publishing and the strong interest their customers of French origin have in the literary life in the European homeland–apparently feel the distance more; newspapers and magazines brought in by air freight distribute reviews and advertisements of new books quite early to their customers, while shipments of the books take more than a month by parcel post.

Bibliography

Br. F. Swan, *The spread of printing, Western Hemisphere: The Caribbean area.* Amsterdam. Vangendt 1970. 47 pp.

3 Retail Prices

There is no intervention in sales prices by the Government of Guadeloupe. By general custom, booksellers grant a 10% discount to students on the normal retail price of any book. The local retail price of imported books, which means all books sold on the islands, is 20% higher than in Europe, to cover the expenses of transports, etc. For the same reason, newspapers brought by surface mail have an extra charge of 10% on the sales prices in Europe.

4 Organization

There is a syndicate of bookstores for the departments of Guadeloupe and Martinique,

Syndicat des Libraires
du Martinique et Guadeloupe
(Syndicate of the Booksellers of
Martinique and Guadeloupe)

Guadeloupe

c/o *Librairie La Cité Universitaire*
86 et 88, rue Victor-Sévère
Fort-de-France, Martinique
which acts occasionally in the name of
members in the case of common problems
with the local government. Half of the
31 companies which form the book trade
in both territories are members. On
Guadeloupe, apart from the fact that the
bookshops are concentrated in the two
cities of Pointe-à-Pitre and Basse-Terre,
collaboration among booksellers is relatively infrequent.

7 Sources of Information, Address Services

Information about the book trade on
Guadeloupe should be sought from professional institutions in France (→BTW I,
France 4). For instance, the
Syndicat National des Éditeurs
(National Syndicate of Publishers)
117, Boulevard Saint-Germain
F 75 Paris V France
has a certain amount of material on the
book trade in the territory of Guadeloupe,
especially in its professional library.

10 Books and Young People

Reading among young people is promoted
occasionally by lectures and other public
activities in the local libraries, principally
in the libraries in various "Maisons des
Jeunes et de la Culture", for instance the
Maison des Jeunes et de la Culture,
Bibliothèque
(Library of the House for Young People and
for Culture)
Pointe-à-Pitre
and in similar institutions in Basse-Terre
and Moule. These libraries have a good
selection of books from France for children
and young people.

12 Taxes

Books enjoy a reduced sales tax of 3.5%
on Guadeloupe. As for the importation of
books, local government does not charge
any taxes, respecting the UNESCO Florence
agreement on the free flow of books,
signed by France in the name of Guadeloupe as one of her Overseas Departments
(→BTW I, International Section 4, 27, 28).

16 Book Production

Because of the non-existence of local
publishers, there is scarcely any local
book production. The exceptions are
brochures printed for the Government or
commercial institutions on the islands.

24 Retail Trade

There are 13 bookstores in Guadeloupe
(1970), 8 of them situated in Pointe-à-Pitre,
island of Grande-Terre. The rest are concentrated in the capital, Basse-Terre, on
the other island of the territory. The three
supermarkets active on the islands sell
paperbacks in their stationery departments, while on the other hand most of
the bookshops realize a good part of their
total sales through stationery.
With the exception of the above mentioned
supermarkets, people in Guadeloupe buy
their books in bookshops only. Books are
offered neither at news-stands nor in the
hotels. One of the important booksellers
offers direct sales, mainly of encyclopedias
and gift books, through salesmen visiting
customers in their homes and offices, and
two firms have installed a department for
second-hand books, although these are
mainly paperbacks.

27 Book Imports

Book imports are the only source of Guadeloupe's book trade, so the figures for this

represent the total sales on the islands. While only a few paperbacks and general titles imported from the United states have reached the islands in recent years, 95% or more of the annual imports come from France. According to her statistics, the islanders of Guadeloupe increased their book acquisitions remarkably as can be seen from the following figures stating French book exports to Guadeloupe:

Year	US$ approx.
1966	180,000
1968	355,000
1969	630,000
1970	728,000

In view of the above mentioned facts, annual sales of books at retail price are estimated at $ 1 ½ million, this being the annual amount spent on books–$ 4.75 per capita.

33 The Reviewing of Books

As for book criticism, Guadeloupe readers depend on French periodicals. The local newspaper, "France Antilles" (published in two editions, one in Guadeloupe and one in Martinique), only occasionally offers book reviews and literary criticism. With 30,000 radio receivers and nearly 8,000 television sets, cultural radio transmissions from near-by stations play a certain role in cultural information.

Guatemala

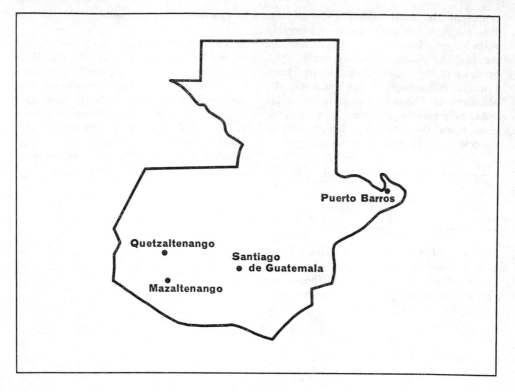

1 General Information

Area 108,889 km²
Population 4,864,000 (45 per km²)
Capital Santiago de Guatemala (768,957)
Largest towns Guatemala (768,957); Quetzaltenango (54,487); Puerto Barros (29,435); Mazaltenango (23,932)
Government Presidential Republic, divided into 22 districts
Religion Roman Catholic predominant, Protestant minorities
National language(s) Spanish (and some Indian dialects)
Leading foreign language English
Weights, measures Metric system; also old Spanish measures
Currency unit Quetzal (Q) = 100 centavos (cts)
Education Compulsory. 23,000 students in 9 universities
Illiteracy 62% (1964 census)

Paper consumption a) Newsprint 1.3 kg per inhabitant (1968)
b) Printing paper (other than newsprint) 0.6 kg per inhabitant (1968)
Membership UNESCO

2 Past and Present

Bibliography

As the site of an ancient Maya civilization, Guatemala must have had an active literary and even "publishing" life, which included papermaking as an independent Mesoamerican invention, before the arrival of the Europeans. In 1524 the Spanish, coming from Mexico, conquered the country, and it is from there that Guatemala was directed during colonial times. These centuries were marked by dependence on the supply of books from the mother country in Europa–part of Spain's policy–so that real local book trade and publishing industry could not develop. The exceptions were mainly religious books, which were printed in Guatemala since the introduction of printing in 1660 by a Spanish bishop. The name of the first printer, José de Pineda Ibarra, is conserved in the name of the official publishing company of the Ministry of Education.

Shortly before independence, booksellers settled in Guatemala, but only thereafter, from 1839 onwards, did book life take an enormous upturn. Thus, it is in the first Republican years that the oldest booksellers' catalogues and popular almanacs were printed. The combination of bookshops with small publishing and printing firms is still characteristic–leaving aside the important role of the government publishers. Booksellers and publishers are concentrated in the capital city, with a small number of firms in Quetzaltenango. Their common problem is a lack of finances, and a dependence on imported books and periodicals. Only in the case of local textbooks do booksellers work under normal conditions, while for nearly all the rest of their sales of imported books they suffer price problems and international monetary movements. Guatemala's first supplier and customer of books is Spain, followed by Argentina and Mexico.

V. M. Diaz, *Historia de la imprenta en Guatemala, desde la colonia hasta la época actual.* (History of printing in Guatemala, from colonial times to the present epoch.) Guatemala City, Tipografía Nacional 1930. 181 pp.

V. Leon de Gandarias, *Jornadas periodísticas.* Etapas notables de la prensa guatemalteca. (Important stages in the development of the Guatemalan press.) Guatemala, Diario de Centro América (1959?). 80 pp.

J. T. Medina, *Historia de la imprenta en los antiguos dominios españoles de América y Oceanía.* (The history of printing in the ancient Spanish dominions of America and Oceania.) 2 vols. Santiago de Chile, Fondo Histórico y Bibliográfico José Toribio Medina 1958. CXLI, 542; XV, 540 pp.
v.II, pp. 17–201: Guatemala.

M. Merida, *Origen de la imprenta en Guatemala.* Su desarrollo hasta la independencia. (Origin of printing in Guatemala. Its development up to Independence.) Guatemala, Biblioteca Nacional 1956. 66 pp.

M. R. R. Morales, *La imprenta en Guatemala.* (Printing in Guatemala.) Guatemala C. A., Ministerio de Educación Pública 1960. 78 pp.
A short history.

J. E. O'Ryan, *Bibliografía Guatemalteca de los siglos XVII–XVIII* (Guatemalan bibliography of the 17th–18th centuries.) 2nd ed. Volume I of the "Colección Bibliográfica del Tercer Centenario de la Introducción de la Imprenta en Centroamérica". Guatemala, Editorial del Ministerio de Educación Pública 'José de Pineda Ibarra' 1961. 124 pp.

J. L. Reyes M., *Anotaciones para la historia de un libro.* El puntero apuntado con apuntes breves. (Notes on the history of a book.) "Colección Bibliográfica

del Tercer Centenario de la Introducción de la Imprenta en Centroamérica". Guatemala, Editorial del
Ministerio de Educación Pública 'José
de Pineda Ibarra' 1960. 112 pp.
This book is one of two special volumes
of the notable series on bibliography
and history of the book in Guatemala,
printed between 1960 and 1964 on occasion of the 300th anniversary of the
introduction of printing in Central
America.

A. A. M. STOLS, *La introducción de la imprenta en Guatemala*. Ensayo en com-
memoración del tercer centenario 1660–
1960. (The introduction of printing in
Guatemala. Essay commemorating the
three hundreth anniversary, 1660–1960).
México, Universidad Nacional Autónoma de México 1960. 37 pp.

L. S. THOMPSON, *Printing in Colonial Spanish
America*. Hamden Conn., Archon Books
1962. 108 pp.
pp. 71–75: Guatemala.

3 Retail Prices

Retail prices of books are not fixed by any
law in Guatemala. However, publishers'
prices are respected by the booksellers
who, by general agreement, charge a 10%
surcharge on imported books. Similarly,
students receive a general 10% discount
on books they buy, and government institutions and libraries receive a 15% reduction on the retail price.
Apart from the standard pricing policy,
there is no regulation for contacts between
publishers and booksellers, nor for booksellers among themselves.

4 Organization

There is no professional organization in
Guatemala's book trade, neither on a
national nor on a local basis. Booksellers
and publishers are obliged to join the
general commercial or industrial organizations. In special cases, irregular meetings are held by the booksellers in the
capital, while, under the leadership of the
government publishing companies, efforts
are made to form an association of firms
belonging to this part of the trade.

7 Sources of Information, Address Services

Commercial information about the book
trade in Guatemala can be obtained from
Cámara de Comercio de Guatemala
(Guatemalan Chamber of Commerce)
10a. Calle 3–80, Zona 1
GCA Guatemala-City
and queries related to the country's litera-
ture from the
Asociación de Autores Nacionales
(Association of National Authors)
9a. Avenida 11–55, Zona 1
GCA Guatemala-City
There are no specialized agencies offering
address services in Guatemala.

Bibliography

The addresses of all branches of the book
trade are contained in
La Empresa del Libro en América Latina. (The
Book in Latin America.) 2nd ed. Buenos
Aires, Bowker Editores Argentina 1974.
VIII, 307 pp.
pp. 165–167: Guatemala.

12 Taxes

The sales of books in Guatemala are
subject to a reduced sales tax. The production of books is charged with a 1.5% tax.
For imported books, taxes are collected
by a system of stamps on the corresponding
invoices. As any shipment of merchandise
to Guatemala has to be accompanied by a
legally valid invoice, further charges are
made–in this case to the exporter–for
registration of these invoices.

15 National Bibliography, National Library

Neither the National Library nor any other institution publishes any regular bibliography of Guatemalan books. However, on the ocasion of the 300th anniversary of the introduction of printing in Central America, this lack was partly filled by the publication of a notable series of bibliographies, covering the years 1660 to 1960 in 10 volumes, with two extra volumes on special themes. These titles give a complete list of national publications and, as regards the first two centuries, include books on Guatemala published outside the country (→2: Bibliography).
The National Library,
Biblioteca Nacional
(National Library)
5a. Avenida 7–26, Zona 1
GCA Guatemala-City
was founded in 1879. Its "Memorias" give some bibliographical information on the country's book trade. The report of the fiscal year 1970/71 shows 84,000 readers, and the acquisition of 2,200 books, while older figures show a total of 85,000 titles in stock. The associated "Hemeroteca Nacional" comprises a number of 28,000 newspaper and periodicals, thus being one ot the most complete collection of this type in Latin America.
National sources report 14 university libraries, 36 school libraries, 89 special and 79 public libraries within the national library system.

Bibliography

P. AVICENNE, *Bibliographical services throughout the world 1965–69*. Paris, UNESCO 1972. 310 pp.
pp. 132–134: Guatemala.
R. BRAN A., *Vida y misión de una hemeroteca.* (Life and mission of a newspaper collection.) Guatemala, Editorial del Ministerio de Educación Publica 'José de Pineda Ibarra' 1967. 96 pp.

G. DARDEN C., *Indice bibliográfico Guatemalteco 1959–60.* (Guatemalan bibliographical index 1959–60.) Guatemala, Instituto Guatemalteco-Americano 1961. 130 pp.
J. E. O'RYAN, *Bibliografía Guatemalteca de los siglos XVII–XVIII.* (Guatemalan bibliography of the 17th–18th centuries.) 2nd ed. Volume I of the 'Colección Bibliográfica del Tercer Centenario de la Introducción de la Imprenta en Centroamérica'. Guatemala, Editorial del Ministerio de Educación Pública 'José de Pineda Ibarra' 1961. 124 pp.
G. VALENZUELA R., *Bibliografía Guatemalteca 1821–1960.* (Guatemalan bibliography, years 1821–1960.) 8 volumes (= vols III to X of the 'Colección Bibliográfica del Tercer Centenario de la Introducción de la Imprenta en Centroamérica'.) Guatemala, Tipografía Nacional 1961–64.
I. ZIMMERMANN, *Current national bibliographies of Latin America.* Gainesville, Florida, University of Florida Press 1971. X, 139 pp.
pp. 78–81: Guatemala.

16 Book Production

The national production of books is characterized by the high portion of private publications, books published directly by the authors or printers. Thus, the figures of 335 titles for 1966, and of 70 in 1968, only give a part of the total of books published in the country.
Average editions are 1,500 copies. 80% of the national books are textbooks for the primary and secondary level. Nearly all the rest are fiction and poetry by local authors.

21 Publishing

Local publishing is firmly based on the direct activity of authors and printers.

Guatemala

Regular publishing companies number about twenty. The main companies are three official organizations, under the direction of the Ministry of Public Education, the National University, and the National Printing Plant.

24 Retail Trade

There are about 65 bookshops in Guatemala. Nearly all of them are located in the capital, but some have branches in Quetzaltenango. While the first bookshops were started by immigrants coming from Spain, present-day book firms were founded in the 20th century, even though a number of owners are of Spanish origin. Spain continues to exert a strong influence on the Guatemalan book trade, as trade rules and information as well as the books sold in Guatemala come mainly from the former mother country. The bookstores are private ventures, of small size and financed by the owners, but during the last years the rise of international book chains (mainly for the sales of periodicals and paperbacks, and credit sales through salesmen) is also beginning to be felt in Guatemala. But public still buy the majority of their books in the bookstores, and only small supermarkets offer paperbacks and periodicals. There are also some companies specializing in technical and medical books. Most booksellers in Guatemala, however, still run general bookshops.

26 Antiquarian Book Trade, Auctions

Although a few booksellers handle antiquarian books as a small sideline, no special antiquarian bookshops exist in Guatemala. But there is one of the few institutions in the world dedicated to the rare book, in this case to American and other early printed books:

Museo del Libro Antiguo
(Museum of Old Books)

Portal Municipal, Plaza Mayor
GCA La Antigua
Situated in the old capital of the country, it was founded in 1956 and has a collection of 4,000–5,000 old books and early manuscripts.

27 Book Imports

The market in Guatemala is dominated by the imported book, mostly in the Spanish language. 90% of the books sold in the country are of foreign origin, the majority coming from Mexico, Panama, the Argentina and Spain. The relatively low position of Spain is surprising (Spanish sources quote sales of about US $ 100,000 in 1969) compared with her exports to other Latin American countries. However, one can presume that Spanish books often reach Guatemala by way of a neighbouring country, delivered by a regional distributor; thus, for example, many shipments are recorded as of Panamerican origin.

Among the non-Spanish-speaking countries, the United States are the leading supplier, followed by the United Kingdom, Germany (F.R.) and France.

The official statistics are as follows:

Year	US $
1967	247,000
1968	1,766,000

The big difference between those two years can only be accidental, but the last figure is nearer to the trends in recent years.

28 Book Exports

The publishing industry has a difficult position among its competitors in the Spanish-speaking countries. The best results have been in neighbouring countries: El Salvador (which, in 1968, received more than half of Guatemala's book exports), Honduras and Mexico.

196

Latest available statistics show a decrease:

Year	US $
1967	197,000
1968	49,000

This difference may not be typical. The national publishers have a difficult position on the foreign book market, due to the high cost of paper and the disadvantage of a small local market. Thus, even minimal results are of special importance to the publishers.

32 Literary Prizes

There are three literary prizes, awarded annually, which have attracted international attention.

The most traditional one is the prize given by the municipality of Quetzaltenango, on 12 September, during the famous *Juegos Florales de Quetzaltenango*, which is a cultural event whith international participation.

An official prize is also awarded by the Ministry of Public Education through its Institute of Fine Arts, in September, which thus bears the name *Premio Literario 13 de Septiembre*. It was founded over twenty years ago.

Furthermore, there is another private venture in this field, the National Association of Journalist's *Quetzal*, named for the small statue of a quetzal bird carved in jade which constitutes the prize. Even though this is the most recent of the literary prizes, it soon became famous when it was awarded to the Nobel Prize author, Miguel Angel Asturias.

34 Graphic Arts

The history of Guatemala's graphic arts dates back to early colonial times, initiated by the local church authorities in 1660. It increased enormously after independence from Spain in 1839. Even though most of the companies are still small firms, their importance to local authors as co-publishers of their books have given to them an important place in the nation's literary life. (→2).

Guyana

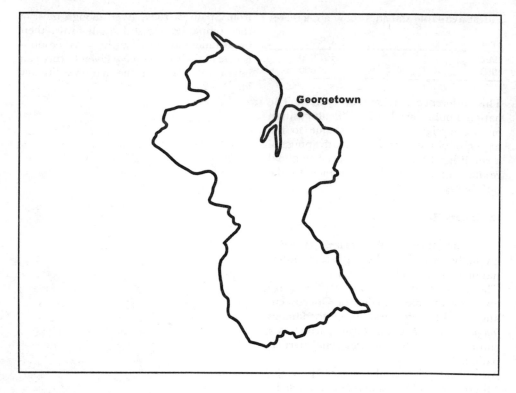

1 General Information

Area 141,000 km²
Population 725,000 (1975: 5.2 per km²)
Capital Georgetown (200,000)
Government Co-operative Republic. Head of the State is the President. The Council of Ministers (Executive Body) is responsible to Parliament.
Religion Principal denominations: Anglican, Roman Catholic, other Christian bodies, Hindus, Muslims
National language English (official language); Hindi, Urdu and Amerindian languages are spoken as well
Weights, measures British Imperial System; metric system to be introduced
Currency unit Guyana dollar ($G) = 100 cents

Education Compulsory between the ages of 6 and 14, free between the ages of 5 and 16. 418 state-aided primary and secondary schools. 190,000 pupils (all schools in 1970). 18 science and technical trade schools. 1 university
Illiteracy 15–20%
Paper consumption a) Newsprint 0.9 kg per inhabitant (1970)
b) Printing paper (other than newsprint) 0.6 kg per inhabitant (1965)
Membership UNESCO

2 Past and Present

As a former British colony (British Guiana) Guyana (independent since 1966) maintains strong ties with the United Kingdom. This is reflected in the importance books imported from Great Britain enjoy with the national readership. Strong cultural relations apart from Britain exist primarily with the Caribbean Islands.

3 Retail Prices

The local selling prices for books are based on landed costs.

7 Sources of Information, Adress Services

Inquiries could be addressed to the
Public Free Library
76–77 Main Street
P.O.B. 110
Georgetown

15 National Bibliography, National Library

The
Public Free Library
76–77 Main Street
P.O.B. 110
Georgetown
acts as national centre for bibliographical information.

Bibliography

A select Bibliography of the Works of Guyanese and on Guyana. Georgetown, Public Free Library 1967. 51 pp.

TH. KABDEBO, *Libraries in Guyana.* In: Encyclopedia of Library and Information Science, vol. 10, pp. 246–249. New York, M. Dekker 1973.

16 Book Production

Guyana published 22 books in 1971. 18 of them were in the field of social sciences.

21 Publishing

Four publishing houses are more or less printers, doing some book and pamphlet publishing occasionally.

24 Retail Trade

The country has 13 bookshops including some mayor firms.

27 Book Imports

In 1970 Guyana imported books für $G 1,245,981. The leading supplies were:

Country	$G
United Kingdom	759,190
USA	255,608
Hongkong	148,400
Canada	20,835

80% of the imports of periodicals came from the United Kingdom (1970).
The Guyana Government has declared that it will be the sole importer of all books coming into Guyana, and that all educational books for use in schools will be provided free of charge to students.

The Government agency for the importation of books is the
Books, Stationery, Sports Equipment and Radio Division
Guyana National Georgetown Trading Corporation Ltd.

28 Book Exports

The country exported "printed books and pamphlets" at the value of US$ 62,000 in 1970.

Haiti

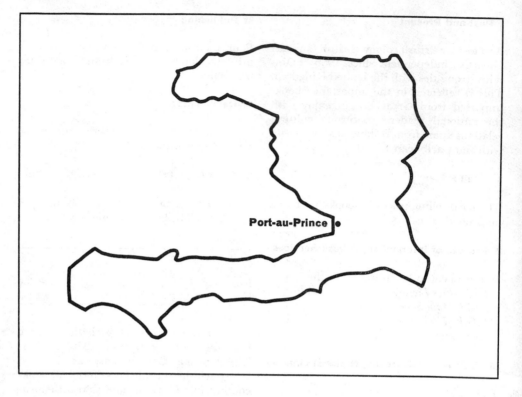

1 General Information

Area 27,500 km²
Population 5,500,000 (1971; 200 per km²)
Capital Port-au-Prince (500,000)
Government A President, elected for life, governs the country, supported by a cabinet
Religion Catholic
Official language French, spoken and written by 10% of the population
National language Creole, French based language of everyday life, spoken by all the inhabitants of the country
Leading foreign language English
Weights, measures Metric system
Currency Gourde (1 gourde = 100 Centimes)
Education Throughout the whole country, the number of those enjoying secondary education does not exceed 35,000, and the number of university students is not greater than 1,700 (figures for 1972–1973)

Illiteracy 90%
Paper consumption a) Newsprint 0.1 kg per inhabitant (1969)
b) Printing paper (other than newsprint) 0.04 kg per inhabitant (1969)

200

2 Past and Present

Even in colonial times, in the second half of the eighteenth century, there were printers in Cabo Francés and Puerto Principe, amongst them "Les Imprimeries Royales du Cap et Port-au-Prince", who published numerous books dealing with scientific and literary themes.

With national independence in 1804, the printing, publishing and circulation of books received great impetus. The first bibliographical document published in Haiti was the "Acta de Independencia" ("Document of Independence"), signed on 1 January 1804 and published by the Government Press in 1814. This was the first publication in the republican history of Latin America.

In the years following, important publications in the fields of history and literature were stimulated by the State of Haiti. Petión, the first republican president, said: "Education gives man the dignity of being a human being." Both he and King Christophe (1806–18) promoted the establishment of printers, the publication of books and the development of education. In 1816 the "L'Imprimerie du Roi" ("Royal Printing-Office") was initiated in Cap Haïtien, which started to publish the "L'Almanach Royal" ("Royal Almanac"). There are also a lot of books by English, French and North American authors on the struggle for independence and the beginnings of the life of the Republic. The first Haitian book translated into another language was probably the "Código Rural de Boyer" of 1826. "The Rural Code of Haiti" (in French and English, London, Macmillan 1827) was published in London in 1827 by His Majesty's Stationery Office. Since then, the publishing trade with regard to Haiti has been characterized by three types of works: a) books published in Haiti, b) books written outside Haiti by Haitian nationals about political and social questions, c) books about the history and ethnology of the country, published abroad by foreigners.

Special mention should be made of the historical studies of Thomas Madiou (1847–8) and in the second half of the nineteenth century, of a series of studies written by outstanding intellectuals against racism.

The most important of these books is "De l'égalité des races humaines" by Anténor Firmin (Paris, Cotillon 1885). It is considered to be one of the most outstanding works of Haitian intellectual life.

Another remarkable literary figure is Jacques Roumain (1905–44). His novel "Gouverneurs de la rosée" has been translated into more than ten languages and is *the* best seller of Haitian literature.

With a rate of illiteracy of 90%, it is quite obvious that any reference to the book market of Haiti must take into consideration the underdevelopment of the country reflected in the cultural and educational fields by a high rate of illiteracy as well as the very low level of consumption.

Bibliography

G. FURLONG, *Orígines del arte tipográfico en América.* (The origins of the art of typography in America.) Buenos Aires, Ed. Huarpes 1947. 225 pp.
Bibliography on pp. 215–225.–Early printing history of Haiti: p. 117.
BR. F. SWAN, *The spread of printing, Western Hemisphere: The Caribbean area.* Amsterdam, Vangendt 1970. 47 pp.
pp. 32–36: Haiti.

3 Retail Prices

Almost the whole book market is supplied by foreign countries, mainly France. No customs tariffs are levied on the import of books. There is no price control either, so that prices are often fixed by the bookshops. Prices are very high, taking into consideration the low living standards of the country and the difference between the value of the local currency and that of the country supplying the books.

4 Organization

In 1972 the
Association des Libraires Haïtiens
(Association of Haitian Booksellers)
c. o. *Librairie "La Pléiade"*
RH Port-au-Prince
was founded with special emphasis on the problems of the rate of exchange and the prices of imported books.

7 Sources of Information, Address Services

Inquiries should be sent to the
Chambre de Commerce d'Haïti
(Chamber of Commerce of Haiti)
Cité de l'Exposition
RH Port-au-Prince
or to the "Association des Libraires Haïtiens" (→4).
→15.

10 Books and Young People

The only books for young people are manuals, textbooks, and some books available in the libraries of certain private schools, or to a lesser extent in bookshops.

12 Taxes

No taxes are levied on the import of books.

14 Copyright

Haiti is a member of the Universal Copyright convention with the effective date of 16 September, 1955 (→BTW I, International Section 14, and annex 5b).
The internal legal stipulations recognize all rights inherent in intellectual property. However, these rights are rarely exercised because of the small number of books produced.

15 National Bibliography, National Library

For bibliographies the following publications may be consulted:
MARX BISSAIN, *Dictionaire de bibliographie haïtienne.* (Dictionary of Haitian bibliography.) The Scarecrow Press, Washington 1951.–Covers the period 1492–1949.
SIDNEY W. MINTZ, et al., *A selective social scientific bibliography of the Republic of Haiti.* Washington D.C., Revista Interamericana de Ciencias Sociales (Interamerican Review of Social Sciences), vol. II, No. 3, 1963.
There are also other bibliographical sources about the Caribbean Area which include Haiti.
LAMBROS COMITAS, *Caribbeana 1900–1965, a tropical bibliography.* Seattle, Publ. for Research Institute for the Study of Man, University of Washington 1968.
Bibliografía de Centroamérica y del Caribe. (Bibliography of Central America and the Caribbean Area.) Madrid 1956. (Junta Técnica de Archivos, Bibliotecas y Museos. Ediciones conmemorativas del centenario del Cuerpo Facultativo, 1858–1959.–Committee for Archives, Libraries and Museums. Memorial publications on the occasion of the 100th anniversary of the College, 1858–1959.) Compiled under the auspices of UNESCO by the "Agrupación de bibliográfica Cubana José Toribio Medina".
The National Library of Haiti is the
Bibliotèque Nationale d'Haïti
(National Library of Haiti)
Rue du Centre
RH Port-au-Prince

For bibliographical information one can contact this library, but also the following institutions:

Institut d'Histoire et de Géographie
(Institute for History and Geography)
RH Port-au-Prince

Centre Haïtien d'Investigations Sociales
(CHIS)
(Haitian Centre of Social Studies)
RH Port-au-Prince

Bibliotèque Institution Saint Louis
de Gonzague
(Library Institution Saint Louis
de Gonzague)
Rue du Centre
RH Port-au-Prince

→7.

Bibliography

I. ZIMMERMANN, *Current national biblio-graphies of Latin America*. Gainesville, Florida, University of Florida Press 1971. X, 139 pp.
pp. 110–112: Haiti.

16 Book Production

From 1963 to 1968 the production of books was as follows*

Year	Total titles	Art	Geo-graphy	Liter-ature	Philos-ophy	Others
1963	25	1	1	14	8	1
1964	25	5	2	5	8	5
1965	19	–	3	10	4	2
1966	84	2	3	68	8	3
1967	18	–	2	8	7	1
1968	14	2	2	2	–	8

Guide Économique de la Republique d'Haïti. (Economic Guide of the Republic of Haiti.) Port-au-Prince, p. 456.
According to the *Dictionaire de Biblio-graphie Haïtienne* (→15), the total number

* Institut Haïtien de Statistique (Haitian Institute of Statistics)

of books and pamphlets published in Haiti or abroad by Haitians between 10 January 1804 and 31 December 1949 is 4,318.
In general, the modern publication of books is financed by subscriptions from friends and by official support. Only books that are published commercially are counted.
→21.

17 Translations

In the whole history of publishing in the country, there have been no translations by foreign authors. Only some official political books were translated from French into English or Spanish, and from French into Creole. The Haitian reader receives French translations from France.

21 Publishing

The most active Port-au-Prince publishing houses are *L'Imprimerie Henri Deschamps (Boulevard Dessalines)*, which produces text-books for schools, and *Les Presses Nationales (Rue du Centre)*. The limited publishing activity in Haiti is due to the restricted book market, and the political atmosphere. Therefore, in the last few years, the pro-duction and market of Haitian books has increased outside the country. The best writers, poets and sociologists are abroad. Thus emigration has led to the fact that in the USA and Canada there is just as large a number of Haitian readers as there is in Haiti–and with a higher purchasing power.
In the last few years the most important literary and scientific works by Haitian authors have been published outside Haiti, mainly in France, Canada and the USA.
Jacques St. Alexis (1922–61), author of *"Compère Géneral Soleil"*, Paris 1955 (two translations into Spanish).
"Les Arbres Musiciens", Paris 1957: transla-ted into Russian and Spanish.

"L'Espace d'un Cillement", Paris 1959: translated into Spanish.

Jacques St. Alexis, a writer assassinated in 1961, was an important contemporary author.

The literature of the poet René Depestre, living in Cuba, and of the poet and writer Anthony Phelps, living in Montréal, should also be mentioned; and, in the field of social science, the books of Gérard Pierre-Charles, which, in French and Spanish, have reached circulations of 14,000 copies.

In Haiti itself among those who have published in the last few years Pradel Pompilus (literature and linguistics) and Roger Gaillard (historical essays) are outstanding. As far as the publishing trade is concerned, Canada is trying to break into the Haitian market.

"Les Éditions Lémac" (371 Quest Rue Laurier, Montréal 15), have been entrusted by a government institution with promoting the publication of Haitian books.

In the last few years Creole has developed as a written language and as a language used for literature and science. Adult education, the publication of magazines and newspapers, the translation of some classical works (drama, political and religious themes) and poetry in Creole have been promoted. Therefore it is likely that this language will make a greater impact on literature, and that the prejudices which have traditionally existed in the country over bilingualism will be reduced, and that a market for books in Creole of some significance will be created.

24 Retail Trade

The market is handled with the help of the foreign suppliers through the 20 bookshops in Port-au-Prince which import and distribute the books. In some provincial towns like Cap Haïtien, Les Cayes or Gonaïves there are one or two bookshops. The import of books is subject to a permit which is granted by the Ministry of Commerce on the basis of a simple application. There is no foreign exchange control so that this authorization is a mere administrative formality.

26 Antiquarian Book Trade, Auctions

The most important dealers in antiquarian books are the following: Albert Mangonès (Port-au-Prince), and Kurt Fisher (Rue du Quaie, Port-au-Prince).

27 Book Imports

As already mentioned ($\rightarrow$ 3, 17, 21, 24) the Haitian book marked depends primarily upon imports.

According to official statistics for the period October 1969 to September 1970 the imports of books and brochures reached a value of 389,047 Gourdes. Main suppliers were

Country	Amount (Gourdes)
France	160,919
USA	94,242
Canada	55,939
Italy	33,616
Belgium	25,872

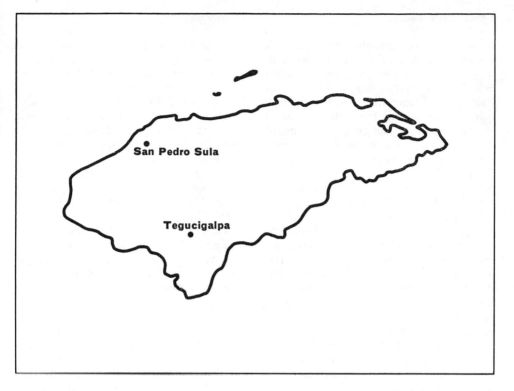

1 General Information

Area 112,100 km²

Population 2,582,000 (23 per km²–Mestizo 89.9%, Indian 6.7%, Negro 2.1%, White 1.3%)

Capital Tegucigalpa (170,538–1970)

Largest towns Tegucigalpa (170,538); San Pedro Sula (102,516)

Government Constitutional Presidential Democracy

Religion Predominantly Roman Catholic

National language Spanish

Leading foreign language English

Weights, measures Metric system

Currency unit Lempira (L.) = 100 Centavos (cts)

Education Obligatory and free for six years (ages 7 to 15), effective in urban areas. 3,457 students (1968) in one national university and two dependances

Illiteracy 64.8% (according to 1950 census; following national references, this figure dropped by 50% during the following ten years)

Paper consumption a) Newsprint 0.5 kg per inhabitant (1970)

b) Printing paper (other than newsprint) 0.4 kg per inhabitant (1970)

Membership UNESCO

Honduras

2 Past and Present

After its discovery during the fourth voyage of Columbus in 1502, Honduras always has been under northern dominion or influence. First as part of the "Grand Capitanía de Guatemala", under Spanish rule, it later became the southern outpost of the Mexican Empire. Independent development of the country could only take place after its separation from the Central American Republics. The first printer established himself in 1840, and the first publisher in 1860, coming from Venezuela and Guatemala, respectively. But during colonial times Honduras received her literary and book-trade influences only from outside. Even today, with about ten publishers and about twenty bookstores with 90% of books sold in the country being of foreign origin, influences of other nations still dominate the national book scene. Trade habits too are adopted from Spanish and Mexican practice.

In general economic life, however, the country has close connections to the United States of America, from which come most of the imports and to which go most of the exports. 60% of these exports consist of banana sales, and this dependence on the harvest of just one fruit plant poses a serious problem in Honduranean international trade and in internal economic development. With annual gross earnings of $150 per capita, the population has also to contend with the fact that one third of the population are children; the annual population increase of 2.7% will further lower the active economic part of the population in future years, so that the actual 19.5% of public expenses spent on education is still insufficient. Yet most of the countryside is never reached by full primary and free education. Cultural life is concentrated among a small group of people in the big cities, so that national literacy can grow only slowly.

Bibliography

Antología del Cuento Hondureño. (Anthology of Honduranean Stories.) Tegucigalpa, Universidad Nacional Autónoma de Honduras 1968. 244 pp.

Banco Central de Honduras, Informe Económico. (Central Bank of Honduras, Economic Report.) Tegucigalpa, Banco Central de Honduras 1950 ff. approx. 200 pp. (mimeograph).

Banco Central de Honduras, Memorias. (Central Bank of Honduras, Annual.) Tegucigalpa, Banco Centra de Honduras 1969 ff. approx. 200 pp.

El Libro de Honduras. Directorio y Guía general de la República. (The Book of Honduras. Directory and general Guide of the Republic.) Tegucigalpa, Tipografía Nacional 1957. 142 pp.

4 Organization

The book trade is concentrated in Tegucigalpa, including its important and historical district of Comayagüela, with the only significant number of bookstores in San Pedro Sula.

A group of booksellers are members of the
Asociación de Libreros de Honduras
(Association of Honduranean Booksellers)
c/o Librería Navarro
Calle Real
Comayagüela

This association was founded in 1960 and is actually trying to reform itself as a "Cámara Hondureña del Libro", that is to say, as an official Chamber of Books, with obligatory membership.

This, apart from all booksellers, would include also the publishers, bookbinders and printers; at present no professional organization for the last three trades exists.

Bibliography

E. A. GARCIA. J. A. PENCE AND E. A. REINA, *The book trade, bibliography, and exchange of publications in Honduras.* Coral Gables, Florida, University of Miami Library 1962. 20 pp.–7th Seminar on the Acquisition of Latin American Library Materials.–Mimeographed.

7 Sources of Information, Address Services

Information about the book trade in Honduras can be obtained from the
> *Asociación de Libreros de Honduras*
> *(Association of Honduranean Booksellers)*
> *c/o Librería Navarro*
> *Calle Real*
> *Comayagüela*

while information on the books of the country should be sought from the National Library
> *Biblioteca Nacional de Honduras*
> *(National Library of Honduras)*
> *6a. Avenida y 5a. Calle*
> *Tegucigalpa*

Information of an economic nature will be given by the official bank of Honduras,
> *Banco Central de Honduras*
> *(Central Bank of Honduras)*
> *Domicilio conocido*
> *Tegucigalpa*

which is involved in sponsoring and publishing a number of books on national bibliography and literary life.

Bibliography

The addresses of all branches of the book trade are contained in
La Empresa del Libro en América Latina. (The Book in Latin America.) 2nd ed. Buenos Aires, Bowker Editores Argentina 1974. VIII, 307 pp.
p. 169: Honduras.
El Libro de Honduras. Directorio y Guía general de la República. (The Book of Honduras. Directory and general guide of the Republic.) Tegucigalpa, Tipografía Nacional 1957. 142 pp.

12 Taxes

The Honduranean government has recognized the importance of the book for the nation's cultural development by granting it exemption from tax for its production and sales. The import of books, too, is free of taxes.

15 National Bibliography, National Library

The official bibliography of Honduras, published by the National Library (→ 7), is relatively new. Since 1968, it is being published as *Boletin Bibliográfico* in weekly lists.

A number of publications complete the references to national book production: firstly, the two manuals *Bibliografía Hondureña 1620–1930* and *Bibliografía Hondureña 1880–1970*, published by the Central Bank of Honduras (→ 7). An annual register is given in the *Colección Bibliográfico Edmundo Durón*, published at the end of every year by the newspaper "El Día" since 1964.

The National Library,
> *Biblioteca Nacional de Honduras*
> *(National Library of Honduras)*
> *6a. Avenida y 5a. Calle*
> *Tegucigalpa*

was founded in 1880 and has collected 55,000 titles. Its obligation to assemble the nation's book production is enforced by a law obliging every author to deposit three copies of his book at the National Library. Apart from this central insitution, there are 3 university libraries, 2 school libraries, 9 special and 4 public libraries serving in the country.

Bibliography

I. ZIMMERMANN, *Current national bibliographies of Latin America.* Gainesville, Florida, University of Florida Press 1971. X, 139 pp.
pp. 81–84: Honduras.

Honduras

16 Book Production

No official statistics on national book production are available. In 1970 the number of titles is estimated to have been 60, and a printing of 2,000 copies per title is normal. There are about 100 titles of national origin on sale in the bookstores, half of them paperbacks. The main field for local publishing is textbooks, mainly for primary and secondary schools, followed by national literature and history of the country and Central America.

21 Publishing

Of the 13 publishers registered in Honduras, only 5 are exclusively publishers of books. The combination of printer-publisher is normal. Three government-owned companies are the main producers of books, the publishing company of the Ministry of Public Education, the Department of Statistics of the Ministry of Economics, and the national printing works, "Tipografía Nacional". They are estimated to publish about 30% of local production, and the main part of the country's textbooks.

It is another characteristic of the local book scene that many authors publish their books themselves or together with the printer. The best-known national authors publish their manuscripts with Mexican and Argentine companies.

24 Retail Trade

"La Empresa del Libro en América Latina" (→7) lists 5 bookshops in Tegucigalpa and 1 in Comayagüela.
→4

Bibliography

Alvarado Garcia, *The book trade... in Honduras*. Coral Gables 1962. 33 pp. (mimeograph).

27 Book Imports

Since 90% of the books sold in Honduras are imported, the statistics for the country's international trade give some idea of total book sales in the country, at cost prices.

Year	US $
1960	40,000
1968	132,000
1969	233,000

This shows that during the last decade the import of books has enormously increased. From the imports of all goods to Honduras in 1969 valued at US $ 651,000, it shows that books have an important place in Honduranean buying abroad. Main suppliers are the United States and Mexico, followed by Panama and Spain.

Bibliography

Anuario Estadístico de la Secretaría de Economía y Hacienda, Tomo IV/V: Indice de comercio exterior, precios... (Statistical Annual of the Ministry of Economics and Finances, vol. IV/V: Index of international trade, prices...). Tegucigalpa, Dirección General de Estadística y Censo 1960 ff. approx. 200 pp. (mimeograph).
Banco Central de Honduras, Informe Económico. (Central Bank of Honduras, Commercial Report.) Tegucigalpa, Banco Central de Honduras 1950 ff. approx. 200 pp. (mimeograph).
Banco Central de Honduras, Memorias. (Central Bank of Honduras, Annual). Tegucigalpa, Banco Central de Honduras, 1969 ff. approximately 200 pp.

28 Book Exports

No statistics for Honduranean exports are available. The sales of national books to foreign countries are very small. National book production consists mainly of locally used textbooks, and books of national concern.

29 Book Fairs

A nationwide book fair is held annually in Tegucigalpa and San Pedro Sula, organized by all booksellers jointly with the Ministry of Education. On this ocasion, a literary prize, *Nuevo Cuento*, is awarded for the best national short story, inaugurated by the Association of the National Press, *Asociación de la Prensa Asociada*.

32 Literary Prizes

→29.

33 The Reviewing of Books

The eight daily newspapers and the many journals published in Honduras have regularly book columns and news about literary events. The majority of books discussed are of foreign origin, due to the situation prevailing in the country's book market. One periodical especially, the bi-monthly

Presente. Revista de Arte y Literatura de Centro América
(Presence. Journal of Art and Literature of Central America)
Apartado Postal 1029
Tegucigalpa

has a high reputation for its criticism of Central American art and literature.
The 126 private radio stations and the 5 television channels also give a relatively big part of their transmission time to books, commenting on new books and literary events in the Spanish-speaking countries.

Jamaica

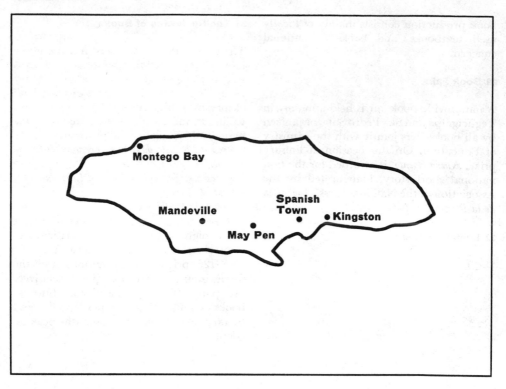

1 General Information

Area 10,962 km²

Population 1,897,000 (1971) (173 per km²)

Capital Kingston (Metropolitan area 1970: 475,548)

Largest Towns Kingston (475,548); Montego Bay (43,754); Spanish Town (40,731); May Pen (26,074); Mandeville (14,421)

Government A self-governing territory within the British Commonwealth of Nations

Religion Protestant 226,000
Roman Catholic 157,593
Smaller religious groups 115,000

National language English

Leading foreign language Spanish

Weights, measures British

Currency unit Dollar (Dollar = 100 cents)

Education Compulsory (6–15 years)

Illiteracy 25%

Paper consumption a) Newsprint 4.4 kg per inhabitant (1971)
b) Printing paper (other than newsprint) 2.6 kg per inhabitant (1971)

Membership UNESCO

2 Past and Present

The Island of Jamaica was sighted on 4 May 1494 by Christopher Columbus on his second voyage to the New World. He took possession in the name of the King and Queen of Spain but it was not until 1509, when Juan de Esquivel was appointed first Governor, that the island was actually occupied.

The original inhabitants of the island, the Arawak Indians, a peaceful people, were exterminated before the arrival of the British in 1655. The first Spanish capital was called Sevilla la Nueva and was located west of the present town of Saint Ann's Bay. Due to its unhealthy site it was soon abandoned and a new capital set up at Villa la Vega, the present Spanish Town. Kingston became the capital in 1872. Jamaica became an independent nation in 1962.

As far as is known, printing in Jamaica has its origins in 1717, when Sir Nicholas Lawes, Governor of Jamaica, prior to taking up his appointment, wrote to the Council of Trade proposing the establishment of a printing press in Jamaica. Robert Baldwin was Jamaica's first printer and started his press shortly after the Governor arrived in 1718. The first thing he printed was "A Pindarisque Ode on the arrival of His Excellency, Sir Nicholas Lawes". Jamaica's first newspaper, "The Weekly Jamaica Courant", appeared on 28 May 1718.

The earliest book produced in Jamaica by a resident was "El Bernado, O Victoria De Roncesvalles Poema heroyco" by Don Bernado de Balbuena, who was abbot of Jamaica from 1608 to 1618. It was published in Madrid in 1674, when Balbuena was Bishop of Puerto Rico. The earliest book printed by a resident in Jamaica under British rule was a book of poems by the Spanish poet, Daniel Israel Lopez Laguna, in 1720.

Up to the late thirties of the present century there was no recognized bookshop service. Prior to this, bookselling was part of general trade, which included stationery and general merchandise. Since then there have been several establishments dealing with the distribution and sale of books. The Booksellers' Association presently consists of 18 recognized firms (→4).

Bibliography

C. BLACK, *The story of Jamaica*. London, Collins 1965.

F. CUNDALL, *A history of printing in Jamaica from 1717 to 1834*. Kingston, Institute of Jamaica 1935.

BR. F. SWAN, *The spread of printing, Western Hemisphere: The Caribbean area*. Amsterdam, Vangendt 1970. 47 pp. pp. 12–14: Jamaica.

3 Retail Prices

Retail prices are arrived at by members of the Booksellers' Association (→4) in consultation with each other.

4 Organization

The main organization for the book trade is the

Booksellers' Association
97, Harbour Street
JA Kingston

7 Sources of Information, Address Services

Secretary, Booksellers' Association (→4).

10 Books and Young People

There is great need for suitable reading material for children. The Ministry of Education, in association with Collins-Sangster Ltd, have published a series of children's books for use in schools. There

211

is special need for the preparation and production of reading material with local relevance for primary and all-age schools.

11 Training

Courses in training in bookselling and management are presently being carried out in conjunction with the Book Development Council of Great Britain (→BTW I, United Kingdom 28).

12 Taxes

No taxes are imposed on books entering the country.

14 Copyright

The Copyright Law, Chapter 76 of the Revised Edition of the Laws of Jamaica 1953, makes it an offence to make, sell, hire, distribute, exhibit or import an infringing copy of a work in which copyright subsists. Under Imperial Statute, the Copyright Act, 1911, the owner of any unpublished original literary, dramatic, musical or artistic work is entitled to copyright therein if at the date of making thereof the author was a British Subject or resident in Jamaica or in some other place in Her Majesty's Dominions to which the act extends. The owner of a published work is entitled to copyright therein if the work was first published in Jamaica or in some other place in Her Majesty's Dominions to which the act extends. The owner of a published work is entitled to copyright therein if the work was first published in Jamaica or in some other place in Her Majesty's Dominions as before.

A New Copyright Act is currently being prepared.

15 National Bibliography, National Library

Following on the transfer of the seat of Government from Spanish Town to Kingston in 1872, the books from the Government-owned library of the Legislative Council and House of Assembly were also transferred from the old capital to the new. Legislation was later enacted, and this collection together with that of other smaller collections formed the nucleus of the stock for the

Public Library of the Institute of Jamaica
12 East Street
JA Kingston
founded in 1879.

The Institute was founded under the "Institute of Jamaica Law 1879", with specific duties to promote the pursuit of literature, science and art "by establishing and maintaining in Kingston an Institution comprising a Public Library, Reading Room, Museum and collection of works and illustrations of science and art; by providing for the reading of papers, and the delivery of lectures and courses of instruction, and the holding of examinations on subjects connected with literature, science and art; by providing and awarding premiums for the encouragement of literary, scientific and artistic work in Jamaica; by providing for the holding from time to time of exhibitions illustrative of the Arts, Crafts and Industries of Jamaica".

A Statutory Board of Governors, consisting of 12 members, is responsible for this work. The library programme was implemented through the establishment of a main general and reference library in Kingston and the provision of branch libraries. Deposit collections were circulated to elementary and secondary schools as well as to training colleges.

Over the years the Institute gradually formulated plans which led to the largest lending library in the island and placed emphasis on the collection of West Indian reference material which, today, comprises the most valuable treasures of Jamaica's National Library.

This collection is recognized as being the largest and most complete in the hemisphere.

In recent years the General Library has changed its emphasis. It now gives priority to its West Indian collection. It has not yet been declared the National Library but is in process of being so converted.

Apart from its reference and research facilities the activities of the Institute have included photo-copying and photographic services, the publication of bibliographies and the abstracting and indexing of its holdings. It has also published material of historical and scientific interest.

Among its many important publications are:

(1) A bibliography of Jamaica entitled 'Bibliographis Jamaicansis' compiled by Frank Cundall and published in 1902.
(2) A guide to Jamaican reference material in the West Indian Reference Library by Ray Delattre, 1965.
(3) Caribbean fiction 1900–1969. (In WIRL'S collection English and American imprints only).
(4) The Jamaica Journal, a quarterly magazine.

Bibliography

J. L. ROBINSON, *Libraries in Jamaica*. In: Encyclopedia of Library and Information Science. vol. 13, pp. 169–204. New York, M. Dekker 1975.

16 Book Production

Book production is carried on an a very limited scale. Most books in circulation are imported. In 1969 a total of 175 titles were produced, 83 of which were concerned with the social sciences. In 1970 the total had dropped to 159, with social science (65) again maintaining the lead.

Applied sciences accounted for 30 and 33 titles respectively in the years 1969 and 1970.

18 Book Clubs

There is moderate subscription to overseas (British and American) book clubs.

19 Paperbacks

In the late 1940s and early 1950s the Pioneer Press, Book Publishing Department of the Gleaner Co. Ltd, started paperback publishing. Despite the fact that over one dozen titles were published, covering a wide range of subjects, the venture resulted in a financial loss. There has been no attempt since then to revive this branch of publishing.

Many popular paperback series published in Britain and the United States are on sale locally. Sales are not only confined to regular bookshops but extend to pharmacies, supermarkets, hotel gift shops and airport kiosks.

21 Publishing

As in the case of book production, very little publishing is carried on in the island. Most of the books in use are published overseas. The publishing industry, such as it is, is concentrated chiefly in the capital city of Kingston and confined mainly to newspapers, periodicals and textbooks. A small number of books, dealing with matters of local interest and providing a vehicle for local literacy effort, are also produced by individual publishers.

The Government Printing Office, the Agency for Public Information, and the Gleaner Company Ltd are among the largest publishing organizations. Publishing is also carried on at the Mona

Campus (Kingston) of the University of the West Indies.

23 Wholesale Trade

This trade is concentrated mainly in the hands of two or three firms operating from headquarters in the capital city of Kingston.

24 Retail Trade

Books, magazines and paperbacks are, for the most part, distributed from the central headquarters of the various organizations. As regards sales policy, members of the Booksellers' Association (→4) are restricted to established practices in order to satisfy standards demanded by their Association.

25 Mail-Order Bookselling

Very limited mail-order business is carried on. Individual booksellers are involved, but there are no statistics to substantiate results.

27 Book Imports

It is estimated that about 3½–4 million dollars are spent annually on the importation of books, including textbooks and magazines. The most important suppliers are the United Kingdom, the USA and Canada.

29 Book Fairs

Following on the promulgation of the year 1972 as "International Book Year" by UNESCO, a Book Fair, sponsored by the Jamaica Library Association (→35a) and supported by the Booksellers' Association (→4) and other interested groups was held in Kingston from 28 April to 2 May 1972. Coinciding with the International Library Conference, then in session, the Fair attracted a wide and interested viewing audience.

Most of the well-known British and American publishing houses, through their local representatives, participated by setting up displays. Librarians and bibliophiles from various countries had the opportunity of meeting with booksellers and publishers' representatives and discussing matters of mutual interest and concern.

30 Public Relations

Book Weeks or Library Weeks sponsored either by the Ministry of Education or by the Jamaica Library Service (→35a) are held from time to time, when renewed emphasis is placed on the importance of reading in the life of the community. The message is reinforced by posters and slogans as well as by short programmes on radio and television.

32 Literary Prizes

Each year the Jamaica Festival Commission, a Government Statutory Board, offers cash awards for the best entries received in the Festival Literary Competitions. Prizes, sponsored by well-known business organizations, are offered for short stories, poems and drama. In all competitions prizes are divided into adult and junior sections. Prizes are also offered for the best radio and television plays.
In recent years prizewinning entries have subsequently been published in the *Jamaica Journal* or on radio and television. Arrangements are also made for drama entries of acceptable standards to be produced.

33 The Reviewing of Books

Most newspapers and periodicals provide sections in their pages for literary reviews. Among these are, The *Sunday Gleaner*, (7 North St, Kingston), The *Daily News* (Sunday edition; 58, Halfway Tree Road,

Kingston 5), *Savacou* (P.O. Box 170, Mona, Kingston 7), *Public Opinion* (2, Torrington Road, Kingston). Books are also reviewed on radio.

35 Miscellaneous

a) *Libraries*
With the establishment of the
   Jamaica Library Service
   JA Kingston
in 1948 a new thrust was given to library development in the island.
Established under the Jamaica Library Service Law, 1949, responsibility was given to a corporate body, the Jamaica Library Board, "to establish, maintain, manage, control and operate a library service". The law also provided for the establishment of local Parish Library Committees to advise and assist in administering the local service under the framework of the Board's policies.
The service is administered from its headquarters in Kingston. There are 442 service points and 850 school libraries in the system.

A union catalogue of the adult book stock is maintained and through an inter-library loan service, operated from headquarters, urgently needed books circulate to all libraries irrespective of permanent allocation.
The total book circulation for 1973 was 2,480,000, an increase of 8.4% over that of the previous year. In the same period membership increased by 6.7% to 450,000.
In addition to house journals the Library Service has published the following:
Jamaica: A select bibliography 1900–1963
   (1963)
Jamaica Library Service; 21 years progress in pictures (1972).
b) *P.E.N.*
Established also in the same year as the Jamaica Library Service (1948) was the
   Jamaica Centre of the International
   P.E.N. Club
   R. L. C. Harong
   33 West Road Mona
   JA Kingston
Besides engaging in a wide range of activities, the club has entertained many distinguished writers from overseas and has been represented at several international congresses.

Martinique

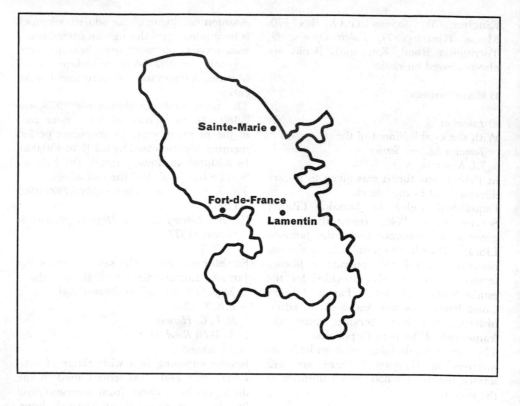

1 General Information

Area 1,102 km²
Population 324,000 (294 per km²)
Capital Fort-de-France (95,000)
Largest towns Fort-de-France (95,000); Sainte-Marie (19,515); Lamentin (18,553)
Government Overseas Department of the French Community
Religion Predominantly Roman Catholic
National language French, also Creole Patois
Leading foreign languages Spanish, English
Weights, measures Metric system
Currency unit Franc français (CFA) = 100 centimes
Education Compulsory for ten years; 865 students in a higher level institute (Institute d'Études Juridiques, as part of the Faculty of Law of the University of Bordeaux)
Illiteracy 15 %

Paper consumption a) Newsprint 1.9 kg per inhabitant
b) Printing paper (other than newsprint) 0.7 kg per inhabitant
Membership UNESCO (→BTW I, France 8)

216

2 Past and Present

Lying in the Lesser Antilles about 300 miles north east of Venezuela, Martinique was probably discovered by Columbus in 1502. It was taken over by France in 1635. Having a semi-autonomous status during the Second World War, it voted in favour of the new Constitution of the French Fifth Republic in September 1958 and remained an Overseas Department within the French Community.

From colonial up to modern times, the importance of Martinique consists in being the first harbour for goods coming from France for her departments and colonies in South America. It connects Guadeloupe, the other French island in the Lesser Antilles, with the European mainland, and is an export point for the agricultural industry (bananas are the main export) on the islands.

The first printing press was installed in 1727, and a newspaper ("France Antilles") covered, and still does so, Martinique and Guadeloupe. Small traders brought books and periodicals from France, and the European homeland is to this day almost the only supplier of literature for the inhabitants. Only in recent years were some connections with United States publishers and distributors established, bringing a very small percentage of books and periodicals from that country to the island. Bookselling companies were founded by private initiative from the first half of the 18th century, and they are still financed by their own capital. They are concentrated in Fort-de-France, the capital and largest city on the island. As in other countries in Latin America, the long distance from their European suppliers creates problems for the booksellers. In view of the lack of a local publishing industry, the cultural interests of the people in Martinique are even more fixed to the literary life in their European homeland than in other, neighbouring countries, and booksellers feel the distance in time between the arrival of literary announcements and that of the books themselves with their customers. Newspapers are mostly brought by air to Martinique, while shipments of books still take more than a month to reach the island by sea.

Trade, customs and professional information too reach booksellers almost exclusively from France.

Bibliography

Br. F. Swan, *The spread of printing, Western Hemisphere: The Caribbean area.* Amsterdam, Vangendt 1970. 47 pp.
p. 32: Martinique.

3 Retail Prices

The Government on Martinique does not intervene in sales price regulation. The local prices of imported books, the only ones sold on the island, are 20% higher than in the European country of origin, to cover trade expenses for transport, insurance, payment etc. Equally, there is a 10% charge on retail prices of periodicals brought by ship. This is imposed by the booksellers as the result of an agreement among themselves. It is a general custom to allow students a 10% discount on the normal price of a book.

4 Organization

There is a syndicate of bookstores for the departments of Martinique and Guadeloupe, the

Syndicat des Libraires
du Martinique et Guadeloupe
(Syndicate of the Booksellers of
Martinique and Guadeloupe)
c/o Librairie La Cité Universitaire
86 et 88, rue Victor-Sévère
Fort-de-France

which occasionally acts in the name of

their members in case of common problems with the local government offices. Half of the 31 companies which form the book trade in both territories are members. On Martinique, as the book trade is concentrated in the capital, collaboration among booksellers is normally close.

7 Sources of Information, Address Services

Special book-trade information on Martinique can be obtained from the professional institutions in France (→BTW I, France 4); for instance, from the
Syndicat National des Éditeurs
(National Syndicate of Publishers)
117, Boulevard Saint-Germain
F 75 Paris VI
General commercial information may be obtained from:
Chambre du Commerce et d'Industrie
(Chamber of Commerce and Industry)
53, rue Victor Hugo
Fort-de-France
→4.

10 Books and Young People

Occasional promotions of reading material for young people are organized by various libraries on the island, chiefly by the territories' leading reference library,
Schoelcher Musée et Bibliothèque
(Schoelcher Museum and Library)
Fort-de-France
The librairies on the island's centres for youth and culture, "Maisons des Jeunes et de la Culture", participate in these promotions. These local centres have a good stock of French books for children and teenagers.

12 Taxes

Books enjoy a reduced sales tax of 3.5% on Martinique. As for the importation of books, the only source of book supplies for the trade in Martinique, the local government does not charge any taxes, thus respecting the UNESCO Florence agreement signed by France including Martinique as one of her overseas departments (→BTW I, International Section 4, 27, 28).

15 National Bibliography, National Library

The small number of books produced in Martinique are only listed in the French bibliographies (→BTW I, France 15). Book lists published on the island, however, mostly listing French books, are issued occasionally by the leading reference library,
Schoelcher Musée et Bibliothèque
(Schoelcher Museum and Library)
Fort-de-France
which up to a certain point acts as a National Library. Furthermore, there are four other libraries on the island, among them one public library and the library of the Institute of Law Studies.

16 Book Production

No figures are available. With only one publishing company on the island (→21), book production is nearly non-existent.
→35.

21 Publishing

There is only one publisher on the island. This company publishes books for students, primary textbooks and a few general titles. The only other local publications are brochures printed and published occasionally by government institutions.
→35

24 Retail Trade

The 17 booksellers on Martinique are concentrated in the capital, Fort-de-France. Their activity, however, covers all the island as well as Guadeloupe, the other French department in the Antilles, where some of the Martinique companies have branches.

People on the island buy nearly all books in the bookshops, the only other sales outlets being three supermarkets which mainly sell paperbacks in their stationery departments. One company on Martinique has specialized in direct sales by representatives visiting offices and private homes, while two others deal in second-hand books (mostly paperbacks) in special departments within their stores.

27 Book Imports

As nearly all books sold on the island are imported, import figures represent more than 95% of the book sales realized in Martinique. Of these imports, 90% come from France, while United States publishers and distributors deliver a small quantity of paperbacks and scientific books to Martinique. (The official figure for 1967 shows a total import of 2.8 million CFA for books and brochures.) During the last years, book imports from France have increased considerably:

Year	Approx. US$
1960	135,000.00
1967	108,000.00
1968	600,000.00
1969	720,000.00
1970	942,000.00

According to these French records, annual sales on Martinique at retail prices could be estimated at nearly two million dollars, i.e. the annual amount spent for books by each of the 324,000 inhabitants would be around US $6.

28 Book Exports

In view of the small amount of local publishing, figures of Martinique's book exports, two thirds of which are sent to France, are not available. European French statistics for the year 1967 give a net value of 178,000 CFA worth imported from the department of Martinique.

33 The Reviewing of Books

Book information and reviews reach Martinique readers from abroad, mostly from French periodicals. The local newspaper, "France Antilles" (published with one edition for Martinique and another for Guadeloupe, with a total of 35,000 printed copies in 1968) occasionally publishes book reviews, as do the local periodicals (21, with a total edition of 79,000 in 1968). With a dense net of radio receivers and television sets, however, cultural transmissions from the local radio station "Radio Martinique" as well as from nearby stations play an important role in disseminating cultural information to the public.

Mexico

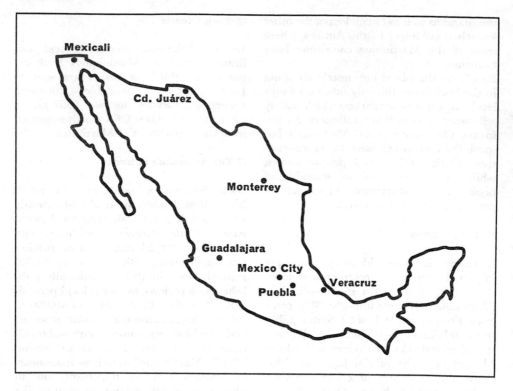

1 General Information

Area 1,972,545 km²

Population 48,225,238 (24 per km²)

Capital Mexico City (México D.F.; 6,874,165 in 1970)

Largest towns México, D.F. (6,874,165); Guadalajara, Jal. (1,199,391); Monterrey, N.L. (853,107); Cd. Juárez, Chih. (424,135); Mexicali, B.C. (396,324); Puebla (287,952); Veracruz, Ver. (230,220)

Government The United States of Mexico are a Federal Republic with 29 states and 2 territories. The president is the supreme authority and is elected for 6 years. The Chamber of Deputies is also elected for 6 years

Religion Roman Catholic

National language Spanish

Leading foreign languages English, French

Weights, measures Metric system

Currency unit Mexican Peso $ (1 Peso = 100 centavos)

Education The educational system extends from primary school up to university level: kindergarten, then "Primaria" for the first six years, then "Secundaria" for the next three years. Up to this level education is free and compulsory. The following three years, "Preparatoria", belong to the university and prepare the student for an academic career

Illiteracy 38%

Paper consumption a) Newsprint: 3.1 kg per inhabitant (1970)

b) Printing paper (other than newsprint): 7.1 kg per inhabitant (1970)

Membership UNESCO; IPA

2 Past and Present

In 1535, shortly after the beginning of the Conquest, book production commenced in Mexico City, before anywhere else in the New World. It is worth mentioning that in those days printing, publishing and bookselling were not separate businesses: the same person performed all these functions. The first printing office was a part of the Episcopal Palace in Mexico City and, to begin with, it belonged to the publisher Juan Cromberger, a native of Sevilla who sent his assistent Juan Pablos to Mexico.

Some people consider that the first book was a work by Saint Juan Climaco entitled *Escala espiritual para llegar al Cielo* ("The spiritual ladder to heaven"), translated from the Latin by Brother Juan de la Magdalena, and that Esteban Martín was the printer.

The first book to come from the presses of Pablos was *La Breve y Más Compendiosa Doctrina Cristiana en Lengua Castellana y Mexicana* ("The short and most compendious Christian doctrine in the Castilian and Mexican language"), in 1539. It is a twelve-page booklet printed in Gothic type. And so to Juan Pablos goes the honour of being the first printer in America. And although this has not been absolutely confirmed, he was, at any rate, the first to set up a printing office to produce work in a regular and continuous fashion. In 1557 Antonio de Espinoza founded the second printing office in Mexico. He produced religious works, grammars, and vocabularies in Indian languages.

Once Mexico gained independence, book publishing increased and diversified. The first magazines appeared. Later, the raw materials were not all imported. At the end of the sixteenth century the first Mexican paper factories went into production.

Examination of the publishing industry in colonial Mexico shows that printing was of great significance in the cultural life of the country, although during that period it suffered from serious limitations.

About 14,420 titles were printed in "Nueva España" during the colonial period, of these 12,256 titles were produced in Mexico, namely,

200 works in the 16th century,
1,845 works in the 17th century,
7,757 works in the 18th century,
2,454 works in the 19th century.

It must also be borne in mind that the number of copies of each title published was very small and rarely exceeded 500.

In 1826, the first independent publishing house was founded by Mariano Galván Rivera, who also started the first bookselling business in the country. He produced the first edition of *Don Quixote* published in Mexico.

During the wars of the Reform and of the Empire not so many books were published. Around 1876, there was more activity, but this declined again shortly afterwards. Publishing remained of little importance up to 1917. It was after the Second World War that an important period began for publishing. It has become more and more extensive in Mexico and is now firmly established. At present, production is sufficient for most of Mexican needs, and the country even exports a considerable amount of printed matter ($\rightarrow$28).

Bibliography

A. B. CARVER, *Esteban Martín, the first printer in the Western Hemisphere*. In: The Library Quarterty, v. 39, No. 4, pp. 344–352. Chicago, University of Chicago Press 1969.

G. FURLONG, *Orígines del arte tipográfico en América*. (The origins of the art of typography in America.) Buenos Aires, Ed. Huarpes 1947. 225 pp.
Bibliography on pp. 215–225. Early printing history of Mexico: pp. 51–70.

J. G. ICAZBALCETA, *Bibliografía Mexicana del siglo XVI*. (Mexican bibliography of the sixteenth century.) New ed. by A. M.

Carlo. Mexico, Fondo de Cultura Económica 1954. 581 pp.
pp. 11–16: bibliographical references;
pp. 23–55: the beginning of Mexican printing.
J. T. MEDINA, *Historia de la imprenta en los antiguos dominios españoles de América y Oceanía.* (The history of printing in the ancient Spanish dominions of America and Oceania.) 2 vols. Santiago de Chile, Fondo Histórico y Bibliográfico José Toribio Medina 1958. CXLI, 542; XV, 540 pp.
v. I. pp. 43–431: Mexico.
F. PEÑALOSA, *The Mexican book industry.* New York, Scarecrow Press 1957. 312 pp.
pp. 260–82: bibliography;
pp. 10–30: history.
L. S. THOMPSON, *Printing in Colonial Spanish America.* Hamden Conn., Archon Books 1962. 108 pp.
pp. 11–33, 66–71: Mexico.

3 Retail Prices

The country's publishing houses decide the retail prices their products will have over a set period, basing their decisions on the costs of materials and labour employed. However, there are no fixed prices as such; there are prices recommended (or suggested) by the publishing houses.
Moreover, fluctuations in the costs of industrial products do not for the most part affect the selling price of books.
The retail price of foreign books is determined by the distributors on behalf of the respective publishers.
Bookshops give a 10% discount to students and teachers and also to libraries and certain educational institutions.

4 Organization

The book industry in Mexico has two organizations which in one way or another look after the interests of institutions or people connected with the production and distribution of published works. These are:

> *Cámara Nacional de la Industria Editorial*
> *(National Chamber of the Publishing Industry)*
> *Vallarta No. 21 – 3er Piso*
> *MEX México 4, D.F.*

This legally constituted institution was founded in 1964; 564 active members were enrolled in 1970. The "Cámara" thus represents the whole publishing industry, books, journals, periodicals and others, in all professional, labour and legal questions.

> *Instituto Mexicano del Libro*
> *(Mexican Book Institute)*
> *Paseo de la Reforma No. 95*
> *Despacho 1024*
> *MEX México 4, D.F.*

The "Instituto" is a private booksellers' organization, founded in 1950. In spite of the fact that there are hundreds of active book dealers in Mexico, the "Instituto" had only 196 members in 1973.

5 Trade Press

Official Journal of the "Cámara" (→4) was

> *México Editor*
> *(Publisher Mexico)*
> *Vallarta 21, 3er Piso*
> *MEX México 4, D.F.*

"Mexico Editor" was founded in 1970, with an edition of 1,500 copies. It was published monthly up to the end of 1972, after which publication was suspended.
Among the private periodicals of book-trade background should be mentioned:

> *Boletín Bibliografico Mexicano*
> *(Mexican Bibliographical Bulletin)*
> *Porrúa Hermanos y Cía., S.A.*
> *Calles Argentina y Justo Sierra*
> *MEX México 1, D.F.*

La Gaceta
(The Gazette)
Fondo de Cultura Económica
Av. Universidad 975
MEX México 20, D.F.
and
Vocero del Libro
(The Book Spokesman)
Librería Internacional, S.A.
Av. Sonora 206
MEX México 11, D.F.

6 Book-Trade Literature

As in nearly all Latin American countries, there is no special literature about the theory and practice of the modern Mexican book trade and its various branches, with the exception of Fernando Peñalosa's work.

Bibliography

F. PENALOSA, *The Mexican book industry.* New York, Scarecrow Press 1957. 312 pp. Table of contents: Introduction (History, literacy, the book industry and the mass media; legal cases; structure of publishing; output; book distribution.) Bibliography on pp. 260–282.
→2.

7 Sources of Information, Address Services

There is no central information office but institutions such as the following offer assistance:
Biblioteca Nacional
(National Library)
República de El Salvador 70
MEX México 1, D.F.

El Colegio de México
(The College of Mexico)
Guanajuato 125
MEX México 7, D.F.

Biblioteca del Congreso
(Congress Library)
Tacuba 29
MEX México 1, D.F.

Biblioteca de la Universidad
(University Library)
Ciudad Universitaria, Villa Obregon
MEX México 20, D.F.

Hemeroteca Nacional
(National Newspaper Library)
Calle del Carmen 31
MEX México 1, D.F.

Bibliography

The addresses of all branches of the book trade are contained in
La Empresa del Libro en América Latina. (The Book in Latin America.) 2nd ed. Buenos Aires, Bowker Editores Argentina 1974. VIII, 307 pp.
pp. 171–215: Mexico.

8 International Membership

Mexico is a member of a wide range of international organizations. In the publishing field, Mexico belongs to the *International Publishers' Association* (→BTW I, International Section 4). Representatives are chosen by the "National Chamber of the Publishing Industry" (→4). It is also a member of the *Federación Iberoamericana de Instituciones Editoriales y Libreras* (FIEL) (Ibero-American Federation of Publishing and Bookselling Institutions; →BTW II, Latin America 4), which was founded as a result of the first "Ibero-American Congress of Associations and Chambers Connected with Books" which took place in Mexico in 1964. Argentina, Chile, Colombia, Mexico, Peru and Venezuela were the founders. The FIEL should act as an international organization of the national book institutes or their equivalents of each country. Since 1970 González Avelar

223

from Mexico is its president, but due to the political situation in Latin America, its activities have been suspended. The address of FIEL is the

Cámara Nacional de la Industria Editorial
Vallarta No. 21 – 3er Piso
MEX México 4, D.F.

Mexico is also studying the advantages of joining the *Centro Regional par el Fomento del Libro en América Latina* (Regional Centre for Book Development in Latin America, → Latin America 4; Colombia 11) which has its headquarters in Bogotá, Colombia. In the latter city, the first course in publishing administration and production took place from 28 November to 18 December 1971. Mexico took part, sending three lecturers and a scholarship student.

9 Market Research

To date there have been no studies on the present-day conditions of the book market in this country. It is hoped that some private institutions or the "Autonomous National University" will undertake research in this field.
→ 35 b.

10 Books and Young People

In Mexico there is no organization which promotes young people's and children's books. Some firms publish stories, novels and other types of children's literature; but there is no organized movement, nor are there publishers who specialize in this type of work.

Books which can be considered as young people's books are published by various firms as part of their general output. As an exception mention should be made of the *Editorial Novaro*, which has produced a considerable amount of reading material in this particular field.

11 Training

There are no schools for training in the promotion and selling of books nor in the organization and running of publishing houses. Some marginal training may be given in educational centres in cataloguing and in marketing schools. Bookshops do not give any systematic training.

The one notable exception is the apprenticeship system which the Librería Internacional, has had for several years. This firm annually takes students who have obtained good results in their first year at the School of Commerce; this practical training lasts two years.

12 Taxes

The publishing and selling of books, journals and magazines is exempt of all sales taxes, but only for the profits proceeding from the distribution and sale of these publications.

Printing houses pay a sales tax of 4%.

Publishing houses for books and scientific material pay half of the corporate global income tax. However, the tax authorities grant a subsidy for all reinvested utilities. There is also an export bonus of 10% (CEDI) for these industries.

Bookstores, printers and related corporations have to pay the full rate.

The fee for social security and retirement has to be paid in the following proportions: ½ by the employee, ½ by the company.

The Government's position concerning customs duties was not to impose fiscal barriers on books entering the country. This was in order to foster cultural links with other nations, and to benefit Mexican books on the Latin American markets, where Mexico competes in price and quality with other countries. In this way Mexico also cooperates with the Latin American policy of creating an integrated common market.

14 Copyright

Mexico signed several international conventions to protect intellectual property of a literary and artistic nature.

The Copyright Convention of Berne, (→BTW I, International Section 14) revised version of Brussels 1948, was signed by Mexico on 20 December 1968.

Two other Latin American conventions have been accepted:

Montevideo, 1947: "Convención interamericana sobre el derecho de autor en obras literarias, científicas y artísticas" (Inter-American Convention about Copyright in Literary, Scientific and Artistic Works). Buenos Aires, 1964: "Convención sobre propiedad literaria y artística suscrita en la 4a conferencia internacional americana" (Convention Regarding Literary and Artistic Property, signed at the 4th International American Conference).

The Mexican federal Copyright law was published on 31 December 1956 and reformed on 4 November 1963.

New proposals are under consideration, but at present it is not known, when the new law will become effective.

Legislation stresses that the greatest care must be taken with regard to what a author can do with his material and intellectual rights. It is absolutely prohibited for the author to concede his intellectual rights in any way whatsoever. The author may not authorize anybody to modify his work, unless specific details are given of the modification; he may not authorize generic and indeterminate modifications. This prohibition is of great importance, for it has frequently happened that a publisher, in the publishing contract, in agreement with the author, puts in clauses that allow him to modify the work. The author may of course authorize certain specific changes, but he cannot give the publisher *carte blanche* to modify the work in general. Many authors are unaware of this legal prohibition, which is the author's absolute right, but their ignorance of it does not affect its legal validity; it can only affect material rights such as the right to reproduce or translate a work (or authorize a translation).

There are two methods of passing on to the publisher all or part of the rights: one is by the publishing contract mentioned above and the other is by ceding the rights. By the latter method, the publisher has absolute rights to protect the material rights of the author. In this way, he can make decisions on his own account regarding how many editions there will be, what appearance the editions will have, at what price they will sell, the frequency of editions, what the terms of the contract for another edition or translation will be, etc. To sum up, the publisher becomes the person who enjoys all the facilities of copyright, with no restrictions except those imposed by the law and the author himself: moral and intellectual rights.

As far as the partial ceding of rights is concerned, the author may grant a publisher the right to a work for a certain period of time. This system is not common because it is against the law. For this reason, the publishing contract is more frequent.

The "Publishing Commission" of the "National Chamber of the Publishing Industry" (→4) has been hard at work lately because the Copyright Head Office has announced that it has now completed: a) a project to reform the Federal Law of Copyright; and b) a project on how to administer the new law. It is hoped that interested parties will collaborate on both projects by studying the proposals and giving their opinions through the above-mentioned Commission.

Mexico

15 National Bibliography, National Library

There is no real national bibliography. However, there have been notable partial efforts, such as the famous *Bibliotheca Mexicana* ("Mexican library") by J. J. Eguiara y Eguren (1695–1763); the *Bibliografía Mexicana del Siglo XVI* ("Mexican bibliography of the 16th century") by J. G. Icazbalceta; the *Ensayo Bibliográfico Mexicano del Siglo XVII* ("Mexican bibliographical treatise of the 17th century") by V. de P. Andrade; the *Bibliografía Mexicana del Siglo XVIII* ("Mexican bibliography of the 18th century") by N. León, whose work was complemented by J. T. Medina with his *La Imprenta en México (1539–1821)* ("Printing in Mexico 1539–1821"). There is no corresponding compilation for the nineteenth century, although in 1889 M. de Olaguíbel published his *Memoria para una Bibliografía Científica de México en el Siglo XIX* ("Monograph for a scientific bibliography of Mexico in the 19th century").

> *Instituto de Investigaciones Bibliográficas*
> *U.N.A.M.*
> *(Institute for Bibliographical Research)*
> *Apartado Postal 29124*
> *MEX México 1, D.F.*

As far as modern times are concerned, since 1958, the *Instituto de Investigaciones Bibliográficas* has been publishing what might well be considered a national bibliography: its *Anuario Bibliográfico Mexicano*, which appeared in 1958 and 1959; subsequently the *Anuario* became a 2-monthly publication, entitled *Bibliografía Mexicana* ("Mexican Bibliography"), six numbers appearing per year.

There is a project to publish a general bibliography of Spanish-speaking countries, emulating the *Bibliografía Española* ("Spanish Bibliography"), which has been published since 1958. A work schedule has already been drawn up and, at the suggestion of Unesco, the results were presented at the "Meeting of Experts for the Promotion of Books in Latin America" (Bogotá, 9–15 September 1969). It was agreed to form a working group with representatives from Argentina, Colombia, Costa Rica, Chile, Spain and Mexico. The

> *Biblioteca Nacional*
> *(National Library)*
> *Isabel La Católica y Uruguay*
> *MEX México 1, D.F.*

enjoys considerable prestige and is firmly established. Since 1929 it has been a part of the National University. It was founded by a decree of 24 October 1833 and inaugurated in 1844. Originally it belonged to the then *Secretaría de Justicia e Instrucción Publica* (Secretariat of Justice and Public Instruction). The University votes it an annual sum of 5 million pesos, of which 1 million pesos is used for buying books and periodicals. At present it has a collection of more than 901,300 volumes.

On average it is used by 1,500 readers per day. On occasions this figure is near to 4,000.

As well as general and specialized bibliographies, it publishes a *Boletín del Instituto de Investigaciones Bibliográficas* ("Bulletin of the Institute of Bibliographical Research"). All publishers (or authors, when they publish their own works) are obliged by law to send two copies to the National Library and the *Biblioteca del Congreso* (Congress Library).

> *Biblioteca del H. Congreso de la Union*
> *(Congress Library of the Union)*
> *Tacuba y Bolivar*
> *MEX México 1, D.F.*

Bibliography

I. Zimmermann, *Current national bibliographies of Latin America*. Gainesville, Florida, University of Florida Press 1971. X, 139 pp.
pp. 65–69: Mexico.

16 Book Production

The output of printed works in Mexico is influenced by various factors, some of which are imponderable, varying not only from year to year but also according to a host of political, social and economic circumstances. General education and the habit of reading (directly proportional to illiteracy) also have important consequences. However, in spite of circumstances at times unfavourable, the output of publishing houses has increased in recent years. A clear indication of this is given in the following figures:

Year	Titles
1955	923
1960	1,964
1965	4,851
1970	4,812

Subject group	Titles		
	1968	1969	1970
General	33	49	60
Philosophy	75	100	141
Religion	27	25	42
Social sciences	591	677	1,102
Philology	47	76	99
Pure sciences	169	104	242
Applied sciences	967	1,287	1,722
Arts	132	133	225
Literature	347	259	286
Geography, history	258	193	253
Total	2,646	2,983	4,812

17 Translations

It is calculated that the annual average production of titles in the last five years has been 3,750. About 10% of the titles are translations into Spanish from works in foreign languages.

Original languages	Titles		
	1967	1968	1969
English	275	279	265
French	30	36	17
German	6	25	8
Russian	4	6	3
Scandinavian languages	1	1	—
Italian	5	9	9
Classical	3	6	2
Spanish	1	1	1
Japanese	—	—	3
Other languages	5	30	3
Total	330	393	311

Subject group	Titles		
	1967	1968	1969
General	8	3	2
Philosophy	12	33	17
Religion	7	4	4
Social sciences	52	118	66
Philology	—	4	2
Pure sciences	19	61	47
Applied sciences	96	55	105
Arts	5	11	11
Literature	104	85	38
Geography, history	27	18	19
Total	330	393	311

18 Book Clubs

There are a few clubs of this nature but they are not very important as regards either size or their internal organization.

19 Paperbacks

Paperbacks are fairly popular in Mexico, although the output and market cannot compare with Europe or the United States. The first paperbacks sold in Mexico were foreign language ones, mainly English. These have continued to be popular, especially since the Second World War. Naturally, various Mexican publishers produce paperbacks in Spanish, a high proportion of which are translations. *Breviarios* (Breviaries), *Colección Popular* (Popular Collection) and *Presencia de*

Mexico

México (Presence of Mexico), three series published by the *Fondo de Cultura Económica*, should be mentioned here. Other publishers produce paperbacks in their own series *(Siglo XXI, Ediciones Novaro, Porrúa, Diana, El Manual Moderno, Extemporáneos*, etc.). For a time the *Secretaría de Educación Pública* (the Department of Public Education) published paperbacks (*"Biblioteca Enciclopédica Popular"* [Popular Encyclopedic Library]). After several years in abeyance, it has recently launched a new series entitled *Sepsetentas*.

21 Publishing

The following information refers to the two basic divisions in the Mexican publishing industry: (a) publishing of "books and related material" and (b) publishing of "newspapers and magazines".

Publishing has progressed steadily in recent years. The figures below show the increase in production of the year 1971 over the year 1970:

Gross production in publishing increased by 12.8%
Amount of raw material used increased by 7.1%
Investments increased by 7.6%
Employment increased by 17.3%
Salaries, wages and loans increased by 28.3%
The apparent consumption of the products of the publishing industry rose by 15.6%.

Details of the evident progress of the publishing industry in Mexico over the two years mentioned–as the most obvious and up-to-date indication–can be appreciated in the following comparative summary of book publishing, 1970 and 1971 (quantities refer to millions of pesos in Mexican currency):

Item	1970	1971	Increase per cent
Number of establishments	250	267	6.8
Employees	5,966	6,141	2.9
Invested capital	999,250	1,060,611	6.1
Total gross production	709,118	914,008	28.9
Wages, salaries and loans	121,187	144,980	19.6
Consumption of raw & auxiliary material	116,345	124,256	8.5
Apparent consumption	733,952	1,023,533	39.4

SOURCE: *Cámara Nacional de la Industria Editorial.* (National Chamber of the Publishing Industry. Information presented by Angel González Avelas before the 8th Ordinary General Meeting, February 1972.)

22 Literary Agents

The output of original work being limited, there is no call for the services of professional intermediaries.

Authors negotiate directly with publishers; the latter, in their turn, represent their authors overseas.

Publishers who deal mainly in translations use their own employees for transactions.

23 Wholesale Trade

There are 70 book distributors in Mexico. Their principal business is to represent certain foreign publishing houses, although some also distribute books produced in Mexico. Noteworthy examples are the *Librería Internacional*, the *Librería Anglo Americana* and the *Librería Francesa*. Besides being institutions selling books to the public, there are also distributors of works in German, English and French respectively. The other bookshops obtain their supplies of foreign books from these centres.

Other distributors do not sell books directly to the public, but merely represent foreign businesses. Some distributors are engaged in both the wholesale and the retail trades.

24 Retail Trade

As is to be expected, the majority of books are sold in the Federal District, where there are about 500 bookshops. About 500 more bookshops exist in the state capitals of the Mexican republic; but only in Monterrey and Guadalajara there exist bookshops of any importance.

Only a few of these firms have direct contact with the publishing houses; the majority obtain their supplies through the distributors described in the previous section.

However, the publishers have felt that their network is not sufficiently extensive, reliable or fast, and so they rely more and more on systems of direct contact with possible customers. At the same time, they make use of self-service shops, in which almost all books published in Mexico can be found.

Imported books, especially foreign-language scientific publications are sold by only a handful of large bookshops.

About half the bookshops in Mexico belong to the *Instituto Mexicano del Libro* (The Mexican Book Institute, →4).

25 Mail-Order Bookselling

There are practically no firms which deal exclusively in mail-order bookselling. Only the most important bookshops offer this service, which for the most part has developed for reference books or for some other types of book which, because of their price or category (they are frequently imported books), are not stocked by provincial bookshops. The bookshops offering this service publish catalogues of new books currently available.

26 Antiquarian Book Trade, Auctions

The buying and selling of antiquarian books is not a very important trade in Mexico. This is because, with the exception of a few bookshops with many years' experience in this field (one of which is the bookshop, Porrúa Hermanos y Cía.), the majority of bookshops do not have enough regular customers for this type of book.

In general there is little public demand for old books, and what demand there is, is primarily for rare books, books of typographical interest or modern books that are out of print. This kind of trade is catered for by second-hand bookshops or even by stalls selling rare books to tourists in popular markets. Some of these enjoy a welle-earned reputation and are visited daily (but especially on Sundays) by a special minority group.

27 Book Imports

In 1971 Mexico imported 59% more books than in 1970. In 1970, the value of imports of books amounted to 194 million Mexican pesos, whereas that of total imports rose to 309.1 million pesos in 1971. Books were imported principally from Spain (60%) and the USA (19%).

28 Book Exports

Exports had been increasing since 1967 and reached their highest result in 1970, with 210.4 million. But in 1971 sales abroad only reached 142.3 million (32.3% lower than 1970). During 1971 Mexico's largest exports were to Peru (13%), Venezuela (10.5%), Argentina (9.6%) and Colombia (9.4%). Details of quantities and percentages were:

Mexico

Country	Pesos
Peru	18,555,138
Venezuela	14,996,126
Argentina	13,628,560
Colombia	13,389,180
Spain	12,750,243
Puerto Rico	11,536,167
Panama	9,306,191
USA	9,120,755
Chile	6,827,535
El Salvador	5,281,370
Guatemala	4,617,269
Costa Rica	3,007,691
Uruguay	3,047,527
Ecuador	1,985,410
Brazil	1,754,312
Bolivia	1,467,996
Nicaragua	1,454,659
Nigeria	1,390,950
Honduras	1,160,634
Paraguay	975,664
Total	142,372,935

The balance of trade was therefore unfavourable, especially when compared with 1970, which was the best year since 1940. It should be noted that the previous figures referring to exports do not include any antiquarian books.

29 Book Fairs

There have been book fairs in the capital and in other important cities for many years. Many form a part of cultural programmes during important festivities. But sometimes the fairs are an event in themselves. The degree of importance that Mexico gives to such fairs can be gauged by the fact that there is an official organization devoted exclusively to them: the *Departamento de Ferias y Exposiciones* (Department of Fairs and Exhibitions), responsible to the *Secretaría de Industria y Comercio* (Secretariat of Industry and Commerce). The private sector has also taken an interest in this aspect of national culture. Recently a *Comisión de Ferias y Exposiciones* (Commission of Fairs and Exhibitions) was formed within the *Consejo Directivo de la Cámara Nacional de la Industria Editorial* (Board of the National Chamber of the Publishing Industry).

The following are some of the 1970 fairs: the Book Fair in the *Casa del Economista* (Economist House), which took place in November in Mexico City, and the First Chihuahua Book Fair, which took place in November in Chihuahua. More important was the First Mexican Book Fair (May, Mexico City) which was inaugurated by the President of the Republic. Mention must also be made of the National Book Convention of Guadalajara 70 (August, Guadalajara).

On an international level, it is worth stressing the interest which Mexico shows in participating in the book fairs of other countries. Several times the country took part in the Frankfurt Book Fair. In 1970 Mexico participated in the Book Fair in Spain (Madrid), in the Eighth International Fair of Bogotá, Colombia and in the First World Exhibition of the Book and International Festival of the Culture (Santo Domingo de Guzmán, Dominican Republic). In 1971 Mexico took part in the Third International Book Fair in Costa Rica (San José) and in the "Culturama Mexico 71" event in Spain (Madrid).

Book exhibitions by private firms are also of considerable cultural importance in Mexico, although they are not fairs as such. These events take place at various times throughout the year for the benefit both of the public at large and for selected groups, specialists and professionals. An example of such exhibitions are the Publishers' Weeks of the Librería Internacional.

30 Public Relations

The book industry has no organized public-relations system. Apart from the exhibitions mentioned in the previous section,

the bookshops support contact between client and publisher. Radio and TV commentaries on this activity and about books themselves are infrequent. However, newspapers devote more space to the subject.
The Mexican Book Institute (→4) could initiate more direct contact with the public, but it is a private organization and has not the economic means to organize such a system.

31 Bibliophily

There are no special organizations for bibliophiles, who are mostly members of the highly educated upper class. The middle class have not yet developed reading habits. At a time when they began to show signs of becoming interested in reading, TV became the book's greatest rival. With its weapons of sound and moving pictures TV has more or less won the battle. In the lower classes book-mindedness is practically non-existent.

32 Literary Prizes

There are half a dozen national and two international literary prizes. The first and most important one is the *Premio Nacional de Letras*. It is one of the group: *Premios Nacionales de Ciencias, Letras y Artes*, which the government awards every year for the complete literary work of a Mexican author (1972: Rodolfo Urigli, 100,000 Pesos). The President sponsors the *Premio Villarrutia*, founded in 1955, while the aforementioned prize was awarded for the first time in 1944. The prize is dedicated to young authors, and the present award is 100,000 Pesos divided among writers of poetry, novels, the theatre and essays.
Apart from these prizes the government also awards the *Belisario Dominguez Medal* for outstanding merits in science, the humanities and literature.

Some other literary prizes are:
Premio Nacional de Letras "Rodolfo E. Goes", Premio "Magda Donato", Premio "Diana Moreno", and *Premio de Novela "Netzahualcoyotl"*.

These prizes are national, but in 1972 two international literary prizes were instituted for authors writing in Spanish:
Premio Internacional de Novela "Mexico", (Editorial Novaro, 10,000 US $), and *Premio Internacional de la Novela "Alfonso Reyes" (Capilla Alfonsina, 100,000 Pesos)*.

33 The Reviewing of Books

Book reviews appear periodically in technical magazines and similar publications. These, to a certain degree, keep professional groups informed about new books. Publications such as those mentioned in section 5 regularly include commentaries of this nature. Various magazines, both technical and general *(Ciencia, Medicina, Prensa Médica Mexicana)*, and nearly all daily newspapers have sections on work published in Mexico *(Excelsior, Mexico en la Cultura)*. Moreover, to a smaller extent, there are a few weekly radio and television programmes that discuss recently published books.

34 Graphic Arts

In Mexico the graphic arts have developed to what might well be considered a remarkable degree. Private firms, especially those concentrating in this field, now produce works of a high technical and artistic level, although in volume and quantity they cannot as yet compare with those of North America or Europe. There are some private organizations through which people interested in this subject can contact like-minded people. Such organizations are the *Cámara Nacional de la Industria de Artes Gráficas*

Mexico

(The National Chamber of the Graphic Art Industry)
Av. Rio de Churubusco 428
MEX México 21, D.F.
and the
Unión de Industriales Litógrafos de México
(Union of Lithographers of Mexico)
Av. H. Suderman 122
MEX México 5, D.F.

35 Miscellaneous

a) Schoolbooks

By presidential decree of 12 February 1959 the "National Commission of Free Text Books" (for Primary Schools) was formed. It is responsible to the *Secretaría de Educación Publica* (Secretariat of Public Education). The importance of this decree is perhaps more of a social or political nature, but it has notable cultural repercussions and, concretely, as far as the publishing industry is concerned, there is a large potential reader public, many of whom will possibly become assiduous readers. In order to enable the publishing industry to expand in Mexico, these will have to be encouraged.

b) Publishers' Opinion

In 1969 the newspaper *El Día* carried out an inquiry among the thirteen most important publishing houses in the country *(Cía. General de Ediciones, Editorial Diógenes, Ediciones Era, Fondo de Cultura Económica, Fondo de Cultura Popular, Editorial Grijalvo, Editorial Jus, Editorial Joaquín Mortiz, Ediciones Novaro, Editorial Nuestro Tiempo, Ediciones Porrúa Hnos., Siglo XXI)* and the publishing house of the National University. It asked five questions, the answers to which are given below.
1. What are the aims of a publishing house? Cultural: 38.5%. Social and political: 38.5%. Commercial: 23%.
2. How do you reconcile the pecuniary interests of the publisher with the cultural aims of publishing?

Publishing everything which is of value: 46.1%. Publishing both books of cultural interest and those which will be a commercial success: 30.8%. Sacrificing lucre on the altars of culture: 15.4%. The publisher reconciles the two opposites subjectively: 7.7%.
3. What subjects does the reader prefer? Socio-political essays: 38.5%. Literary works: 38.8%. Contemporary problems: 23.3%. Cheap selected works: 7.7%.
4. What subjects do you choose as publisher? About Mexico: 30.8%. Subjects which appeal to young people: 23.8%. Contemporary problems: 15.4%. Literary: 7.7%. Latin American problems: 7.7%.
5. What kind of public do you appeal to? Students and professionals: 46.1%. The cultured middle class: 38.5%. Every type of public: 15.4%.
In theory, the majority of Mexican publishers (77.7%) are motivated by their interest in spreading culture and only 23% have economic incentives as their basic motivation. 53% consider that publishing houses would not be viable if they only published books which were of cultural value. The public prefers political subjects to literary works and to a lesser extent it favours cheap editions.
The subjects chosen by the publisher pertain principally to socio-economic questions (61.5%) and to Mexican problems. Only to a very slight extent do they choose literary subjects (7.7%). The reading public is mainly composed of students, professional people and the cultured middle class (84.6%). It is considered that the remaining 15.4% is made up of people from all sections of the community.

c) Financial Support

In May 1970, preliminary measures were taken in conjunction with officers of the Foreign Department of the *Banco Nacional de México, S.A.* (National Bank of Mexico) in order to obtain credit for book publishers and enable them to finance exports. A similar meeting was planned with the Foreign Department of the *Banco de Comercio, S.A.* (Bank of Commerce). The *Cámara Nacional de la Industria Editorial* (National Chamber of the Publishing Industry, →4) took an active part in these talks with directors of the publishing companies. It is hoped that results will be encouraging, so that the production and trade in books in Mexico will increase in the next few years.

Netherlands Antilles

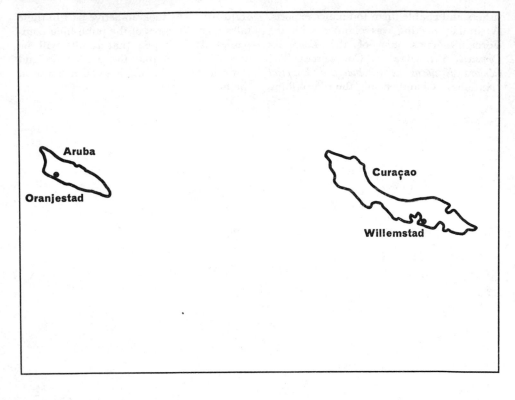

1 General Information

Area 961 km² (Aruba 184 km²; Bonaire 290 km²; Curaçao 461 km²; Saba 13 km²; San Eustaquio 31 km²; Saint Maarten, South part 41 km²)

Population 218,000 (Aruba 53,199; Bonaire 5,812; Curaçao 125,481; Saba, San Eustaquio, Saint Maarten 4,722; 227 per km²)

Capital Willemstad, Curaçao (43,547)

Largest towns Willemstad (43,547); Oranjestad; Aruba

Government Autonomous part of the Kingdom of the Netherlands, directed by a Governor of the Queen, with a delegate on every island

Religion Roman Catholic 80 %

National language Dutch, also Papiamento

Leading foreign languages English, Spanish

Weights, measures Metric system

Currency unit Antillian Guilder (NA fl) = 100 cents (cts)

Education Non-compulsory. No academic educational institution (12,966 students in 2nd level and 572 in four special professional institutions in 1966)

Illiteracy Nil

Paper consumption a) Newsprint 2.8 kg per inhabitant (1968)
b) Printing paper (other than newsprint) 5.2 kg per inhabitant (1968)

Membership UNESCO–jointly with the Netherlands and Surinam (→BTW I, Netherlands 8)

2 Past and Present

From the arrival of the Spaniards at the Windward Islands (Aruba, Curaçao and Bonaire) in 1527 up to the final assumption of the six Antilles islands by the Netherlands crown in 1816, these territories changed hands frequently. This, however, did not prevent the spread of printing and books over the islands, which flank the South American continent.

San Eustaquio, one of the two smallest islands of the group–its only importance was as a harbour on the routes of British, French and Spanish vessels–is the first to have had printing at the end of the 18th century with the publication of "The St Eustatius Gazette". Nowadays on this island there is no printer on the island, nor any other publishing activity. Curaçao was next: in the time of British rule, William Lee, a Scotsman, arrived from Caracas and in 1812 founded the first printing press. He published the English "Curaçao Gazette", which still exists today under its Dutch title "De Couraçaosche Courant". It is the most important paper of the Netherlands Antilles, as well as one of the biggest printing plants and publishing companies.

Also from Venezuela, on the South American continent, came the first publishers and booksellers, in 1830, extending their activities quickly over the six Antilles islands. The islands of Aruba and Curaçao, with its capital cities, soon became the Antilles' centres of book production and book trade, where 5 publishers and 12 bookshops now exist, with at least one bookseller on every island of the group. During colonial times, which ended in 1954 when the islands became an autonomous part of the Kingdom of the Netherlands, they always had an independent book trade, mainly influenced by the Netherlands, but with connections to the United States of America and to the United Kingdom; the latter is most evident on the English-speaking Leeward Islands.

These international influences, and the Netherlands Antilles being on the crossroads of American and European commercial, tourist and cultural connections, supported by an open-minded private initiative, give the book trade on the Netherlands Antilles its special character.

Bibliography

J. Hartog, *Journalistik leven in Curaçao.* (Journalistic life in Curaçao.) Nijmegen 1944.

J. Hartog, *Verspielding van de drukkunst in de Nederlandse Antillen.* (Development of the graphic arts on the Netherlands Antilles.) In: Tété (Amsterdam) 1963, pp. 22–26.

Br. F. Swan, *The spread of printing, Western Hemisphere: The Caribbean area.* Amsterdam, Vangendt 1970. 47 pp. pp. 37–41: Netherlands Antilles.

J. van de Walle, *De Nederlandse Antillen; land, volk, cultuur.* (The Netherlands Antilles; land, people, culture.) Baarn, Het Wereldvenster 1954. 204 pp.

3 Retail Prices

There is no legal retail-price maintenance. Booksellers, however, by agreement among themselves, respect retail prices fixed by the publishers. As for the majority of imported books, a general price schedule is observed by the trade which is based on the prices in the countries of origin. As regards the trade's own agreements, no discount is given on these retail prices of books, with the exception of a 15% discount on sales to public and scientific libraries.

7 Sources of Information, Address Services

While there is no individual institution for the documentation of book statistics and information thereon, local booksellers as well as publishers estimate their activities individually. General cultural information can be obtained from the main public libraries,

Openbaare Bibliotheek van het
Eilandgebied Curaçao
(Public Library for the Island
Territory of Curaçao)
Johan van Walbeeckplein 13
NA Willemstad, Curaçao

and

Openbaare Leeszaal en Boekerij
(Public Reading Room and Library)
Wilhelminastraat 6
NA Oranjestad, Aruba

There are also some institutions in the Netherlands that collect material about books and literature on the Netherlands Antilles (→BTW I, Special Libraries "Books about Books": Netherlands). One of them is a special foundation for cultural and scientific cooperation with the Netherlands Antilles,

Nederlandse Stichting voor Culturele
Samenwerking met Suriname en de
Nederlandse Antillen (STICUSA)
(Netherlands Foundation for Cultural
Cooperation with Surinam and the Nether-
lands Antilles)
J. J. Viottastraat 41
NL Amsterdam-Zuid

which by its special publications and in individual cases may be able to provide information.

Bibliography

Opgave van Litteratuur betreffende de Nederlandse Antillen. (Books and periodicals on
the Netherlands Antilles.) Amsterdam,
Sticusa 1967. 42 pp.

10 Books and Young People

Booksellers as well as librarians are conscious of the growing importance of youth as readers. Furthermore, as young people on the Netherlands Antilles mostly under-stand Dutch, the official language at school, they are the main recipients of reading campaigns. The centres of these activities are the public libraries on Curaçao, Aruba, Bonaire and Saint Maarten. Juvenile books are on sale in every bookshop on the islands, and young readers are an important target for publishers.

12 Taxes

Books are absolutely tax free on the Netherlands Antilles. This applies to the sale and the publication of books, as well as to the importation of books and periodicals.

14 Copyright

The Antilles are a member of the Berne Convention (→BTW I, International Section 14) and have signed international conventions in combination with the Kingdom of the Netherlands (→BTW I, Netherlands 14).

15 National Bibliography, National Library

Local book production is generally incorporated in the Netherlands' bibliographies (→BTW I, Netherlands 15). A bibliography of books *in* and *on* Papiamento is being prepared in Aruba.

No national library exists on the islands. The two most important public libraries in Curaçao and Aruba

Openbaare Bibliotheek van het
Eilandgebied Curaçao
(Public Library for the Island
Territory of Curaçao)
Johan van Walbeeckplein 13
NA Willemstad, Curaçao

and

Openbaare Leeszaal en Boekerij
(Public Reading Room and Library)
Wilhelminastraat 6
NA Oranjestad, Aruba

to some extent serve as national libraries,

since they buy everything published on the islands and about them. However, there is no depository law in the Netherlands Antilles.

Bibliography

H. E. COOMANS, *Het Bibliotheekwesen op de Nederlandse Antillen.* (The Library system in the Netherlands Antilles.) In: Bibliotheekleven (Amsterdam) 1961, pp. 564 –568.

16 Book Production

No statistics are available. Some 10 to 15 titles are published annually on the islands, including school books. A number of books are published by the authors themselves, and these are not registered. Various institutions connected with the churches are also active contributors to local book production.

Bibliography

G. DEBROT, *Literature of the Netherlands Antilles.* Edited by the Department of Culture and Education. Willemstad, De Curaçaosche Courant 1964. 28 pp.

19 Paperbacks

The pocketbooks sold on these six islands are nearly all imported in foreign languages, i.e. in Dutch and English, the latter mainly imported from the United States of America. Publishers in Aruba have recently begun to publish general titles in paperbacks. The only sale outlets for pocketbooks are bookshops.

21 Publishing

Of the five publishing companies, only two publish primarily books, and at the same time act as booksellers. Since authors, and to some extend the churches, often publish their books privately, there exists some publishing apart from the commercial channels. Government institutions, other than in most of the American countries, do no publishing, neither directly nor by subsidizing publications. So financing is only by private initiative.

The books published in the Netherlands Antilles are mainly textbooks, the average edition of general titles being about 1,000 copies per title.

24 Retail Trade

As in publishing, bookselling activities are purely private. There are about 12 bookshops, one at least on each of the six islands. In the book-trade centres of the Antilles (Willemstad on Curaçao and Oranjestad on Aruba) specialized and well-stocked bookshops exist. 90% of all books sold are bought in bookshops.

27 Book Imports

Of books sold in the island territories up to 99% are imported. Annual imports of books are relatively high; worth aproximately US $ 500,000 (estimated figure) in 1970. The books are mainly in Dutch, the Netherlands being the most important supplier (80% of the Antilles' imports). Other imports are in English and Spanish: imports from the United States make up about 15% of all book imports, while for books in Spanish Mexico is the main supplier. The value of imported periodicals is worth about US$ 50,000 annually (1970).

Bibliography

G. STUIVELING, *Nederlandse Letteren in de Antillen.* (Dutch literature on the Antilles.) In: Schakels (The Hague) 1959, pp. 42–48.

J. TERLINGEN, *Las Antillas Neerlandesas en su vecindad.* Lengua y literatura Españolas en las Antillas Neerlandesas. (The Netherlands Antilles and their neighbours.

Spanish language and literature on the Netherlands Antilles.) Willemstad, Regeringsvoorlichtingsdienst der Nederlandse Antillen 1961. 39 pp.

28 Book Exports

Of the few books published on the Antilles a small part is sold to the Netherlands. The quantities vary widely, and it is not possible to give annual figures.

32 Literary Prizes

Only one prize for cultural events exists on the Netherlands Antilles, instituted in 1968 by the Island Government of Curaçao: the *Cola Debrot-Prize* awarded every year alternately for music, sculpture, literature, etc.

33 The Reviewing of Books

Book reviews are only published in the daily papers (there are 6 local papers with a total edition–in 1968–of 34,000 copies). Cultural reviews in the Antilles rarely review books (there are 42 weekly and other periodicals with a total edition of 97,000 copies). Many books published on the Netherlands Antilles, however, are reviewed by periodicals in the Netherlands. There are two daily papers with a special page for book reviews, totaling about 160 reviews per year.
Book reviews on radio (6 transmitters and 3 TV stations) are broadcasted once a week. In every case, the newspaper or the radio station will ask for review copies: little is done by the publisher to promote his books.

Bibliography

J. Hartog, *Journalistiek leven in Curaçao.* (Journalistic life in Curaçao.) Nijmegen 1944.
A. G. Jansen, *De Pers of Curaçao.* (The press at Curaçao.) In: Christoffel (Curaçao) 1947, pp. 154–170.
J. A. J. Verschoor, *Gedenkboek ter gelegenheid van het 150-jarig bestaan van de Curaçaosche Courant.* (Memorial volume for the 150th anniversary of the "Curaçaosche Courant".) Willemstad, Drukkerij de Curaçaose Courant 1966.

34 Graphic Arts

Printers were the first to bring books to the Netherlands Antilles, the Leewards Islands, and the Lesser Antilles. Their place in publishing as well as in bookselling is thus very important. Today, about six private printers work on the islands, together with two bookbinders. A considerable activity of printing is done by the churches, which began to print and publish soon after the establishment of the first private printer. The graphic arts have a regular standard on the islands, their chief output being publications for daily use.

Bibliography

J. Hartog, *Verspielding van de drukkunst in de Nederlandse Antillen.* (Development of the graphic arts on the Netherlands Antilles.) In: Tété (Amsterdam) 1963, pp. 22–26.
J. A. J. Verschoor, *Gedenkboek ter gelegenheid van het 150-jarig bestaan van de Couraçaosche Courant.* (Memorial volume for the 150th anniversary of the "Couraçaosche Courant".) Willemstad, Drukkerij de Couraçaose Courant 1966.

Nicaragua

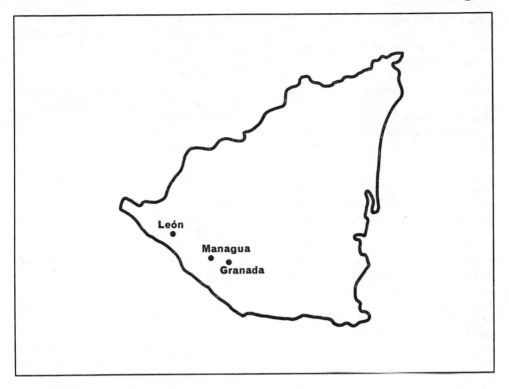

1 General Information

Area 148,000 km²
Population 1,842,000 (14 per km²; Mestizo 70%, White 17%, Negro 9%, Indian 4%)
Capital Managua (300,000 in 1967)
Largest towns Managua (300,000); León (79,939); Granada (47,573)
Government Presidential Republic
Religion Roman Catholic predominant; Protestants 54,100
National language Spanish
Leading foreign language English
Weights, measures Metric system
Currency unit Córdoba (C$) = 100 centavos (cts)
Education Compulsory for six years. 4,056 students (1967) in two universities and a college of academic level (Escuela Nacional de Agricultura y Ganadería)
Illiteracy 63.7% (1960)

Paper consumption a) Newsprint 2.9 kg per inhabitant (1967)
b) Printing paper (other than newsprint) 0.9 kg per inhabitant (1968)
Membership UNESCO

Nicaragua

2 Past and Present

Nicaragua was first discovered and visited by the Spanish in 1522. The chief of the then leading Indian tribe gave his name to the country. A Spanish colony up to the year 1838, Nicaragua became independent after some years of participation in the short-lived Central Amercian Republic. During long periods, the country later suffered strong United States influences and interventions.

Due to Spain's colonial political influences on the country's culture, it was only after independence that Nicaragua could develop a book-life of its own. The first newspaper to appear was "El Porvenir" in 1865; the first printers settled in the city of León in 1880; and the first publisher/bookseller of Spanish origin, came to Nicaragua in 1886. The traditional city of León, at that time the cradle of the Nicaraguan book and printing industry, now occupies third place as a book-trade centre in the country, after the capital and Granada.

Although Nicaragua's general trade is mainly with the United States, Germany (Federal Republic), her Central American neighbours, and Japan, a strong influence in commercial patterns is still exercised by Spain on her book trade. These patterns are only slowly changing in favour of contact with American countries, among whom the chief supplier is Mexico, whose trading habits and sales system, influenced by the United States, are now beginning to make their appearance in Nicaragua.

The two second-largest book-trade centres, León and Granada, once again grew in importance, after the heavy damage wrought on the capital by the tragic earthquake of December 1972. The reconstruction of the capital will undoubtedly change the face of the Nicaraguan book world. The information given below, including addresses, however, refers to the situation shortly before the 1972 disaster.

Bibliography

Anuario Statistico. (Statistical Yearbook). Managua, Ministerio de Economía y Comercio 1936 ff.

7 Sources of Information, Address Services

Book information can be obtained from the
> *Biblioteca Nacional*
> *(National Library)*
> *Calle del Triunfo, 302*
> *NIC Managua*

or, information of a more general natural, from the
> *Archivo Nacional*
> *(National Archive)*
> *6a. Calle No. 402*
> *NIC Managua*

Some of the daily newspapers of Managua have close ties with local writers and frequently publish poems and short stories. Thus their archives, for instance that of
> *La Prensa*
> *Domicilio conocido*
> *NIC Managua*

offer a wide range of items on this subject.

Bibliography

The addresses of all branches of the book trade of are contained in
> *La Empresa del Libro en América Latina.* (The Book in Latin America.) 2nd ed. Buenos Aires, Bowker Editores Argentina 1974. VIII, 307 pp.
> p. 217: Nicaragua.

12 Taxes

In Nicaragua, books are subject to a reduced sales tax of 2.2%. Production, however, and the import of books are absolutely free of taxes.

15 National Bibliography, National Library

Bibliographies on Nicaraguan books are very rare. Only occasionally do the reports of the National Library contain a bibliography of any one year. At present (1972), the National Library together with the Ministry of Education are preparing a conference for publishers and printers to guarantee an annual national bibliography for the future.
The

Biblioteca Nacional
(National Library)
Calle del Triunfo, 302
NIC Managua

was founded in 1882 and houses nearly 100,000 volumes. As the publisher, author or printer of any book published in Nicaragua is obliged to deposit by law two copies in the National Library, it has a complete collection of the country's books.

Bibliography

Bibliografía Americana de Nicaragua. Libros y folletos publicados 1942 (ó antes). (American bibliography of Nicaragua. books and brochures published 1943 or before.) Managua, Editorial Nuevos Horizontes 1945. 157 pp.
Bibliografía de Trabajos publicados en Nicaragua en 1943. (Bibliography of works published in Nicaragua in 1943.) – "Serie de la Bibliografía Americana 1". Managua, Biblioteca Nacional/Editorial Nuevos Horizontes 1944. 50 pp.
Published yearly up to 1948 (for the year 1947).
Boletin Informativo 1963/64. (Information Bulletin 1963/64.) 2 vols. Managua, Biblioteca Nacional/Ministerio de Educación Pública 1965. 60, 74 pp.
I. ZIMMERMANN, *Current national bibliographies of Latin America.* Gainesville, Florida, University of Florida Press 1971. X. 139 pp.
pp. 84–86: Nicaragua.

21 Publishing

Since they enjoyed relative liberty in their activities, Christian schools play an important role in Nicaraguan publishing history, as far as their textbooks and religious literature are concerned, during colonial times in León and Managua. Nowadays most of the companies also run small printing plants or newspapers all over the country. Furthermore, state institutions (such as the Ministry of Education, the Statistical Offices, the National University) publish a fairly large proportion of the country's books, their title output being estimated at about a third of total production.

27 Book Imports

Imported books dominate the national book market, due to the small number of books published locally. Though Spain remains an influential supplier in the trade, Latin American countries and the United States are constantly increasing their book sales to Nicaragua. The latest official statistics available, for 1970, give the following figures (total imports: US $ 654,844):

Country	US $
USA	185,981
Mexico	159,325
Panama	157,997
Argentina	46,174
Costa Rica	36,818
Guatemala	18,784

Bibliography

Memoria de la Direccion general da Aduanas, 1970. Managua, Ministerio de Economía y Comercio 1971.

28 Book Exports

Because of the low number of books produced locally, exports are very small. The statistics for 1970 give a total of US $ 17,426, with Honduras, Costa Rica and Guatemala as the main countries of destination.

29 Book Fairs

A nation-wide book exhibition is organized annually in Managua by the Ministry of Education. Local exhibitions are very occasionally organized by some booksellers.

Bibliography

F. COLOMA GONZALEZ, *Exposición del Libro Nicaraguense 1964.* (Exhibition of the Nicaraguan Book 1964.) Managua, Ministerio de Educación Pública 1965. 4 pp.

32 Literary Prizes

Among a number of small and private literary prices, the most important is the official annual prize, *Premio Nacional de la Patria*, awarded since 1960.

33 The Reviewing of Books

The 11 dailies, with a total of 91,000 copies, and the 39 magazines give wide coverage to books. Some newspapers, especially in the capital, publish short stories and poems by national authors, thus providing the only platform for young local writers who wish to present their work to the public. Very few local book publishers are prepared to print their work. The leading newspapers are: *La Prensa, Novedades,* and *La Noticia.*

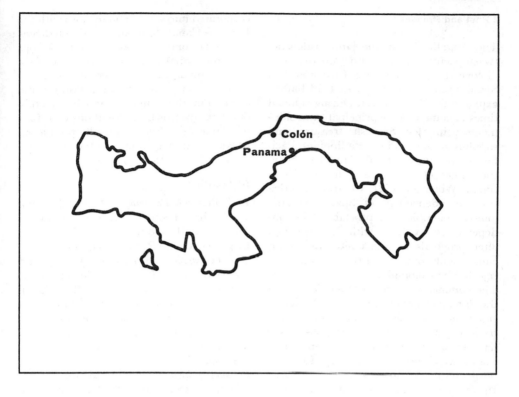

1 General Information

Area 75,650 km²
Population 1,414,000 (18.7 per km²; Mestizo 65.3%, Negro 13.3%, White 11%, Indian 9.5%, others 0.8% = 1970)
Capital Ciudad de Panamá (492,000 = 1970)
Largest towns Panamá (492,000), Colón (65,600)
Government Presidential republic
Religion Roman Catholic 93%, Protestant 6%
National language Spanish (official), some Indian dialects
Leading foreign language English
Weights, measures Metric system, also British units
Currency unit Balboa (B$) = 100 cents (cts); at par with the US $, therefore also US-coinage in use
Education Compulsory from 7 to 15 years. 9,265 students (1967) in two universities
Illiteracy 23% (1960–excluding certain tribes)

Paper consumption a) Newsprint 3.2 kg per inhabitant (1969)
b) Printing paper (other than newsprint) 2.6 kg per inhabitant (1968)
Membership UNESCO, CERLAL
→ Panama, Canal Zone

243

Panama

2 Past and Present

The Atlantic side of the land bridge between Central and South America was discovered by Columbus in 1510, and then Spanish settlement began. In 1513 Balboa explored the Pacific coast. During colonial times Panama was the principal trans-shipment point for Spanish treasure and supplies from and to the Philippines, Pacific South and Central America, being the target of attacks by pirates several times. When in 1821 Central America became independent of Spain, Panama joined Colombia, but proclaimed her independence in 1903 with US backing, after proposals by the United States for canal rights over the isthmus had been rejected by Colombia.

The commerce of the 16 km-wide strip of the Panama Canal is the republic's biggest economic asset. Also in its general foreign trade–exports (mainly bananas, 58%)–she has strong connections with the United States, which takes over 76.6% of her exports and makes up 38.4% of all imports. In the book trade, too, Panama's relations with the United States are very close. Apart from being among the three most important suppliers of books, a number of big US publishers and printers maintain branches in Colón, in the Free Trade Zone, for their production and sales operations with Central and South America. The Free Zone of Colón is an important factor within Panama's international trade. The government's offer of a 20 years' exemption from taxes for companies settled in the Zone has attracted a number of producing and service firms–also some companies related to the book.

Unlike other Central American states, Panama is a less important customer for Spanish books, and only after the end of colonial times (when Spanish-realm policy no longer restricted an independent book trade), did a national book life begin, incorporated into strong connections with the Panama Canal Zone and the United States. Today one can observe the bookshops near the Canal Zone as directed to book buyers among the employees of the Canal Company and the tourists visiting the canal. But the country's activity steadily develops towards better relations with Latin America's leading book producers, Mexico and Argentina, and with neighbouring Costa Rica.

Bibliography

J. H. BIESANZ, *Panamá y su pueblo*. (Panama and her people). Mexico, Editorial Letras 1961. 308 pp.

E. J. CASTILLERO REYES, *Origines y desarrollo de la imprenta en Panamá*. (Origin and development of printing in Panama.) Panamá, Imprenta Nacional 1958. 35 pp.

A. M. JAEN Y JAEN, *Breve historia de la situación del libro en Panamá*. (Short history of the situation of the book in Panama.) Panamá, Universidad Nacional 1949. 44 pp.

Panamá en Cifras. (Panama in figures.) Panamá, Dirección de Estatística y Censo 1948 ff.

4 Organization

Panama has a professional organization of booksellers, the

> *Asocación Nacional de Librerías*
> *(National Association of Bookshops)*
> *Apartado Postal 2052*
> *Calle 23, No. 56–28*
> *PA Ciudad de Panamá*

which is based on private initiative.

6 Book-Trade Literature

Professional literature in the book field is very rare as regards bookselling and publishing. There are, however, very active university studies and a great many academic theses on library questions and those related to the cultural importance of the book, chiefly in the Library department of the National University and its Library School.

Bibliography

Boletín de la Escuela de Bibliotecología Panameña. (Bulletin of the Panamanean Bibliotechnical School.) Panamá, Biblioteca de la Universidad Nacional 1958 ff. Irregular.

El Heraldo. Boletín de Información Literario y Bibliográfico (The Herald. Bulletin of literary and bibliographical information.) Panamá, El Heraldo 1959 ff. Monthly.

C. D. DE HERRERA a. o., *The book trade, bibliography, and exchange of publications in Panama.* Coral Gables, Florida, University of Miami Library 1962. 14 pp. – 7th Seminar on the Acquisition of Library Materials. – Mimeographed.

Primeras Jornadas de Bibliotecarios Panameños. Febrero 1967. Información general. (First Panamanean Librarian Days February 1967. General information.) Panamá, Ministerio de Educación Pública 1967.

7 Sources of Information, Address Services

Information about the book trade can be obtained from the booksellers' association,

Asocación Nacional de Librerías
(National Association of Bookshops)
Apartado Postal 2052
Calle 23, No. 56–28
PA Ciudad de Panamá

As to Panamanean book production and literature in general, information is obtainable from the

Biblioteca Nacional
(National Library)
Apartado Postal 3435
PA Ciudad de Panamá

General questions of a commercial nature are handled by the

Cámara de Comercio de las Américas
(Commercial Chamber of the Americas)
Avenida 5a, No. 338–18
PA Ciudad de Panamá

Information about the Free Zone of Colón, is obtainable from the

Free Zone Authority
Apartado Postal 1108
PA Colón

Address services specialized in books do not exist. General services, however, might have enough material on book-buying groups and can be contacted through the Commercial Chamber of the Americas. On the other hand, in non-competitive cases, some of the big credit-sales organizations working in Panama City and in Colón offer to combine any circular.

Bibliography

The addresses of all branches of the book trade are contained in

La Empresa del Libro en América Latina. (The Book in Latin America.) 2nd ed. Buenos Aires, Bowker Editores Argentina 1974. VIII, 307 pp. pp. 219–222: Panama.

H. ESPINOZA, *Estudio y organización del sistema bibliotecario en Panama.* (Study and organization of the library system in Panama.) Panamá, Universidad Nacional (thesis) 1951. 93 pp.

F. PERAZA Y SARAUSA, *Directorio de bibliotecas en Panama.* (Directory of libraries in Panama.) La Habana, Ediciones de la Asociación de Bibliotecarios Cubanos 1948. 48 pp.

10 Books and Young People

Apart from the isolated ventures of private book-trade firms, it is primarily the libraries and the Ministry of Education that are active in promoting reading habits among young people.

There is an interesting government institution, the

Banco del Libro
(Bank of the Book)
Vía España
PA Ciudad de Panamá

Founded in 1967 by the Ministry of Education, the "Banco del Libro" was first established to concentrate state buying of textbooks for primary schools. According to official reports and orders, this institution annually placed a bulk order for the textbooks needed in the country directly with the publishers. Later on, it participated in the creation of school libraries, and at present (1972) it is engaged in forming a basic library of children's books in all primary schools in the republic. Apart from government subsidies, the institution counts on a good number of donations from private individuals (who are asked to assign a part of the value of a basic stock for such libraries), but also from shipments supported by other countries.

Bibliography

O. CEDENO, *Directorio de labor educativa de las bibliotecas de la Provincia de Herrera.* (Directory of the educational work of the libraries in the Province of Herrera.) Panamá, Universidad Nacional 1972. 92 pp.

El Libro como Agente de Progreso de un Pueblo. (The book as agent of progress of a nation.) Edited by the Normal School "Juan Demóstenes Arasemena". Santiago de Veraguas (Panamá), Tipografía Santiago 1946. 11 pp.

15 National Bibliography, National Library

Apart from special investigations concentrating on certain years, no annual bibliography is published for Panamanean books. The only source, then, is the catalogue of the National Library and its book lists, issued from time to time in mimeographed form. An almost complete legal deposit of Panamanean books can be found there. The

Biblioteca Nacional
(National Library)
Partado Postal 3435
Calle 22
PA Ciudad de Panamá

was founded in 1892, taking over the books and the rooms of the then "Bibliotéca Colón". It has a stock of 160,000 volumes (1969).

Apart from the National Library, and the well-organized library of the National University, the country has 18 school libraries, 24 specialized and 127 public libraries. The librarians in the Republic are members of the

Asociación Panameña de Bibliotecarios
(Panamanean Association of Librarians)
c/o Biblioteca de la Universidad Nacional
Apartado Postal 3277
PA Ciudad de Panamá

Bibliography

G. ANDREVE, *Biblioteca, cultura nacional.* (The library, national culture.) Panamá, Tipografía Moderna 1918. 33 pp.

Bibliografía Bibliotecológica. (Bibliotechnical bibliography.) Panamá, Biblioteca Nacional 1959.

Boletín de la Escuela de Bibliotecología Panameña. (Bulletin of the Panamanean Library School.) Panamá, Biblioteca de la Universidad Nacional 1958 ff. Irregular.

E. J. CASTILLERO REYES, *Orígenes y desarrollo de la imprenta en Panamá.* (Origin and development of printing in Panama.) Panamá, Imprenta Nacional 1958. 35 pp.

H. G. DOYLE, *A tentative bibliography of the belles-lettres of Panama.* Cambridge, Mass., Harvard Council of Hispanic-American Studies 1934. 21 pp.

M. A. GALVEZ G., *Impresiones de un viaje de estudios bibliotecarios en Panamá.* (Impressions of a journey by library students in Panama.) 2 vols. Guatemala, Tipografía Nacional 1951. 221, 224 pp.

G. PATINO, *Panamá necesita bibliotecas.* (Panama needs libraries.) Panamá, Asociación de Bibliotecarios 1944. 28 pp.

F. PERAZO Y SARAUSA. *Directorio de bibliotecas en Panamá.* (Directory of libraries in Panama.) Series "Biblioteca del Bibliotecario", vol. 21. La Habana, Editorial de la Asociación de Bibliotecarios Cubanos 1948. 48 pp.

Primeras Jornadas de Bibliotecarios Panameños. (First Meeting of Panamanean Librarians.) Febrero 1967. Información General. Panamá, Ministerio de Educación Publica 1967.

G. SUCRE REYES, *La biblioteca como medio efectivo en el desarrollo cultural del país.* (The library as an effective medium in the development of the country.) Panamá, Universidad Nacional 1969. 3, 110 pp.

J. A. SUSTO, *Panorama de la bibliografía de Panamá 1619–1967.* (Panorama of the bibliography of Panama 1619–1967.) Panamá, Editorial Universitaria 1971. 19, 102 pp.

L. VANEGAS LOPEZ, *Organización y reforma administrativa de la Biblioteca Nacional.* (Organization and administrative reform of the National Library.) Panamá, Universidad Nacional 1971. 64 pp.

I. ZIMMERMANN, *Current national bibliographies of Latin America.* Gainesville, Florida, University of Florida Press 1971. X, 139 pp.
pp. 86–88: Panama.
→6: Bibliography.

16 Book Production

No official figures are available. For the year 1969 195 titles are listed, seven of which were published in English.
In 1970 Panama published 132 titles:

Subject group	Titles
Generalities	18
Philosophy	1
Religion	2
Social sciences	46
Philology	11
Pure sciences	9
Applied sciences	15
Arts	4
Literature	13
Geography, history	13
Total	132

Bibliography

A. M. JAÉN Y JAÉN, *Breve historia de la situación del libro en Panamá.* (Short history of the situation of the book in Panama. Panamá, Universidad Nacional 1949. 44 pp.

21 Publishing

While private publishing in Panama is relatively small, government institutions play an important part in this field. This refers not only to textbooks, where the state as publisher and as bookseller (concentrating on the buying of textbooks, including imported books in the so-called "Banco del Libro" →10) owns the main sources. Nearly all kinds of official and historical publications are published by an official institution, under the aegis of the Ministry of Education, or by the Autonomous National University, and the National Printing Plant.

Bibliography

Informe de la Comisión Nacional de Reforma Educativa. Subscomisión "Fomento y Producción del Libro Panameño". (Report of the National Commission of Educational Reform. Subcommission "Origination and Production of the Panamanean Book".) Panamá, Editorial Educativa 1971.

Panama

E. C. Paredes S., *La industría tipográfica en Panamá.* (The graphic industry in Panama.) Panamá, Universidad Nacional 1967. 4, 133 pp.

Year	US $
1967	836,346
1968	631,223
1969	302,178
1970	325,228

24 Retail Trade

Retail bookshops work on a private basis. One characteristic of the Panamanean book trade is the importance of chains of bookshops which dominate the sales of tourist books, for instance, as well as the distribution of paperbacks and magazines within the same firm. On the other hand, a number of branches of United States companies are working in the country (→25) mainly in direct sales. Most of the bookshops are in the capital, with a number of them, also distributors, in the Free Zone of Colón.

25 Mail-Order Bookselling

Panama is the centre for Central America in the activity of direct-sales companies, not only by mail but also by door-to-door salesmen. These companies, mostly of US-origin and partly with headquarters in the Free Zone of the city of Colón, constitute a second and very important market for the sales of encyclopedias and high-priced books on credit, which as in some other Central American countries, already outnumber the sales to the public through the traditional bookshops.

27 Book Imports

Imported books constitute the main part of book sales in Panama, both in Spanish and English, the latter being sold mainly to tourists and to the employees of the Canal Company (→ Panama, Canal Zone 24). The figures are as follows:

Among the total imports of the year 1968, Mexico is the main supplier, with 194,000 US $, followed by the United States with 160,000 US $, and by Costa Rica with 152,000 US $ worth of books. The latter can be supposed to deliver books partly from Central American distributors of Spanish books, and partly for shipments of the Publishing Company of Central American Universities (→ Costa Rica 21) printed and published for the Panamanean universities. Spain, in the same year, reports, sales worth 10 million Pesetas to Panama. In 1968 the Free Trade Zone of Colón contributed 49,000 US $ worth of books to national sales.

28 Book Exports

Exports of books from Panama are relatively small, due to the national publishing situation. Even though the country is a central channel for international book trade within the Americas, the figure for 1968 is only 68,000 US $. Nevertheless, from printing plants in Colón owned by big American companies, and including the part of their production that counts as being of Panamanean origin, the total export of printed materials was 267,533 US $.

As a unique fact in Latin America, Spanish sources report that her imports from Panama outnumbered by nearly four times the sales to that country, being a total of 37.5 million Pesetas.

30 Public Relations

Public-relations activities in the book trade are rather small, as the National Association of Bookshops (→ 4) is formed mainly to represent the trade vis-à-vis the government and to discuss internal problems of the trade.

Panamanean libraries, however, have a great variety of programmes to promote the book to the public. Invitations to use the public and school library system are distributed everywhere. Many efforts are made to form school libraries and reading habits from primary-school age onwards (→ 10).

Bibliography

G. ANDREVE, *Biblioteca–cultura nacional.* (The library and national culture.) Panamá, Tipografía Nacional 1918. 33 pp.

C. CEDENO, *Directorio de labor educativa de las bibliotecas en la Provincia de Herrera.* (Directory of the educational work of the libraries in the Province of Herrera.) Panamá, Universidad Nacional 1972. 10, 92 pp.

El Libro como Agente de Progreso de un Pueblo. (The book as agent of progress of a nation.) Edited by the Normal School "Juan Demóstenes Arasemena". Santiago de Veraguas (Panamá), Tipografía Santiago 1946. 11 pp.

G. PATINO, *Panamá necesita bibliotecas.* Ideas sobre un positivo servicio moderno. (Panama needs libraries. Ideas for a positive modern service.) Panamá, Asociación de Bibliotecarios 1944. 2, 8 pp.

G. SUCRE REYES, *La biblioteca como medio efectivo en el desarrollo cultural del país.* (The library as an effective medium in the development of the country.) Panamá, Universidad Nacional 1969. 3, 110 pp.

34 Graphic Arts

The Panamanean printing industry has a good tradition within Central America. Due to the situation of the isthmus, even in late colonial times, with their restrictions, the graphic arts maintained a high standard. Nowadays, with the influence of the plants in the Free Trade Zone of Colón, printing is of a relatively high standard, although for the lack of publishers there is a scarcity in local books. But the export figures of printing material (267,533 US $ in 1968) show its importance in Central America.

Bibliography

E. J. CASTILLERO REYES, *Orígenes y desarrollo de la imprenta en Panamá.* (Origin and development of printing in Panama.) Panamá, Imprenta Nacional 1958. 35 pp.

R. MIRO, *La imprenta y el periodismo en Panamá durante el periódo de la Gran Colombia.* (Printing and periodicals in Panama during the period of Great Colombia.) Panamá, Editorial Panamericana 1963. 301 pp.

E. C. PAREDES S., *La industria tipográfica en Panama.* (The graphic industry in Panama.) Panamá, Universidad Nacional 1967. 4, 133 pp.

Panama, Canal Zone

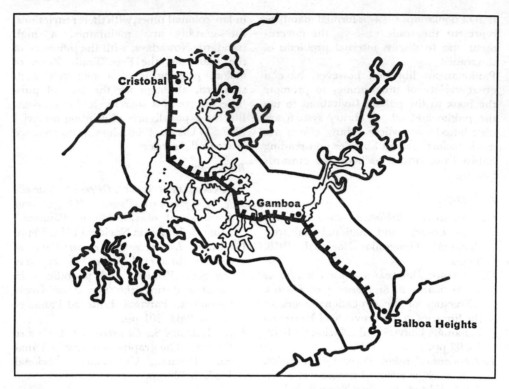

1 General Information

Area 1,432 km²
Population 56,000 (39 per km²–US-citizens 41,002 = 1968)
Capital Balboa Heights, C.Z.
Largest towns Balboa Heights, Cristobal, Gamboa
Government US Government reservation, directed by a Governor appointed by the US President, who is also ex officio President of the Panama Canal Company
National language English

Leading foreign language Spanish
Currency unit US Dollar ($) = 100 cents (c.), also Panamanean Balboa (B$) = 100 cents (equal to 1 US $)
Weights and measures United States measures used
Education 10 years obligatory administrative policy, not enforced by law. 1,284 students (1967) in 3 higher-level institutes
Illiteracy Nil
Membership (→USA 1,4)

2 Past and Present

In 1903 Panama successfully revolted against Colombia, with US backing. Shortly thereafter Panama and the United States signed a treaty for Panama's independence, and after the purchase of the French Canal Company rights (under which construction of the waterway had been started formally in 1880), the US Government was granted perpetual sovereign rights over the Canal Zone, a 50-mile strip between the Atlantic and Pacific Oceans, extending roughly 10 km on either side of the Panama Canal.

As by the 1903 treaty between Panama and the United States no private enterprise is permitted in the Canal Zone, except that relating directly to the operation of the canal, commercial–and therefore also publishing as well as bookselling activity–is restricted to the needs of the employees of the Panama Canal Company, only under the direction of the latter.

Bibliography

Current Publications of General Interest of the Panama Canal Company/Canal Zone Government. Balboa Heights, C.Z., Panama Canal Company 1966 ff. aprox. 11 pp.

Panama Canal Company–Canal Zone Government. Annual Report of the Fiscal Year... Balboa Heights, C.Z., Printing Plant Canal Zone 1921 ff. (1921–1924, Annual Report, Panama Canal Company).

Panama Canal Review. Annually. Mount Home, C.Z., Printing Plant, Office of Publications 1962 ff.

7 Sources of Information, Address Services

Because there are no special book information centres, general information can be obtained from
Panama Canal Information Office
PA Balboa Heights, C.Z.,

and information relating to books and periodicals, especially bibliographical dates of the Panama Canal, from the
Canal Zone Library and Museum
Civil Affairs Building
Box M
PA Balboa Heights, C.Z.

15 National Bibliography, National Library

The official bibliographical source on Panama Canal Zone publications is the Library of Congress in Washington, D.C. ($\rightarrow$ USA 15). Run by the Canal Zone Government, there is a Library and Museum in Balboa Heights, which to some extent acts as a "National Library", in so far as it collects not only publications printed in the Canal Zone, but also books on the Panama Canal. The last-mentioned collection is the most complete one on this subject in the world, backed by a good selection of books on Latin America. Thus its mimeographed "Library Bulletin" forms a useful bibliography on local matters:
Canal Zone Library and *Museum*
Civil Affairs Building
Box M
PA Balboa Heights, C.Z.
The small region of the Canal Zone has a dense network of libraries, 14 of which are administrated by the Canal Zone Government–apart from nine public libraries for general use under the head administration of the Canal Zone Library, three College libraries, and the Canal Zone Law Library in Ancon. There are, furthermore, fifteen Army libraries of general and special character, such as, for instance, the Latin America Collection of the US Army School of the American Military Library, and the Amador-Washington Library of the US Information Service, whose lending departments are situated outside the Canal Zone in the City of Panama.

Panama, Canal Zone

Bibliography

Canal Zone College Library Handbook. La Boca, C.Z. (mimeogr). 22 pp.

Canal Zone Library. A report. Balboa Heights, C.Z. 1951 ff.

Current Publications of General Interest of the Panama Canal Company/Canal Zone Government. Balboa Heights, C.Z., Panama Canal Company 1966 ff.

S. THURMOND, *Bibliography of Panama Canal Works.* Excerpt from Congress Record, 9 July 1964 to July 1966. Washington, D.C., Government Printing Office 1967. 79 pp.

21 Publishing

The only publications published within the Canal Zone are official ones, for the use of the Panama Canal Zone Company and the Canal Zone Government, and some annuals of the Canal colleges, partly printed outside, in the Republic of Panama. The Canal Zone Government printing plant forms the only "publishing company" in the Zone territory.

24 Retail Trade

Bookselling is restricted to the needs of the employees of the Canal Company and their families. The only bookshop, exists in the Canal Zone College, the "Canal Zone College Bookstore" in La Boca. Paperbacks and periodicals are sold in the three department stores of the Canal Zone. Canal Zone residents as well as the 280,000 annual visitors chiefly buy their books at the entrances to the Zone, e.g. on the Panama City side, where there are a good number of well equipped bookstores handling titles popular with Canal Zone residents (→ Panama 24).

Paraguay

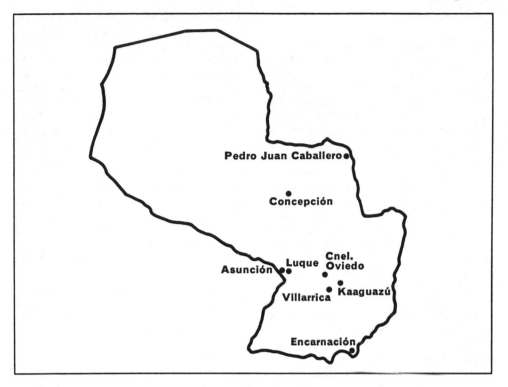

1 General Information

Area 406,752 km²
Population 2,354,071 (5.8 per km²)
Capital Asunción (392,753)
Largest towns Asunción (392,753); Kaaguazú (58,752); Cnel. Oviedo (54,690); Pedro Juan Caballero (49,245); Concepción (44,861); Encarnación (40,902); Luque (40,493); Villarica (33,553)
Government Democratic, Representative and Unitary Republic. Government is by the Legislative, Executive and Judiciary.
Asunción, the capital of Paraguay, is the seat of State. The National territory is divided into Departments. These are divided into Districts, which are further divided into Companies and Colonies. The National Constitution recognizes municipal autonomy, political as well as juridic, economic and administrative
Religion Roman Catholic 90%; Non-Catholic 10%
National language Paraguay is a bi-lingual country. Guaraní (native language). Spanish (official language)
Leading foreign languages English, French, German, Italian. These languages are studied as an elective subject in high schools and are spoken primarily among European immigrants.
Weights, measures Metric system
Currency unit Guaraní (G) = 100 Céntimos
Education Primary education is compulsory and free (491,600) for children from 7 to 14 years old (1968). The State supports and encourages Secondary, Vocational, Agricultural, Industrial and Professional Schools, and the University (58,130 secondary students and 8,011 university students in 1971).
Illiteracy 17.9% of the population over 15
Paper consumption a) Newsprint 1.7 kg per inhabitant (1970)
b) Printing paper (other than newsprint) 0.2 kg per inhabitant (1970)
Membership UNESCO, CERLAL

253

Paraguay

2 Past and Present

Paraguay gained her freedom on 14 and 15 May 1811. In 1700, when still a Spanish Colony, Paraguay already had a printing office in the Jesuit Mission, where books and pamphlets in Guaraní and Spanish were printed. The development of the printing industry, since then, has been much influenced by the political and social events that the country lived through since it became independent. The National Government was the principal factor in this development, specially Carlos Antonio López's government under whose direction on 26 April 1845 the first newspaper "El Paraguayo Independiente" appeared. This newspaper set up its own printing plant in 1846. Here the first printers in the country were trained.

In the State printing enterprise other periodical publications and a great variety of books, pamphlets etc. were published.

Today there are a large number of private printing enterprises in the capital. Most of them have the necessary equipment and technicians for printing books, magazines and other works.

The main newspapers of the country ("La Tribuna"; "ABC Color"; "Patria", among others) have their own up-to-date plant.

In some towns there are small firms which produce newspapers, pamphlets, bulletins, and commercial print. There are a few publishing houses in the country.

Few books are printed in Paraguay, and there is a great unbalance between these and imported books. The price of books, national as well as imported is very high.

There are a considerable number of bookshops in the capital, but they ought really to be spread over the country. Public and private libraries are limited, and they benefit only a limited section of the population.

There has been a considerable increase in school libraries in the last few years, in number as well as in trained and specialized people to do this job. Some efforts are being made to reach a satisfactory distribution of books through the country. The *Paraguayan Book Chamber* (Cámara del Libro del Paraguay →4) and the *Association of Graphic Industries of Paraguay* (Asociación de Industriales Gráficos del Paraguay →4) are organizations serving that purpose. The training of graphical workers and bookshop personnel, a modern system of sales and promotion, the increase of the number of bookshops, the lowering of production costs and book prices, the enlargement of the market for nationally produced books are long–range problems, whose solution has been faced in the last years, both in the country itself and at international level.

At present, promotion of the book and the publishing industry are a very important part of the National Plan of Economics and Social Development.

Bibliography

E. Cardozo, *Historia cultural del Paraguay.* (Cultural history of Paraguay.) Asunción, F.V.D. Editions 1963.

R. Centurión, *Historia de la cultura Paraguaya.* (Paraguayan cultural history.) v. I. Buenos Aires, Lumen 1961. 295 pp.

G. Furlong, *Orígines del arte tipográfico en América.* (The origins of the art of typography in America.) Buenos Aires, Ed. Huarpes 1947. 225 pp. Bibliography on pp. 215–225.–Early printing history of Paraguay: p. 93.

J. T. Medina, *Historia de la imprenta en los antiguos dominios españoles de América y Oceanía.* (The history of printing in the ancient Spanish dominions of America and Oceania.) 2 vols. Santiago de Chile, Fondo Histórico y Bibliográfico José Toribio Medina 1958. CXLI, 542; XV, 540 pp. v. II, pp. 203–210: Paraguay.

L. S. Thompson, *Printing in Colonial Spanish*

America. Hamden Conn., Archon Books 1962. 108 pp.
pp. 45–55: Paraguay.

3 Retail Prices

There is no special rule concerning price fixing either officially or in connection with trade organizations. The book trade is free to fix book prices according to the costs involved.

The discount for the bookseller generally varies according to the kind of book between 15% and 40%.

4 Organization

There are two principal organizations concerned with the development and distribution of books in the country.
The

Cámara del Libro del Paraguay
(Paraguayan Book Chamber)
Estrella 380
P.O. Box 1730
PY Asunción

established in 1968 represents all branches of the book trade and related trades. Its concern is the development of an interest in book reading, the legal protection of copyright, the statistics, development of a bookshop network, particularly for the benefit of the country's own writers (→2).
The

Asociación de Industriales Gráficos
del Paraguay (Association of Graphic
Industries of Paraguay)
Avenida España 248
PY Asunción

established in 1959 is concerned with the technology of book production and the promotion and protection of the graphic arts (→2).

6 Book-Trade Literature

→ 2, 7, 14, 15.

7 Sources of Information, Address Services

Information may be obtained from the following addresses:

Cámara del Libro del Paraguay
(Paraguayan Book Chamber)
Estrella 380
P.O. Box 1730
PY Asunción

Asociación de Industriales Gráficos
del Paraguay
(Association of Graphic Industries of
Paraguay)
Avda. España 248
PY Asunción

Sindicato de Obreros Gráficos
(Graphical Labour Union)
Ministerio de Justicia y Trabajo
PY Asunción

Secretaría Técnica de Planificación de la
Presidencia de la República
(Technical Secretariat of Planning of the
Republic's Presidency)
Iturbe y Eligio Ayala Street
PY Asunción

Bibliographical inquiries could be addressed to:

Biblioteca Nacional
(National Library)
Sarmiento 122
PY Asunción
and
Asociación de Escritores Guaranies
(Guarani Writers' Association)
Chile 850
PY Asunción

Bibliography

The addresses of all branches of the book trade are contained in
La Empresa del Libro en América Latina. (The Book in Latin America.) 2nd ed. Buenos Aires, Bowker Editores Argentina 1974, VIII, 307 pp.
pp. 223–225: Paraguay.

Paraguay

10 Books and Young People

The production and distribution of reading material for the young is of great importance, since the greater part of Uruguay's population consists of young people. The chief aims are the provision of better and cheaper textbooks; the spreading of school and popular libraries, local production of general cultural magazines, and the control of imported reading material for young people. Another problem of national interest in view of Paraguay's intensification of its drive to increase literacy, is the provision of reading material specially suited for newly literate readers.

12 Taxes

There are no taxes on the importation or production or selling of books.

14 Copyright

The Public Registry of Intellectual Rights, under the Ministry of Education, was created to administer the law of intellectual rights that protects scientific, literary and artistic creations. This law recognizes and protects the copyright of unpublished works, if they are registered. Translations, adaptations, compilations, adjustments and other versions of literary, scientific or artistic works are also protected.
This law came into force in July 1951.
Paraguay is a member of the Universal Copyright Convention (11 March 1962; →BTW I, International Section 14).

Bibliography

Ministry of Education, Law No. 94. Derechos intelectuales. (Intellectual rights.) Asunción 1951

15 National Bibliography, National Library

The main function of the
Biblioteca Nacional
(National Library)
Sarmiento 122
PY Asunción
is to collect nationally produced books and to edit the national bibliography, including foreign works about Paraguay. It has about 40,000 books, many of which are out of print, rare and of great value.
The National Library belongs to the
Dirección General de Archivos,
Bibliotecas y Museos Nacionales
(General Direction of Archives, Libraries and National Museums)
PY Asunción
New Paraguayan books are regularly listed in *Libros Paraguayos*
Librería La Cultura
Palma esq. Montevideo
PY Asunción

Bibliography

I. ZIMMERMANN, *Current national bibliographies of Latin America.* Gainesville, Florida, University of Florida Press 1971. X, 139 pp.
pp. 50–54: Paraguay.

16 Book Production

Books for elementary and secondary schools form the bulk of national book production. Annually about 235,000 copies are printed. All other subjects comprise 100 titles as an annual average, with approximately 150,000 copies printed.

Bibliography

S. MARESKI, *The present situation of book publication (in Paraguay).* St. Louis, Miss., Washington University Libraries 1964. 11 pp.–9th Seminar on the Acquisition of Latin American Library Materials.– Mimeographed.

17 Translations

Insignificant.

21 Publishing

The very small local publishing industry (5 publishing houses in Asunción) and its development are principally affected by the following problems: the lack of an internal market means that profits from publication do not cover the publishing cost; the total absence of an external market; the need of a subsidy to the publishing companies (this would be the only way to lower book prices); the need to promote the sale of Paraguayan books to other countries.

Of every 100 books sold in Paraguay 90 are imported and only 10 locally produced.

24 Retail Trade

Asunción has 9 bookshops. No book outlets of any quality exist outside of the capital.

27 Book Imports

According to official Paraguayan statistics the import of books and periodicals in 1970 was worth US$ 253,500.

The leading countries of origin were

Country	US $
Argentina	183,900
USA	29,800
Germany, (Fed. Rep.)	23,400
Japan	4,400
Mexico	2,100

28 Book Exports

Some books and newspapers are exported to Argentina, and, to a lesser extent, to other countries in America.

29 Book Fairs

They are occasionally organized, with the help of the "Cámara del Libro" (→4) or some special bookshop. The national and foreign publishers, booksellers and authors take part in these fairs, which usually last one or two weeks.

32 Literary Prizes

Occasionally literary contests are organized with the help of cultural, official or private institutions, and prizes are given to the winners. The *Academia Literaria* (Literary Academy), which works with several secondary schools, organizes competitions in order to encourage literary taste and creativeness among students.

33 The Reviewing of Books

The bibliographical bulletin *Libros Paraguayos* (→15) gives information about new books. Newspapers like "ABC Color" and "La Tribuna" occasionally carry book reviews.

34 Graphic Arts

→4.

Peru

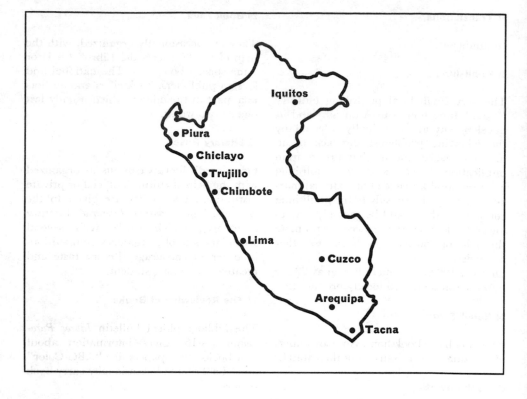

1 General Information

Area 1,285,215 km²
Population 14,010,000 (11 per km²)
Capital Lima (2,836,374)
Largest towns Lima (2,836,374); Arequipa (304,653); Chiclayo (189,685); Chimbote (159,045); Trujillo (241,882); Piura (126,702); Cuzco (120,881); Iquitos (111,327); Tacna (55,752)
Government Republic, 23 Departments and 150 Provinces. Education under the control of the Ministry of Public Education; Police under the control of the Ministry of the Interior
Religion Catholic 97%; Protestant 2%; Others 1%
National language Official language: Spanish, however, a large number of the native Indian population in the high Andes plateau speak Quechua and Aymara. In the Amazon region there are a number of tribal languages
Leading foreign languages English, French

Weights, measures Metric system
Currency unit Sol (S/.) = 100 centavos
Education Compulsory. There were 32 universities with a total enrolment of 96,402 students in 1969
Illiteracy Approx. 50%
Paper consumption a) Newsprint 3.5 kg per inhabitant (1970)
b) Printing paper (other than newsprint) 1.4 kg per inhabitant (1970)
Membership UNESCO, CERLAL

258

2 Past and Present

Peru occupies a special position in South America, as it was virtually its centre during the time of colonial occupation by Spain, Lima being the seat of the Viceroy. Lima was the first city in the Western hemisphere to be granted the charter of a university by the Crown of Spain, and this Universidad San Marcos in Lima is the hemisphere's oldest centre of higher education. Needless to say, books were already being printed in Peru in the 16th century. There are records of bookstores in the 18th century, and it seems that, in addition to books brought in from Spain, a good many with modern ideas were also introduced from France. This seems to account for the fact that in the late 18th century and following the French Revolution movements appeared which demanded independence from Spain. Therefore, by the time San Martín landed in Peru, he rapidly gathered support for his war of independence with Spain; in 1821 he proclaimed Peru's independence from Spain.

Several important bookstores but little publishing existed in Peru in the early part of the 20th century. The Civil War in Spain and Hitler's persecution brought publishers and booksellers to Latin America, and the former concentrated in Buenos Aires, Mexico and Habana. While a number of the important bookstores and wholesale businesses in Peru belong to Peruvian nationals, others are owned by companies of Spanish origin, especially in the very successful operation of door-to-door, selling and these are mostly branches of publishers who were immigrants to Argentina and Mexico as a result of becoming exiles after the Spanish Civil War. Publishing as a business is relatively new in Peru, and only during the last years have a few full-time publishers, mostly of school textbooks, developed. Previously the larger bookselling companies published schoolbooks as a sideline, and most books had to be published either by universities or the authors themselves. In 1946 the Cámara Peruana del Libro (→4) was founded. This, today, has 77 members, comprising 95% of the retail, wholesale and publishing business in Peru.

Bibliography

G. Furlong, *Orígines del arte tipográfico en América.* (The origins of the art of typography in America.) Buenos Aires, Ed. Huarpes 1947. 225 pp.
Bibliography on pp. 215–225. – Early printing history of Peru. pp. 71–82.

J. T. Medina, *Historia de la imprenta en los antiguos dominios españoles de América y Oceanía.* (The history of printing in the ancient Spanish dominions of America and Oceania.) 2 vols. Santiago de Chile, Fondo Histórico y Bibliográfico José Toribio Medina 1958. CXLI, 542; XV, 540 pp.
v. I, pp. 433–487: Peru (Lima).

L. S. Thompson, *Printing in Colonial Spanish America.* Hamden Conn., Archon Books 1962. 108 pp.
pp. 34–44: Peru.

3 Retail Prices

There is no price-fixing law in Peru. 90% of the books sold in bookstores, aside from primary and secondary schoolbooks, are imported and are sold at a surcharge over the original price. This is fully justified when one remembers that it takes from one to four months until books ordered from abroad are received in Peru, which accounts not only for high transportation and clearing charges, but also for the need to carry large stocks. Surcharges on original prices are between 20% and 50%, and depend on the country of origin, the type of book, the discount granted to the importer, etc. The average discount grant-

259

ed to bookstores by importers is 30% at 60 days sight draft. Libraries are usually granted a 20% discount, and the same applies to schools and universities, which has led to certain student co-ops buying their books in bulk. Another factor that increases the price is that a lot of books are lost in transit. The surchage is much greater in the widely developed door-to-door type of operation, which accounts for about 50% of all sales in monetary terms. Since the seller has no guarantee except personal reference as far as the buyer is concerned, he has to take into account: a commission of 15–20% to the salesman, a hedge against uncollected debts, a commission for collecting monthly instalments, etc. Another way, though expensive, of importing books is by airfreight, and this again justifies a relatively high retail price.

4 Organization

The only organization is the
Cámara Peruana del Libro
(Peruvian Book Chamber)
Jirón Washington 1206 Of. 507
Apartado 10253
PE Lima 1
founded in 1946. It is run by a Board of Directors, with a President in charge, a Vice-President, Secretary, Treasurer and 8 Members. The Board is elected every year; however, the President and Members can be re-elected. In addition the Cámara employs a full-time Manager, who is a lawyer, as well as some secretaries. The task of the Cámara is to promote the book trade with local book fairs; to defend the interests of the book trade; to defend the freedom of circulation of books; to defend the free import and export of books; to maintain contact with other similar organizations in other countries; to induce the government to make laws that help the publishing and circulation of books. In addition to the Board of Directors there are

special committees for publishers, booksellers, wholesalers and door-to-door organizations, all of which have their own chairman and members of the board; however, for each of these boards the President of the Cámara names his representative. The Cámara also receives a copy of each book published in Peru, with which it makes up a library of publications. In addition it has started an inquiry to establish the value of imports of books into Peru, as well as exports. It publishes monthly bulletins, which keep its members informed about its activities, new laws pertaining to the book trade, etc. All in all, the Cámara has become an indispensable part of the book business in Peru and is consulted by the local authorities as well.

The Book Chamber has been officially recognized as being the representative of the book trade under Supreme Resolution 2140 of 26 September 1946 of the Ministry of Public Education.

The principal activities of the Peruvian Chamber of Books:

1. Distribution to its members, Ministries, Embassies and other Book Chambers of legislation and information pertaining to the book trade and the results of its work in as many as four bulletins per month, reporting discussions with the authorities, international conventions, fairs, statistics, etc.

2. The Book Chamber is constantly engaged in discussions with authorities with regard to the production and circulation of books, and the principal legislation existing in the country has come about largely thanks to its activities.

3. The Book Chamber organized the First Book Fair in Peru in 1947. In 1972 it organized a book fair in which 50 companies participated. This fair will now be repeated yearly and is expected to attract 100 companies. A prize of US$ 450 has been instituted for "The Best Story".

4. The Book Chamber collects from

amongst its members and donates 1,000 books yearly in order to create a basic library in one of the shanty-towns around Lima. The Association of Librarians is cooperating in this effort.

5. The Book Chamber supplies information about books.

6. The Book Chamber is working on a national bibliography.

7. The Book Chamber took part in the Frankfurt Book Fair in 1970 and 1972, and in the Sofia Book Fair of 1972.

5 Trade Press

Aside from occasional publications of the "Camara Peruana del Libro" (→4), there is no regular publication that deals with the book trade. Some of the larger book-sellers and publishers issue catalogues. The only publication that is read regularly is the *Fichero Bibliográfico Hispanoamericano* (→BTW II, Latin America 5; Argentina 5), published in Buenos Aires, in which local publishers both advertise and publish information about their activities.

6 Book-Trade Literature

No book-trade literature is published in Peru.

7 Sources of Information, Address Services

Again the only source of information is:
Cámara Peruana del Libro
Jirón Washington 1206 Of. 507
Apartado 10253
PE Lima 1

Bibliography

The addresses of all branches of the book trade are contained in
La Empresa del Libro en América Latina. (The Book in Latin America.) 2nd ed. Buenos Aires, Bowker Editores Argentina 1974. VIII, 307 pp.–pp. 227–237: Peru.

8 International Membership

Peru is a member of UNESCO and of CERLAL (→ Latin America 4).

9 Market Research

There is no scientific research into the book and its market, except by private companies.

10 Books and Young People

There is no particular promotion of books for young people.

11 Training

Except for occasional training by private firms in either retail bookselling or door-to-door selling, there is no system of training people for the book trade.

12 Taxes

The sale of books and magazines both at retail and wholesale level is exempt from Peruvian sales tax. Apart from that, book importers, wholesalers and retailers pay all taxes like other businesses in Peru.

However, publishing can take advantage of certain tax exemptions under the new "Industry Law", where it is being classified as a "second essential" item. Since this law is rather complicated and fills a book, thorough study before starting a publishing company in Peru is recommended. Under this law, compulsory for all industry, 15% of profits before tax must be set aside for the "industrial coummunity" made up of employees and workmen, who then buy shares of up to 50% of the company and have proportional representation on the board of the company. The General Industrial Law is contained in Decree-Law 18350 of 27 July 1970. Its regulations are

Peru

contained in Supreme Decree 001–71–IC/DS of 25 January 1971.

14 Copyright

Peru subscribes to the Berne Convention (→BTW I, International Section 14). Peru is a member of the Universal Copyright Convention (UCC) since 16 October 1963. As to membership of Inter-American Conventions →BTW I, International Section 14.
Ley No. 13714 covers the internal copyright laws (Ley de derechos de autor).

15 National Bibliography, National Library

The "Biblioteca Nacional" must receive two copies of each book published in Peru. Similarly the Library of the San Marcos University must receive one copy of each book published in Peru. Both publish annuals listing all books published in Peru. The addresses are:
Biblioteca Nacional
(National Library)
Avenida Abancay
PE Lima
and
Universidad Nacional Mayor de San Marcos
Biblioteca Central
PE Lima

Bibliography

P. AVICENNE, *Bibliographical services throughout the world 1965–69*. Paris, UNESCO 1972. 310 pp.
pp. 206–208: Peru.
I. ZIMMERMANN, *Current national bibliographies of Latin America*. Gainesville, Florida, University of Florida Press 1971. X, 139 pp.
pp. 55–57: Peru.

16 Book Production

In 1970 885 titles were produced in Peru:

Subject group	Titles
General	24
Philosophy	9
Religion	18
Social sciences	366
Philology	38
Pure sciences	35
Applied sciences	142
Arts	23
Literature	120
Geography, history	110
Total	885

17 Translations

A very limited number of books is translated in Peru each year. In 1969 35 titles were counted in this group, mainly in the fields of literature, social sciences, applied sciences and geography/history.
15 titles were translated from English, 9 from Spanish and the rest from French, German, Italian, and Arabic.

19 Paperbacks

There are no regular series of mass-market or quality paperbacks produced in Peru, except for occasional titles.

21 Publishing

The publishing industry in Peru only started a few years ago and probably 90% of the books published are published in Lima. A sector that has come out very strongly is school textbooks, especially primary and secondary books. Many publications come from government agencies–ministries as well as the Universities. There are now about six major publishers (considering the smallness of the market), all of whom, however, are either printers or booksellers or distributors as well, and there is no one who really only publishes books, this part usually being the minor occupation of the firm. Some good printing equipment has been brought to Peru, mostly from the German Federal Republic, but there is still a great lack of printing facilities. A major problem is the nationalistic trend in most countries in South America that makes it impossible to import paper; thus only national paper of poor quality can be used; in addition many jobs cannot be done as the paper is not available. Therefore art books, etc., published by Peruvian publishers are usually manufactured in Spain or Germany. It is–under present laws–impossible to import sheets partially printed to be finished and bound in Peru. → 2.

Bibliography

B. S. Pagés, *The publishing industry in Peru.* St. Louis, Miss., Washington University Libraries 1964. 3 pp. – 9 th Seminar on the Acquisition of Latin American Library Materials. – Mimeographed.

23 Wholesale Trade

The wholesale trade is an important factor in the book business in Peru, comprising about a dozen firms, most of them importers of books. There are about a dozen importers of books who distribute and wholesale them all over the country. Only the few major bookstores of Peru (frequently connected with the wholesalers as subsidiaries) import their own books; the so-called bookstores all over the country are supplied by the wholesalers of Lima, who have travelling salesmen serving the country. Volume in sales of these wholesale firms runs into figures of over a million US $ in some instances.

24 Retail Trade

There are about 500 retail bookstores in the Republic of Peru. Admittedly practically all those outside of Lima, which account for the majority of the 500, are not merely retailers of books, but also sell magazines, newspapers, stationery, stationery supplies, school supplies, records, etc. However, due to the practice of calling such stores "Librerías" in Peru, they are all named after the book end of their various lines. In Lima, however, a number of large, middle-sized and small bookstores exist that sell only books, and here again we find some specializing in medical, technical, etc., books.

The 45 bookshops mentioned in "La Empresa del Libro" (→ 7) are the very important ones catering solely for books. Only the very important bookshops will import some of the books they sell; the balance will usually be bought from the local wholesalers, therefore they have no major problems as long as they do not get involved in selling certain political material or sex books and magazines which are prohibited, but still seem to come in. → 2.

25 Mail-Order Bookselling

This has never been tried in Peru. Basically speaking, very little mail-order advertising is done in Latin America. Deficiency in the postal system is probably the main factor. → 2.

26 Antiquarian Book Trade, Auctions

The antiquarian book trade is confined to two well-organized houses which publish catalogues on antiquarian books, mainly those of Peru, as well as modern publications (by ministries, government departments, universities) that are hard to obtain. In addition, Lima has a number of small second-hand bookstores, where one can find interesting items, if one has enough time to go through their stock.

27 Book Imports

According to the customs authorities, in 1972 the following import were realized:

Category	Sol
Books	9,598,423
Pamphlets	142,285
Magazines and periodicals	4,313,621

Main suppliers were Spain, Argentina, Mexico and the USA.

28 Book Exports

Peru exports small quantities of books and periodicals, primarily to the USA, to Ecuador, Argentina, Bolivia and Brazil.

29 Book Fairs

No regular book fairs are held in Peru; but occasional ones, especially exhibitions sponsored by embassies of foreign countries take place. Peru, however, takes part in book fairs, especially in Latin America, and in 1970 for the first time took part in the Frankfurt Book Fair (→BTW I, International Section 29).

30 Public Relations

A number of activities are carried on by the "Camara Peruana del Libro" (→4).

32 Literary Prizes

There are several Government National Prizes, for instance in Literature, Essays, History, Medicine, etc. The most important prize is the *Concurso Nacional de Premios de Fomento a la Cultura*, which is subdivided into 18 sections. Other prizes are the *Concurso Bienal de Novela Jose Maria Arguedas* and the *Concurso Bienal de Novela Universo*.

33 The Reviewing of Books

Apart from technical and specialized magazines, the two principal newspapers of Lima, *La Prensa* and *El Comercio*, especially in their Sunday supplements, have a regular section for book reviews. This book section also carries advertising of the local book trade. Likewise journals such as *Caretas* and *Oiga* have book sections.

34 Graphic Arts

The
Asociación Gráfica Unión de Imprentas,
(Association of the Graphic Union)
Avenida Garcilaso de la Vega 1494, 2° Piso
PE Lima 1
represents the graphic arts in Peru and publishes the bulletin "Artes Gráficas del Perú".
A similar institution is
Sociedad Impresores del Perú
(Society of Peruvian Printers)
Avenida Nicolás de Piérola 938
PE Lima 1

Puerto Rico

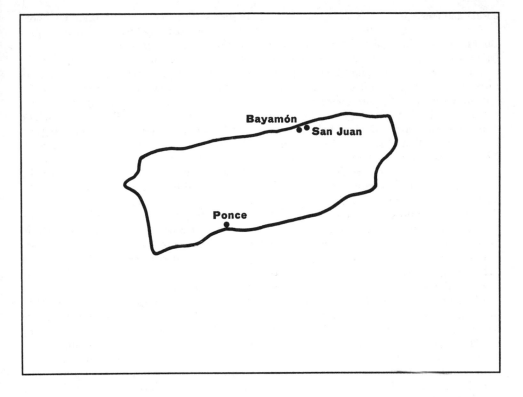

1 General Information

Area 8,897 km², including adjacent islands
Population 2,913,000 (1973; 327.3 per km²)
Capital San Juan (421,144)
Largest towns San Juan (421,144); Bayamón (147,552); Ponce (126,219)
Government Semi-autonomous commonwealth under the United States within framework set up by Puerto Rican–Federal Relations Act and United States Constitution. Representative democracy with bi-cameral legislature. All Puerto Ricans are citizens of the United States of America
Religion It is estimated that 70% of the population are nominally Roman Catholic, 20% Protestant and 10% belong to other groups or are non-affiliated
National language Spanish
Leading foreign language English

Weights, measures English system, except road distances, which are in metric system
Currency unit US dollar (US $) = 100 cents
Education Compulsory and free. Elementary (grades 1–6), Secondary (Junior High School: grades 7–9; and Senior High School: grades 10–12); 88,254 (1973) higher education (3rd level) students in one state-supported (50,439) and seven private (37,815) colleges and universities
Illiteracy 10% of population over age 10 in 1970 census

Puerto Rico

2 Past and Present

Books arrived in Puerto Rico with the friars who always followed the Spanish conquistadores and settlers. The island was discovered in 1493 during Columbus' second voyage, and Juan Ponce de León established the first settlement in 1508. The oldest known book collection belonged to the island's first bishop, Fray Alonso Manso, who came to take charge of his diocese in 1513. There is evidence of other collections of some significance, particularly one at the Dominican Convent.

But the social and economic conditions of the colony were not favourable to the development of a dynamic cultural life where books and their trade could flourish. When larger and richer lands were conquered, the island's strategic location in the Caribbean Sea led Spain to turn the main city into a mighty military bastion while forgetting almost every other aspect of the colony's development. Consequently, throughout the 16th, 17th and 18th centuries, book trading was minimal and book production non-existent. The small population, the extremely limited opportunities for any kind of education, and the censorship laws imposed by the Spanish Monarchy were factors contributing to this state of affairs.

There was a dramatic change in the 19th century when concurrently with the gradual development of a distinctly Puerto Rican national identity there was a cultural and political awakening which gave birth to newspapers, books and a national literature. The establishment of a printing press in 1806 immediately led to the island's first publications: the official newspaper *La Gazeta de Puerto Rico*, and a 120-page book of poems: *Ocios de la juventud*. But the market for books was limited and publishers often called for subscriptions through newspaper ads in order to secure printing costs before venturing publication.

It seems that many of the planned books never made it to the presses and book production remained insignificant.

A more important development was the establishment of bookstores, the growth of a retail trade and the appearance of the specialized book merchant who could give advise about books as well as sell them. The first bookstore was established in San Juan in 1837 and soon afterwards there were several more in the Capital, as well as in other major towns. The role played by these establishments in the promotion of culture and liberal ideas was quite significant; nevertheless, books must have been a commodity which only a minority could possess, since the large majority of the population could not read. Even at the end of the century from 80 to 85 per cent of the people were illiterate.

As a result of the Spanish-American War of 1898, Puerto Rico became a colony of the United States. The American policy of rapid expansion of the public school system to achieve universal education could have created an expanding book market and certainly a textbook industry could have developed. But this possibility did not materialize due to the American government decision that English be the language of instruction in Puerto Rican schools. This meant that most, if not all the textbooks, including those used for teaching the Spanish language, were produced in their entirety by publishing houses in the United States. When this policy was changed and Spanish became the language of instruction throughout the elementary and secondary levels (1948) there was no book industry which could take over book production. Consequently, this has remained to a large degree in the hands of a few American companies. The Puerto Rican Government's Department of Public Education organized a textbook production division and set up modern printing equipment capable of producing most of the textbooks needed for the public school system, but inefficient operation and lack of expertise have limited their output significantly.

Local book production prior to 1960 was for the most part an individual venture with the writer himself acting as publisher of his works. After paying the printing costs he would distribute the copies to bookstores and to individual would-be buyers. There were, to be sure, a handful of publishing groups, but except for one or two exceptions these were not really commercial enterprises.

During the last 15 years book trade and publishing have increased significantly. Undoubtedly a crucial factor in this development has been the growth of higher education (tertiary level). In 1973 there were 88,254 higher-education students out of an estimated population of 2,900,000 or one student for every thirty-three persons. It is estimated that these students buy over US $ 4,000,000 in books every year. Another factor is the increase in the number of elementary and secondary students in private schools which do not provide free textbooks. In order to supply the growing demand, new bookstores have been established, especially in the large urban centres, and new publishing companies have been organized. All indications are that the market for all kinds of books is increasing and that book trade and publishing are finally becoming a profitable business.

There are, however, several difficulties which must be overcome if the above-mentioned possibility is to become a reality. The book industry must adopt modern techniques of advertising and merchandizing in order to reach the potential market of university graduates in the middle and professional classes. Systematic market research and aggressive sales methods should be able to expand sales considerably. A more efficient system of distribution and the increase in the number of outlets are also an urgent task which should be undertaken jointly by the two recently organized trade associations representing the publishers and the retailers respectively. An area of high potential is the large Puerto Rican population in the United States whose younger members are developing a strong interest in Puerto Rican past and present cultural life.

Bibliography

J. T. Medina, *Historia de la imprenta en los antiguos dominios españoles de América y Oceanía*. (The history of printing in the ancient Spanish dominions of America and Oceania.) 2 vols. Santiago de Chile, Fondo Histórico y Bibliográfico José Toribio Medina 1958. CXLI, 542; XV, 540 pp.
v. II, pp. 471–475: Puerto Rico.

L. Cr. Monclova, *El libro y la cultura literaria puertorriqueña*. (Books and Puerto Rican literary culture.) In: Editorial Coquí, Catálogo, San Juan de Puerto Rico 1972, pp. 4–8.

L. Cr. Monclova, *La introducción de la imprenta en Puerto Rico y el primer periódico puertorriqueño*. (The introduction of the printing press in Puerto Rico and the first Puerto Rican newspaper.) In: Revista del Instituto de Cultura Puertorriqueña, San Juan de Puerto Rico, Jul.–Sept. (1969), No. 44: 4–6.

L. Cr. Monclova, *Nuestros libros perdidos*. (Our lost books.) In: ibid., Jan.–Mar. (1970), No. 46: 17–18.

E. J. Pasarell, *El libro más antiguo de Puerto Rico*. (The oldest Puerto Rican book.) In: Puerto Rico Ilustrado, San Juan de Puerto Rico, 27 May 1950, pp. 13–15; 25.

Qué pasa con los libros puertorriqueños? (What is the problem with Puerto Rican Books?) In: Isla Literaria, San Juan de Puerto Rico, No. 1, (Sept. 1969) 14–17.

P. Vivo (ed.), *The Puerto Ricans: an annotated*

bibliography. New York, R. R. Bowker 1973. 352 pp.

Both Spanish and English-language materials are contained in this annotated bibliography about Puerto Rico and Puerto Ricans. Entries–both print and non-print items–are arranged alphabetically by subject, with headings ranging from arts to government and politics, from folklore and tradition to music, and from religion and philosophy to migration.

3 Retail Prices

There is no general policy among publishers to fix the retail price of books. There is also no fixed discount policy for specialized libraries, public libraries or other wholesale buyers. All such price arrangements are made on an individual basis.

4 Organization

There are two associations representing different sectors of the book trade:
The
> Asociación de Editores de Puerto Rico
> (Publishers' Association of Puerto Rico)
> P. O. Box S
> Hato Rey, Puerto Rico 00919

is incorporated as a non-profit organization under the Laws of Puerto Rico to promote the local and international book trade.
It has been avtive since 1971.
The
> Asociación de Libreros de Puerto Rico
> (Booksellers' Association of Puerto Rico)
> P. O. Box BO
> Río Piedras, Puerto Rico 00928

was recently organized to promote all aspects of the book trade.

7 Sources of Information, Address Services

Interested persons may obtain information and addresses through the two organizations mentioned under →4.

Bibliography

The addresses of all branches of the book trade of are contained in
> *Le Empresa del Libro en América Latina*. (The Book in Latin America.) 2nd ed. Buenos Aires, Bowker Editores Argentina 1974. VIII, 307 pp.
> pp. 239–242: Puerto Rico.

12 Taxes

Foreign books are duty free if in a language other than English. Puerto Ricans do not pay US Federal Taxes; book-trade firms are subject to current revenue laws of the Commonwealth of Puerto Rico, which are generally one-quarter to one-third lower than Federal ones. There is a graduated personal and business tax and a property tax. In 1954 book printing and bookbinding were exempted from revenues.

14 Copyright

The copyright legislation in force in Puerto Rico is the Copyright Law of the United States of America, (→USA 14).

15 National Bibliography, National Library

The *Bibliografía Puertorriqueña* (Puerto Rican Bibliography) by Antonio S. Pedreira lists most works published before and up to 1930. There is a gap between 1930 and 1948 which is not included in a more recent compilation, *Anuario Bibliográfico Puertorriqueño* (Puerto Rican Bibliographical Yearbook) published up to 1960 and compiled up to 1965. The *Revista del Insti-*

tuto de Cultura Puertorriqueña (Journal of the Institute of Puerto Rican Culture) may be consulted for more recent years. The Puerto Rican bibliographer, Gonzalo Velázquez, is preparing what should be the most complete bibliography of books by Puerto Rican authors.

The *Biblioteca General de Puerto Rico* (General Library of Puerto Rico) has been recently organized under the supervision of the Institute of Puerto Rican Culture. Together with the *Archivo General de Puerto Rico* (General Archives of Puerto Rico), of which it is a sister institution, it is intended to function as the depository of all documents and books published in Puerto Rico. Until this intention becomes a reality, the largest collection of Puerto Rican books is the *Colección Puertorriqueña* (Puerto Rican Collection) of the University of Puerto Rico at Río Piedras General Library, which holds over 100,000 items.

Bibliography

I. ZIMMERMANN, *Current national bibliographies of Latin America*. Gainesville, Florida, University of Florida Press 1971. X, 139 pp.
pp. 102–104: Puerto Rico.

16 Book Production

There are no readily available statistics on book production but a sampling of the catalogues of several of the publishing firms leads us to believe that the larger companies average between 25 and 40 titles per year. A total of 250 titles per year seems to be a reasonable estimate. A survey made in 1969 by the literary journal *Isla Literaria* revealed that the average book impression was 1,000 copies, but in 1974 this figure had increased to 2,000. Almost all publishers print their books in Mexico or in Spain due to the high costs of printing in Puerto Rico. Although literary works, short stories, novels, and poetry, in that order, ranked first, there is a significant increase in the production of non-fiction and more academic books in the social and humanistic disciplines.

20 Book Design

Due to the high production costs, most Puerto Rican books are printed in Mexico and Spain and too often book design and illustration are also foreign. There is, however, a group of book designers and illustrators whose work has achieved international recognition in book exhibitions in Europe and Latin America. The Division of Community Education of the Department of Public Education and the Institute of Puerto Rican Culture promote the development of a graphic arts tradition. The

Casa del Libro (House of the Book)
Calle del Cristo 255
P.O.B. 2265
Old San Juan, Puerto Rico

was established by a private group of citizens interested in the graphic arts and has become one of the leading book museums in the Americas. It holds over 5,000 rare books and manuscripts including 200 different examples of the printing styles of the 15th century. The *Casa* regularly holds exhibitions of its collections, as well as items on loan from other similar institutions (→BTW I, International Section: Book Museums, p. 66).

21 Publishing

With a growing capacity of Puerto Rican book production in Spanish the number of publishing houses has a tendency to grow. Approximately seven publishers supply a substantial market.
→2, 16.

24 Retail Trade

Books are retailed through privately owned bookstores, university and school bookstores, supermarkets, and drugstores. There are around 60 bookstores throughout the island, most of them concentrated in the cities where there are public or private universities. Statistics concerning the book trade are not compiled by the government, nor by the trade organizations. A reasonable estimate of overall trade volume would be US$ 10,000,000.

Bibliography

J. TOME, *En defensa de las librerías.* (In defense of bookstores.) In: Avance, San Juan de Puerto Rico, No. 15, oct 25, 1972, pp. 48–49.

27 Book Imports

The major external provider of books according to 1973 statistics was the United States. The imports from the USA totalled US$ 3,054,516 distributed as follows:

Category	US $
Textbooks	2,271,283
Technical, scientific and professional	88,584
Religious	319,643
Dictionaries	68,853
Childrens' picture painting books	236,407
Music	3,906

The second largest provider was Spain, followed by Mexico and Argentina and 16 other countries. Total of non-US imports was US$ 5,807,258. It should be noted, however, that these statistics include as "imports" books published by Puerto Rican publishers but printed in Spain and Mexico (→ 16).

28 Book Exports

The total volume of book exports was US$ 355,266 excluding sales to the US mainland, which are not compiled.

29 Book Fairs

The *Asociación de Mujeres Graduadas de la Universidad de Puerto Rico* (Association of Women Graduates of the University of Puerto Rico) sponsors an annual book fair in October with the cooperation of publishers, booksellers and several government agencies. In conjunction with the fair—which is usually held in Old San Juan, but which often is also taken to other major cities–the Department of Public Education celebrates Book Week with activities to promote reading among school-children and the adult population.

The fair is strictly a local exhibition of books published in Puerto Rico and foreign books regularly sold at bookstores.

32 Literary Prizes

Literary prizes are awarded every year by three institutions: The *Ateneo de Puerto Rico* (Puerto Rican Atheneum), the *Instituto de Literatura* (Institute of Literature, established by law), and the *Instituto de Cultura* (Institute of Culture). Usually there are three prizes for every literary genre, but they do not seem to influence book sales to any significant degree. Some of the prizes are awarded for unpublished manuscripts and the award includes publication.

33 The Reviewing of Books

Book reviewing primarily takes place in the specialized journals, which regularly include reviews of Puerto Rican and foreign books. The most important journals are: *La Torre*, general journal of the

University of Puerto Rico; *Revista del Instituto de Cultura Puertorriqueña*, specializing in Puerto Rican history, folklore and literature; *Revista de Ciencias Sociales*, a social science journal published by the Social Science Research Center of the University of Puerto Rico; *Sin Nombre*, a literary monthly review; *Isla Literaria*, published by the Writers' Association, and *Diálogo*, a philosophy journal published by the Department of Philosophy of the University of Puerto Rico at Río Piedras.

Large newspapers carry a weekly literary section devoted primarily to local book production. The most important is the *El Mundo* literary section under the direction of book critic, Juan Martínez Capó.

271

St. Pierre et Miquelon

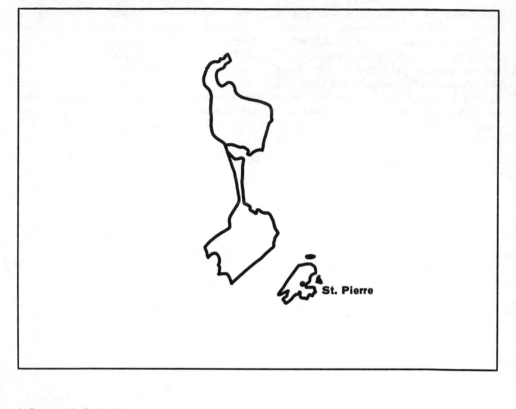

1 General Information

Area 242 km² (St. Pierre 26 km², Miquelon 216 km²)

Population 5,235 (Island of St. Pierre 4,362, Miquelon Group 628 = 20.7 per km²)

Capital St. Pierre, Island of St. Pierre (4,051)

Largest towns St. Pierre (4,051)

Government Overseas Territory of the French community

Religion 100% Roman Catholic

National language French

Leading foreign language English

Weights, measures Metric system

Currency unit Franc C.F.A. (CFA) = 100 centimes

Education Compulsory and free. No academic level institutions (142 pupils in 6 technical schools)

Membership UNESCO (→BTW I, France 8)

2 Past and Present

The sole remnant of the French colonial empire in North America, the two islands were first occupied by the French in 1664. Their importance arises from the proximity of the Grand Banks, located 10 miles south of Newfoundland, making them the centre of the French Atlantic cod fisheries. In September 1958, St. Pierre and Miquelon voted in favour of the new Constitution of the French Fifth Republic and remained an Overseas Territory within the French Community.

In early times, the reading public of the islands depended for books and periodicals delivered directly from French book exporters, receiving them only occasionally by way of a local general merchant. In 1939 the first bookseller, coming from France, established his shop in the harbour city of St. Pierre. Today there are four bookshops, all of them in the capital, selling stationery and photographic materials as well as books. Since there is practically no publishing–this is confined to the local government and a small printing company–the booksellers depend on imports. Though today a small number of books and periodicals are imported from the United States of America, most of them continue to come from France, to which the booksellers have to turn for professional information.

Bibliography

J. Y. RIBAULT, *Les Isles de St. Pierre et Miquelon.* (The Islands of St. Pierre and Miquelon.) St. Pierre, Imprimerie du Gouvernement 1965.

3 Retail Prices

Prices, including those of books, are fixed by law. As regards imports, the booksellers respect the publishers' prices, and by local agreement they charge their costs of delivery from abroad at the same percentage.

4 Organization

There is no professional association on the islands, and only one bookseller is a member of a French commercial organization. The fact, however, that there exists only one bookselling centre, the capital city of St. Pierre, together with a remarkable amount of goodwill among the local trade, has led to effective collaboration between the four booksellers in resolving their common problems.

7 Sources of Information, Address Services

Since there are no local book organizations or trade institutions, information about the book world of St. Pierre and Miquelon may be obtained from

*Bibliothèque du Gouvernement du
St. Pierre et Miquelon
(Library of the Government of
St. Pierre and Miquelon)
St. Pierre*

A further helpful contact is the

*Bureau Touristique
(Tourist Office)
St. Pierre*

Other trade information can be found in France ($\rightarrow$ BTW I, France 4).

12 Taxes

Books are absolutely free of taxes, as regards their import and their sale. The trade has only to pay a tax of 7% on final annual net earnings.

15 National Bibliography, National Library

The few titles published during the last thirty years on the islands can be found in the French bibliographies ($\rightarrow$ BTW I, France 15). There is no local bibliography, apart from circulars listing new acquisitions of the Government of St. Pierre and Miquelon's library, which consist mostly of French books and include those dealing in any way with the islands.

The government library, the

Bibliothèque du Gouvernement du
St. Pierre et Miquelon
(Library of the Government of St. Pierre
and Miquelon)
St. Pierre

serves as a kind of national library whose chief purpose is to collect books about the territory.

16 Book Production

No figures are available. A very small number of books and pamphlets are published either by the Government Office (→2) or by a private local printer. Most of them are brochures about the islands, additional primary textbooks, commercial reports, etc.

21 Publishing

There is no real publishing company in St. Pierre and Miquelon. Two printing plants, one owned by the local government, occasionally publish books and brochures (→16), and there is a daily paper in St. Pierre.
→2.

24 Retail Trade

The four bookshops, all of them located in the capital city of St. Pierre, also sell stationery and photographic materials. Their sales are based almost entirely on imports from France, the major part of them being French newspapers and periodicals.
→2.

27 Book Imports

Nearly all books and periodicals sold on the islands are imported. France supplies 90% of these books, so her figures can be taken to give an idea of the yearly turnover of book sales in the territory (the other 10% of imports are from the USA.) According to French statistics, her sales to St. Pierre and Miquelon are in the increase:

Year	Appr. US $
1960	6,500
1965	23,000
1968	12,000
1970	36,500

According to these figures, imports of books and periodicals have had a fivefold increase during the last ten years. Furthermore, the annual amount spent on books and periodicals must thus be around seven dollars per capita.

33 The Reviewing of Books

The local newspaper has a weekly page for book reviews and literary articles, mostly dealing with books published in France and written by French authors.

Surinam

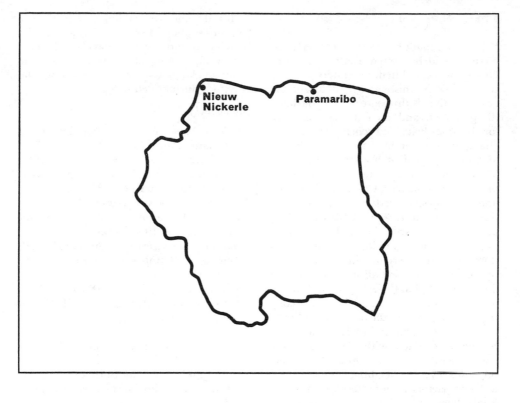

1 General Information

Area 163,265 km²

Population 375,000 (2 per km²; Creoles 39%, East Indians 30%, Indonesians 16%, indigenous Indians 10%, Chinese 2%, Europeans and others 2%)

Capital Paramaribo (110,867)

Largest towns Paramaribo (110,867), Nieuw Nickerle (30,100)

Government Part of the Kingdom of the Netherlands, directed by a Governor of the Realm of the Hague

Religion Protestants 80,000, Roman Catholics 71,000, Hindu 88,000, Moslems 67,000

National language Dutch

Leading foreign languages English, also "Negro English" as lingua franca, Javanese, Hindi

Weights, measures Metric system

Currency unit Surinam florin (S.fl) = 100 cents (cts)

Education Compulsory for five years. 667 students (1964) at a university-level School of Medicine

Illiteracy 25% (1950)

Paper consumption a) Newsprint 1.2 kg per inhabitant (1968)

b) Printing paper (other than newsprint) 0.7 kg per inhabitant (1968)

Membership UNESCO (→BTW I, Netherlands 8)

275

Surinam

2 Past and Present

When the Spanish came to Guiana, the territory which is often also called Dutch Guiana was inhabited by scattered Indian tribes. The Spanish who had looked for gold in the 16th century left Surinam disappointed, and then it was competed for by the British, French and Dutch, changing control five times, till it was awarded to the Dutch at the Congress of Vienna in 1815. In later years, after the prohibition of slavery, Chinese, Hindustani and Indonesian settlers emigrated to Surinam. From 1936 to 1950 the colony progressed towards internal autonomy, and in 1954 it was united with the Kingdom of the Netherlands in a new statute on a footing of equality. The ten-year development plan then started has brought a rising level of industrial and commercial activity to the area (mainly the bauxite and sugar industries), increasing Surinam's contacts with neighbour countries other than the European homeland. So nowadays her neighbour Venezuela is a strong partner in her international trade. Booksellers and printers settled relatively early in the colony, but their strongholds are still in the European homeland. In the professional circles of the latter, companies and personalities not only of the Netherlands Antilles but also from Surinam play an important role. The typical local firm has either combined a printing plant with a daily newspaper or with a periodical, or it is a bookshop and a small publishing company–all of them, about a dozen companies, concentrated in the capital of Paramaribo. Lacking a professional organization, they cooperate with the Dutch associations (→BTW I, Netherlands 4). There are also a number of bookshops in the Netherlands that handle direct exports to customers in Surinam and thus contribute to the local book trade.

Cultural and educational efforts are strongly supported by organizations in the homeland, and together have reached an increasing grade of unification of the different language groups, opening the way to a Surinam ethnology.

Bibliography

Bevolking van Surinam. (Population of Surinam). Amsterdam, STICUSA 1967.
A. van Eyck, *Surinam, de Vraagbakk 1955.* Surinam Almanak (Surinam almanac.) Paramaribo 1956. 257 pp.
Facts and Figures about Surinam. Paramaribo, Surinam Government Information Service R.V.D.S. 1960 20 pp.
Newsletter from Surinam. Paramaribo 1960 ff. Surinam Chamber of Commerce and Industries.
Suriname: Cultureel Mozaik. (Surinam, cultural mosaic.) Amsterdam, STICUSA 1966. 4 pp. folder.

7 Sources of Information, Address Services

Two organizations in Surinam may be consulted about book-trade matters. First, for cultural information, the
Stichting Cultureel Centrum Suriname
(Surinam Cultural Centre Foundation)
Postbus 1241
Gravenstraat 112–114
SME Paramaribo
and, on the commercial side, the
Kamer van Koophandel en Fabrieken
(Chamber of Commerce and Industry)
D.J.C. Mirandistraat 10
SME Paramaribo
There are no address services in Surinam, but the equivalent institutes in the Netherlands (→BTW I, Netherlands 7) in many cases carry a good number of items on the territory.

15 National Bibliography, National Library

Apart from occasional booksellers' catalogues, no bibliographies are published in Surinam. In Amsterdam, however, there is an institution for cultural contacts with Surinam and the Netherlands Antilles which, apart from publishing material about the territory, issues booklists on Surinam matters including the most important local publications:

*Nederlandse Stichting voor
Culturele Samenwerking met Suriname en
de Nederlandse Antillen (STICUSA)
(Netherlands Foundation for Cultural
Cooperation with Surinam and the Netherlands
Antilles)
J. J. Viottastraat 41
NL Amsterdam-Zuid*

The normal obligations of a national library are maintained by institutions in the homeland (→ BTW I, Netherland 15). One local public library,

*Stichting Cultureel Centrum Surinam
(Surinam Cultural Centre Foundation)
Postbus 1241
Gravenstraat 112–114
SME Paramaribo*

can be regarded as a general, nation-wide library, collecting all local literature.

21 Publishing

Publishing in Surinam, apart from the activities of some official government institutions, is carried out by half a dozen companies, either as a sideline to bookselling, or of a printing plant or newspaper publishing. No annual figures are available. The booklists of STICUSA (→ 15) reveal that about 1,200 titles were published within the last ten years in Surinam.

24 Retail Trade

About ten companies in Paramaribo sell books, among them a number of shops offering books only as a sideline. Three firms are exclusively or mainly attending to books. However, as books are also delivered to local readers directly from the Netherlands by companies exporting to the territory, the local market is really supported by a major number of bookshops. There is no local professional organization, apart from the general Chamber of Commerce and Industry. But the most active book firms are members of the homeland organizations (→BTW I, Netherlands 4).

27 Book Imports

According to official statistics Surinam in 1970 imported books valued at S.fl. 3,381,000, with the Netherlands as the main supplier (S.fl. 3,293,000).

33 The Reviewing of Books

The five daily newspapers as well as nearly 50 periodicals published in Surinam have a relatively high cultural standard, reviewing books of both local and European origin. The five radio stations and the local television channel regularly allot time to book and literary criticism.

Trinidad and Tobago

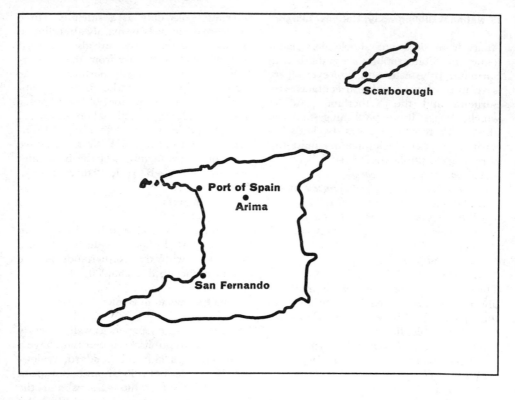

1 General Information

Area 5,126 km² (Trinidad 4,828 km²; Tobago 300 km²)

Population 1,089,300 (1970; 197 per km²)

Capital Port-of-Spain (100,000)

Largest towns Port-of-Spain (100,000); San Fernando (39,890); Arima (11,792); Scarborough (Tobago)

Government An independent (August 31, 1962) member state of the British Commonwealth. There is a bicameral legislature comprising a Senate and a House of Representatives

Religion Roman Catholics (36%), Protestants (35%), Hindus (23%), Muslims (6%)

National language English is the official and commercial language. Some French Patois is still spoken. There are a limited number of Spanish speaking nationals. Among the older Hindus, Hindi dialects are spoken and a modern trend is the study of Hindi by young persons.

Chinese dialects are spoken mainly by older persons and newest arrivals

Weights, measures Imperial system is used but the change to Metric is actively under way

Currency unit The monetary unit is the Trinidad & Tobago dollar (TT$) comprising 100 cents

Education Education is free at both primary and secondary levels. The compulsory ages are 6–12. There are 471 Primary Schools (Government and Assisted–210,679); 44 Secondary Schools (Government and Assisted–27,435); over 200 Primary and Secondary Schools (Private–20,130); 6 Teacher Training Colleges (Government and Private). 2 Technical Institutes (Government, full time and evening classes); and since 1970, 16 Junior Secondary Schools (Government–30,720) have been constructed. At the University of the West Indies, St Augustine Campus, Trinidad, there

2 Past and Present

Of the three major pillars of the book trade, retailing or bookselling is by far the oldest in Trinidad and Tobago. One bookshop is at least 125 years old and is still today one of the leading concerns.

Another, a division of a large department store, has already marked its golden jubilee.

In addition to school texts which account for the bulk of the business, these shops not only carried mainly fiction and popular reading, but arranged periodical subscriptions for their customers, a large proportion of which were transient residents. The leading library of popular books maintained over a number of years by one of the older shops for its customers, was closed down in the 1950s.

The predominance of British books on the market has in part been influenced by restrictions with the United States Market which was closed after World War II, opened on a quota basis in 1951/2, and freely opened in 1956. Although attractive discounts were and are offered, the problems of hard currency affected the selling price making United States publications more expensive than British.

In the 1940's too, Government's import policies from Great Britain included the obtaining of books, stationery and supplies through the Crown Agents. The channelling of orders for the public libraries through local booksellers was an innovation which brought about speedier deliveries and the development of local expertise in handling large quantities of books.

The general growth and spread of education, increased provision of secondary schools and technical institutes and courses, the expansion of the public and special library services, the establishment of the St Augustine Campus of the University of the West Indies in 1961, the establishment of the television service, have all contri-

are 1,800 students. The Faculties of Agriculture and Engineering are located here and there is a College of Arts and Sciences. Spanish is now a compulsory subject on the school curriculum

Illiteracy 20%

Paper consumption a) Newsprint 6.4 kg per inhabitant (1971)

b) Printing paper (other than newsprint) 2.8 kg per inhabitant (1971)

Membership UNESCO

279

buted to changes in the book trade. More buyers know what they want and can ask for specific books, browsing has increased, impulse buying continues especially at the miscellany of outlets, the increased personal expectations of nationals affecting purchasing ability. More children and young people go on their own to bookshops, knowing what they want.

Trends indicate an increased demand for purposeful books over the traditional classics.

While books have generally become more easily available, the problems of distance from the publishers, time lapses in deliveries–affected by strikes of all kinds–continue.

The general interest by booksellers in taking advantage of training courses made available recently is a positive step towards overall improvement in the book trade.

3 Retail Prices

The larger, general bookshops have had, up to 1974, a gentleman's agreement for mark-ups and discounts. The mark-up on school textbooks was 25% on the published price. In mid-1974, it was reported that school texts would be subject to price control allowing a maximum 25% mark-up on the published price. Prices of general books, fiction and non-fiction are dependent on discounts offered by exporters or book agents. Libraries and government departments, which purchase books in quantity, receive discounts which are influenced by (a) the discounts received, or (b) the type of purchase–i.e.–order placed (10% on published price),–shelf purchase–(15% on retail price).

The proposed price control of school texts, while acknowledging some of the public complaints about the rising cost of books, ignore the representation by booksellers in recent years, for an increased mark-up to absorb some of the increased rates they experience for freight, postal and brokerage charges, and losses due to pilferage, higher applicable salaries and rental costs. The Booksellers Association is considering an appeal to the Brokers' Association for a reduction in the brokerage fee for School Texts.

4 Organization

The
Booksellers' Association of
Trinidad and Tobago
c/o Metropolitan Bookshop
17 Chacon Street
Port-of-Spain
first organized in 1956, soon became defunct. Between 1958 and 1973, however, problems affecting booksellers were dealt with at informal meetings. The revival of the BATT was one of the constructive effects of the August 1974 announcement that school texts would be subject to government price control.

5 Trade Press

This is not existent in the literal sence. The Booksellers' Association of Trinidad and Tobago ($\rightarrow$4) proposes the issuing of a publication to advertise books. One of the larger bookshops issues a weekly "Book Bulletin" in the local press announcing new arrivals or topical books, and runs a "Top Books of the Week" column in the same paper. A publishing company-cum-bookshop which deals with national, often controversial issues of all kinds, regularly runs in its weekly paper, lists of books, pamphlets and publications available from its bookshop.

7 Sources of Information, Address Services

These include individual, better known bookshops, larger libraries, the Library Association of Trinidad and Tobago ($\rightarrow$15) and persons in the book world. More often the information requested is about local books and authors than about the book trade. The role for the Booksellers' Association (→4) is clearly indicated and it has already prepared a list of bookshops on which its members are indentified.

10 Books and Young People

The large bookshops traditionally support any activity in the area which is undertaken by the children's departments of public libraries or by the Library Association of Trinidad and Tobago (→15) e.g. in the first National Library Week, 1969 and in International Book Year, 1972. The trade has initiated promotional displays on behalf of publishers or groups of publishers and, in some instances, books for young people have been emphasized; no separate formal programming of these has so far been undertaken.

One library sytem maintains Parent-Teacher-Librarian Reference Collections at its major service points. These collections include award winners world-wide in range. This library system also supported a highly successful Travelling Book Exhibition which visited several primary schools throughout Trinidad and Tobago. The exhibition included selected and recommended reading for children up to age twelve and a comprehensive book list "Books for All: a Catalogue of the Travelling Book Exhibition" was published.

In 1973, to mark the 25th Aniversary of one of the system's branch libraries, the West Indian section of the "Books for All" catalogue was up-dated and published separately as "My own West Indian literature". A recent innovation has been the publishing of the series of children's books with local backgrounds and themes, by local authors, which has been started by one of the two indigenous publishing houses.

11 Training

A five-day residential Bookselling Course arranged in 1968 was the first ever attempt at formal training and was very successful. There were seventeen participants from six Caribbean countries and there was total local involvement in the programme. Despite its success, five years were to go by before there was any continuation. In 1974, three five-day non-residential courses were offered, two for junior assistants and one for middle and upper management. Conducted by the Bookselling Officer of the "British Book Development Council", local involvement was limited to interest, support and co-ordination. Registrants totalled 53 from 19 bookshops and actually involved 48 persons, five of whom took both courses. The courses have again been offered in 1975. At the middle-management and management levels, (often owners of bookshops) little formal training has applied but there has been some exposure for varying periods to overseas booksellers, mainly in the United Kingdom. In 1966 a British Council Scholarship in University Bookselling was awarded.

Bibliography

R. E. Martin, *Bookseller training in the Caribbean*. Report 1974. London, British Book Development Council 1974.

12 Taxes

Books are duty free. There are customs and excise duties on gramophone records, tapes and also books of crossword puzzles.

14 Copyright

The Trinidad and Tobago Copyright Ordinance, Chap. 31 No. 16, is based on the 1911 Copyright Act of Great Britain. The Act, with its later amendments, covers the legal deposit of six copies of works locally published–two to the Minister of Education and Culture, and one each to the Archives, the Central Library of Trinidad and Tobago, the University of the West Indies Library (St Augustine) and the Registrar General.

15 National Bibliography, National Library

Trinidad and Tobago's Fifteen-year Plan für Educational Development published in 1968, includes provision for a National Library. Focal point will be the
Central Library of
Trinidad and Tobago
P.O.B. 547
Port-of-Spain
The nucleus of the National Literature Collection will be the Trinidad and Tobago materials acquired over many years by the three public libraries. One library system issues a bimonthly accessions list of material received in its West Indian Reference Collection. This cumulates annually and 5-year cumulations are proposed. One academic library published a Trinidad and Tobago Imprint List. A Medical Literature Index has been compiled. A National Bibliography is planned from 1975.
The *Library Association* of
Trinidad and Tobago (LATT)
P. O. Box 1177
Port-of-Spain
Trinidad

Bibliography

P. Avicenne, *Bibliographical services throughout the world 1965–69*. Paris, Unesco 1972. 310 pp.–pp. 255–256: Trinidad–Tobago.

16 Book Production

As local development of the post World War II period, the growth of book production has been extremely slow. An important factor influencing output is that printers are willing to accept this material only in their slower months (January to April) before the non-book, promotional type of material–especially for the seasonal Christmas and Carnival business is received. It ist estimated that in 1973/74, between 50–75 titles, describable as books and pamphlets were published. This low figure still represents considerable growth over the 1960's by at least 50%.

Bibliography

The Report of the 1972 Seminar on "Regional problems of book production and distribution" which had been organized by the Trinidad and Tobago National Commission for Unesco to mark International Book Year has been published in book form.

19 Paperbacks

In the past there was no difference in the ordering of books in any format. In recent years the book-wholesaler has evolved offering paperback titles (and periodicals) to retail outlets throughout the country on a sale or return basis. These outlets include bookshops large and small, supermarkets, drug stores, hardware and general shops, and more recently, gift shops and department stores without book departments. Both US ann U.K. paperbacks are available. A general annual increase in sales is reported but no figures are available. Light fiction, bestsellers and the 'book-of-the-film' account for the greatest turnover. Exports to other Caribbean countries are made on the same basis.

21 Publishing

Historically, out of necessity, publishing has been undertaken by printers. Local authors, writing at home, are in the main forced to act as their own publishers by depositing an agreed amount with the printer on placing of the order, and paying

the balance on delivery, pre-selling or pre-booking copies and listing contributors in the work, securing a sponsor by their own efforts. There are two local publishers. A few well-known British publishers take a special interest in the Caribbean, travel out regularly seeking new authors and issue Caribbean catalogues or lists. Others have established subsidiary "Caribbean" companies, three of which are located in Trinidad. These publishers may also adapt books especially for this market and the finished work which may be printed in smaller European countries, Japan or Hong Kong (to take advantage of lower production costs) are exported to this market.
→ 16,23.

23 Wholesale Trade

Most of the general and traditional book-shops order stocks of books especially school texts in sufficient quantity to supply smaller shops in suburban and rural areas. Publishers representatives who operate from local offices in Trinidad or from regional offices (in other neighbouring countries) keep in close touch with libraries, schools, bookshops and the Ministry of Education and Culture. There are also Caribbean branches of British publishers set up here. A development of the last fifteen years is the establishment of firms representing groups of British publishers. All publishers' representatives maintain a standing collection of the current publications of their principals at showrooms. Booksellers, teachers, and librarians utilise this service by which books may be examined before orders are placed. Items that have served their purpose, are donated to selected and appropriate institutions or sold to libraries at reduced rated. They are never offered to the individual purchaser and offer no competition with the established book-seller. The paperback book trade is handled by whosesalers who use this medium

exclusively but may have retail outlets as subsidiary or parent companies.

24 Retail Trade

There are approximately 17 traditional bookshops, including one in Scarborough, Tobago, and two in San Fernando. Eight other bookshops handle Primary and Secondary School textbooks almost exclusively. Special bookshops include five Religous, the University Bookshop, and political publishers who offer for sale their own publications as well as other dealing with controversial and/or political issues. A number of small outlets call themselves "bookshops" but carry mainly periodicals of all kinds including comics, with some paperbacks, especially second hand ones.

25 Mail-Order Bookselling

The traditional larger bookshops accept orders by mail. These are received from libraries and bookshops in other Caribbean Islands, and, in the case of West Indian or Trinidad and Tobago works, also from universities, colleges and individuals in other countries, especially the United States of America.

26 Antiquarian Book Trade, Auctions

There is no antiquarian book trade as such. Air conditioning is a development of the last three decades and the survival of old, rare books against tropical book pests, and against mildew, is a rare thing. Older leather bound books have literally "fallen to bits".

27 Book Imports

As for all "finished goods" Trinidad and Tobago, along with the rest of the English speaking Caribbean, has been a market for British books. Imports from other than the

Trinidad and Tobago

United Kingdom and the United States of America are negligible. Influences on public demand are British and American, their education programmes (formal, correspondence, etc.) their mass media, and travel to these countries.

According to official figures issued by the Government of Trinidad and Tobago the country in 1970 imported books and pamphlets for $ 2,612,914. The two principal suppliers were the United Kingdom ($ 706,249) and the USA ($ 295,188).

28 Book Exports

The turnover of business is represented mainly by books imported from abroad and exported to neighbouring countries. In 1970 books and pamphlets were exported for $ 215,957. At least six bookshops accept and execute orders for local publications from other parts of the world.

29 Book Fairs

Exhibitions have been mounted by booksellers to promote a particular book, an author's works collectively, the books of a single publisher, or groups of publishers overseas. The first Book Fair, the International Book Year "Book Festival" was very successful. Most of the traditional bookshops actively participated.

32 Literary Prizes

To mark the country's Independence in 1962, a prize was awarded by a local trans- or multi-national Cooperation for the best work of fiction contributed to the country's literature. Other than this, there is an annual national contest between villages for a trophy. The competitions for which this trophy is awarded include short stories, plays and verse. In 1972, International Book Year, awards were made for the best short story, and the best children's story.

33 The Reviewing of Books

Books published locally and in the West Indies, books by West Indian writers, and books about the West Indian countries are reviewed from time to time in the following newspapers: Sunday Guardian, Trinidad Guardian, Tapia, and Express. In the 1969 "National Library Week" a book review competition for selected West Indian titles was arranged.

34 Graphic Arts

Few of the country's many printers publish books. A number of the newer printing shops publish booklets and pamphlets but mainly concentrate on promotional material. More recently, pervasive periodicals of a very general appeal are being published. Most of the older printers do not have modern equipment, and in the main, a one-shift workday pattern applies. Maintainance costs of equipment are high and there is an economic loss, awaiting the arrival of spare parts from abroad. The local production of textbooks is proposed and development here will influence improvements in the standard quality of the product. However, there has been rapid growth and development in the printing industry in recent years, from approximately twenty firms in the 1950's to over one hundred today. Most firms handle job printing, some accept pamphlets and fewer still books. Re-organized and newer companies can now handle engraving, printing, plate and offset negatives manufacture, die–cutting, four-colour printing and embosing –work which traditionally had to be imported. Contributing factors to this development include the establishment of the Heidelberg Company of Germany (Federal Republic) locally, and the Governments' encouraging diversification programme of aid under which small business men are encouraged to go into business.

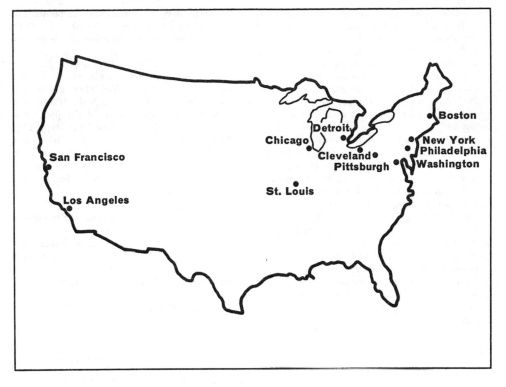

1 General Information

Area 9,363,169 km²

Population 205,022,000 (21.9 per km²)

Capital Washington, D.C. (2,751,000)

Largest towns New York (11, 551,000); Los Angeles (6,860,000); Chicago (6,815,000); Philadelphia (4,829,000); Detroit (4,127,000); Boston (3,239,000); San Francisco (2,999,000); Washington D.C. (2,751,000); Pittsburgh (2,387,000); St Louis (2,327,000); Cleveland (2,068,000)

Government United States of America (USA) comprising 50 states. The National Government consists of an elected President and Vice-President, an elected Senate, and an elected House of Representatives. The Senate consists of 100 members, 2 from each of 50 States. The House of Representatives consists of 431 members, apportioned among the 50 states on the basis of population. The state of California

elects 38 representatives, the state of Alaska elects 1. Within the states there are also counties, and cities. Police services are primarily handled at the city level. There are national and state income taxes, also state and local sales taxes and property taxes

Religion Protestant 54.0%, Roman Catholic 37.3%, others 8.7%

National language English

Leading foreign languages Spanish, French

Weights, measures The USA reckons distances and areas in miles and square miles, yards and square yards, feet and square feet, inches and square inches. There are 12 inches to the foot, 3 feet to the yard, 5,280 feet to the mile, 1,760 yards to the mile. Another measure of area is the acre. Weight is most commonly reckoned in pounds, according to the avoirdupois system. One pound is 16 ounces. 2,000 pounds make one ton. Printing paper is ordinarily sold by the pound, or ton, also by the ream, which (as regards book papers) is 500 sheets. A so-called "60-pound" paper would be paper of which one ream, 500 sheets, in size 25 inches by 38 inches, would weigh 60 lb. A ream of the same paper in size 38 × 50 inches would, of course, weigh twice as much but would still be described as "60-pound"

Liquid measure is most commonly reckoned in pints, quarts and gallons. Two pints make one quart. In America four quarts make a gallon. Temperature is reckoned on the Fahrenheit system in which the freezing point of sea water is 0°, the freezing point of fresh water is 32°, and the boiling point of water is 212°

In printing, the sizes of type are reckoned in points, there being 72 points to the inch, or about 28.35 to the centimeter. Type sizes in common use range from the 6-point often used in telephone directories, to the 10-point often used in novels. A description of a page of standard book type might be: 10-point, leaded 2 points, on a 24-pica line, 36 lines to the page. A pica is 1/6 inch, or 12 points. The same page might also be described as 10/12, meaning type with a 10-point face, cast on a 12-point body

Currency unit Dollar ($) = 100 cents (c)

Education There are free public schools through the 12th year of schooling. There are tuition-free state universities through the 16th year of schooling in many states. Of the population aged 25 years or older, as of 1969, about 11% had received 16 or more years of education, another 43% had received 12 to 15 years, 31% had received 8 to 11 years, and 9% had received 5 to 7 years. About 5.6% had received 4 years or less

Illiteracy Estimated at 2%

Paper consumption a) Newsprint 43.6 kg per inhabitant (1970)

b) Printing paper (other than newsprint) 48.6 kg per inhabitant (1970)

Membership UNESCO, IPA, ICBA, ILAB

→ Puerto Rico; Virgin Islands.

2 Past and Present

Successful colonization of North America began in 1620. By 1636 Harvard College had been founded, near Boston. By 1776 there were 13 British colonies in America, and in that year they declared their independence of England. By 1776 there was a good deal of printing and publishing and bookselling in Boston, New York and Philadelphia. For the next century the USA freely pirated books of English origin. In 1891 the USA extended copyright protection to British and other foreign authors, with the limitation that to enjoy such protection their works had to be printed in the USA.

In 1871 a man named Frederick Leypoldt, who had served an apprenticeship in the German book trade, started the US booktrade journal which became the "Publishers' Weekly" (→5). Among his early associates were Henry Holt and Richard Rogers Bowker. In 1876 he issued the first volume of the "Publishers' Trade List Annual", which ultimately became the basis of "Books in Print USA".

About 2,000 books were published by US publishers in 1876, including editions imported from England. By 1901 this number had grown to about 8,000–and there were approximately 68,000 entries in a 1902 index to the "Publishers' Trade List Annual". In that year was begun H. W. Wilson's "Cumulative Book Index", which continues today and provides an index by author, title and subject to all books published in the English language. In 1972 some 38,000 new titles and new editions were issued in the USA, and 345,000 titles were listed in Bowker's "Books in Print".

US retail booksellers have never been as successful as their European colleagues in organizing for effective control of their markets. When the public schools began to provide free textbooks, they tended to buy direct from the publishers, not through the bookstores. Later, the publishers of encyclopedias set up sales forces which went directly into homes and offices, bypassing the retailers. Still later, the publishers of low-priced paperbacks emphasized distribution through newsstands, using local wholesalers specializing in handling newspapers and magazines. Low-priced children's books came to be sold primarily through chains of food stores, Woolworth stores, etc.

At the same time, independent book retailers often found themselves undersold, when department stores would cut the list prices of bestsellers. Attempts to take legal action to prevent such price-cutting were unsuccessful.

Retailers also found themselves gradually losing their library customers. Today, US libraries of all kinds probably spend more than $ 250,000,000 a year for books–but they largely buy through firms which had originally been wholesalers to booksellers, but then found it more profitable to concentrate on selling to libraries.

Despite the competition from other kinds of outlets, there has been a steady growth in the number and size of bookstores also. From 1960 to 1970 the membership of the "American Booksellers' Association" (→4) grew from 1,500 to 3,800. Many of the newly opened stores are in the new shopping centres outside the cities.

Bibliography

O. H. CHENEY, *Economic survey of the book industry*. 3rd printing. (Originally published in 1931 by the National Association of Book Publishers.) New York, N.Y., R. R. Bowker Co. 1960. 356 pp.

H. LEHMANN-HAUPT, *The book in America*. 2nd ed. New York, N.Y., R. R. Bowker Co. 1951. 493 pp.

W. MILLER, *The book industry*. New York, N.Y., Columbia University Press 1949 156 pp.

J. A. NIETZ, *The evolution of American secondary school textbooks*. Rutland, Vt., Charles E. Tuttle Co. 1966. 265 pp.

J. M. REID, *An adventure in textbooks*. New York, N.Y., R. R. Bowker Co. 1969. 198 pp.

D. SHEEHAN, *This was publishing*. Bloomington, Ind., Indiana University Press 1952. 288 pp.

G. TH. TANSELLE, *Guide to the study of United States imprints*. 2 vols. Cambridge Mass., Harvard University Press 1971. LXIV, 1050 pp.

J. TEBBEL, *A history of book publishing in the United States*. Vol. 1: The creation of an industry, 1630–1865. Vol. 2: The expansion of an industry, 1865–1919. New York, N.Y., R. R. Bowker Co. 1972–75. XVI, 646; XII, 813 pp.

→6.

3 Retail Prices

Despite several attempts to secure government approval of some kind of re-sale price maintenance for books, there have been only very brief interludes of such protection, and in general US book retailers have never enjoyed such protection for very long and do not enjoy it today.

To be sure, price-cutting has generally been prevented wherever a publisher has had full control of his channels of sale–as for example in the sale of free textbooks to the public schools, the sale of encyclopedias direct to homes, and the sale of books offered only direct-by-mail-to-the-consumer and without discount to wholesalers or retailers.

The basic pattern is to set list prices on general books which will permit giving retailers discounts of about $33\frac{1}{2}\%$ on one, 40% on 2–5, and up to 46% on larger quantities. Some of the higher priced technical books carry trade discounts in the 25 to 35% range. College textbooks are commonly sold to college bookstores at list less 20%. School textbooks are usually sold to the schools at a nominal list price (which nobody pays) less 25%. Books published primarily for sale at list price direct by mail (including library reference books) sometimes carry no discount to retailers or wholesalers, and sometimes carry a discount like 10 or 15% intended to cover the dealer's costs, but leave no room for underselling the publisher.

The best-stocked US bookstores do generally sell only at list prices. In some cities they face price-cutting by the book departments within department stores, where discounts of 30% or so on bestsellers may be offered. There are also several booksellers specializing in soliciting mail-orders at cut prices–sometimes at list price less 30% plus a flat amount (like 40 cents) for packing and postage.

Libraries can count on being able to buy general trade books at discounts of 30 to 36%, depending on volume and service. Of course, they get less discount when the wholesaler supplying them gets less. Quite commonly wholesalers specialized in servicing libraries find they can work on mark-ups averaging about 10% of retail prices.

Book clubs are, of course, another channel through which books move at less than list prices.

The best place to seek the price of forthcoming US publications is in Bowker's "Forthcoming Books", which attempts to look six months ahead. Prices of current books are, of course, given in all the current bibliographies. In view of the recent inflation in all prices it is a good plan to look in Bowker's "Books in Print", revised annually in October, to see whether the original price of an older book has since been increased. Even more current information about paperback prices is to be found in Bowker's "Paperbound Books in Print", revised three times a year.

Publisher's discount policies are given in the "Book Buyer's Handbook" published annually by the "American Booksellers' Association".

Retail price averages of hardcover books increased 38% between 1967 and 1970 from $8.43 to $11.66. Retail prices for mass market paperbacks increased 26% from 1967 to 1970.

4 Organization

In July of 1970 the two principal book industry associations–the "American Book Publishers' Council" and the "American Educational Publishers' Institute"–consolidated to become the

Association of American Publishers Inc.
(AAP)
1 Park Ave.
USA New York., N.Y. 10016

With more than 250 members, the Association now represents nearly all the major publishers of general books, textbooks, and other educational materials.

The Association holds two annual membership meetings in addition to a number of conferences and seminars.

The governing body of the Association is a 21-member Board of Directors elected annually by the membership in two to four year staggered terms. Membership in the Association is open to any American firm which, for at least one year, has been actively engaged in the creation, production, and publication of books or other copyrightable types of educational materials. Foreign publishers doing business in the United States may become associate members.

The AAP's activities are organized vertically by special interest (trade books, school texts, college texts, reference books, scientific, technical and medical books, religious books, mass-market paperbacks, maps) as well as horizontally by common interest (copyright, freedom to read, international trade, reading development, marketing, postal matters, management and administration, credit).

The AAP has a member on the Executive Committee of the "International Publishers' Association" (→BTW I, International Section 4), and it organized the Central Exhibit of US books at the Frankfurt Book Fair up to 1972, followed by the Book Combined Exhibit, Briarcliff Mauer, N.Y. It represents the publishers in their cooperation with the "American Library Association" (→35), the "American Booksellers' Association", the "National Education Association", the "National Book Committee", the "Council for Great Cities", and many others. Its Washington office maintains liaison with government at both the legislative and operating levels, on both international and domestic matters, and produces a newsletter covering such activities and developments.

US retail booksellers are mainly organized in the following associations:

The *American Booksellers' Association (ABA)*
800 2nd Ave.
USA New York N.Y. 10017

has 2,850 members (founded in 1900). It works towards establishment, improvement and maintenance of favorable trade conditions, combats unfair competition and price-cutting by vigilant support of Fair Trade laws, strives for the maintenance of sound bookseller–publisher relations, and sponsors promotional campaigns to increase the sale of all books.

Publications:
1) *ABA Bulletin*, monthly
2) *Book Buyer's Handbook*, annual
3) *ABA Sidelines Directory*, annual
4) *Basic Book List*, annual
5) *Staff Manual*, irregular

The
National Association of College Stores (NACS)
55 E. College St.
USA Oberlin, Ohio 44074

has 2,207 members (founded in 1923), in-

cludes institutional, private, and cooperative college stores (1,830) selling books and stationery to college students and faculty, as well as publishers and manufacturers (377) as associate members. NACSCORP, Inc., a wholly owned corporation, distributes paperback books for 80 publishers.
Publications:
1) *College Store Journal*, bimonthly
2) *Confidential Bulletin*, weekly.
The
Antiquarian Booksellers' Association of America (ABAA),
Shop 2 Concourse, 630 Fifth Ave.
USA New York N.Y. 10020
has 400 members (founded in 1949). Includes dealers in rare and out-of-print books. Affiliated with: International League of Antiquarian Booksellers (→ BTW I, International Section 26).
Other organizations are:
Association of American University Presses (AAUP)
1 Park Ave.
USA New York, N.Y. 10016
with 69 members (founded 1937), scholarly publishing divisions of colleges and universities of the United States, Canada and Mexico. Activities include seminars, workshops and research programmes. Operates *American University Press Services*, including a cooperative mailing list service open both to members and non-members.
Bureau of Independent Publishers & Distributors (BIPAD)
122 E. 42 St.
USA New York.) N.Y. 10017
with 813 members (founded 1946). Publishers of magazines, comics and children's books, and small paperbound books, and wholesalers who distribute these publications.
Book Manufacturers' Institute (BMI)
161 E. 42 St.
USA New York, N.Y. 10017
with 110 members (founded 1920). Independent book printers and binders, also

mechanical departments of book publishers.
Publication:
BMI Newspacket, 10 per year.

Christian Booksellers' Association (CBA),
2031 W. Cheyenne Rd.
USA Colorado Springs, Colo. 80906
with 1,000 members (founded 1950). Retail bookselling, Protestant books, Bibles, gifts, Sunday School and church supplies.
Publications:
1) *CBA*, monthly
2) *Bookstore Journal*, 10/year
3) *Suppliers Directory*, annual
also publishes bookkeeping manual and Christian bookstore manual.

Society of Authors' Representatives (SAR)
101 Park Ave.
USA New York, N.Y. 10017
with 42 members (founded 1928). Literary and dramatic agents, who market books, plays, and other literary material.
The
Children's Book Council (CBS)
175 Fifth Ave.
USA New York, N.Y. 10010
with 90 members (founded 1945). Publishers of books for children. To encourage the reading and enjoyment of good children's books. The Children's Book Council is the headquarters for the National Children's Book Week. For over twenty years, this Book Week has been sponsored by the Council. In 1964 the Children's Book Council initiated a vacation reading programme to help teachers and librarians plan summer-reading programmes.

Franklin Book Programs → 28.

5 Trade Press

The most important trade journal for all matters concerning the book trade is the
Publishers' Weekly
1180 Avenue of the Americas
USA New York, N.Y. 10036

PW was founded in 1871 by Frederick Leypoldt, and has ever since remained independent of either the publishers' associations or the booksellers' associations. The more important forthcoming trade books are first announced in the advertising pages of PW, and also reviewed in the editorial pages, together with news about promotion plans.

PW's news columns cover trade events, and news of the sale of book rights to reprinters, book clubs, foreign publishers, motion picture producers, etc.

About 4,000 new books of major interest to booksellers and libraries are reviewed each year in the "Forecast" columns of PW, and others are briefly described in the seasonal Announcement Numbers. For example, in the Spring Announcement Number of 26 January 1971 some 700 titles were briefly previewed by month and publisher for the period February to September. In addition, 174 publishers placed 176 pages of book advertising, announcing 4,500 coming titles, and these 4,500 titles were also indexed in the editorial pages by title and by author.

The circulation of PW is more than 30,000 copies (1973).

Another book-trade journal, formerly part of PW but independent since 1948, is

AB, Bookman's Weekly (formerly
Antiquarian Bookman)
Box 1100
USA Newark, N.J. 07101

which is more fully described in Chapter 26 on the antiquarian booktrade. However, AB's "Bookman's Year Book" should be mentioned here, inasmuch as some 500 publishers of new books and reprints advertise here their publications of special interest to bookmen and book collectors.

There are several other trade publications, as follows:

The official journal of the National Association of College Stores is the

College Store Journal
55 E. College Street
USA Oberlin, Ohio 44070

Its editorial and advertising pages feature books of special interest to college bookstores, also other kinds of merchandise sold in college stores ranging from stationery to sporting goods and clothing. Bimonthly, circulation 3,100.

The Christian Booksellers' Association publishes the

Bookstore Journal,
1722 Ridge Road
USA Homewood, Ill. 60430

10 issues a year, circulation 6,500.

The *Christian Bookseller*
Gundersen Dr. & Schmale Rd.
USA Wheaton, Ill., 60187

circulation 7,100.

Knowledge Industry Report (semi-monthly) and *The Educational Marketer* (semi-monthly): Newsletters published by Knowledge Industry Publications, Inc., Tiffany Towers, White Plains, N.Y. 10602.
(→15).

6 Book-Trade Literature

In the US the first book about publishing that is usually recommended to the neophyte is not even a US book—it is a British book, namely, Sir Stanley Unwin's "The truth about publishing", which has remained a classic even outside Britain through all its many revisions over the past 50 years. There are, however, a number of US books that would come high on anyone's list of books relevant to understanding the current publishing scene. They are:

Bibliography

C. B. ANDERSON (ed.), *Bookselling in America and the world.* NewYork,Quadrangle 1975. XII, 214 pp.

C. B. ANDERSON, J. A. DUFFY, J. D. KAHN, *A manual on bookselling.* New York, N.Y.,

R. R. Bowker Co. 1969. 271 pp.

H. S. BAILEY JR., *The art and science of book publishing*. New York, N.Y., Evanston and London, Harper & Row 1970. 216 pp.

Bowker Annual of Library and Booktrade Information. 18th ed. New York, N.Y., R. R. Bowker Co. 1973. 548 pp.

C. B. GRANNIS, *What happens in book publishing*. 2nd ed. New York, N.Y., Columbia University Press 1967. 467 pp.

G. GROSS (ed.), *Publishers on publishing*. New York, N.Y., Grosset & Dunlap, 1961. 491 pp.

W. JOVANOVIC, *Now Barabbas*. New York, N.Y., Harvest Books, Harcourt Brace Jovanovic 1960. 228 pp.

M. LEE, *Bookmaking: the illustrated guide to design and production*. New York, N.Y., R. R. Bowker Co. 1965. 399 pp.

CH. A. MADISON, *Book publishing in America*. New York, N.Y., McGraw-Hill 1966. 628 pp.

D. SMITH, *A guide to book-publishing*. New York, N.Y., R. R. Bowker Co. 1966. 244 pp.

J. TEBBEL, *A history of book publishing in the United States*. Vol. 1: The creation of an industry 1630–1835. Vol. 2: The expansion of an industry, 1865–1919. New York, N.Y., R. R. Bowker Co. 1972–75. XVI, 646; XII, 813 pp.

One more volume to be expected.

→2, 7.

7 Sources of Information, Address Services

Bowker's "Literary Market Place", revised and re-issued annually in June, provides close to 900 pages of guidance to every facet of US publishing, with the names, and addresses of about 1,000 active US and Canadian publishers, classified by name, by field of activity, and area. Other features include advertising agencies, literary agents, associations, book clubs, book lists, book manufacturers, paper merchants, book reviewers, booktrade events, mailing-list sources, consultants, exhibits, exporters and importers, awards and prize contests, magazines by name and interest (about 700), magazine subscription agencies, foreign literary periodicals, news services, newspapers reviewing books, motion-picture companies, record, film and tape producers, radio and TV stations, shipping services, wholesalers, translators and much else.

The LMP also has a section describing about 150 "Reference books of the trade" among which the following are perhaps the most used:

American Book Trade Directory, R. R. Bowker Co., 21st ed. 1973. Contains complete directory of booksellers in US and Canada, by states and cities; information on sidelines, wholesalers, private book clubs and dealers in foreign-language books.

American Library Directory, R. R. Bowker Co., 28th ed. 1972. Contains detailed information about US, Canadian and selected overseas libraries; library schools.

Bowker Annual of Library and Booktrade Information, R. R. Bowker Co., annually in spring.

Guide to Reference Books, American Library Association, 8th ed., 1967. Lists and describes some 7,600 currently useful reference works in all fields and includes books in the major European languages as well as English.

Ulrich's International Periodicals Directory, R. R. Bowker Co., 14th ed. 1971. Subject-arranged list of over 40,000 periodicals published throughout the world. Provides price, frequency, editors' names, addresses, etc. 2 vols. Revised biannually.

8 International Membership

The USA is a member of UNESCO. The Association of American Publishers is a member of the International Publishers'

Association (→BTW I, International Section 4), and has a member on its Executive Committee, and a member on the International Committee (→4).

The American Booksellers' Association (→4) is a member of the International Community of Booksellers' Association (→BTW I, International Section 4).

The Antiquarian Booksellers' Association of America (→4) is a member of the International League of Antiquarian Booksellers (→BTW I, International Section 26).

9 Market Research

The US book industry as such has not had any sustained general programme of co-operative book-market research. The only industry-wide study was that made by Cheney in 1931 (→2).

However, much information of relevance to book-market research is to be found in government census data, as summarized in the annual volume "Statistical Abstracts", published by the US Government Printing Office. In this source, for example, can be found data and trends regarding population, income, education, professions, schools, libraries, titles published, copies printed, book imports and exports, paper consumed, etc.

There have been specialized studies from time to time, sometimes by industry groups, sometimes by foundations. Some research into the college market is currently being done in the College Publishing Division of the Association of American Publishers (→4). All such efforts are usually summarized in the Bowker Annual (→7) which has a 5-year cumulative index to help in locating them. Many market research questions can also be answered by study of the various trade directories, or of the offerings of some of the brokers of mailing lists of book buyers (→7).

10 Books and Young People

In 1970 Bowker's "School Library Journal", which had a paid circulation of 68,000, reviewed about 2,500 new books for children and young people, and Bowker's "Children's Books in Print" indexed 37,000 available titles by author, title and illustrator. School libraries and public libraries form the primary US market for the higher-priced clothbound children's books, and are estimated to spend more than $ 200 million on such books. Parents, reached through newsstands, department stores and food markets, form the primary market for the lower-priced, paper-covered children's books, and probably spend between $ 50 and $ 100 million on such books.

Until about 1930, children's books were generally conceived and published in the expectation that the primary sale would be through bookstores to parents. From about 1930 to 1950 publishers increasingly began to pay more attention to the suggestions and demands coming from the children's departments of public libraries. After 1950 there was a very strong rise in the number and size of school libraries, first in high schools, then in elementary schools, and the expenditures of school libraries overtook and greatly surpassed those of public libraries.

The publishers of children's books are organized in the Children's Book Council (→4). Within the American Library Association (→35a) the children's librarians are organized in the Children's Services Division, which presents the annual Newbery and Caldecott Medals (→32) for the year's most distinguished children's books, and in the American Association of School Librarians (→35a). The former has a journal called "Top of the News" and the latter has a journal called "School Libraries". Librarians in public libraries who work with teen-age young people are organized in the Young Adult Service Division.

Since 1919 one week in November has been set aside as "Book Week" during which special displays and programmes are planned emphasizing the importance of children's books in the home.

The "Booklist" of the American Library Association reviews about 900 children's books a year.

The

Horn Book Magazine
585 Boylston Street
USA Boston, Mass. 02116

and the "New York (Sunday) Times" each review about 500 children's books.

The Horn Book Magazine combines four or five articles about children's books and reading per issue with 75 to 100 reviews of children's books.
→20.

Bibliography

Best Books for Children. Annual. R. R. Bowker Co.
4,000 approved juvenile and young adult titles in print.

Children's Catalog. 12thed.Bronx,N.Y.,W.H. Wilson Co. 1971.
4,274 titles proven useful in public and elementary school libraries.

El-Hi Textbooks in Print. Annual, R. R. Bowker Co.
14,000 textbooks and related teaching materials for elementary and high schools.

V. HAVILAND, *Children's literature;* A guide to reference sources. Washington, D. C., 1966. 341 pp. First supplement, 1972. 315 pp.
A bibliography listing children's literature published through 1965 and available at the Library of Congress. Supplement updates the main volume through 1969.

C. L. MEIGS, *A critical history of children's literature;* a survey of children's books in

English. Rev. ed. New York, Macmillan 1969. 708 pp.

A. PELLOWSKI, *The world of children's literature.* New York, N.Y., R. R. Bowker Co. 1966.
Comprehensive bibliography of materials dealing with children's literature and children's libraries throughout the world.

11 Training

For some years the National Association of College Stores (→4) has held periodic seminars to which members could come, or send employees for a week or so of intensive instruction in bookselling methods. Since 1968 the American Booksellers' Association (→4) has joined in sponsoring these courses. One is held on the East Coast and one on the West Coast, and the combined attendance is about 250 students a year. For many years there has been a six-week summer course in publishing at Radcliffe College which graduates about 70 each year.

In general, very few of the people in US bookselling and book publishing have any formal training or apprenticeship, and are expected to learn on the job or from the literature (→6). There are, however, many schools for librarians since advancement in a school, public, or college library generally requires a degree in librarianship. In 1968 some 5,000 Master's Degrees were conferred.

Courses for the book trade and the graphic arts are offered by the Harvard Summer School (Cambridge, Mass.), the Graphic Arts Education Center (Philadelphia, Pa.), the Hunter College (New York), the New York University (New York) and Syracuse University (Syracuse, N. Y.).

12 Taxes

Within the US, books are generally subject to the same kind of taxes as other merchandise.

Most of the 50 states have sales taxes, which are collected from the ultimate consumer at the time of the sale. These are usually in the 5% to 7% range. Sales taxes are levied by the states, not by the national government, and need not be collected where the buyer is in one state, and the seller is elsewhere, as for example, in selling by mail.

The US does not tax exports as such. It taxes many imports, but not books. It prohibits the import of any book in violation of US copyright. For example, copies of a British edition may not be imported if there is a copyrighted US edition of the same book. However, this restriction does not prohibit US libraries from acquiring imported editions.

In the USA, the national government and most state governments rely for their revenue primarily on income taxes, which may be levied both on businesses and on individuals. Businesses pay about 50% of their net profits in Federal taxes. An unmarried individual earning $ 100 a week would commonly have about $ 20 or more withheld for income taxes, and in New York State an individual with net taxable income exceeding $ 50,000 a year would pay about 78% of the excess in national and state income taxes. Most state governments also levy sales taxes, and city governments rely primarily on taxes on real property–land and buildings. There are also national and state inheritance taxes.

In 1970 the overall tax picture for the USA was as follows:

National: (in million US $)

Receipts	
From income taxes	129,200
From employment taxes	38,914
From sales taxes (excise taxes)	15,940
From import duties	2,260
Miscellaneous receipts	13,072

Difference between undistributed intragovernmental transactions and net lending	1,225

Outlays	
For community development and education	10,583
For national services including Social Security	75,361
For national defence including the Vietnam war, military pensions, military aid to other countries etc.	88,114
Miscellaneous outlays	25,553

State and local: (in million US $; 1968)

Receipts	
From Federal Government	17,168
From property taxes	27,747
From income taxes	9,826
From licences	7,087
From sales and gross receipts taxes	22,911
From charges and miscellaneous	16,511
From operation of state-owned public utilities and liquor stores	7,502
From insurance trust revenue	8,815

Outlays	
For education	41,158
For highways	14,481
For other services	46,772
For operation of state-owned public utilities and liquor stores	8,170
For insurance trust expenditure	5,635

Bibliography

Statistical Abstract of the United States 1970, US Department of Commerce, Bureau of the Census 1970. Washington, D.C.

13 Clearing Houses

The Association of American Publishers (→4) operates a Credit Information Service for the benefit of its members. There are no arrangements for payments clearing, or orders clearing. There is a plan called SCOP; meaning Single Copy Order Plan, under which booksellers get a larger discount if they order in a way that reduces the publishers' paperwork. The National Association of College Stores (→4) operates a cooperative wholesale house handling the kind of paperbacks not available through local news wholesalers.

14 Copyright

The USA is not a member of the Berne Convention. Apart from the USSR, it is the only major nation which has never joined—and has no present plans to do so. However, the US did become a signatory of the Universal Copyright Convention (UCC) as of 1955, and since that date books copyrighted in the US have enjoyed protection in UCC countries (→BTW I, International Section 14).

In general, no book by an author who is a citizen of, or a resident in the US may enjoy full copyright protection under US law unless manufactured within the US. Limited, "ad interim", protection, up to five years, may be obtained under certain circumstances, provided no more than 1,500 copies are imported. Manufacture within the US, within the five-year period, can secure full-term protection. Whether the requirement of domestic "manufacture" means type composition as well as presswork and binding has never been tested in the courts.

A book by a foreign author who resides outside the US, and who is a resident of a UCC country, will be protected under the UCC. If the foreign author does not himself reside in a UCC country, he may still gain UCC protection if his book is properly published and copyrighted in a UCC country.

In general, US books published prior to 1955 did not and do not enjoy copyright protection in other countries unless simultaneously published within a country adhering to the Berne Convention. However, such "simultaneous" publication in New York and London was often arranged.

The US copyright law of 1909 originally provided protection to the owner of a copyright for a total of 56 years from date of publication. This protection consisted of one term of 28 years, renewable for another term of another 28 years. Application for renewal had to be made in the 28th year, otherwise the work fell into the public domain.

Beginning in 1968, legislation was introduced in the US to change the term of copyright protection from this 56-year basis to the more common basis of 50 years after the death of the author. This legislation failed of passage, but has been reintroduced in each subsequent session of the Congress and is expected to pass eventually. Because of this expected change in the duration of copyright, temporary legislation has provided for an extension of the 28-year renewal term of any copyright which would otherwise have expired subsequent to 1962. It is contemplated that the second term existing copyrights will be extended from 28 years to 47 years.

The basic action required to copyright a book under US law is to print it with a notice on the title page or the verso of the title page in the form "Copyright 1971 by . . . .". For most secure protection in other countries as well it is considered best to use the form "Copyright © 1971 by (name of proprietor). All rights reserved." Two copies of the best edition, together with a fee of US $ 6, are then to be deposited with the Register of Copyright at the Library of Congress in Washington, D.C. However, delay in registering does not invalidate the protection. Publication of a work without a notice of copyright, or with an incorrect notice of copyright, can invalidate the copyright.

Bibliography

An excellent source of further information about copyright practice in the US which also lists other sources, is:

H. F. PILPEL and M. D. GOLDBERG, *A copyright guide*. 4th ed., New York, N.Y., R. R. Bowker Co. 1969. 40 pp.

15 National Bibliography, National Library

The Library of Congress is the "national library" of the US. However, its "National Union Catalog" does not stop with listing publications of US origin, but includes books from all countries in all languages. It is therefore less widely used than two less extensive and less expensive privately produced sets of bibliographies, namely those produced by the H. W. Wilson Co., whose "Cumulative Book Index" undertakes to cover only books in English, and the R. R. Bowker Co., whose various services attempt to cover only books published in the US, or at least having one exclusive sales agent in the US.

During 1970 the Library of Congress added 174,000 books to its collections. This included books received from other countries, about 80,000 of them in English. During 1970 some 88,000 books, including pamphlets, were deposited in the US Copyright Office. This figure must be viewed in the light of the fact that such deposit is not compulsory, nor would government documents be thus deposited.

During 1970 some 36,000 books, excluding pamphlets under 49 pages and government documents, were listed in the Weekly Record of Bowker's "Publishers' Weekly". During 1970 some 36,000 books, excluding pamphlets under 100 pages and government documents, were listed in the H. W. Wilson Company's "Cumulative Book Index". During 1970 the publishers who supplied information to the editors of Bowker's "Literary Market Place" reported their title output for 1970 at 49,000 titles. During 1970 the US Government Printing Office listed 27,000 titles in its Monthly Catalog of US Government Publications, most of which were pamphlets rather than books.

These various counts, different though they may be, are not necessarily in conflict with each other. At first glance, the 36,000 count for Wilson's CBI might seem low by comparison with the 36,000 count for Bowker's PW Weekly Record, inasmuch as Wilson aims to cover the output of the English-speaking world, not just the output of the USA. However, Wilson counts a title only once, even if it appears under both British and US imprints, and probably counts fewer reprints and pamphlets. (Wilson offers a separate bibliography of pamphlets called the "Vertical File Service", which indexes about 4,000 items a year.) Those publishers whose counts of their own activity were higher than Bowker's may have been counting each volume in a multi-volume set, where Bowker counted only the set.

Since there is no one place in the USA to which copies of published materials must be sent—it is not even required that the deposit of books in the Copyright Office be done promptly—many materials often get into the bibliographies long after they have appeared.

The first notice of a forthcoming publication is usually the listing in Bowker's "Forthcoming Books", which appears every two months and attempts to index all books which the publishers expect to publish within the next six months. The entry is under both author and title, and gives tentative price and publication date. There is also a "Subject Guide to Forthcoming Books". The information in these indexes is gathered and updated by questionnairing the publishers.

Once a book is actually printed, experienced publishers send the earliest possible advance copies to the Library of Congress cataloguing office and Wilson and Bowker. Books received at LC are catalogued by LC, and advance proofs of the cataloguing are sent by LC to Wilson and Bowker so that entries can appear in the CBI and Bowker's Weekly Record, recording the fact that the book is actually available. The CBI appears monthly, arranged by author, title and subject. The entries in the Weekly Record, themselves arranged by author only, are cumulated monthly into the "American Book Publishing Record", in which the basic arrangement is by subject, with an author and title index.

A far more complete record of the books catalogued by LC (including books originating outside the US) is provided also by LC in its monthly "National Union Catalog". This also includes entries supplied by the other large research libraries in the US.

Each year there are annual accumulations of these various monthly publications, and there is also a Bowker annual which lists not only the new titles, but also older titles which continue to be available from the publisher. This is called "Books in Print" and is arranged by author and title. It also has a companion called the "Subject Guide to Books in Print". In 1972 some 265,000 titles were listed in "Books in Print".

The
Library of Congress (LC)
USA Washington D.C. 20541
was created by Congress in 1800 as a parliamentary collection for the national legislature. In the 19th century the Congress established legal deposit for copyrighted and official publications. This together with special purchases, private gifts, and transfers from other government agencies led to a large and comprehensive national reference collection. Probably the world's largest library, it serves today not only the Congress, but also government agencies, libraries everywhere, and the general public.

In 1970 the total holdings had reached more than 61 million items, among which were more than 15 million books and pamphlets. It has outstanding collections in American history, law, music and music literature, and cartographic material.

The Library issued nearly 2 ½ million volumes to visitors in its public reading rooms in 1970. 267 bibliographies containing more than 95,000 entries were prepared.

Since 1901 LC has made its cataloguing available to other libraries in the form of printed cards. They are used by some 10,000 other libraries. In 1969 LC sold some 63 million cards.

LC's bibliographies for the past years are available both in reprint and in microform. The years from 1901 to 1942 are available as a set. The years from 1943 to 1962 are available as another set. Further cumulations are in work.

16 Book Production

The statistics of American book titles output in 1972 are given as follows in the Annual Summary number of Publishers' Weekly:

Subject group with Dewey Deeimal Numbers	New books	1972 New editions	Total
Agriculture (630-639; 712-719)	286	104	390
Art (700-711; 720-779)	1,097	373	1,470
Biography (920-929)	1,086	900	1,986
Business (650-659)	529	155	684
Education (370-379)	1,041	251	1,292
Fiction	2,109	1,151	3,260
General works (000-099)	802	246	1,048
History (900-909; 930-999)	906	723	1,629
Home economics (640-649)	479	117	596
Juveniles	2,126	400	2,526
Language (400-499)	354	125	479
Law (340-349)	418	298	716
Literature (800-810; 813-820; 823-899)	1,398	1,127	2,525
Medicine (610-619)	1,404	435	1,839
Music (780-789)	215	187	402

Subject group with Dewey Decimal Numbers	New books	1972 New editions	Total
Philosophy, psychology (100-199)	829	335	1,164
Poetry, drama (811; 812; 821; 822)	883	601	1,484
Religion (200-299)	1,233	472	1,705
Science (500-599)	2,143	443	2,586
Sociology, economics (300-339; 350-369; 380-399)	4,688	1,727	6,415
Sports, recreation (790-799)	686	255	941
Technology (600-609; 620-629; 660-699)	1,184	241	1,425
Travel (910-919)	972	519	1,491
Total	26,868	11,185	38,053

Bibliography

In the annual summary of "Publishers' Weekly" (→ 5) a lot of information can be found concerning book production. These statistics are also given in the *Bowker Annual* (→ 7) and *Printing and Publishing* (→ 27).

17 Translations

Books translated into English may, of course, be simultaneously published both in the US and in the United Kingdom, leading to some complication of the count as between the two countries.
In 1970 the "Publishers' Weekly" counted 1,232 translations from other languages, as follows:

Language(s)	1971	1972
French	280	277
German	295	272
Italian	16	26
Oriental	48	63
Russian	126	135
Scandinavian	40	50
Spanish	47	38
Other languages	274	232
Total	1,126	1,093

The most important subjects were literature (27% of all translations), religion (17%), geography and history (13%), pure science (11%), and arts (10%).
According to the UNESCO Statistical Yearbook 1970 15,279 books were translated from English into other languages in 1967, 57% of these being in the field of literature. The most important of these were:

Language(s)	Titles (1967)	Percentage
French	986	6.5
German	1,969	12.9
Italian	898	5.9
Japan	1,081	7.1
Russian	486	3.2
Scandinavian	2,263	14.8
Spanish	934	6.1
Other languages	6,662	43.5
Total	15,279	100.0

Bibliography

Both "Publishers' Weekly" (→ 3) in its Annual Summary number and the Bowker Annual (→ 7) give the total amount of translations in a year, classified into languages of origin.
The UNESCO *Statistical Yearbook* (→ BTW I, International Section 17) gives a lot of information about translations from all languages, also classified into sources and even more into subject. (The numbers of UNESCO and PW do not correspond).

18 Book Clubs

Book Clubs reported sales, at retail, of about US $ 220 million in 1969, perhaps about one-quarter the volume of book sales in retail outlets, and one-third the volume of sales achieved by door-to-door selling of encyclopedias and other sets.
The first US book club was the Literary Guild, started in 1927, now a division of Doubleday, and still a major factor. It was closely followed by the Book-of-the-Month

Club, now a public company, which reported sales of US $ 39,000,000 in 1970.

Larger than either in terms of membership is the Readers' Digest Condensed Book Club.

There are 138 US book clubs, large and small, and 28 additional book clubs for children, with a total membership of about ten million.

Book clubs typically send each member an advance description of each selection. The member may write and say he does not want it, or that he wants some other book instead, but if he takes no action the announced selection is sent to him with a bill. By way of inducement to agree to this arrangement, the member usually receives a free bonus book at the start, and additional bonus books or price reductions in proportion to the number of selections he accepts and pays for.

A development of a few years ago is the condensed book club, notably the Reader's Digest Condensed-Book Club, which issues condensations of four or five books in a single volume.

In 1970 the Federal Trade Commission, a US Government agency, began an inquiry as to whether the so-called "negative option" selling was contrary to policy—whether it might be deceptive in the sense that it exploited human inertia in such a way as to lead people to buy and keep books they did not really want. Of course, the book clubs are pointing to four decades of public acceptance–decades during which hundreds of thousands of members uncomplainingly sent in from four to twelve payments a year even though free to cancel at any time. As these word are written, the inquiry has not made any determination one way or the other.

The larger clubs negotiate with the publishers for the right to print their own editions and they pay a reduced rate of royalty in return for a comparatively large advance or guarantee.

Book clubs' royalties range from 4 ½ cents a copy to as much as 10 % of the club's selling price, with guarantees based on sales of a few hundred copies to 400,000 of 500,000.

The smaller clubs tend to buy part of the original publisher's edition at a special discount, or arrange for print runs jointly with a book publisher.

Since discounts given by book clubs range from 12 to 40 % off the list price of the book, the book clubs must be able either to manufacture or to purchase books from the publisher for about 25 % of retail list price.

The story of the Book-of-the-Month Club has been told in the book "The hidden public" by Charles Lee.

Bibliography

I. HAAS, *Book clubs*. In: Encyclopedia of Library and Information Science. vol. 2. New York and London, Marcel Dekker. 1969. pp. 661–672.

C. LEE, *The hidden public*. Garden City N.Y. 1958, 236 pp.

Literary Market Place (→ 7).

19 Paperbacks

The July 1971 edition of Bowker's "Paperbound Books in Print" indexed some 91,000 paperbacks, issued by about 1,400 publishers. This number of titles was about a third as large as the count of titles recorded in "Books in Print 1970" (305,000). By contrast, only 4,500 paperbacks were listed in the first edition of "Paperback Books in Print", when it appeared in 1955, a number which at that time was only about 2 % of total books in print.

The so-called "mass market" paperbacks are, of course, only a sub-category within the above totals. These brightly jacketed, low-priced editions are intended primarily for display alongside magazines in the nation's 100,000 newstands and drugstores, though of course bookstores now sell them, too. New mass-market titles are published at the rate of about 200 titles a month –although some don't stay in print very long. Since many of the mass-market outlets have no more than 100 "pockets", there is intense competition between the various publishers for those pockets. One form which this competition takes is intense competition for bestsellers, because the publisher who has a bestseller has the best chance of getting the retailers to take his other titles as well.

The so-called "paperback" revolution really began in 1939, when a group of "pocket books" were distributed exatly as if they were magazines (→BTW I, International Section 19). The same wholesalers who were sending out trucks every day to deliver newspapers and magazines were happy to deliver books as well, provided the books could, like newspapers and magazines, be returned if they were still unsold when it was time to put later editions into the same display racks.

In mass-market book distribution, the basic principle is that the outlet makes the space available, and the wholesaler does the work.

The wholesaler decides what titles to put on display, how long to leave them, and when to take them away and substitute more saleable titles. For making the space available, the outlet (drugstore, news-stand, candy store, etc.) keeps 20% of list price. The wholesaler keeps another 20%. The national news distributor gets 60%, out of which he pays the publisher. In 1971 there were about a dozen national news distributors supplying 900 local news distributors with the lines of about 30 publishers of mass-market paperbacks. The annual dollar volume of publishers' receipts was estimated at about US $ annual volume of publishers' receipts was estimated at about US $ 170,000,000.

In addition to the 200 or so paperbacks published each month for distribution through mass-market channels, another 500 or 600 are published for sale through other channels. Many are aimed primarily at the college market, some at the general bookstore market, some at more specialized outlets such as hobby shops, hardware stores, and churches.

Most of the higher-priced paperbounds are sold by the publishers directly to the outlets, with the outlets getting discounts of 40% or better.

Out of the 2,400 new mass-market paperbacks issued in 1970, about 900 (37%) were new titles as distinct from reprints. Out of the 6,900 other paperbacks issued in 1970, about 5,200 (74%) were new titles. Within the mass-market group, there was twice as much fiction as non-fiction. Within the other group, fiction was a negligible factor–under 2%.

The largest wholesaler of paperbacks, stocking more than 40,000 titles in both the mass-market and higher-priced category, is A&A Distributors, Inc., Holbrook, Massachusetts (near Boston).

Another is Raymar Book Co., Monrovia, Calif. The National Association of College Stores (→4) also has organized a cooperative to wholesale paperbacks to its members (NACSCORP).

Bibliography

a) Catalogue

Paperbound Books in Print. Twice annually. R. R. Bowker Company, New York.–91,000 titles listed in the July 1971 volume.

Entries are indexed by author, title and subject, and give title, author, series, illustrator, ISBN, pages, sizes, publisher, price, whether an original or reissue.

b) Other literature

M. T. CURLEY, *The public library reporter. The buckram syndrome.* Chicago, American Library Association 1968. 65 pp.

A critical essay on paperbacks in Public Libraries of the United States.

F. Lewis, *Paperbound books in America.* In: Bowker Lectures on Book Publishing. New York, R. R. Bowker Co. 1957.

F. Lewis, *Mass market paperbacks.* P. Johnson jr. *The trade paperback.* In: Ch. B. Grannis (ed.), What happens in book publishing. 2nd ed. New York & London Columbia University Press 1967.

The New York Times, annual issue: The New York Times Book Review–Paperback Books.

F. L. Schick, *The paperbound book in America.* New York, R. R. Bowker Co. 1958. The history of paperbacks and their European background.

20 Book Design

The year 1914 saw the founding of the
American Institute of Graphic Art (AIGA)
1059 Third Avenue
USA New York, N.Y. 10021
which had as one of its major goals the recognition and encouragement of good book design. For fifty years, now, it has sponsored annual exhibits of the "Fifty Books of the Year" (→34).

The audience for the shows has expanded steadily and the Fifty Books are now shown throughout the US in public and school libraries, universities, museums and book and graphic art centres and also in the US Department of State's Information Agency Centres in many parts of the world.

Every year the Fifty Books Committee selects three jurors from the book trade, book design, publishing or book manufacturing industries. Publishers are asked to submit what they considered the best books from their publications in the last calendar year. The books must have been offered for sale in editions of not less than hundred and their design and manufacture planned and supervised in the United States. Out of the about 800 books annually submitted,

the jury selects the Fifty Books, which represent "the highest standard of design and manufacture".

Since 1938 an "Annual Textbook Show" gathers together the outstanding examples of textbooks. The books are evaluated in terms of their skill in presenting technical material accurately, concisely and effectively to students and adults.

Every two or three years the best children's books are collected and shown throughout the whole country (→10).

Two series of monthly meetings are held under AIGA auspices; namely, the Trade Book Clinic, founded in 1920, and the Textbook Clinic, founded in 1938.

Bibliography

Yearly *Catalogue of the Fifty Books of the Years,* New York, N.Y., American Institute of Graphic Arts.

Journal of the American Institute of Graphic Arts, published bimonthly by the AIGA for the members of the AIGA.

21 Publishing

According to government figures for the year 1969 some 1,050 US publishers had about 54,000 employees and total sales of about US $ 2,522 million, of which about US $ 790 million was in textbooks, US $ 232 million was in encyclopedias, US $ 276 million was in technical, scientific and professional books, and subscription reference books, US $ 108 million was in religious books, and US $ 810 million was in general trade books.

Further break-downs were given in the 1967 Census, which recorded US $ 591 million of general trade sales, including US $ 156 million in sales to book clubs, US $ 68 million in mass-market paperbacks, US $ 80 million in other paperbacks, US $ 102 million in juveniles priced above US $ 1, and US $ 35 million in juveniles priced under US $ 1.

In terms of copies, the 1967 distribution amounted to about 222 million textbooks, 133 million workbooks, 31 million subscription reference books, 33 million technical, scientific and professional books, 55 million religious books, 114 million book-club books, 201 million mass-market paperbacks, 48 million adult trade hardbounds, 144 million adult trade paperbacks, 62 million juveniles priced at US $ 1 or higher, and 144 million juveniles priced under US $ 1. (Within sales reported were also some sales not specified as to kind, and yet more sales for which the number of copies was not supplied.) With allowance for the under-reporting, the per capita book consumption was estimated at about 7.5 copies.

In general, the book industry is less concentrated than magazines, though more concentrated than newspapers. There has been a small but steady trend towards increasing concentration. In the period from 1958 to 1967, the four largest book-publishing companies increased their share of total industry shipments from 16 % to 20 %. The eight largest increased their share from 29 % to 32 %. The 20 largest increased their share from 48 % to 75 %.

Book publishing is strongly concentrated in the New York area. The 1971 issue of LMP (→ 7) lists 945 publishers who issued 5 or more titles in 1970. Among these 486 are in New York or the New York metropolitan area. Other important publishing centres are the Chicago area with 87 publishers, the Boston area with 49, the San Francisco area with 44, the Los Angeles area with 42 and the Philadelphia area with 25 publishers.

Regarding the title output of these geographical units, the importance of New York is still greater. Although there are no exact statistics about the geographical distribution of the title output in the last three years, the share of New York can be deduced from former statistics given in the annual summary numbers of PW as about 75 %. Furthermore, New York is the organizational centre of the American book trade, for it is the headquarter of both the AAP and the ABA (→ 4). A lot of other organizations concerning the book trade also have their offices in New York.

The LMP also gives the areas of special interest of each publisher. These are summarized in the following table. Publishers may be counted under more than one heading.

Field of activity	Number of publishers	Percentage
Americana, regional	77	8.1
Art, photography	89	9.4
Bibles	16	1.7
Book trade, library, bibliographical	26	2.8
Encyclopedia	27	2.9
Foreign language	23	2.4
Foundation presses	8	0.8
Juvenile	167	17.7
Law	33	3.5
Map	9	0.9
Medicine and psychiatry	41	4.3
Paperbound books and reprints	189	20.0
Hardbound reprints	33	3.5
Fine editions	6	0.6
Scholary	34	3.6
Plays	17	1.8
Programmed learning and multimedia materials	63	6.7
Religious	122	12.9
Scientific, technical, business	175	18.5
Sports, hobbies, recreation and pets	70	7.4
Subscription, reference, mail order	97	10.3
Textbook	226	23.9
Trade	75	7.9
University Presses	79	8.4

Estimated book-publishing industry sales by US Census of Manufactures Categories:

USA

Category	1972 million US$	Percent change from '71
Adult trade (Total)	298	6
Hardbound	243	5
Paperbound	55	14
Juvenile (Total)	152	1
Under $ 1 retail	24	−17
$ 1 and Over retail	128	6
Religious (Total)	126	8
Bibles, testaments, hymnals, prayer books	63	13
Other Religious	63	3
Professional (Total)	350	7
Law	94	4
Medicine	65	10
Business	41	17
Technical, scientific and vocational	150	4
Book clubs	304	3
Mass market paperbacks	253	10
University presses	41	5
Elementary and secondary textbooks	498	0
College textbooks	375	−1
Standardized tests	27	8
Subscription reference	606	0
Other	147	9
Total	3,177	3

22 Literary Agents

About 120 literary agents are listed in the Literary Market Place (→7), many of whom are organized in the
Society of Authors' Representatives, Inc.
101 Park Ave.
USA New York 10017.
Literary agents are essentially business managers for authors, helping them find markets for their material, helping them negotiate contracts, and helping them with their personal finances, tax returns, etc. They tend to be helpful in more or less direct proportion to the amount of money involved, and the complexity of the transactions–they can seldom be really helpful to an author unless their 10% of his earnings from royalties and rights could justify their time. (Artists' agents get substantially higher commissions.)

One of the reasons authors work through agents is in the expectation that the agent will find and exploit markets beyond the obvious–perhaps selling not only book rights but also serial rights, motion-picture and TV rights, translation rights, etc. Often the publisher feels he can do this even better. Complicating the picture is the fact that book-publication contracts often give the publisher greater incentives, e.g., 50% of the income from subsidiary rights against the agent's 10%.

A common complaint in the "developing" countries is that inquiries about translation rights are not answered. This seems to stem from the fact that the employees to whom such requests are referred for action, whether in the publishing house or in the office of the author's agent, are overworked and tend to defer action on inquiries they consider vague, or complex, or unlikely to amount to much in terms of money. Sometimes they extend credit to fly-by-nights or refuse it to long-established publishers out of simple ignorance of how to check on credit standing.

In an effort to ensure that inquiries about minor translation rights are dealt with in a businesslike way, the Association of American Publishers (→4) has set up a group called INCINC (International Copyright, Incorporated) and invited overseas publishers to call upon it in case of trouble.

23 Wholesale Trade

The book wholesalers like the American News Company, Baker & Taylor, and A. C. McClurg, who once played an important role in supplying US bookstores, began about 50 years ago to compete with their bookstore customers instead, using their extra discount to take the library business away from the retailers (→3).

Today there is effective wholesaling of general trade books to general bookstores to only a limited extent, in only a few cities. Retailers can and do get better discounts by dealing direct with the publishers.

The listing of "wholesalers to bookstores" in the "Literary Market Place" (→7) must therefore be interpreted. The above-mentioned "wholesalers" are predominantly library suppliers. The most active wholesalers to retailers are Bookazine and Dimondstein in New York, and Raymar in Los Angeles.

Wholesaling is an important factor in the distribution of paperbacks (→19). It is also a factor in the distribution of medical books. The LMP gives a list of "wholesalers in special subjects", also a list of wholesalers specializing in remainders.

The LMP's category of "wholesalers to schools and libraries" could be misleading in countries where the word "wholesaler" means "wholesaler to retailers". This is really a list of retailers specializing in the sale of books to schools and libraries at cut prices. The biggest of them is the Baker & Taylor Company, which is active in selling to schools, public libraries and colleges. BroDart and Campbell & Hall concentrate more on serving school and public libraries. About 60 other "wholesalers to libraries" are listed in the LMP, together with about ten "prebinders to schools and libraries" which specialize in putting re-inforced library bindings on publishers trade editions.

Bibliography

American Book Trade Directory (→7)
Literary Market Place (→7).

24 Retail Trade

Bowker's *American Booktrade Directory* (→7), revised every two years, lists about 10,000 retail book outlets of all kinds in some 2,500 cities, and also about 900 of the local news wholesalers specializing in carrying mass-market paperbacks and juveniles into about 200,000 newsstands, drugstores, supermarkets, etc.

Many of the 10,000 listed outlets are quite small or quite specialized, and the number includes dealers in old and rare books (→26). Perhaps a more realistic impression of the number of real bookstores in the USA is implicit in the fact that the American Booksellers' Association (→4) has some 3,800 members.

The USA has fewer "real bookstores" than the most advanced European countries. On the other hand it has many more libraries of all kinds, and more book "outlets". It may be that more books move through other channels, including door-to-door selling, mail-order, and especially mass-marketing.

The names of booksellers specializing in foreign language books are to be found in the *American Book Trade Directory* (→7). There are several chains of bookshops, notably the Doubleday, Brentano, Waverley, Walden and Pickwick stores.

The

American Booksellers' Association
800 2nd Ave.
USA New York 10017

offers a special, flat-rate, $ 30-a-year membership to qualified overseas booksellers, and has about 100 such members. The ABA publishes an *ABA Book Buyer's Handbook*, which gives the discount schedules of all the publishers, also an *ABA Sidelines Directory*, and ABA basic booklists of both hardbounds and paperbacks. Its "Manual on Bookselling" (→6) was published jointly with Bowker.

The ABA is a charter member of the International Community of Booksellers' Associations.

There are also special associations of college bookstores and religious bookstores (→4).

Bibliography

American Book Trade Directory (→7)
→6.

25 Mail-Order Bookselling

The selling of books by mail is a very active business in the USA, and, consequently, the selling of mailing lists of people known to respond to mail-order sales promotion is also an active business. Mail-order promotion is, in fact, the primary way of selling specialized books to libraries and professionals. Publishers tend to have an advantage over retailers when it comes to selling by mail inasmuch as they routinely allow themselves a margin of about 50% of list price for the cost of the mail promotion, and retailers simply do not have this kind of margin except as the publisher's promotion material may be available to them and suited to their needs.

The US consumer would not be surprised to find in his mail box, even on one and the same day, book advertising from publishers, from book clubs, from department stores, from bookstores, from the US Government Printing Office, even from magazines using their subscriber lists to offer books as well. He would also see advertisements in (for example) the Sunday Book Section of the *New York Times* giving the names of mail-order booksellers anxious to fill his orders for current trade books at list price less 25%.

The US Government Printing Office sells entirely by mail-order, and has 830,000 people on the mailing list to receive its free "Selected List of Government Publications". People overseas may request and receive this. In 1970 government publi-

cations to a total of 80 million were sold for US $ 23 million.

The mailing-list brokers listed in the *Literary Market Place* (→7) will send their "lists of lists" on request. So will the R. R. Bowker Company, which itself has a mailing-list department offering lists of booksellers, libraries, schools, colleges, publishers, etc.

26 Antiquarian Book Trade, Auctions

The members of the antiquarian book market are organized in the
Antiquarian Booksellers' Association of America (ABAA)
Shop 2 Concourse, 630 Fifth Ave.
USA New York, N.Y. 10020
The chief trade publication of the antiquarian book trade is
AB Bookman's Weekly
Box 1100
USA Newark, N.J. 07101
The circulation is 5,500. AB includes the annual two-volume *AB Bookman's Yearbook*. AB runs to about 4,000 pages a year, including over 3,600 pages of "books wanted and for sale". It carries about 600,000 lines of such advertising each year, plus news and reviews (→5).
AB's Bookman's Yearbook, part one, carries the advertising of some 500 publishers of books and reprints of special interest to bookmen and collectors. Part two carries advertising by some 500 antiquarian book dealers who take space to put their special interests on record. Part two also provides a 35-page section entitled "The O.P. (out-of-print) Market", in which subscribers to AB can list themselves under their speciality. There are about 2,500 listings under 1,000 subjects.
Another publication in the antiquarian book area is
The Library Bookseller: TAAB Weekly
Box 7791
USA Philadelphia, Pa. 19101

This invites libraries to list their wants, without charge, and circulates this information to book dealers.

Major auctions of literary property are held at frequent but irregular intervals at Park Bernet Galleries, Inc., in New York City. In Philadelphia, auctions are held irregularly at Samuel T. Freeman & Company. A record of literary property sold at auction in England, the United States, and Canada is published annually in *American Book Prices Current* (latest edition for the season 1972–73; publishers Bancroft-Parkman, Inc.).
→4.

27 Book Imports

According to the counts kept by the book-listing staff of PW, 3,402 of the 24,288 new titles recorded in 1970 and 557 of the 11,783 new editions were imported. The number of imported titles increased by about 9% over the prior year, though there were reductions in the number of titles in science and technology.

US book imports in 1970 amounted to US $92 million, up from US $60 million in 1966. About 88% of the imported titles were in English; about 44% came from English-speaking countries.

The major sources were:

Country	Amount US $ 1,000	Percentage
United Kingdom	34,062	37.1
Netherlands	8,868	9.6
Japan	7,696	8.7
Germany (Fed. Rep.)	7,392	8.0
Italy	6,782	7.4
Canada	5,330	5.8
France	4,145	4.5
Switzerland	4,098	4.5
Spain	3,599	3.9
Mexico	1,538	1.7

Bibliography

Statistics on international trade are regularly given in *Printing and Publishing*, a quarterly issued by the US Department of Commerce, Business and Defense Services Administration, Washington D.C.

28 Book Exports

According to the US Government Department of Commerce, American book exports amounted in 1970 to US $174.2 m. However, this figure does not include freight shipments valued below US $240 nor shipments by book post. Because of these exclusions, the true value is assumed to be at least 50% higher, perhaps amounting to about 10% of total book sales in that year. The following breakdown gives the amount of the different categories within the shipments counted:

Category	Amount US$ m	Percentage
Encyclopedias	46.1	26.5
Textbooks	37.2	21.3
Technical, scientific and professional books	24.9	14.3
Bibles, testaments and other religious books	5.8	3.3
Dictionaries	4.2	2.4
Other books, including childrens painting and picture books and music books	56.0	32.2
Total	174.2	100.0

The value of exported periodicals was put at US $83.7 m, and the value of exported cartographic products at US $3.0 m, all adding to US $260.9 m. The volume of US book exports has been growing steadily. From 1965 to 1970 it increased 70%.
The countries receiving the larger part of 1970 US book exports were:

Country	Amount US$ 1,000	Percentage
Canada	73,722	42.3
Japan	28,325	16.2
United Kingdom	16,900	9.7
Australia	10,390	6.0
Italy	3,420	2.0
South Africa	3,332	1.9
Mexico	3,085	1.8
Brazil	3,071	1.8
Netherlands	2,956	1.7
Germany (Fed. Rep.)	2,749	1.6
Philippines	2,520	1.4
India	2,095	1.2
Argentina	1,599	0.9
Singapore	1,335	0.8
Venezuela	1,175	0.7
Colombia	1,082	0.6
New Zealand	1,056	0.6
France	883	0.5
Other countries	14,561	8.3
Total	174,256	100.0

These figures show the dominant position of the English-speaking countries. About 60% of all exports went to these countries, among which Canada is the most important market with a share of about 42%. 82% of all textbook exports, 72% of the technical, scientific and professional books, 75% of the general books and 24% of the encyclopedias went to these countries. In the different categories there were the following dominating countries:

Encyclopedias:

Country	Amount US$ 1,000	Percentage
Japan	23,079	50.1
Canada	5,883	12.8
Australia	2,459	5.3
South Africa	1,729	3.8
Brazil	1,377	3.0
Mexico	1,257	2.7
United Kingdom	928	2.1
Argentina	926	2.1
Philippines	905	2.0
Korea (South)	870	1.9

Textbooks:

Country	Amount US$ 1,000	Percentage
Canada	23,176	62.2
United Kingdom	5,344	14.4
Australia	1,537	4.1
Netherlands	842	2.3
Japan	535	1.4
Mexico	526	1.4
Philippines	413	1.1
Germany (Fed. Rep.)	368	1.0
India	353	0.9
Colombia	343	0.9

Scientific, technical and professional books:

Country	Amount US$ 1,000	Percentage
Canada	9,783	39.4
United Kingdom	5,897	23.8
Japan	2,198	8.9
Australia	1,779	7.2
Netherlands	1,191	4.8
Germany (Fed. Rep.)	666	2.7
India	523	2.1
South Africa	327	1.3
Philippines	203	0.8
Switzerland	182	0.7

Bibles, testaments and other religious books:

Country	Amount US$ 1,000	Percentage
Canada	1,605	27.6
Brazil	589	10.1
Australia	463	7.9
Mexico	458	7.9
France	248	4.3
United Kingdom	242	4.2
Colombia	229	3.9
South Africa	183	3.1
Philippines	176	3.0
Venezuela	167	2.9

Dictionaries:

Country	Amount US$ 1,000	Percentage
Canada	935	22.2
Brazil	782	18.5
Japan	552	13.2
Australia	245	5.8
United Kingdom	233	5.5
Colombia	218	5.2
Argentina	177	4.2
Angola	141	3.3
Mexico	122	2.9
South Africa	119	2.8

General books:

Country	Amount US$ 1,000	Percentage
Canada	32,340	57.7
United Kingdom	4,256	7.6
Australia	3,906	7.1
Italy	2,267	4.1
Japan	1,882	3.4
Germany (Fed. Rep.)	1,272	2.3
India	1,043	1.9
Singapore	1,004	1.8
Netherlands	859	1.5
South Africa	805	1.4

The export statistics for periodicals are as follows:

Country	Amount US$ m	Percentage
Canada	56.1	67.1
United Kingdom	4.4	5.3
Australia	3.4	4.1
Mexico	2.7	3.2
Venezuela	2.2	2.6
Germany (Fed. Rep.)	1.2	1.4
Japan	1.1	1.3
Netherlands	1.1	1.3
Panama	1.0	1.2
South Africa	0.8	1.0
France	0.7	0.8
New Zealand	0.7	0.8
Argentina	0.6	0.7
Other countries	7.7	9.2
Total	83.7	100.0

The
Franklin Book Programs
801 2nd Ave.
USA New York, New York 10017
is a non-government, non-profit educational corporation whose primary purpose is to assist international book publishing development. Through programmes carried out both in the USA and overseas it undertakes to increase the number, quality, availability, and use of books and related educational materials in developing countries in the conviction that economic development depends upon education; and education, in turn, depends upon books. Franklin was founded in 1952 and is governed by a board of directors consisting of twenty-five leading publishers, educators, and corporation executives. Its work is supported by foundations, governments (US and other), universities corporations, and individuals. Operating offices are maintained in Cairo, Dacca, Djakarta, Kabul, Islamabad, and Tehran, although its activities are not restricted to those areas. In Latin America it has worked through cooperating organizations in Rio de Janairo, São Paulo, Buenos Aires, and Mexico City. In Africa, Franklin formerly supported programmes in Nigeria and Kenya and has conducted surveys in several other countries.
To fulfill its purpose, Franklin pursues four basic objectives:
1. The increase of local capabilities.
2. The increase of international exchange.
3. The strengthening of marketing and distribution.
4. The development of the reading habit.

Bibliography

→ 27

29 Book Fairs

The USA has nothing so international as the Frankfurt Book Fair (→BTW I, International Section 29), but it has several rather large-scale book exhibits in connection with various association conventions.

Probably the closest USA analogy to the Frankfurt Book Fair is the Annual Book Exhibit held each year in May in connection with the annual convention of the American Booksellers' Association (→4).

Another major annual book exhibit takes place each year in June in connection with the Annual Convention of the American Library Association (→35). At the 1971 event in Dallas there were exhibits by about 200 US book publishers and about 140 other firms interested in the library market including library-book wholesalers, periodical subscription services, rebinders and prebinders, importers, library supply houses, and firms offering microforms, films, and filmstrips, slides, recordings, tapes, etc. Information about this exhibition can be obtained from the American Library Association (→35).

Within the above-mentioned ALA exhibit there is also an international section. In 1971, there were 26 exhibitors from Britain, Canada, France, Belgium, Holland, New Zealand, and Japan. This is organized by the A.P. Wales Organization (26 Charing Cross Road, London, W.C. 2., England).

There are a good many book exhibits, also, at the Annual Convention of the American Association of School Administrators, held in February of each year in Atlantic City, N.J., about half-way between New York and Washington. Of course, the emphasis here is on materials for use in schools. Information can be obtained from the AAAS, care of the National Education Association (1201 16th St, N.W., Washington, D.C. 20036).

310

30 Public Relations

The public relations arm of the US book industry is the
National Book Committee
1 Park Ave.
USA New York 10016
This organization aims to promote the wiser and wider use of books by making books widely available, and encouraging readership. It sponsors National Library Week, National Book Awards, National Medal for Literature, and a variety of reading research and development projects.

31 Bibliophily

Some associations of book-lovers:
The
Grolier Club (GC)
47 East 60th Str.
USA New York, N.Y. 10022
was founded in 1884 and has 630 members. The members are collectors of books and prints and persons who are interested in books. The club maintains a library and publishes books to illustrate and encourage the arts of book production.
The
Bibliographical Society of America (BSA)
P.O. Box 397, Grand Central Station
USA New York, N.Y. 10017
was founded in 1904 and has 1,510 members. The members are collectors, librarians, rare-book dealers, and others interested in books and bibliography. They promote bibliographical research and issue bibliographical publications.
The
Bibliographical Society of the University of Virginia
c/o University of Virginia Library
USA Charlottesville, Va. 22901
was founded in 1947 and has 920 members. It is an international society of bibliographers, book collectors, librarians, schol-

ars, and others interested in books and bibliography.
The
Society of Jewish Bibliophiles (SJB)
c/o Hebrew Union College, 3101 Clifton Ave.
USA Cincinnati, Ohio 45220
was founded in 1961 and has 209 members. The society provides bibliophilic fellowship for collectors of Jewish books, prints, manuscripts, and art, keeps alive the tradition of excellence and beauty in the production of modern Jewish books, sponsors lectures and discussions and prepares exhibits.
There are many magazines and publications catering for the interest of booklovers. The following is a short selection:
AB Bookman's Weekly
Box 1100
USA Newark, N.J. 07101

American Book Collector
1822 School Street
USA Chicago, Ill. 60657

Harvard Library Bulletin
505 Lamont Library
USA Cambridge, Mass. 02138

Papers of the Bibliographical Society of America
P.O. Box 397, Grand Central Station
USA New York, N.Y. 10017

32 Literary Prizes

About 230 US literary prizes having more than merely local interest are listed in Bowker's LMP. (→7).
The most important:
Pulitzer Prizes
which are annual awards for great achievements in American journalism, letters, and music. They were established at Columbia University by Joseph Pulitzer, an American newspaper publisher. Each May since 1917 these prizes have been awarded by the Columbia trustees on the recommendation of a board composed of distinguished American newspapermen and the president of Columbia University.
Book awards are given in the areas of biography or autobiography, drama, history, fiction, and poetry.
The National Book Awards
These awards are sponsored by the Association of American Publishers Inc., American Booksellers' Association, Inc., and Book Manufacturers' Institute, Inc. (→4). The awards were originated by the three sponsoring book-industry associations in 1950.
They give recognition to the most distinguished books of fiction, non-fiction, poetry, arts and letters, history and biography, science, philosophy, children's literature, translation, and religion.
A cash award is presented to each year's winner in each category.
Carey-Thomas Awards
The purpose of these annual awards is to honour creative book publishing at its best. Nominations are made by the book-review staff of the R. R. Bowker Company, which also presents the awards.
The John Newbery Medal
The John Newbery Medal has been awarded annually since 1922 for the most distinguished contribution to American literature for children.
The Caldecott Medal
The Caldecott Medal has been awarded annually since 1938 to the illustrator of the year's most distinguished picture book.
Both were originated by the late Frederic G. Melcher, and are sponsored by the Children's Services Division of the American Library.

Bibliography

Literary and Library Prizes. 7th ed. New York, N.Y., R. R. Bowker Co. 1970.

33 The Reviewing of Books

There are literally thousands of newspapers and magazines and technical and scientific journals in America which review books regularly or run syndicated book-review columns. Only a few, however, review even as many as 100 books a month–which would be less than 5% of the new titles actually published.

The most comprehensive reviewing is not found in the consumer publications, but rather in the more specialized book-trade and library publications. The *Publisher's Weekly* (→4) reviews about 4,000 titles a year. The *Library Journal* (→35) reviews about 6,000 adult books each year plus 2,400 children's books. *Choice*, a publication of the Association of College and Research Libraries (→35) reviews about 6,200 titles.

The *Kirkus Reviews*
  60 W. 13th Street
  USA New York, N.Y. 10011
cover about 4,500 titles.

The *Booklist*, a publication of the American Library Association (→35), covers about 3,600 titles.

The
  Book Review Digest
  H. W. Wilson Co.
  950 University Avenue
  USA Bronx, N.Y. 10452
published monthly by the H. W. Wilson Company, covers about 5,500 books a year, as reviewed in some 70 different magazines and newspapers. *Technical Book Review Index*, published by the Special Libraries Association (→35), monitors 2,500 trade and technical journals.

The various book review media are identified and listed in Bowker's "Literary Market Place" (→7). Among the consumer media, the most comprehensive is probably the Book Review section of the Sunday *New York Times*, which runs about 2,500 reviews each year.

34 Graphic Arts

The US book manufacturers are organized in the
  Book Manufacturers' Institute (BMI)
  161 E. 42nd Street
  USA New York, N.Y. 10017
This institute was founded in 1920 and has 110 members, who are manufacturers of hardbound books. Publisher-owned plants engaged in the printing and binding of textbook, subscription, reference, and general books may belong to the BMI.

Publications:

BMI Newspacket, 10 times a year.

Commercial printing firms plus allied firms in the graphic arts are organized in the
  Printing Industries of America (PIA)
  1730 N. Lynn Street
  USA Arlington, Va. 22209
The association was founded in 1887 and has 7,621 members. It provides extensive management and industrial-relations services; it sponsors sales, production, and financial conferences.

Publications:

1) *DPM Newsletter*, weekly
2) *PIA Bulletin*, monthly
3) *PAR-Lance*, monthly

Book designers, art directors, artists, photographers and executives of printing, publishing, and advertising firms are organized in the
  American Institute of Graphic Arts (AIGA)
  1059 Third Ave.
  USA New York, N.Y. 10021
The Institute was founded in 1914 and has 1,900 members. It sponsors exhibits, workshops, and clinics to advance the graphic arts.–Affiliated organization: Guild of Book Workers (subsidiary).

Publications:

AIGA Journal, bimonthly.

The
National Association of Photo-Lithographers
(NAPL)
230 West 41st St.
USA New York, N.Y. 10036
was founded in 1933 and has 1,500 members.

Publications:

1) *NAPL Member Bulletin*, irregular
2) *NAPL Labor Relations Bulletins*, irregular; also publishes numerous pamphlets and books.

35 Miscellaneous

a) Libraries
To understand many aspects of the US book trade, it is important to understand the importance of the library market, especially the big increase in the book spending of school and university libraries. Many books are currently being published with no expectation of any sale whatever beyond the sale to libraries. This is especially true of scholarly books, and many higher-priced juveniles.

In recent years the number of university libraries with resources enough to "gather" books rather than "select" them has increased sharply. Within their defined fields, there are several hundred institutions which routinely buy everything published, at whatever price.

The sharp increase in the number of research collections has paralleled the sharp rise in the number of advanced degrees granted. The number of science doctorates, for example, increased from 6,276 in 1960 to 15,982 in 1969. Needless to say, the institutions attempting to attract the kind of faculty necessary for any programme of advanced research could not fail to promise them a library with funds adequate to build a research collection.

For some kinds of books the library market is the only market. Even for more general books, the library market may be 40 or 50% of the total market as regards the first printing, even though libraries might take only a small percentage of the copies of a bestseller.

However, there are indications that more advanced degrees have been granted in recent years than are really needed, and cut-backs in government support to some of the programmes of advanced research are imminent. The total of doctorates conferred in 1969 was 25,734. The total of Master's Degrees conferred in 1968 was 177,150.

The addresses of the leading library associations and library journals are:
Library Associations:
American Library Association
50 E. Huron Street
USA Chicago, Ill. 60611
and
Special Libraries Association
235 Park Avenue South
USA New York, N.Y. 10003
Library journals:
American Libraries
American Library Association
50 E. Huron Street
USA Chicago, Ill. 60611

Library Journal
R. R. Bowker Company
1180 Avenue of the Americas
USA New York, N.Y. 10036
and
Wilson Library Bulletin
H. W. Wilson Company
950 University Avenue
USA Bronx, N.Y. 10452

Uruguay

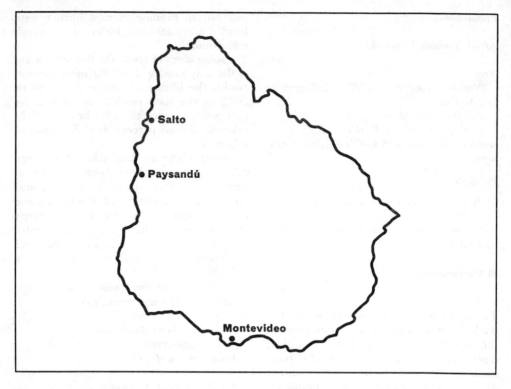

1 General Information

Area 186,926 km²
Population 2,851,600 (15 per km²; 1969)
Capital Montevideo (1,375,000)
Largest towns Montevideo (1,375,000); Paysandú (52,000); Salto (58,000)
Government Centralized, representative, democratic government. The President of the Republic is the head of the National Executive State Power. There is also a General Assembly formed by two Chambers of Senators and Deputies and an independent Judicial Power. The country is divided into 19 departments
Religion Nearly all Uruguayan Christians are Roman Catholics. There are small Protestant communities and an important number of agnostics
National language Spanish
Leading foreign languages English, French
Weights, measures Metric system

Currency unit Urugayan Peso (Urug. $) = 100 centésimos
Education Primary and secondary; agrarian or industrial instruction is compulsory
The number of pupils in public and private schools is: 376,999 (1967); Secondary school students in public and private schools: 117,247 (1967); Technical schools: 30,054 (1967); Teaching: 7,868 (1967); at university level: 13,100 (1967)
Education expenditures in the National Budget (Central Administration): 25.1% (1968)
Illiteracy 8.6%
Paper consumption a) Newsprint 7.2 kg per inhabitant (1970)
b) Printing paper (other than newsprint) 6.6 kg per inhabitant (1970)
Membership Unesco, CERLAL

314

2 Past and Present

The territory now occupied by Uruguay was discovered by the Spaniards in 1516, but its first settlements began with the foundation of the cities of Colonia in 1680 and Montevideo in 1726. The inland towns were founded in the second half of the 18th and the beginning of the 19th century.

The first printing press in the River Plate area was operated by the Jesuit Missions beyond the northern part of Uruguay about 1700. The first schools started their activities in Montevideo in 1743 and 1746. In 1807 the English conquered Montevideo and brought the first local press, which published the periodical "*The Southern Star*". After being defeated, the English took back with them their press, which was replaced by another one in 1811, which published *La Gaceta*. The first public library was opened in 1816.

After 20 years of war, during which the country was consecutively under the domination of Buenos Aires, the Portuguese and the Brazilians, a free Republic was founded in 1830. From that moment on and notwithstanding the civil wars, the population quickly increased, mainly because of the European immigration, mostly of Spanish, Italian and French origin.

In those years a high cultural level was reached by the educated population of Montevideo, which gave birth to the book trade. Several bookstores maintained close relationships with the European publishing houses, fundamentally from Spain and France. Further, the State University was founded and started its activities between 1838 and 1849 in the Nation's capital.

Another important milestone in the country's cultural progress was the reform of primary education, which took place in 1877.

Until the end of the 19th century small-scale local book production constantly increased. This was due to the influence of booksellers, authors and printers, but not publishers.

Law No. 1962 of 5 January 1888 gave rather favourable customs treatment to printed books, with discrimination between soft-cover and hard-cover books: a duty of 8% for the first and 6% for the latter.

This system was changed by law No. 3.681 of 23 June 1910, proposed at the House of Representatives by the famous writer José Enrique Rodó. This law conferred exemption from customs levies on imports of soft-cover books with the exception of books written by national writers or published by local publishers but printed in foreign countries. Books in deluxe bindings were also excluded from the benefits of the law. This efficient law, still in force today, promoted widespread diffusion of books and afforded economic protection to local printing and publishing activities. The birth date of this law came about at the beginning of an era of civil peace, an extraordinary cultural development and institutional progress, which was interrupted by the world crisis of 1931 and continued until the middle of the 1950–60 decade, when economic conditions became stagnant in Uruguay, creating social and political tensions.

Some publishers began in the first quarter of our century, most of them booksellers at the same time.

The majority of books published were educational. Books about Uruguay's history, political and civic subjects, essays and poetry represented a second group of less importance, while other kinds of literature, such as novels, were relatively few.

This situation did not change substantially until a few years ago, when an important movement began in publishing, which put emphasis on novels, stories, political and social essays, and weekly instalment collections, sold at news-stands in the streets.

This increase in publishing activity, at the

time called "the publishing boom", originated as a result of factors, including a public policy of book promotion, the main aspects of which were the reduction of the paper price for publishing purposes, the creation of a system which exempted from most taxes the publishing trade, and the creation of a Paper Commission for the administration and handling of the system. The Paper Commission instituted by the article 79 of law No. 13.349 of 5 July 1965 had three aims:

a) to lower the cost of paper used in the printing of literary, scientific, artistic, and educational books, booklets and periodicals, and general educational material

b) thus to lower the price to the public of these books, booklets and educational material

c) to encourage the development of a big national and international publishing centre in Uruguay.

The law, in its article 79, states: "Article 45 of law No. 13.319 of 28 December 1964 must be amended in the following way: printing works, publishing houses and bookstores shall be exempted from paying taxes on their capital, sales, revenues, acts, services and business, with the sole exception of income tax, and in the amount of money related to the printing and sale of literary, scientific, artistic, educational books, booklets, periodicals and educational material.

These firms shall only pay these taxes on assets, sales, revenues, acts and business of any kind which are not directly related to the exempted turnover. Where assets, acts or operations are partially affected by or related to the exempted turnover, these taxes shall be paid proportionally.

The exemptions do not include contributions for pensions and for the Family Allowance Compensation Funds.

Raw material for the manufacture of paper and boards for the sole purpose of printing the above-mentioned publications and educational material shall be exempt from every tax and duty that burden the import, manufacturing and trading of said paper and boards and shall also benefit with the exemptions indicated in the preceeding paragraphs.

Paper manufacturers shall reduce by 30% their selling prices, in force on 1 May 1965, on paper and boards solely used for the printing and publishing of books and/or educational material already mentioned, without impairing in any way the quality of every grade of paper or board.

Printing works, publishing houses and bookstores shall use the paper and boards benefited by the deduction above indicated only to print the publications and educational material already mentioned.

If the Executive Power with the help of the Paper Commission verifies non-justified paper and board shortages at discount prices as well as substandard quality, it shall free from taxes and duties imported paper and board for book printing and educational material.

Within the term of seven days from the enactment of this law, paper manufacturers shall submit to said Commission or by default to the Ministry of Industry and Commerce a paper and board manufacturing cost breakdown with percentages of each item making up its cost. On every price increase which may take place in the future, an advance notice of thirty days must be given to the Paper Commission and the Executive Power, which must exert the controlling action conferred by the foregoing paragraph, if it is found that those increases do not exactly correspond to those actually experimented in the cost of production or are not in bearing with the components which integrate it at present.

The Paper Commission is charged with the task of controlling and enforcing the preceeding rules and shall be formed in the following way: a deputy of the Ministry of

Industry and Labour who shall be its Chairman, a deputy of the Ministry of Education and Culture, a deputy of the Ministry of Economy and Finance, a deputy of the Paper Manufacturers' Association and a deputy of the Uruguayan Printers' Association. This Commission shall be installed within the term of 30 days following the enactment of this law.

Infringements to this rule are subject to penalties established by the Ministry of Industry and Labour, ranging from Urug. $ 10,000 (ten thousand pesos) to $ 30,000 (thirty thousand pesos). In the case of repetition of transgression, the transgressing firm may be closed for a period up to one year.

The Executive Power shall regulate the application of this article within the term of thirty days.

This law was implemented by the decree No. 379/65 of 24 August 1965 published in the Official Journal of 16 September 1965.

The Paper Commission is the only official register for statistical data about publishing production in Uruguay.

Every month bulletins with the number of copies and list of books published during the previous month are distributed in the country and abroad among international organizations.

The official policy of promoting book activities includes two new statements in the decrees No. 26/970 of 19 February 1970 and No. 265/971 of 14 May 1971.

The first declares that publishing firms shall be considered as industrial producers of literary, scientific, artistic and educational books, booklets and periodicals as well as educational material that they shall publish. For said purpose their production activity enjoys all the benefits granted by law No. 13.268 and all other laws and decrees which grant other benefits to export transactions.

These benefits consist chiefly of reimbursements paid by the State to the exporters of non-traditional goods (a percentage of the f.o.b price under the form of a certificate in the amount of the refund valid for the cancellation of taxes); in the exemption from export charges and the granting of credits. This decree provides special credit aid by the Bank of the Republic, under the rules to be laid down to permit the attainment of the aims of this decree.

Credits are granted on the basis of the firm's past export activities of submitting publishing plans duly evaluated in connection with existing publishing funds. Final decisions rest in the hands of the Advisory Commission for the Publishing Industry created by this decree, which falls within the sphere of the Ministry of Industry and Commerce.

As regards postal tariffs for books and publications under this decree and for export purposes there is a provision which grants preferential mail rates under this category.

This scheme has already been put into practice: loans have been granted under most favourable conditions as compared with current market financial conditions for export editions, and very economic postal rates have been enacted in accordance with the decree.

It should be borne in mind that the financing also includes the cost of translation and that the system of temporary admission, free from duties, allows the purchase of paper and other high quality materials in the world market at the best prices.

With this credit availability at low cost and the refunds granted for export, not only can the promotion of local publishing for export be expected, but also the stimulation of publishing business from abroad resulting from the advantages offered.

The aim of the second decree, dated 13 May 1971, was to promote the country's book production, and in order to expand it inside and outside the country, it created the

Uruguay

Advisory Commission of National Publishing Policy, which will work under the aegis of the Ministry of Education and Culture. Its task is similar to that of the Advisory Commission of the Publishing Industry of the Ministry of Industry and Commerce.

Bibliography

G. FURLONG, *Orígines del arte tipográfico en América*. (The origins of the art of typography in America.) Buenos Aires, Ed. Huarpes 1947. 225 pp. Bibliography on pp. 215–225. Early printing history of Uruguay: pp. 119–120.

J. T. MEDINA, *Historia de la imprenta en los antiguos dominios españoles de América y Oceanía*. (The history of printing in the ancient Spanish dominions of America and Oceania.) 2 vols. Santiago de Chile, Fondo Histórico y Bibliográfico José Toribio Medina 1958. CXLI, 542; XV, 540 pp.
v. II. pp. 463–469: Uruguay (Montevideo).

L. S. THOMPSON, *Printing in Colonial Spanish America*. Hamden, Conn., Archon Books 1962. 108 pp.
pp. 57–70: Uruguay.

3 Retail Prices

Until 1968 there was no price control on books, except for some primary and secondary school textbooks, whose prices were under the control of a State office and afterwards of a mixed public and private membership Commission.

Under this system, the resale price was imposed by the owner of the publication for locally produced books and in the case of foreign books by the importer-distributor. A discount on the public sale price was included in the invoice for the benefit of the retail bookseller.

For foreign imported books there was a general tariff for converting the cover price in foreign currency (or catalogue price) into national Uruguayan currency. This tariff included a percentage to cover the shipping and marketing charges and the risk of devaluation of the exchange rate. These rules were put into practice but their fulfilment was irregular and incomplete because the participants were not bound by any formal agreement.

It must be added that there is a very widespread practice which consists in granting a 10% discount on the retail price to teachers, professors, libraries and teaching establishments.

Law No. 13.720 of 16 December 1968 established the

Comisión de Productividad, Precios
e Ingresos (COPRIN)
(Productivity, Prices and Incomes
Commission)
Calle Paysandú 919
U Montevideo

This Commission consists of five members appointed by the Government, two more selected by the business sector, and another two proposed by the labour sector. One of its main tasks is to fix maximum prices to the goods or services which are obviously essential or desirable for popular consumption. This law confirms the stability system for prices, services and goods imposed by the decree of 28 June 1968, which established a price freeze.

Books, both Uruguayan and foreign, now have to sell at prices approved by COPRIN.

In practice the system works as follows: the prices of books produced locally must be approved by COPRIN on the submission by the publisher of a declaration detailing in absolute figures the various cost and discount items on the production and trading of the book in question. The initial price fixed by COPRIN may be raised, no more than twice a year, if the labour costs and the paper costs rise. For each percentage point of increments in costs (authorized by COPRIN) the sales

318

price to the public can be augmented by 0.66% on the labour items of costs and 0.34% on the paper items of costs (Resolución Ordinaria No. 284 of COPRIN). It must be emphasized that all the books which are printed on economy publishing paper must have printed on their back cover the retail selling price with the following text "subject to modifications according to law No. 13.720 of COPRIN".

With regard to imported books, COPRIN has approved an exchange rate of the cover price in foreign currency to national currency at the official exchange rate in force plus 40% to cover expenses.

The fixed resale price imposed by the publisher or the importer-distributor remains in effect, within the limits allowed by the system already described.

4 Organization

At the present time there is a trade association in Uruguay for everyone engaged in book activities. It is the

Cámara Uruguaya del Libro
(Uruguayan Book Chamber)
Ibicuy 1276, Piso 1. Oficina 4
U Montevideo

This institution was founded on 23 November 1944 by a meeting to which all firms or persons engaged in book production, sales and distribution were invited. It has 104 members at present.

The object of this organization is, according to article 1 of its by-laws "to bring together all those who are engaged in book work". Its activities shall be confined to the trade-association type.

The purpose is described in article 2: "to bring together all the publishers, booksellers and also as members all the writers, printers, artists, binders and other persons or firms contributing with their manual or intellectual work, to present books to the public and to represent them in order to defend the trade's interests; to foster and

improve the development of book production and distribution in every aspect; to study and demand from the public authorities measures leading to a better defence of the proposed purpose; and in general to interest itself in all the professional activities related to books and their public."

The Chamber's authorities are: a) the Board of Directors; b) the Category Deliberative Bodies; c) the Plenaries; d) the General Meeting; e) the Arbitration Courts.

The Board of Directors is composed of nine members, whose posts are distributed as follows: five for the publishers' section and four for the booksellers' section. There is a Secretary-Director, a Treasurer-Director and a Library-Director and the other Directors act as Chairman by rotation.

The publishers and bookseller members separately form the Category Deliberative Bodies, who meet to discuss matters connected with the problems in their own categories. If the decisions of the Category Deliberative Bodies are rejected by the majority of the Board's members not belonging to the Deliberative Category, the matter must be submitted for decision to the Chamber's Plenary. This Plenary shall be constituted by both the whole Board of Directors acting in a special session and the Category of the Deliberative Body as convened for that purpose. The General Meetings are ordinary and extraordinary and are the supreme authority of the Chamber.

The Book Chamber has deputies on the following official commissions: Advisory Commission of the Publishing Industry of the Ministry of Industry and Trade; the Book Commission of the Ministry of Education and Culture; the Honorary Advisory Commission for National Publishing Policy of the Ministry of Education and Culture. The "Uruguayan Book Chamber" has participated in several international Congresses related to books; among them the "Ibero-American Federation of Publishing and Bookselling Institutions" (→ Latin America 4) Congress deserves special mention. The Uruguayan Government secured through the "Cámara" the participation of Uruguay in the Frankfurt Book Fair (→ BTW I, International Section 29).

The Ministries of Education and Culture, Industry and Trade, and Economy and Finance are all involved in the book organization's activities.

The Ministry of Education and Culture runs the Instituto del Libro, created by the law 13.318, of 28 December 1964.

The Book Institute's address is:

Instituto del Libro
(Book Institute)
Avda. 18 de Julio 1790
U Montevideo

Its tasks are to foster and develop public libraries adequate to the cultural level of the people; to distribute within the country and abroad the works published by the State, and the books that the State may buy; to carry out the international exchange of publications and advise the Executive Power in the buying of books by national authors.

These tasks were regulated by decree 100/967 of 21 February 1967.

The publishing activities of the State began in 1950 with the issue of the "Colección de Clásicos Uruguayos, Biblioteca General Artigas". In the period 1963–67 it maintained a publication rate of two titles per month. The Ministry also has published a "Colección de Autores de la Literatura Universal", a "Colección Cultural Uruguaya", a "Biblioteca Jurídica", and other books, among them the "Archivo Artigas", a collection of historical documents concerning the history of the country.

Law 13.586 of 13 February 1967 gives the "Book Institute" the right to retain up to 10% monthly of the wages and salaries of public employees who have purchased, in instalments, books published by the Ministry of Education and Culture.

The Paper Commission established by law 13.349 of Publishing and Promotion (→ 2) works at the

Ministerio de Educación y Cultura
Comisión Asesora Honoraria de la
Politica Editoral Nacional
(Ministry of Education and Culture,
Honorary Advisory Commission of
National Publishing Policy)
Sarandi 444
U Montevideo

In the same Ministry, the Honorary Advisory Commission of National Publishing Policy was created by decree 265/971 of 13 May 1971 with the task of advising the Executive Power about national publishing policy; studying the possibilities of expanding the internal book trade; promoting the export of local books and the lowering of the cost of educational books. This Commission shall be composed of a deputy from the Ministry of Education and Culture who shall be its Chairman, the Director of the National Library, the Director of the Book Institute, the Chairman of the Honorary Paper Commission, a deputy of the Book Chamber and a deputy of the National Printers' Association.

The

Comisión Asesora de la Industria Editorial
(Advisory Commission of the Publishing
Industry)
Rincon 747 esq. Ciudadela
U Montevideo

under the Ministry of Industry and Trade consists of a deputy each from the Ministry of Industry and Trade who shall be its Chairman, one of the Bank of the Republic, the Culture Ministry's representative from the Paper Commission, one of the Uruguayan Exporters' Union, and one from the Book Chamber (→ 4).

This Commission shall perform the following functions:

1) To give its opinion on the granting of

credits for the development of the publishing industry and its products
2) to determine if the publications for which aid is requested are within the categories established
3) to advise the Advisory Commission for export allowances to non-traditional exports on everything connected with the book industry, specially as regards quality
4) to advise the Ministry of Industry and Trade on the possible use of mechanisms of temporary admission in publishing operations
5) to propose to the proper authorities new ways of fostering the development of the publishing industry, especially those that may benefit its international importance, culturally as well as commercially.

5 Trade Press

There is no publication in the trade press category. There is only a news bulletin which is circulated among its members by the Uruguayan Book Chamber (→4).

6 Book-Trade Literature →2, 15, 21.

7 Sources of Information, Address Services

Cámara Uruguaya del Libro
(Uruguayan Book Chamber)
Ibicuy 1276, Piso 1, Oficina 4
U Montevideo

Bibliography

The addresses of all branches of the book trade are contained in
La Empresa del Libro en América Latina. (The Book in Latin America.) 2nd ed. Buenos Aires, Bowker Editores Argentina 1974, VIII, 307 pp. pp. 247–255: Uruguay.

8 International Membership

Uruguay is a member of UNESCO.
The Uruguayan Book Chamber has participated in the first "Ibero American Congress of Associations of Publishers and Booksellers" held in 1964 (→Latin America 4).–Uruguay is a member of the "Centro Regional para el Fomento del Libro en América Latina (CERLAL)", Bogotá (→Latin America 4).

10 Books and Young People

There are some public and private institutions which have dealt with problems of books for children and young people.
Among them the
Consejo del Niño
(Child Council)
Piedras 482
U Montevideo
is concerned with the confiscation of pornographic magazines which are prohibited by law.
The Pedagogic Museum Library, which belongs to the Primary and Normal Education Council is at the following address
Biblioteca del Museo Pedagógico
(Pedagogic Museum Library)
Plaza Libertad 1175
U Montevideo
A private institution carries out activities to orientate children and young people in book reading. It has published a guide of books classified according to morals and selected by age for children and young people. Its address is
Secretariado Católico del Libro
(Catholic Book Secretariat)
Cerrito 475
U Montevideo

11 Training

In this field there is little worth mentioning. Private firms engaged in instalment credit book sales pay special attention to the preparation and training of their staff.

Uruguay

The
Escuela de Dirigentes de Empresa
(Business Executives' School)
Avda. Uruguay 1829
U Montevideo
has at times organized courses for the training of book sales clerks.

12 Taxes

Activities related to books have a favourable tax system. The fundamental law is the so-called "Law for Promotion of Publishing Activities" (article 79 of law 13.349 of 29 July 1965). The basic principle of this system is exemption from capital, sales, revenues, acts, services and business tax, but not from income tax. For this law and its decree 379/65 of 24 August 1965 →2, for the exemption of value-added tax →law 14.100, article 87, G.

Law 13.420 of 2 December 1965, article 32 has a text complementary to article 79 of law 13.349 and declares that tax exemption established by this law covers the contracts and other documents related to the selling of books.

Confirming the Rodó Law 3.681 of 30 June 1910, the import of books, booklets and literary magazines, etc., determined by law 13.586 of 13 February 1967, is exempted from import taxes (→2).

14 Copyright

In Uruguay literary and artictic property is recognized in article 33 of the Constitution. The juridical system is principally contained in law 9.739 of 17 December 1937.

In the international field, Uruguay confirmed the Treaty of Montevideo on Literary and Artistic Property signed in 1889 with other Latin American countries; and the Treaty of Montevideo which replaced it in 1941. The Buenos Aires Convention, which referred to the same matter, was signed and ratified in 1910.

Law 9.739 declares in its first article the moral right of the author of any literary, scientific or artistic creation, and recognizes his right of property in work of any kind, subject to the common law and the following articles:

The right is limited in time: it lasts all the author's life, and the heirs or legatees maintain it for 40 years from the death of the person from whom the right is derived. But the state, cities or any other public organization that are owners of such rights have them in perpetuity.

If there are no heirs or legatees or if the above-mentioned term of 40 years has elapsed, the books enter the public domain, and any person can publish them upon paying the tariffs which shall be fixed by the Copyright Council and meticulously respecting the entirety of the work reproduced.

Legal protection is the same irrespective the nature or origin of the book or the author's nationality. It is compulsory to enter it in the respective register in order to protect it by this law. In the case of foreign books, it will be sufficient to prove that the conditions demanded for its protection in the native country according to the rules in force there have been fulfilled. The contract of transference of the author's rights must be in a written document and it cannot be opposed by third persons before registering it. When the contract is executed abroad, registration can be made before the diplomatic or consular authorities of the country.

The right of publishing the book of the acquirer shall belong to him during 15 years after the author's death, passing to the heirs at that moment.

In every sale, the right of participating in the plus value of the book, obtained by the consecutive acquirers, is reserved to the author (25%). The law establishes a number of cases of illicit reproduction, and other special cases.

Infringements of the law shall be punished by fines or equivalent prison sentences, without prejudice to the civil actions for damages and the devolution of all the benefits unduly cashed by the infringer.

Illicitly reproduced copies shall be confiscated except from those who purchased them in good faith.

The Copyright Register is in the National Library. The enforcing of this law lies with the Copyright Council.

Uruguay is a member of the Berne Union. As to the membership to Inter-American Conventions →BTW I, International Section 14.

Bibliography

E. VALDES, *Derecho de autor-régimen jurídico Uruguaya*. (Copyright in Uruguay). Otero 1953.

15 National Bibliography, National Library

The compulsory legal deposit of printed books in the National Library was instituted by law 2.239 of 14 July 1893, and re-stated by law 13.385 of 7 January 1970 (articles 191 and 193).

The owners or lessees of printing houses etc., as well as state printing presses, shall observe the compulsory free legal deposit of printed copies: 3 copies for current printings and one copy for minor printings. This obligation is sanctioned by fines and the forbidding of the selling, distribution or any other way of trading, if the compulsory deposit has not been made.

Books in condition of infringement shall be deprived of the benefits established by law 13.449 for Publishing Promotion and law 9.737 of Artistic and Literary Property. The decree corresponding to the law 13.835 of 21 October 1971 establishes a Registry of Firms in which the persons obliged to make the legal deposit must be inscribed.

The National Library shall be in charge of the administrative service and must give to the Library of the Assembly of the Legislative Power a copy of items subject to legal deposit.

According to the works deposited the
Biblioteca Nacional
(National Library)
18 de Julio esq. Tristán Narvaja
U Montevideo
publishes the *Uruguayan Bibliographical Annual* in which deposited books and magazines are classified by authors and publishers.

The
Biblioteca del Poder Legislativo
(Library of the Legislative Power's Assembly)
Avda. Agraciada s/n
U Montevideo
publishes the *Uruguayan Bibliography*.

The Paper Commission, created by law 13.349 of Publishing Promotion in article 79, publishes a monthly list of books, magazines and booklets printed in Uruguay under the protection of the above mentioned law.

The bibliography classifies in alphabetical order by authors, mentions publishers, date, number of pages, format, illustrations, collections, and offers subject classification.

The address of the Paper Commission is the
Ministerio de Educación y Cultura
La Comisión del Papel
(Ministry of Education and Culture, Paper Commission)
Sarandi 444
U Montevideo

Bibliography

P. AVICENNE, *Bibliographical services throughout the world 1965–69*. Paris, Unesco 1972. 310 pp.
pp. 292–94: Uruguay

I. ZIMMERMANN, *Current national bibliographies of Latin America*. Gainesville, Florida, University of Florida Press 1971. X, 139 pp.
pp. 58–61: Uruguay.

323

Uruguay

16 Book Production

Statistics regarding books and magazines published, the total of titles and numbers of copies produced, have only been available since the enactment of law 13.349 on Publishing Promotion.

These are the numbers: books and magazines published under law 13.349:

Year	Copies	Titles
1966	2,022,690	430
1967	2,972,270	715
1968	3,783,015	721
1969	3,245,023	645
1970	2,150,211	535
1971	1,894,836	550
1972	1,528,235	447

The figures show that the Publishing Promotion Law has succeeded in promoting the production of books and magazines; in 1968 3,783,015 copies and 721 titles were produced. This is a very significant figure for a population of 2,800,000.

The figures fell in the following years. General economic restrictive monetary and credit policy must have influenced this decline. It must also be borne in mind that most of the reading capacity of the population is absorbed by newspapers, magazines and books imported from abroad.

Until a few years ago Uruguay had the highest index of newspaper copies per inhabitant in the whole of Latin America.

17 Translations

Books translated from their original language into Spanish constitute an important proportion in the total of books imported from abroad. These books come from the big publishing centres of the Spanish-speaking areas: Spain, Argentina, Mexico, etc.

Translations published in Uruguay represent a small number and a low percentage of the total of publications. Translation of Uruguayan books into foreign languages is also very rare.

19 Paperbacks

The modern concept of paperbacks as understood in Anglo-Saxon countries does not apply in Uruguay. The devaluation of the national currency and the rise of the original cost of foreign books on the one hand, and on the other hand the relatively low price of paperbacks, have resulted in their constituting a growing proportion in the import of foreign books. It must be noted that in the last years the distributors have tried to improve distribution and points of sale, using supermarkets, magazine stands, drugstores and retail outlets other than typical bookstores.

The number of weekly publications sold in instalments similarly to newspapers and magazines at news-stands, bookstores, etc., has also increased.

20 Book Design

Book design has shown some progress in the course of the last few years.

A factor which limits advances in this field is the small number of printed copies due to the limited size of the local market and the high cost per copy resulting from this.

The "National Book and Engravings Fair" (→29) gives an annual prize for the best-designed book; the prize is awarded by the "Uruguayan Printers' Association" (→34).

21 Publishing

Uruguay has not reached an advanced degree of specialization as regards work in the book trade.

Though most bookstores are neither distributors nor publishers, there are a number which are publishers, distributors and bookstores at the same time.

35 publishers and distributors are members of the "Uruguayan Book Chamber" (→4), all of them established in Montevideo. There are ten firms not affiliated to this institution, and statistics about publishers' and distributors' sales or numbers of employees are not available.

Mention has already been made of the biggest restrictive factor in publishing and book distribution, namely, the small size of the internal market. In spite of that, the country has a good cultural basis and a good intellectual level in the Latin American world. It is therefore thought that a publishing centre may be built in Uruguay, provided foreign markets can be conquered and a systematic policy for promoting publishing production can be organized.

It is expected that international publishers may be interested in operating in Uruguay. To encourage them they have been given advantageous terms in the field of materials, credits, taxes, post tariffs, and a local graphic industry with excellent achievements (→1, 2, 4).

Bibliography

M. A. PIÑEIRO AND L. A. MUSSO, *Book publishing in Uruguay*. St. Louis, Miss., Washington University Libraries, 1964. 10 pp.–9th Seminar on the Acquisition of Latin American Library Materials.– Mimeographed.

22 Literary Agents

There are no literary agents in Uruguay.

23 Wholesale Trade

The wholesale trade in effect goes together with imports and representation of foreign publishers.
→2, 21, 24, 27.

24 Retail Trade

There are 110 retail bookstores affiliated to the "Uruguayan Book Chamber" (→4), located in Montevideo. In the interior of the country there are approximately 100 establishments. The volume of their business is not known, and many of them combine other business lines, mainly stationery, but also other kinds of small retail trade or news-stands.

It has been stated (→19) that selling in supermarkets, drugstores, news-stands in the streets, etc. has lately been introduced, using specially designed bookstands. The importance of the collections of works sold in weekly instalments, similar to magazines, in every shop, including the traditional bookstores, must also be emphasized.

A branch of the book trade which has acquired great importance is instalment credit sales, through door-to-door salesmen. There are firms representing the big foreign publishers which develop this activity, especially at the universities and among the middle class.

The very high rates of interest, characteristic of a strongly inflationist economy and the high renumeration for salesmen decreed by the public authority make the final price very high.
→1, 2, 4, 21, 24, 27.

26 Antiquarian Book Trade, Auctions

A firm trading in antiquarian books is:
Librería Anticuaria
Adolfo Linardi
Juan Carlos Gomez 1418
U Montevideo
Auctions of old books do not exist as a speciality. From time to time complete libraries of old books are sold in general auctions.

Uruguay

27 Book Imports

Book imports, specially from the Spanish-speaking areas, are the most important sector in the Uruguayan book market.

Book importers are obliged to register at the Bank of the Republic.

There is no need to ask for a permit to import books. This has been the practice followed up to this moment. Books are an exception to the general system of import permits.

However, imports are subject to three conditions: the first is the certification of the trade invoice in its native country by the respective Book Chamber or the Chamber of Commerce if a Book Chamber does not exist. The second is the stamping of the receipt and its verification by the Bank of the Republic at the Uruguayan Post Office.

The third condition is that imports shall not exceed the maximum quotas fixed by the Central Bank of Uruguay and allocated to each registered importer for a yearly period.

The fulfilment of these conditions enables the importers to ask for foreign currency at the official rate of exchange at any local bank, to which the Central Uruguayan Bank supplies the exchange bills.

The rules now in force were established by circular No. 381, of 25 May 1972, of the Central Bank of Uruguay.

The official rate of exchange fluctuates.

As a consequence of the decline of currency reserves early in 1971, the foreign trade authorities have made decisions which include the book imports corresponding to the years 1970 and 1971, before 13 May 1971, not yet paid, in a special system.

Book-import debts up to US $ 25,000 by creditors are authorized by the Central Bank to be paid in cash; and those debts to foreign publishers exceeding US $ 25,000 will be settled by the issue of bills of exchange to be paid in six instalments, the first one US $ 3,000 or its equivalent in other currencies.

The bills will be subscribed by the Central Bank. Payment is therefore guaranteed by the State, and can be discounted in the financial markets.

There are no statistics referring to the value and physical units of imported books. The value of imports is estimated at an annual amount of US $ 2,000,000 in recent years, i. e. about 1 % of the country's total imports.

Spain has first place as a book exporter to Uruguay, followed by Argentina and then Mexico, France, the United Kingdom and the United States.

28 Book Exports

Book exports are limited to national book production, because exports of foreign books are as a general rule prohibited.

Exports must be certified by the Post Office and the exporter is obliged to give up the corresponding foreign currency to the Official Bank.

Book exports have many advantages and incentives, established by decree 26/960 of 19 February 1970 ($\rightarrow$ 2). The export bounty to books printed by photolithography is 36 % or 30 % of the f.o.b. value, according to the paper used, local or foreign, which is paid in the form of a certificate for the corresponding value destined to cancel taxes.

There are no statistics about the value and physical volume of Uruguayan book exports.

29 Book Fairs

There is a "National Book and Engravings Fair", held by a private organization which has the patronage of the Montevidean Municipal Government, which provides the site for the Fair in the Municipal Esplanade and Palace.

The fair takes place early in December and lasts until early January, the beginning of summer.

Only national books are admitted in this fair. The address is the following:

Feria Nacional de Libros y Grabados
(National Book and Engravings Fair)
Palacio Municipal
U Montevideo

From time to time book exhibitions are organized inland.

30 Public Relations

In this field there have been sporadic initiatives such as a Book Week or a Book Day, but they have not been long-lived.

On "Children's Day" there is some advertising, designed to sell children's books. There is also a "Friends of Books' Association".

32 Literary Prizes

Periodic and permanent prizes in Uruguay were instituted by the State and some Departmental Government. In the private sphere there are sometimes contests in specialized subjects.

The literary prizes given by the State have been established by law 11.648 of 19 February 1951. The most important ones are the following:

The *Gran Premio Nacional de Literatura* (Great National Literature Prize) which has so far been conferred every three years for general work done by a writer.

The *Premio Nacional de Literatura* (National Literature Prize) conferred every two years for the general work of a writer of literary works of great importance whether for books published, lectures or any other work of national importance during that time.

Thirteen awards confer a certain amount of money as reward for books published: three for poetry, poems and prose; four for stories, novels, fictionalized biographies; one for legends, children's literature and imaginative prose; two for aesthetic or literary essays; and three for plays.

There are also seven money awards for the printing of hitherto unpublished books of published or unpublished authors, and five money awards for scientific, sociological, historical, educational and philosophical books. There is also a special prize for the best literary work of a foreign author who has been resident in the country for more than a year.

There are four boards of juries who award the prizes. Each of these boards is composed of five members: two are appointed by the Ministry of Education and Culture, one by the National Academy of Letters, and two by institutions representing writers and authors.

The "Great National Literature Prize" and the "National Literature Prize" are awarded by the four boards gathered into one, presided over by the Rector of the University.

These official literary prizes carry some prestige, and their beneficiaries are writers with established literary reputations.

33 The Reviewing of Books

Book criticism is limited to the literary sections of the daily press and literary magazines and periodicals.

Dailies: "El País", "La Mañana", "El Día"; weekly: "Mancha".

Magazines: "Revista Nacional", "Revista de la Biblioteca Nacional".

34 Graphic Arts

In the capital of Uruguay there are two groups of firms engaged in printing activities:

a) The periodical press, engaged in the publishing of newspapers; and b) the book-printing industry, engaged in the production of books and commercial or official printing.

The latter belong to the
Asociación de Impresores del Uruguay
(Uruguayan Printers' Association)
Ciudadela 1410
U Montevideo

As mentioned elsewhere, Uruguayan printing has reached a high technical level and printers use nearly all the graphic processes currently available.

35 Miscellaneous

a) Authors
The address of the national authors' association is
Asociación General de Autores del
Uruguay
(General Uruguayan Authors' Association)
Canelones 1130
U Montevideo

Venezuela

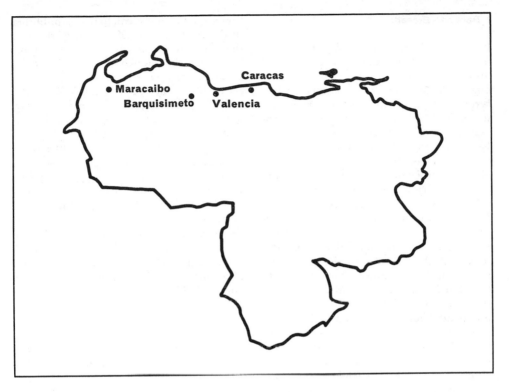

1 General Information

Area 912,050 km²

Population 7,524,000 (11 per km²)

Capital Caracas (2,000,000)

Largest towns Caracas (2,000,000); Maracaibo (421,872); Barquisimeto (198,981); Valencia (164,322)

Government Federal Republic comprising twenty States, two Federal Territories, one Federal District in which Caracas is located. Each entity elects its representatives to the National Congress as well as to the Legislative Assemblies and Municipal Councils; the Governor, however, is appointed by the President of the Republic

Religion Although the National Constitution guarantees complete freedom of religion, it can be said that the official religion is Roman Catholic

National language Spanish

Leading foreign languages Because of strong immigration from that country, Italian is perhaps the most widely diffused foreign language. Although English and French are fairly common, both are restricted to professional groups and international relations

Weights and measures Metric system

Currency Bolívar (B$) = 20 centavos = 100 céntimos

Education For the year 1969–70 the student population was made up as follows: elementary (compulsory): 1,726,410; secondary: 263,324; technical schools: 146,421; teachers' training colleges: 14,000; university: 71,000.

Illiteracy 36.7% (1961)

Paper consumption a) Newsprint 6.8 kg per inhabitant (1971)

b) Printing paper (other than newsprint) 4.5 kg per inhabitant (1971)

Membership UNESCO, CERLAL

329

Venezuela

2 Past and Present

In Venezuela the history of printing and the book is closely linked to its political history and its birth as a nation at the beginning of the 19th century, when favourable conditions for the armed insurrection and the struggle for independence from Spain were created.

In fact it was in the year 1806, that political documents appeared for the first time –leaflets, proclamations, speeches, but not one book–printed on a press which General Francisco Miranda carried aboard the *Leander* at the time of the intended invasion.

However, it was not until two years later that, with the help of the colonial government, the first printing office was established in Caracas, after transferring it from the near-by island of Trinidad to the mainland. This explains why no books, but newspapers of undoubtedly special importance for the history of Venezuela were printed, as for example the *Gaceta de Caracas*, and thus they could in one way serve the cause of the acting government.

And from that moment, until very recently, it was the Venezuelan government which, through different organs, acted as the principal publisher. This is explained by the fact that during the 19th and well into the 20th century there were very few printers–individuals or companies–and at the same time there were many authors who did their own publishing and distributing. This kept Venezuelan publishing activities within a concept of craftsmanship already superseded by other Spanish American countries, especially Mexico and Argentina.

At the end of the 19th century the *El Cojo Company*, originally a manufacturer of Havanna cigars, started the publication of one of the most significant Spanish American magazines, entitled *El Cojo Ilustrado,* as well as books of Venezuelan writers. Although we cannot speak here of a publisher in the modern sense of the word, this was the first support which local authors found for the launching of their books. Unfortunately, the economic difficulties created by the First World War also hit the unsophisticated national economy, and thus the project was seriously impaired. It is only fair to mention other pioneer companies in so difficult a field: *Editorial Elite, Avila Gráfica, Editorial Nueva Segovia*. But all of them together hardly satisfied the local needs, without even crossing the country's geographic boundaries. It is only with the advent of the sixties that one can begin to speak of a publishing industry proper, in which book production is characterized by the demands of a market which is no longer just Venezuelan, but comprises all Spanish-speaking countries.

Bibliography

G. Furlong, *Orígines del arte tipográfico en América.* (The origins of the art of typography in America.) Buenos Aires, Ed. Huarpes 1947. 225 pp.
Bibliography on pp. 215–25.–Early printing history of Venezuela: pp. 121 –122.

P. Grases, *Origines de la imprenta en Venezuela y primicias editoriales de Caracas.* (The origins of printing in Venezuela and the first publishers of Caracas.) Caracas, El Nacional 1958. 428 pp.

J. T. Medina, *Historia de la imprenta en los antiguos dominios españoles de América y Oceanía.* (The history of printing in the ancient Spanish dominions of America and Oceania.) 2 vols. Santiago de Chile, Fondo Histórico y Bibliográfico José Toribio Medina 1958. CXLI, 542; XV, 540 pp.
v. II. pp. 475–478: Venezuela (Caracas).

L. S. Thompson, *Printing in Colonial Spanish America.* Hamden, Conn., Archon Books

1962. 108 pp.
pp. 74–86: Venezuela.

4 Organization

The principal organization which unites the publishers and booksellers of the country is the
Cámara Venezolana del libro
(Venezuelan Book Chamber)
Edificio San Bernardino
Avenida Andrés Bello
YV Caracas
which fulfils the task of coordinating the activities of the trade in a satisfactory manner. Every year the Chamber organizes a Book Fair which is the most representative exhibition of the work achieved within that period.

7 Sources of Information, Address Services

General information on the book trade in Venezuela may be obtained from the
Cámara Venezolana del Libro
(Venezuelan Book Chamber)
Edificio San Bernardino
Avenida Andrés Bello
YV Caracas
Since the National Universities as a group make up the most important Venezuelan publishing group, general information may also be obtained from the
Servicio de Distribución de Publicaciones
(Publications Distribution Service)
Biblioteca Central
Universidad Central de Venezuela
YV Caracas
Likewise, any bibliographic information may be obtained from the
Biblioteca Central
(Central Library)
Sala de Referencia
(Reference Room)
Universidad Central de Venezuela
YV Caracas

For commercial inquiries, the most comprehensive source of information for the acquisition of Venezuelan books can be obtained from:
Síntesis Dos Mil
Apartado 68717
YV Caracas, 106

Bibliography

The addresses of all branches of the book trade are contained in
La Empresa del Libro en América Latina. (The Book in Latin America.) 2nd ed. Buenos Aires, Bowker Editores Argentina 1974. VIII, 307 pp.
pp. 257–268: Venezuela.

9 Market Research

Although one cannot say with entire objectivity that there exists in the country an institution specifically dedicated to the scientific investigation of the book and its influence on society, it is worth mentioning the modest studies rendered by the
Escuela de Biblioteconomía y Archivos de la Facultad de Humanidades y Educación de la Universidad Central de Venezuela ("School for Library Sciences and Archives of the Humanities and Education Department of the Central University of Venezuela").
The *Consejo Nacional de Investigaciones Científicas y Tecnológicas* (CONICIT "National Council for Scientific and Technological Research") is at present making special efforts towards the organization of a *Centro de Documentación* ("Documentation Centre"), which will have a considerable influence on Venezuelan publishing activities.

10 Books and Young People

In the *Escuela de Biblioteconomía y Archivos* (→9) a course in juvenile literature and libraries has been taught for some years now, which, in the long run, will create greater awareness of such a difficult problem.

The major efforts in this direction, however, are being undertaken by the

Banco del Libro
(Book Bank)
Sur Avenida Avila
Altamira
YV Caracas, 106

11 Training

Even though specific professional training does not exist either in the commercial field or the book trade, the *Escuela de Biblioteconomía y Archivos de la Universidad Central de Venezuela* (→9) is offering training courses for persons with a medium-level general education who later on will be capable of handling books in libraries, academies, universities, research institutes and similar institutions.

The studies are carried on over a period of four years and comprise courses in specific and complementary subjects. At the end the graduates receive the degree of a *Licenciado* which entitles them to exercise the profession of a librarian.

12 Taxes

In Venezuela customs duties on imported books are very low compared to other countries. Apart from the fact that the books are exempt from taxation, only 2% of the declared value or B^s 0.40 per kg is levied.

14 Copyright

Venezuela is a member of the Universal Copyright Convention (UCC) since 30 September 1966.

As to the membership to Inter-American Conventions →BTW I, International Section 14.

15 National Bibliography, National Library

The National Library is located in the old quarter of Caracas, in a building annexed to the ancient seat of the *Universidad Central de Venezuela* before the latter was transferred to the *Ciudad Universitaria* ("University City"). As the legal depository (copyright library) for the complete publishing production of the country and of Venezuelans residing in a foreign country, the library is regarded as housing the most complete national bibliographical collection. A law of the Republic prescribes the fulfilment of this condition.

The *Biblioteca Nacional* also has a section of books which are circulated and the *Hemeroteca Nacional* ("National Newspaper Collection").

However, the deficiencies of the ancient building and its limited budget have led to the *Biblioteca Central* ("Central Library") of the Central University extending and modernizing its structure so as to offer several additional services which would satisfy not only the demands of the university students, but also those of the non-university and polytechnic students, and of the general public. The Central Library of the University is the copyright library for the publications of the teaching and scientific staff of the Institution (→7).

From 1942 to 1948 the National Library published six volumes of the *Anuario bibliográfico venezolano* ("Venezuelan Bibliographic Annual"), but its publication was interrupted after that.

The Library of the Central University also published a *Catálogo de obras ingresadas* ("Catalogue of Works Deposited") during the years 1952—1964.

Bibliography

P. AVICENNE, *Bibliographical services throughout the world* 1965–69. Paris, UNESCO 1972. 310 pp.
p. 294: Venezuela.

I. Zimmermann, *Current national biblio-graphies of Latin America.* Gainesville, Florida, University of Florida Press 1971. X, 139 pp.
pp. 61–63: Venezuela.

20 Book Design

Until very recently (1961) the incipient and irregular publishing industry of Venezuela did not pay great attention to the design of title pages nor to the layout of books in general. All the same, some books whose publication was supervised by the authors themselves, stood out among the others on account of an attractive design and a neat graphic expression. In 1961 the *Universidad Central de Venezuela* started publishing on a commercial basis which took the demands of the market into consideration. At the time there was a great need for a good layout, which then for the first time became a compulsory part of ordinary programming.

The impact produced by the University's innovation forced the other publishers to follow suit and devote more care to title pages, format, and the harmony of a page, so that books would not just be printed material, but would be provided with an aesthetic component that would place Venezuelan production on a level with foreign standards.

21 Publishing

There are 11 publishing houses in Caracas. Most of them are of very small size. →2, 28.

22 Literary Agents

Because of limited local production and the very recent start of an organized publishing trade in Venezuela, there are no literary agents to attend to the relations between writers on the one side, and natio-nal as well as foreign publishers on the other. Generally speaking, it is customary to establish direct contact between the parties concerned.

24 Retail Trade

According to "La Empresa del Libro en América Latina" (→7) 59 bookshops or book outlets exist in Venezuela, 44 of them in Caracas, 6 in Maracaibo, and the rest in 6 other communities.

26 Antiquarian Book Trade, Auctions

Although Venezuela was noted for its regular and satisfactory market of antiquarian and rare books in the 19th century which was of limited proportions because of the constant state of effervescence within the new nation during the first fifty years of the 20th century this field of bibliographic activities was drastically abandoned. While it was common to offer out-of-print or rare Venezuelan editions in many foreign specialized bookshops, in the country itself it became almost impossible to find any book at all in the extremely few establishments which dealt with this type of material.

Old private libraries, which are generally the source for secondhand and antiquarian book-dealers, were conserved by the heirs with senseless zeal and false vigilance over an already lost integrity. However, some foreign universities, especially North American ones, were lucky enough to acquire fine collections, which explains the fact that some of these centres possess material not available in the country itself.

It is only during the last twenty years that dealing in rare and antiquarian books has begun to establish itself as a trade, though without the existence of associations or unions.

Venezuela

27 Book Imports

During the entire pre-industrial period mentioned above (→2) the country's book supply was met almost entirely by imports. Thus the book represented just another commodity among others needed in the country. The general structure of the book trade was characterized by an emphasis on craftsmanship and by provincialism, unfavourable for a development which should permit the commercial viability of the product. Not even the few printing offices which called themselves publishing companies were adequate. Their work was costly, of mediocre quality, save for a few exceptions, and unsatisfactory from both an aesthetic and a technical point of view.

Therefore, authors came to prefer foreign printers who produced a better quality at a lower cost and who promoted the commercial possibilities of their books.

It can be said that the import of books is almost completely exempt from taxes, as only a duty of fourty céntimos (B$ 0.40) per kg or 2% on the value declared must be paid.

The official import statistics for 1970 contain the following leading countries of origin:

Country	US$
USA	1,634,921
Argentina	1,060,075
Panama	919,674
Mexico	818,094
Spain	721,161
Italy	253,002
Colombia	179,380
Panama (Canal Zone)	147,230

The total amount for book imports was US$ 5,972,747.

28 Book Exports

The scene as described in the preceding chapter (→27) has changed considerably in the course of the last twenty years. This is especially true for the sixties, when the *Ediciones de la Biblioteca de la Universidad Central* (EBUC–"Central University Publications") appeared in 1961; this, chronologically speaking, was the first book organization based on commercial criteria encompassing the whole range of activities: the programming of the material to be published down to the problems of distribution outside of Venezuela. At an earlier date *Monte Avila Editores C.A.*, the publishing company of the Venezuelan State, had helped to expand and authorize this new image and concept of book production.

It has only been for ten short years now that Venezuelan books–written, designed and printed in the country–have begun to circulate in the rest of the world.

The export of Venezuelan books is totally exempt from taxes and customs duties.

Another vehicle for the promotion of Venezuelan books in foreign countries was an Exhibition of the Venezuelan Book organized by the *Instituto Nacional de Cultura y Bellas Artes* ("National Institute for Cultural Affairs and Fine Arts") which covered Europe, the United States, Canada and Spanish American countries.

Book exports covered US$ 235,781 in 1970, with Argentina as leading country of destination.

29 Book Fairs

Every year the *Cámara Venezolana del Libro* organizes a *Feria del Libro* ("Book Fair") in the *Palacio de las Industrias* ("Exhibition Hall of the Industries"), which comprises not only local production but also that of the foreign publishers established in the country.

Venezuela participated in the Frankfurt Book Fair (→BTW I, International Section 29).

32 Literary Prizes

Literary and journalists' prizes abound in Venezuela. The majority of them, however, have no influence in the book industry –especially the provincial ones–but seem rather to be intended as recognition for a work completed.

The *Premio Internacional de Novela Rómulo Gallegos*, set up by the *Instituto Nacional de Cultura y Bellas Artes* in honour of the distinguished Venezuelan writer, and consisting of the publication of the work plus one hundred thousand Bolívares is at present probably the highest prize for literature. It has been awarded only once: in that instance the special distinction went to the Peruvian writer Mario Vargas Llosa for his novel *La casa verde* ("The green house").

Other important prizes are: *Premio Nacional de Literatura* (honourable mentions for prose and poetry); *Premio Municipal de Literatura* (honourable mentions for prose and poetry); *Premio Asociación de Profesores de la Universidad Central de Venezuela* (honourable mentions for the humanities and the natural sciences); *Concurso de Cuentos* ("Short-Story Competition") of the newspaper *El Nacional*; *Premios de la Universidad del Zulia* (honourable mentions: drama, poetry, essays, short stories).

33 The Reviewing of Books

Basically, all of the capital's and provinces' newspapers with a sizable edition, and the principal news magazines, have a section on cultural topics where books are reviewed which have received wide attention. From the very first day of its appearance, the newspaper *El Nacional* has published a weekly supplement entitled *Papel Literario*. Apart from short essays, this supplement presents articles on national cultural affairs and the most salient events in countries closely related to Venezuela, as well as book reviews of national and foreign books. In the same newspaper a special feature entitled *Página de Arte* appears daily, except on Mondays. This section often includes articles on the appearance of some notable literary work and interviews with authors. On page four, the editorial page, a weekly column, *Crítica*, is published which is also a book review.

With less regularity than the *El Nacional*, another newspaper, *Ultimas Noticias*, also publishes articles about books which are included in the cultural supplement of the Sunday edition. *El Universal* is the third newspaper of Caracas which has been doing useful work over a long period of time in the difficult field of book promotion.

In 1938 the writer Mariano Picón Salas founded the *Revista Nacional de Cultura* ("National Review for Cultural Affairs") as a publication of the Ministry of Education. Although it is considered to be a cultural organ controlled by the Government, this review has been one of the most significant vehicles in diffusing the work of Venezuelan writers. Among the permanent sections of the *Revista*, one is dedicated to *Notas bibliográficas*. The *Revista Nacional de Cultura* was put under the control of the *Instituto Nacional de Cultura y Bellas Artes* after its foundation in 1960. This Institute publishes another monthly magazine, *Imágen*, which includes a book section.

With greater or lesser regularity each of the National Universities publishes a cultural magazine in which there is always a section reserved for book articles. The principal magazines are: *Cultura Universitaria* (Universidad Central de Venezuela, Caracas); *Actual* (Universidad de Los Andes, Mérida); *Revista de la Universidad del Zulia* (Maracaibo); *Oriente* (Universidad de Oriente, Cumaná). The University of Zulia publishes *Resenciones* ("Book Reviews"), which is, strictly speaking, the only magazine dedicated entirely to the reviewing of books.

Virgin Islands of the USA

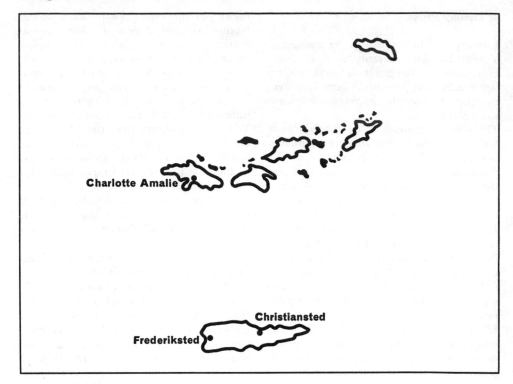

Charlotte Amalie

Christiansted
Frederiksted

1 General Information

Area 344 km² (St. Croix 207 km², St. Thomas 83 km², St. John 52 km²)

Population 58,000 (St. Thomas 39,000, St. Croix 27,000, St. John 7,000; 174 per km²–80% Negroes, 10% White)

Capital Charlotte Amalie (on St. Thomas; 12,700)

Largest towns Charlotte Amalie (12,700), Christiansted (on St. Croix; 5,088), Frederiksted (on St. Croix; 1,925)

Government Non-selfgoverning territory of the United States of America, directed by an elected governor

Religion Roman Catholic and Jewish in St. Croix and St. Thomas

National language English

Leading foreign languages Spanish, Danish

Weights, measures US System

Currency unit US Dollar (US $) = 100 cents (cts)

Education Compulsory for seven years. 1,065 students (1968) in the College of the Virgin Islands

Membership → USA

2 Past and Present

Discovered during the second voyage of
Columbus in 1493, and since 1671 part of
the Danish West Indies, the three islands
which form the US part of the Virgin
Islands were sold to the United States in
1917 for $25 million. Farming is the main
livelihood, with small industries manufacturing rum, watches, costume jewelry,
pharmaceutical and chemical products.
Tourism is now the main industry.
There are no booksellers.

Bibliography

J. P. KNOX, *A history and account of St. Tho-
mas, West Indies, and incidental countries of
St. Croix and St. John.* New York, Negro
University Press 1950. 272 pp.

15 National Bibliography, National Library

There are 11 libraries, mainly public and
school libraries, on St. Thomas, and 6 on
St. Croix, directed from the cities of
Charlotte Amalie and Christiansted, re-
spectively. There is one school library on
St. John.

27 Book Imports

No figures available.

33 The Reviewing of Books

There are three daily newspapers (total
edition 9,000) in circulation, and five
periodicals (1969); 9,300 radio receivers
and 18,000 TV sets; 3 radio stations and
2 TV channels (private).

West Indies Associated States

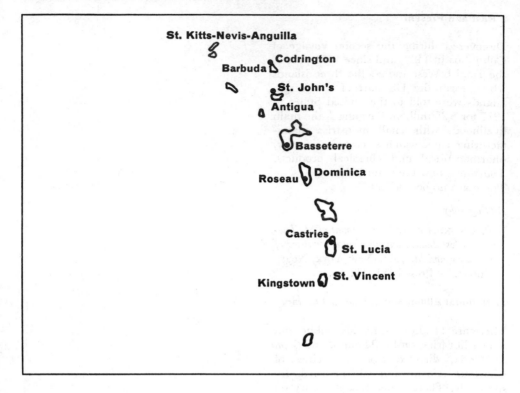

St. Kitts-Nevis-Anguilla

Codrington
Barbuda
St. John's
Antigua
Basseterre
Roseau — Dominica
Castries
St. Lucia
Kingstown — St. Vincent

1 General Information:

Area, Population, Capitals, Largest towns

a) Antigua (Leeward Islands) and dependencies (Barbuda; Redonda)

b) St. Kitts, Nevis and Anguilla (Leeward Islands)

b²) Anguilla

c) St. Lucia (Windward Islands)

d) Dominica (Windward Islands)

e) St. Vincent (Windward Islands) (including the Grenadines Dependencies)

a) 440 (160) km²; population: 61,664 (1,145); capital: St. John's (25,000); largest town: Parham

b) 396 km²; population: 57,617 15,072; capital: Basseterre; (15,897); largest town: Charlestown in Nevis (1530)

b²) 91 km²; population: 5,810;

c) 616 km²; population: 100,000; capital: Castries (40,000); largest town: Soufrière (7,325), Vieux Fort (6,981)

d) 728 km²; population: 70,177; capital: Roseau (13,200); largest town: Portsmouth (5,000), Grand Bay

e) 389 km²; population: 89,129; capital: Kingstown (23,000); largest towns: Georgetown, Chateau Belair

Total area: 2,569 km²; population: 378,587 (147 per km²)

Government Ministerial Government was introduced in 1956. In 1967 the West Indies Associated States (except St. Vincent) were given full internal self-government in voluntary association with Britain which retains powers and responsibilities for defence and external affairs. Government is exercised through a Parliament comprising the British Sovereign, an elected House of Assembly or Representatives and for executive government, through a Premier and a Cabinet. A Governor, appointed

338

by Her Majesty the Queen, is her respresentative in each state.

St. Vincent became an Associated State in 1969 with full self-government for control of internal affairs and with the right to amend its own constitution and the power to end the Association with the U.K. and declare itself independent.

In 1967 Anguilla announced its independence from the Federation of St. Kitts, Nevis & Anguilla. After many efforts to solve the Anguilla problem, under the Anguilla Act 1971, the U.K. Government provided for the Government of Anguilla through a Commissioner and a council for Anguilla. The arrangement is to come up for review.

Religion
  Antigua: Anglican (predominant), Methodist, Moravian, Petecostal, Pilgrim Holiness, Roman Catholic, Seventh Day Adventist
  St. Kitts Nevis & Anguilla: Anglican, Baptist, Church of God, Methodist, Moravian, Pilgrim Holiness, Roman Catholic, Seventh Day Adventist
  St. Lucia: Anglican, Methodist, Roman Catholic (predominant)
  Dominica: Anglican, Methodist, Roman Catholic
  St. Vincent: Anglican, Baptist, Church of God, Jehovah Witnesses, Methodist, Pentecostal, Pilgrim Holiness, Plymouth Brethren, Roman Catholic, Seventh Day Adventist, Salvation Army

National Language English is the official and commercial language in all the States. In Antigua an English Patois is spoken and a French Patois in Dominica and St. Lucia

Currency unit The monetary unit is the Eastern Caribbean Dollar (EC$) which comprises 100 cents with a fixed exchange rate of $4.80 to the £ Sterling

Weights, measures British Imperial System

Education With the exception of St. Vincent, Primary Education is compulsory in all the states. It is free throughout. There are 287 Primary Schools and 32 Secondary Schools, further more 3 Junior Secondary Schools. There is a Technical College in St. Kitts and, in Dominica, a Technical Wing is provided at one of the secondary schools. Teacher Training Colleges are provided in all states with the exception of Antigua. Special provision includes a School for Deaf Children in Antigua and for the Blind in Dominica. In St. Vincent there are six Craft Centres. Adult Education and/or Universities of the West Indies Extra-Mural Classes are available in St. Vincent and Antigua

Illiteracy Illiteracy has been described as "low" or "decreasing" generally. In Antigua a 40% figure is given

Paper consumption Details are not available for the states. It is noted that under the description "Paper, paperboard and manufactures thereof", Dominica imported 1,897,400 lbs. in 1967. Of this quantity 1,765,300 lbs. was from the United Kingdom and the rest from Canada and the USA. Dominica reports 3 weekly newspapers and 2 periodicals. The newspapers undertake commercial printing, there is a Government Printer and at least one other printer

2 Past and Present

Trace of Arawaks, Caribs, Amerindians are to be found in most of the Islands, although there are very few of pure strain. In Dominica and St. Vincent, Carib reserves or settlements are maintained. Other influences include Spanish, French and British (the early European settlers) and later Portugese, East Indians and Syrians. In all the states the population is predominantly of African descent.

A post-World-War II development is the concerted effort by all the Governments to reduce their dependence on agriculture and to diversify the economy by encouraging industrial programmes. These programmes include the promotion of secondary industries from agricultural produce, the introduction of manufacturing industries and the development of tourism and its ancillary industries. In St. Vincent encouragement of the tourist industry has resulted in the lifting of all but token duties on tourist goods, construction of new hotels, and improved facilities.

The "Winds of Change" blowing through these states have also brought developments and improvements in education and training, in social sciences, in communications and the mass media and constitutionally. These sophisticated trends have affected the field of printing. In the past most of the local work has been official printing and the Government Printers have been responsible for this output. Commercial printing has been small and undertaken mainly by the newspaper publishers. (Dominica reports that in 1765 a Printing Press was set up in Roseau and a publication "Free Port Gazette or Dominica Advertiser" issued. Later the title has changed to "Freeport Gazette or Dominica Chronicle". The press also undertook local commercial printing). The increasing demands for printed materials, brochures, booklets, guides, directories and reports, and the inability of local printers to cope with the situation has led to the utilizing of regional resources, that is, the printing presses of the more developed countries of the Caribbean viz.

Barbados, Guyana, Jamaica and Trinidad & Tobago, and these have responded ably.

With regard to books the Associated States have been and still are markets for British books with some imports also being made from North America. The development of Eastern Caribbean Library services which took place in the late 40's and early 50's with the establishment of 'free' public libraries led to more demands on the local publishers. The construction of new school buildings with provision for school libraries, the adult education programmes, technical institutes, the general spread of education, increased travel and visitors to the area, suggest a continuing demand for more books and a desirable effect on the book trade.

Recently there has been a greater demand for St. Vincent's arrowroot from the United States of America. This, it is reported, is influenced by the fact that the Arrowroot starch is an important base for the manufacture of paper used in computers. The unit price offered by the USA has been raised and this has acted as a stimulant or encouragement to crop growth.

Bibliography

Br. F. Swan, *The spread of printing, Western Hemisphere: The Caribbean area.* Amsterdam, Vangendt 1970, 47 pp. pp. 21–25: Antigua.

3 Retail Prices

As far as can be determined no standard policy obtains. The 'mark-up', influenced by the discount offered by the overseas bookseller/publisher/agent, is arbitrary, or is the published price plus postage, plus percentage, plus tax, if any. No changes are anticipated in the immediate future.

One accepted policy is apparent–a variable discount, not less than 10%–is granted to libraries by the local bookseller/agent.
In Antigua, in the case of educational books, a 15% mark-up on the published price obtains.

7 Sources of Information, Address Service

Support may primarily be expected from the Central/Public Library Headquarters in each state, and the local press.

11 Training

In St. Kitts, the S.P.C.K. Bookshop, prior to its closing down, conducted training sessions for its staff. In St. Vincent, bookshops staff have been given the opportunity to train overseas. Some persons have sought training on their own.

12 Taxes

Reports indicate
  in Antigua: 7% tax
  in Dominica: Package tax
  in St. Vincent: no tax on duty if sent "book post", otherwise a stamp duty and traders' rates apply.

14 Copyright

Copyright Acts are based on the British Act of 1911, modifications apply in some instances. In St. Vincent the Act is operative but not enforced (→BTW I, International Section 14).

15 National Bibliography, National Library

No library is designated the National Library in any of the Associated States. However, in St. Kitts & Nevis, Dominica and St. Vincent, the Public Library carries out some functions of a national library. No bibliography or booklists are issued but every effort is made to collect locally published material.

16 Book Production

Subject group	1973 Antigua	Dominica	St. Vincent	Total
Applied sciences	1			1
Literature		1	1	1
History		1	1	2
Total	1	2	2	4

In St. Vincent several booklets of poetry have been published of under 49 pages.

21 Publishing

Throughout the Caribbean, the field of publishing is a development of the last decade or so. The negligible regional publishing makes it necessary for authors to seek publication overseas, especially in the United Kingdom, the major publication area for Caribbean writers from English-speaking states. Local demand for local authors has been influenced by U.K. acceptance but this picture has changed in recent years. After a slow beginning, the growth of publishing is accelerating. Production is however dependent on the local printers whose schedules are often overcrowded by non-book and business records orders.
Throughout the Caribbean the pattern has been that both printers and authors act as 'publishers' because of the few publishing houses. This action has been necessary merely to make their works available at all. Publication by persons in each of the Associated States or about these states, is often actually published and/or printed in one of the larger independent regional countries. Publishers reported are: Antigua 2 and Dominica 3.

West Indies Associated States

24 Retail Trade

A total of 26 bookshops: Antigua 10; St. Kitts, Nevis & Anguilla 3; Dominica 2; St. Lucia 5; and St. Vincent 6, are reported. Traditionally few shops market only books. The business is often described as "Booksellers and Stationers". The pattern in these areas is to accommodate patrons by stocking other miscellany. "Seasons" are concentrated on Christmas and the start of the school year when the greatest turnover of business takes place.

The public libraries tend to place their orders through the local booksellers, a discount is given for this 'bulk' business but no fixed policies apply. Bookshops are mainly concentrated in the capitals.

Booksellers serve another function–that of promoting locally published booklets, pamphlets, etc. In these areas, it is the bookseller whom the author approaches and on whom he relies to draw attention to his work. In this role, the bookseller also keeps librarians aware of the items available. This is most useful especially if press announcements are delayed.

Periodicals are sold and orders for subscriptions to periodicals are accepted by some shops.

26 Antiquarian Book Trade, Auctions

No second-hand bookshops are reported. Mention should however be made of an existing avenue for second-hand purchases of books from bookstalls at bazaars, fairs, etc. Contributions are sought from individuals and bookshops, etc. and sold at cheap attractive prices.

27 Book Imports

Figures of imports are not available. Since local publishing is negligible, bookshop sales are mainly of works imported from the United Kingdom, the USA and from countries within the Caribbean area. Antigua reports 20,000 books imported in one year.

30 Public Relations

Occasional book displays arranged by public libraries have contributed to increase in sales of books by booksellers.

31 Bibliophily

St. Kitts reports a Poetry-Lovers Club, "The Lucky 13".

32 Literary Prizes

In Dominica, an annual *Short Story* and *Poetry Competition* is included in its National Day Celebrations. Contributions are later issued by the Government Printer in annual volumes "Dies Dominica".

33 The Reviewing of Books

Reviews of books appear in the local newspapers and weeklies of each state:
Antigua: *Antigua Star; Worker's Voice*
St. Kitts, Nevis and Anguilla: *Democrat; Labour Spokesman; Nevis Review*
Dominica: *Dominica Chronicle; Star; Wahseen; School Magazines*
St. Lucia: *Voice of St. Lucia; Herald; Standard*
St. Vincent: *Vincentian*
In one or more of these states reviews of books of regional interest are regularly available by means of the reviews in news media–press and/or radio–of some of the larger countries in the Eastern Caribbean e.g. Barbados, Jamaica, Trinidad & Tobago.

35 Miscellaneous

a) *Broadcasting*
Broadcasting stations are reported in 3 States. In Antigua there are two stations including one private company, and a television station operated by the Leeward Island Television Service.
Originally founded by Government in 1961, the St. Kitts, Nevis & Anguilla Government Broadcasting Station conducts sponsored programmes since 1963.
In St. Lucia, programmes are received from Antigua, Barbados, Grenada, Martinique, Montserrat, St. Kitts and Trinidad. Radio Caribbean International broadcasts in French and English.
There is a relay station of Grenada's West Indian Broadcasting Service in Dominica and this transmits local news bulletins and brief programmes.

b) *Newspapers, Magazines*
Antigua
  Antigua Star (P.O. Box 114 St. John's)
  Workers Voice (46 North Street St. John's)
St. Kitts, Nevis & Anguilla
  Democrat (Basseterre, St. Kitts)
  Labour Spokesman (do)
  Nevis Review (Charlestown, Nevis)
Dominica
  Dominica Chronicle (P.O. Box 124, Roseau)
  Star (26 Bath Road, Roseau)
St. Lucia
  Voice of St. Lucia (Bridge Pt., Castries)
  Herald (do)
  Standard (do)
  Catholic Chronicle (do)
  Crusader (do)
St. Vincent
  Vincentian (Lot 113, Bay Street, Kingstown)

Australia

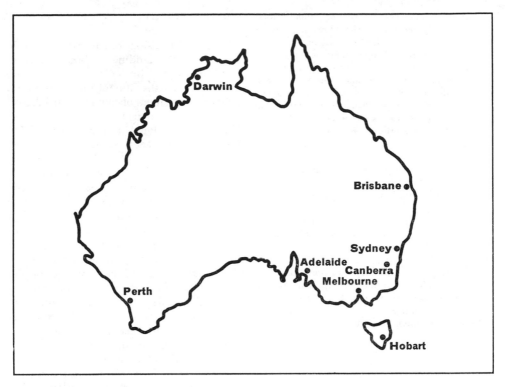

1 General Information

Area 7,695,099 km²
Population 13,040,000 (1.69 per km²)
Federal Capital Canberra (159,000)
State Capitals NEW SOUTH WALES: Sydney (2,800,000); VICTORIA: Melbourne (2,498,000); QUEENSLAND: Brisbane (867,000); SOUTH AUSTRALIA: Adelaide (843,000); WESTERN AUSTRALIA: Perth (702,000); Tasmania: Hobart (153,000); NORTHERN TERRITORY: Darwin (35,000)
Major towns in addition to capital cities
NEW SOUTH WALES: Albury (27,500), Armidale (18,000), Broken Hill (30,000), Gosford (39,000), Goulburn (22,000), Orange (24,000), Tamworth (25,000), Wagga Wagga (28,000); VICTORIA: Ballarat (58,500), Bendigo (46,000), Geelong (122,000), Moe (21,000), Shepparton (19,500); QUEENSLAND: Bundaberg (27,000), Cairns (33,000), Gold Coast (69,000), Too-

woomba (58,000), Townsville (68,500); SOUTH AUSTRALIA: Mount Gambier (18,000), Whyalla (32,000); WESTERN AUSTRALIA: Bunbury (18,000), Kalgoorlie (21,000); TASMANIA: Burnie (20,000), Launceston (62,000); NORTHERN TERRITORY: Alice Springs (11,500)

Government The Commonwealth of Australia is a federation of six states; the Australian Capital Territory and the Norther Territory are directly controlled by the Commonwealth. There are six state parliaments, and a Commonwealth Parliament consisting of the House of Representatives, and the Senate. The chief political executive of each state is the Premier, of the Commonwealth the Prime Minister. The Head of State is Queen Elizabeth II, represented in the states by a governor and in the Commonwealth by the Governor-General. Primary and secondary education and public libraries are under the control of the states or municipalities respectively; secondary-school libraries, science laboratories and other educational facilities receive assistance through the federal Department of Education. The whole cost of tertiary education, to include an allowance for students and, for the first time, a textbook allowance, was passed from the Australian states to be borne by the central government in 1974.

National language English

Leading foreign languages German, French, Indonesian

Weights, measures Imperial (1971), metric system being introduced by 1976

Currency unit Australian dollar ($A) = 100 cents (C.)

Education Compulsory. There are 168,000 tertiary-level students at 17 universities and colleges of adult education

Illiteracy Nil

Paper consumption Australian production (excluding newsprint, but including fine papers other than those in book production) 857,000 tons; imports, 218,000 tons.

Membership UNESCO, IPA, ICBA

2 Past and Present

The recorded history of Australia begins in 1770 with the landing in Botany Bay of Captain Cook, who took possession of the eastern coast in the name of King George III. The first settlement of convicts, officials and marines arrived in 1788 in what was to become the colony of New South Wales. Other colonies (now states) were formed by the middle of the 19th century; they federated into the Commonwealth of Australia on 1 January 1901. It has been a long but now completed political process for Australia (she still shares her Head of State with the United Kingdom and other so-called Commonwealth countries) to reach the stage of full national independence; in the narrow non-political confines of the book trade this independence has not yet been fully achieved. Australia continues to depend for her books on the United Kingdom, and more recently on the United States, and although since the end of the Second World War she has claimed to become a "third force" in English language publishing, the ownership of the Australian book trade is progressively slipping into British and American hands.

The first book to be published in Australia was issued by George Howe in 1802, but well into the late nineteenth century Australian publishing consisted mainly of official publications and subsidized publishing. Australia's first regular publisher was George Robertson of Melbourne, Victoria, who published his first book in 1856, and the real founder another George Robertson of Sydney, New South Wales, whose successes in the 1890s laid the foundation of Angus & Robertson Ltd., still Australia's largest publishing house. All early publishers had such other interests as bookselling, printing, or a connection with an overseas publisher, a situation which still persists.

It is essential towards the understanding of

the facts and interpretation which will follow, that in the first century of its history Australia imported virtually all her books from the United Kingdom, that the great majority of books sold in Australia to the beginning of the Second World War were likewise of United Kingdom origin, and that in spite of a spectacular expansion of Australian book publishing in the last three decades, the value of books imported–from Britain and America–is four times the value of books published, if not necessarily printed, in Australia.

Australia's book-printing industry offering a reasonable choice of type-faces, automated binding equipment, and the basic professional know-how in book production has only been in existence for the last thirty years. Because of high labour costs Australian book printers have witnessed a substantial loss of business to printing works in Hong Kong, Singapore, and other countries in South East Asia; some Australian publishers do all their printing, if not the design and typesetting, outside Australia (→34).

Bibliography

Australian Encyclopedia 10 volumes. Sydney, Grolier Society 1965.

The Modern Encyclopedia of Australia and New Zealand. Sydney, Horwitz-Grahame 1964.

D. H. BORCHARDT, *The spread of printing. Eastern hemisphere: Australia.* Amsterdam, Vangendt & Co. 1969. 45 pp.
A bibliography of some reference works on p. 45.

A. FABINYI, *The Australian book.* In: Texas Quarterly, special issue "Image of Australia". pp 77/84. Austin, University of Texas 1962.

J. HOLROYD, *George Robertson of Melbourne.* Melbourne, Robertson & Mullens 1968. 64 pp.

W. KIRSOP, *The Australian book trade: prosspects for a history.* Sydney, Wentworth Press 1969, 96 pp.

3 Retail Prices

In 1971, an Australian Commonwealth law was proclaimed which made all retail price maintenance illegal. It was based on similar legislation in the United Kingdom, where, however, after protracted legal proceedings the "Net Book Agreement", so called, was upheld as being in the "public interest"; similar decisions have been reached in such other largely English-speaking countries as New Zealand and South Africa.

It is essential for what are now historical reasons to state that an Australian equivalent of a "Net Book Agreement", called "Statement of Terms" (i.e. a statement by publishers on the conditions under which they supply books to booksellers), was in force till may 1972. Unlike the U.K. Net Book Agreement it did not distinguish between "net" and "non-net" books, but on the other hand dealt with three other categories:

a) Books published by an Australian publisher, of which the publisher fixes and maintains the retail price, with certain allowable discounts to institutions, teachers and some others.

b) Books published in the United Kingdom and available "on indent"; their prices are fixed on a schedule which was based on the *cost* of the book to the bookseller, and *not on the United Kingdom retail price;* and yet under certain conditions the same books could also be sold at the retail price in the United Kingdom converted into Australian currency.

c) Books published in the United Kingdom but "marketed" by the Australian offices of the United Kingdom publisher who fixes an Australian retail price and who has the sole right to sell the books in Australia; they may not be "indented" direct from the United Kingdom.

The "Statement of Terms" did not cover books published in the United States;

many of these are not available in Australia because of copyright restrictions, the United States publisher having sold the rights to the "British Traditional Market Area"; those which may be sold, most in the college textbook field are normally "marketed" by the proliferating Australian branches of American publishers (→ 14).

No "Statement of Terms" or any other agreement covered books imported from New Zealand, Germany and other non-English-speaking countries, although in actual practice booksellers marked them up closely in line with the "schedule" for U.K. books.

The "schedule", that is the conversion rate to retail price of books imported from the United Kingdom, as well as the discounts allowable on retail prices, had been the source of constant negotiation and friction ever since the parity of £A (now $A) went below that of the £Stg.

Before then, as a rule of thumb, 1 shilling (Stg. retail price) was converted, to provide for the cost of freight, into one shilling and three-pence (Australian retail price). There was however a varying pricing structure for books supplied by United Kingdom publishers at the "colonial discount" (usually 50%) or short-discounted schoolbook.

To establish some system, eventually a so-called Australian Joint Advisory Committee (AJAC) was formed to bring into being the first "Schedule". After the Second World War the matter came under the supervision of the Publishers (i. e. U.K. Publishers) Association Committee (PAC) comprised of British publishers' and Australian booksellers' representatives. The growth of Australian publishing changed its constitution to turn it into the Australian Book Trade Advisory Committee (ABTAC) of which the present writer was chairman from 1966 to 1968, to bring together representatives of the Australian book publishers, the Australian booksellers, the Publishers' Association, the British publishers' representatives in Australia, and the Wholesalers' Association. Unresolved differences between publishers and booksellers and exacerbated trade politics led in 1969 to the formation of the Joint Publishers' Committee (JPC) which dissolved itself early in 1971.

It is necessary to look at the current situation in this historical context outlined above.

As soon as legislation prohibiting all retail price maintenance in Australia was proclaimed in 1971, the Australian Book Publishers' Association (→4), which had the responsibility for the orderly marketing of books in Australia, applied to the Trade Practices Tribunal to exempt books from the provisions of the legislation.

At a protracted hearing, lasting some eight weeks, the majority of the book trade argued for maintaining the status quo but a minority of publishers and booksellers argued that the retail price maintenance and the validity of the Statement of Terms was no longer in the public interest.

In a judgment brought down in May 1972 the Trade Practices Tribunal made the retail price maintenance of books in Australia illegal.

The Australian publishing and bookselling trade was, at the time of writing (1973) still probing to assess the full implications of this judgment. Whatever the final outcome may be, a number of bookshops have already closed down and the output of Australian book publishers (→16) has already declined.

It is likely that the Australian book trade will now develop on the United States pattern, with the enormous difference, however, that the United States publishers and booksellers serve a population of over 200 million while the Australian population is only a fraction of that number.

The Australian Booksellers' Association (→4) still publishes a so-called schedule of prices for books imported from Britain and the United States which is subject to variation according to changes in the value of currency.

The legality of such a schedule being in existence is doubtful, and its possible enforcement is beyond doubt illegal.

Bibliography

R. PAGE, *Australian bookselling*. Melbourne, Hill of Content 1970. 187 pp.

4 Organization

There is no association in existence to embrace all book-trade interests, although in the associations listed hereunder there is, to an extent, an interlocking membership; the same firms may belong having regard to their differing activities, to more than one association.

The

Australian Book Publishers'
Association (ABPA)
163-165 Clarence Street
AUS Sydney 2000

states as its objectives, *inter alia*, the promotion of "Australian books in Australia and overseas having regard to the social, cultural, educational and literary values these books represent", "to maintain constant liaison with other bodies associated with the manufacture and distribution of books and to contribute to the improvement of the Australian book industry as a whole".

Founded in 1946, it now (1973) has 55 full and 19 associate members. Of the 55 full members, representing the major publishers, 27 are either wholly owned by United Kingdom interests, or are branches of a United Kingdom firm, 9 are wholly owned by United States interests or are branches of a USA firm, 4 are Australian university presses, 2 are branches of New Zealand firms, and only 14 are Australian owned.

The 19 associate members, representing firms and organizations with a small turnover, are all Australian owned and include one university press.

The ABPA meets regionally in Melbourne, Victoria and Sydney, N.S.W., and annual meetings are held in one of the capital cities; a national executive of twelve meets usually every second month. It has a number of specialized committees of which the Book Export Development the Book Design and Book Manufacturing Advisory Committees are the most important. The

Association of Australian University Presses
c/o Australian National University Press
P. O. Box 4
AUS Canberra

is constituted within the framework of the ABPA.

The Australian Book Publishers' Association now has a professional director, Mr. G. A. Ferguson, former chairman of Angus & Robertson Ltd., Australia's oldest and still largest publishing house.

The

Australian Booksellers' Association
Box 1386 G.P.O.
AUS Sydney, 2001

is the national body bringing together the N.S.W. Booksellers' Association (NSWBA), the Victorian Booksellers' Association (VBA), the South Australian Booksellers' Association (SABA), the Western Australian Booksellers' Association (WABA), the Queensland Booksellers' Association (QBA), and the Tasmanian Booksellers' Association (TBA). Because conditions vary widely from state to state in such matters as the supply of school textbooks, or the methods of government tendering, state associations meet independently and control their regional policy. A Federal Council of five meets at regular intervals and an annual conference is being held, rotating between various capital cities. The ABA has a membership of 130.

A survey commissioned by the ABA disclosed what amounted to a crisis in the profitability of Australian bookselling (→24) and the main efforts of the ABA are concentrated on obtaining reasonable terms from publishers. It publishes an annual *ABA Handbook* giving all the relevant information, including trade discounts, return terms, freight charges, etc., of all publishers located or represented in Australia. It runs, in conjunction with the Education Department of Victoria a training scheme for booksellers, leading to the Certificate of Bookshop Practice and occasionally organizes Booksellers' Overseas Study Tours.

The Wholesale Booksellers' Association of
Australia (WBA)
c/o Samuel Wood Pty. Ltd.
8 Bunn Street
AUS Pyrmont, N.S.W. 2009

is a small association which includes wholesalers who supply other bookshops as well as being library suppliers; it usually holds an annual meeting only in Melbourne or Sydney.

Bibliography

The ABA Handbook. Sydney, Australian Booksellers' Association 1973.
Australian Book Publishers' Association, Directory of Members, Sydney, ABPA 1973.

5 Trade Press

The only genuine trade journal is the
Australian Bookseller and Publisher
D.W. Thorpe Pty Ltd
Stationers' Hall
384 Spencer Street
AUS Melbourne, Victoria, 3003
for Australia, New Zealand and the Pacific; monthly (formerly published as "Ideas".
In addition to being both Australian and overseas publishers' main advertising medium, it publishes news commentaries, bestseller lists and a monthly list of Australian books published. The monthly

lists are published as *Cumulative Australian Books* every three months.
Its yearly publication *Australian Books in Print* (latest edition 1975) is a list of all Australian books in print, listed thrice, alphabetically by author, title and subject matter, with physical details against title and author entries. It also includes a combined list of British, American, European and Asian publishers, with their Australian representatives; Australian publishers and their addresses; Australian magazines; all series of books, trade associations, literary societies, literary awards. Other journals which carry book-trade information are:

Australian Book Review
27 Park Road,
AUS Kensington Park, South Australia 5068
(formerly monthly, now quarterly; now [1973] Vol. 11).
The
Australian Newsagent
Horwitz Publications,
155 Miller Street,
AUS North Sydney, N.S.W. 2060

Advertising & Newspaper News
Yaffar Building,
AUS Surry Hills, N.S.W. 2010
and
Newsagent & Bookseller
Peter Isaacson Publication
46-49 Porter Street,
AUS Prahran, Victoria, 3181

6 Book-Trade Literature

The relevant literature is listed in the bibliographies to the various chapters (→3, 4, 5, 7, 10, 15, 21, 24, 26, 34, 35).

7 Sources of Information, Address Services

Addresses, where available, are given in the relevant chapters. Australian diplomatic posts and trade commissioners abroad carry Australian reference libraries of various sizes and are provided by both the Department of Trade and Industry and the Australian Book Publishers' Association with up-to-date information on the Australian book trade.

The National Library of Australia has liaison officers in London (Australia House, London, WC2) and in New York (Rockefeller Center, Fifth Avenue); the Australian News and Information Bureau has officers attached to most Australian diplomatic missions; information on the current Australian book-trade situation is available from these officers.

Bibliography

Official Year Book of the Commonwealth of Australia No. 58 Canberra, Commonwealth Bureau of Census and Statistics 1972.

8 International Membership

The Australian Book Publishers' Association (> 4) is a member of the International Publishers' Association (→BTW I, International Section 8), and is normally represented at its meetings.

The Australian Booksellers' Association (→4) is a member of the International Community of Booksellers' Associations (BTW I, International Section 8).

The ABPA is a member of the Australian National Advisory Committee of UNESCO, and its representative is currently (1973) chairman of the UNESCO Communication Committee: earlier, as then President of the ABPA, he represented Australia at the UNESCO Asian Book Development Conference in Tokyo (→BTW III, Asia 8), also at a recent meeting of the IKAPI (Indonesian Publishers' Association) in Tretes, Indonesia (→BTW III, Indonesia 4).

The ABPA sends official representatives to the national stands at book fairs and exhibitions in Frankfurt, Tokyo, Mexico, Djakarta, Singapore, Kuala Lumpur and Bologna, always in co-operation with the Commonwealth Department of Overseas Trade and/or the Australian Foreign Office.

9 Market Research

No meaningful research in the Australian book market has yet been undertaken.

The Australian Booksellers' Association has published a survey on book-trade economics (→24) and there is in existence an unpublished thesis "Australian book publishing", by D. H. Barker (University of Melbourne, 1970) which contains a somewhat inconclusive chapter on the subject.

Assessments of the Australian book market can be found, however, in many items quoted in the bibliographies; conclusions may also be drawn from the relevant statistics under 16, 27 and 28.

10 Books and Young People

There is an element of complexity in the provision of Australian books for young Australian readers. An Australian children's book is defined by some as one by an Australian author, illustrated by an Australian artist or published by an Australian publisher, any one of these qualifications justifying its being billed "Australian". Others adhere to the definition that an Australian children's book is one written, conceived or commissioned in Australia, and published, if not necessarily printed in Australia by a resident if not necessarily Australian-owned publisher.

Using the second definition, Australian children's book publishing would appear to be insignificant. According to the statistical returns of the Australian Book Publishers Association (→4) the number of new children's books published per annum has increased from 39 titles in 1964 to only 57 titles in 1972, and of reprints from 28 to 60.

The most significant development in Australian publishing has been in the field of school textbooks, by any definition "books for young people"; new titles, 205 in 1964, stood at 425 in 1972, while reprints increased from 292 titles to 659. In the last ten years the concentration of both local and overseas capital and editorial manpower was directed towards educational publishing, and the process is still accelerating, rather to the detriment of "general publishing", which of course covers the so-called "quality" children's book.

Local production however meets only a fraction of the existing market for books for young readers, which is expanding rapidly. Children's books, particularly of the popular kind, billed in Australia as "dollar flats", sell in more diverse outlets apart from bookshops.

The long neglected Australian school library service (controlled by the states, or in the case of so-called "independent schools" by churches or similar authorities) has in 1968 received an infusion of $27 million federal funds, and this has in 1971 been renewed at the rate of $30 million for the next three years. As a result of a report submitted to the Australian government by the so-called "School Commission" federal funds, which until then covered secondary schools only, will now be extended, from 1974, to primary-school libraries. The expansion of the Australian market for books suitable for primary and secondary school libraries ought to be one of the widest, if not the widest in the English language for the next decade.

Hence Australia represents a very large outlet for children's books published in the United Kingdom but both copyright restrictions and high retail prices exclude most United States material.

A *Childrens' Book Council*
  50 Booroondara Street
  AUS Reid A.G.T. 2601
was first formed in N.S.W. in 1942, and is now operating on a federal basis in every state. Once a year, usually in July, it runs a Children's Book Week, when the "Book of the Year Award" given to the Australian children's book, judged by a panel of librarians to be the best book published in the preceding year, is announced. This is accompanied by wide publicity and usually generates sales of 15,000 copies or more for the book selected.

During the week there are extensive exhibitions of both Australian and overseas children's books, and the Council regularly publishes excellent book-lists either as separate publications or in Education Gazettes; these have proved invaluable tools for librarians' book selection and in the important but still badly overlooked field of parent education.

The library service departments–they may operate from state to state under different names–also publish lists of recommended children's books; the education departments once a year issue a list of recommended or prescribed textbooks, although the choice of textbooks, with the exception of those for matriculation level, is being increasingly left to individual schools and teachers.

Bibliography

A. FABINYI, *The development of Australian children's book publishing*. Sydney, University of N.S.W. 1971. 28 pp.

M. MUIR, *A bibliography of Australian children's books*. London, Deutsch 1970. 1038 pp.

H.M. SAXBY, *A history of Australian children's literature*. Sydney, Wentworth Press 1969. 224 pp.

R. WIGHTON, *Early Australian children's literature*. Melbourne, Lansdowne 1963. 40 pp.

11 Training

Apart from two courses in Victoria, a Bookselling Course at the Royal Melbourne Institute of Technology and an Editors' Course at the Caulfield Institute of Technology, Australia as a whole offers no formal training for booksellers and editors. The
Book Trade Group,
384 Spencer Street
AUS Melbourne 3003
also located in Victoria, does run occasional seminars on book-trade topics. The
Imprint Society,
346 St Kilda Road
AUS Melbourne 3004
a small group of typographers and book designers, also in Victoria, from time to time organizes lectures on graphic arts. Printing schools in technical colleges are not orientated towards book design.
Publishers normally recruit their editorial staff from university graduates, and in the wake of the expansion of educational publishing many come from the teaching profession; they all receive only "in service" training.
The adequate staffing of bookshops in the current Australian situation of over-employment is presenting considerable difficulties. Bookshop hours (9-7.30 weekdays, 9-12 Saturdays) are longer, but salaries and status are lower than those of office jobs.
With a few exceptions Australia's top booksellers or bookshop managers are self-made men; their lack of formal qualification is usually well compensated by their genuine love of books.

12 Taxes

Australia levies no import duty, sales tax, currency restriction or any other impost on books.

14 Copyright

The Commonwealth Copyright Act 1968 came into force on 1 May 1969.
On that date Australia ratified its adherence to the Brussels revision of the Berne Copyright Convention and to the Universal Copyright Convention formally requiring proprietors to place on the works the symbol © together with their name and the year of first publication, in such a manner and location as to give reasonable notice of their claim of copyright in the works so identified. The legislation contains no provision for the registration of copyright and the Copyright Office, so called, ceased to exist on 1 May 1969.
Commonwealth legislation requires that a copy of each Australian book be deposited with the National Library of Australia (→ 15), while individual states have similar legislation requiring publishers to deposit copies published within the state to one or more libraries. These latter provisions are becoming difficult to implement and police, as there is some doubt whether a book needs to be "published" or "printed" in a particular state for the state legislations to apply.
Although books by Australian authors or on Australian subjects published outside Australia are technically exempt from the provisions of compulsory deposit copies, the National Library is expecting, and is trying to enforce the practice that all Australian material locally distributed, wherever published, be deposited.
In Australia as elsewhere both publishers and authors are increasingly concerned about photocopying and other breaches of copyright. Their interests are being watched by the
Australian Copyright Council
252 George Street
AUS Sydney, 2000
of which both the Australian Book Publishers' Association (→4) and the Australian

Society of Authors (→ 35) are contributing members.

There has been for some time strong agitation in Australia to amend the Copyright Act or bring down some other legislation which would include provisions for a Public Lending Right, that is that authors and publishers would be paid some fee for multiple lendings by public libraries.

A new government, elected in Australia in December 1972, announced its intention to legislate in the matter by 1974 on the principle that all fees paid to Australian authors will come from federal funds and will not be a charge on individual libraries.

An agreement exists between British and American publishers which restricts the sale in Australia of United States books for which a British publisher has acquired the "British Traditional Market" rights. This means that some American books, including paperbacks, are not available in Australia till some time after publication, and if a British edition fails to appear, as could happen, may not be available at all.

The matter is the subject of a great deal of public controversy, and from time to time booksellers deliberately or inadvertently import books from the United States, for which the American original publisher does not hold the right to sell it in Australia, which is the largest of the British Traditional Market area.

Such action in Australian common law is a breach of copyright. Nevertheless at the time of writing (1973) action is being considered and negotiations between Australian publishers and British publishers are at an advanced stage which will make this so-called "British Traditional Market" agreement at least more flexible, and it is likely, if not certain, that Australia, vis-à-vis British publishers, will occupy the same position which Canada has been occupying for a long time.

15 National Bibliography, National Library

The *Australian National Bibliography* is issued by the National Library of Australia four times a year, including monthly cumulations together with annual volumes. In an alphabetical, self-indexing arrangement it lists books and pamphlets, items of Australian association published overseas, sheet music of Australian origin, and the first issue only of each new annual, periodical and newspaper. Through the co-operation of Australian publishers items about to be published are also included; these are marked with an asterisk.

Whilst government publications are included in the *Australian National Bibliography*, their coverage is generally more comprehensive in the National Library's annual *Australian Government Publications*, which covers the publications of both Commonwealth and State Governments and statutory authorities. Since 1971 it is being issued quarterly.

Australian Books, issued by the National Library annually, is designed as an authoritative current reference and reading list of works dealing with Australia or of Australian authorship; it is selective, classified broadly by subject, and gives the principal standard works in print as well as significant current publications.

For *Australian Books in Print* (including Bookbuyers' Reference Book) → 5.

The

Australian Advisory Council on Bibliographical Services (AACOBS)
AUS Canberra Act 2600

was established in 1950 to plan and recommend to appropriate authorities measures for the further development of Australian library and bibliographical services and to co-operate with international bodies such as the UNESCO International Advisory Committee on Libraries, Documentation and Archives.

It now (1971) has a membership of 49,

which, in the opinion of some of its professional members, makes for a body too large to do more than discuss bibliographical policy, without having the executive power to implement it. AACOBS is administratively part of the National Library. The

National Library of Australia
AUS Canberra Act 2600

had its origins in the Commonwealth Parliamentary Library established in 1901; its Australian collection had its beginning with the 10,000 volumes acquired from E. A. Petherick. It was formally established as the Commonwealth National Library in 1923, when Federal Parliament moved from Melbourne to Canberra. It was housed, until 1968, within the precincts of the Commonwealth Parliament, but now occupies a building of its own, which is one of the most impressive public buildings in Australia.

Its functions were consolidated in the National Library Act 1960-67 "to maintain and develop a national collection of library material relating to Australia and the Australian people". It has perforce a special responsibility for Australian materials, particularly current publications in the widest sense of the word. It is assisted in this by the deposit provisions of the Copyright Act 1968 (→14).

Beyond its Australian responsibilities the National Library has achieved considerable progress towards a complete coverage of the current world output of scholarly publications, with special emphasis on the social sciences and humanities, and including the publications of overseas governments. In addition, its programme for retrospective collecting is continually being expanded to supplement its present research collections and to support and anticipate research programmes within Australia.

The National Library's holdings (1971) are 1,250,000 volumes.

Bibliography

National Library of Australia Tenth Annual Report. Canberra, 1970.

D. H. Borchardt, *Australian bibliography. A guide to printed sources of information.* Melbourne, Cheshire 1966. 96 pp.

J. Ferguson, *Bibliography of Australia.* 7 vols. Sydney, Angus & Robertson 1941-1969. 5,834 pp.

E. M. Morris Miller, *Australian literature from its beginning to 1935. A descriptive and bibliographical survey.* Sydney, Angus & Robertson 1956. 513 pp.

J. Nicholson (ed.) *Australian books in print 1974 (Including Bookbuyers' Reference Book).* Melbourne, D. W. Thorpe 1975. 322 pp.

16 Book Production

Statistics about Australian book publishing are prepared by the Commonwealth Bureau of Census and Statistics and by the Australian Book Publishers' Association (→4).

The Bureau of Census and Statistics bases its figures on data supplied by the National Library of Australia. The method of counting conforms to international practice: each title is counted as one unit; the figures cover all books and pamphlets published in Australia and the External Territories. A book is a non-periodical publication of at least 49 pages, and a pamphlet of no less than 5 and no more than 48 pages. As the figures include government publications, including pamphlets, these statistics are not a very reliable measure of the output of Australian book publishers.

Of the total number of items recorded at 4,523 in 1971, a dissection, made for the first time, discloses that only 1,059 books were produced by trade publishers, including books by university presses and other statutory authorities. The classifications of the *totals* (first editions and re-editions) were as follows in 1971:

Subject group	Titles
Bibliography, libraries, general	93
Philosophy, psychology	34
Religion, theology	180
Social sciences	1,978
Linguistics, philology	74
Science	372
Technology, business	755
Art, amusement	182
Literature	
History of literature, literary	
criticism, anthologies, school editions	39
Australian literature	264
Other literature	63
Total, literature	356
Geography, travel	203
History, biography	196
All publications	4,523

No dissection between first and new editions is available for 1971. The National Library introduced a new system for recording Australian book publishing statistics in 1972.

According to the National Library Australian books *and* pamphlets published in 1973 are stated as follows:

Type of publisher	Titles
Commercial	918
Commonwealth government	261
State government	150
Local government	8
Society, institution, company, private	311
Total	1,648

No subject dissection is available.

A breakdown of the 1973 statistics, based on the Australian National Bibliography lists 5,695 individual titles. Of these, 5,329 were published in Australia and 366 were books of Australian interest or association published overseas. Analysis of the 5,329 Australian titles by type of publication gives 2,902 books, 1,886 pamphlets (5–48 pages), 110 leaflets (1–4 pages), 259 periodicals and 172 other serials (e.g. annuals, newspapers). Of the 4,898 monographic (i.e. non-serial) titles, 87 were published in 1970, 447 in 1971, 2,716 in 1972, 1,648 in 1973 and 2 will be published in 1974.

The statistics compiled by the Australian Book Publishers' Association (→4) need to be qualified in two ways: although most major publishers are members of the Association, there are exceptions, and the Association does not record books by occasional or institutional publishers; even within the membership there is a variation in the number of publishers who submit their reports. Nevertheless the ABPA statistics do reflect the general trend of Australian book publishing. The figures given cover the end of the Australian financial year, that is the twelve months ended 30 June each year.

The following are comparative figures for 1962, 1969 and 1972, with the number of reporting publishers shown in brackets under the year.

New books and new editions:	1969 (42)	1972 (48)	1973 (55)
Fiction	34	18	26
Poetry, drama, belles-lettres	34	39	36
General literature	231	310	424
Children's books	46	57	154
Scientific and technical	171	151	148
Educational	340	425	547
Paperbacks	211	95	281
Total	1,067	1,095	1,616

Reprints:			
Fiction	10	3	3
Poetry, drama, belles-lettres	14	20	19
General literature	69	113	124
Children's books	25	60	211
Scientific and technical	44	122	56
Educational	598	659	1,002
Paperbacks	54	67	161
Total	814	1,044	1,576
Total new books and reprints	1,881	2,139	3,192

17 Translations

Australian publishers do not, as a rule, publish translations. Although Australian geographical, political and to an extent publishing contacts in South East Asia have brought forth the concept that translations from languages such as Bahasa Indonesian, Malayan or Chinese be first published in Australia, this has not yet produced any meaningful practical results. According to UNESCO statistics Australia published 24 translations on 1969.

There is a minimal amount of book and pamphlet publishing by immigrant groups in European languages; these are not, normally, translated into English.

18 Book Clubs

No book clubs exist in Australia which could in any way compare with those in the United States or in the United Kingdom. The one book club specializing in Australian creative writing is the

Australasian Book Society
104 Bathurst Street
AUS Sydney, 2000

Overseas book clubs advertise in Australia, many of them have resident agents and command a sizeable Australian membership.

In 1973 an American and a British Book Club started local operation.

19 Paperbacks

The impact of the "paperback revolution" on Australia is similar to the one experienced by other English-speaking countries. Paperbacks have created a new reading public, and are being mass-marketed through outlets other than bookshops, although the majority of the business is still being retained by booksellers all of whom have ever-extending paperback departments displacing current hardbound books.

The significant difference is that the majority of paperbacks sold in Australia are imported from the United Kingdom and the USA. In the financial year ending 30 June 1970 of the total imports from the USA and U.K. at publishers' invoiced prices, at $A 37,605,000, paperbacks represented $A 11,619,000, equivalent to not less than 25 million volumes. As against this, in the same period, 320 paperback titles were published in Australia at a total print run (but not necessarily sales) of 1,774,000 copies.

The only Australian publishing house bringing out paperbacks only is Sun Books, now (1971) owned by Macmillans of London. Founded by a former managing director of Penguin Books Australia, they work to the Penguin-Pelican pattern, publishing reprints but mainly original non-fiction.

Penguin Books Australia is also building up a strong Australian list, in addition to its main task of distributing the parent company's books in Australia.

Of the major Australian publishers, Angus & Robertson ("Pacific Books") Rigbys ("Seal Books"), and the Horwitz Group publish series of mass-market paperbacks.

20 Book Design

Book designers, typographers and even trained book printers were virtually non-existent in Australia at the end of the Second World War when indigenous publishing began to take shape. The development in the last three decades is therefore the more impressive.

The provincial look, so typical of the early Australian book, has been replaced by sophisticated design and typography expressed in an Australian idiom, which is somewhere between the American and British styles. In some fields, such as school textbooks, young Australian book designers have done some pioneering work.

The development has been strongly influenced by two book-design awards.

The Australian Book Publishers Association's *Book Design Awards* were first given in 1951. Three judges selected by the Book Design Committee of the ABPA usually representing a typographer, a designer, occasionally a bookseller or a publisher, and a layman assess the books published in the previous year, and select those which receive awards or commendation. The results of the judging are published in an attractively designed booklet presented at the Australian Book Publishers' Association annual meetings normally held in April each year.

Until 1970 only books printed in Australia were eligible, but because of the widespread practice of printing Australian designed books abroad, this practice has now been abandoned. Since 1971 there has been a winning book chosen as the *Book of the Year,* and all books chosen receive a Certificate of Award. The ABPA's best-designed books are from time to time displayed at Frankfurt and other international book fairs (→BTW I, International Section 29). The *Australian Book Review Transfield Award* was a monetary award of $A 2,000 donated by the Transfield Company and administered by the editors of the "Australian Book Review", given to the best-designed Australian books. The adjudicators have been overseas book designers in the United Kingdom, United States, Italy, Canada and Hungary. The last award was made in 1970.

The *Australian Book Review* had published for seven years, under the headline "The Shaping of Books", a monthly critical design evaluation of books published and printed in Australia. It was because of the uniformly high standard achieved by professional, if not by occasional and institutional publishers, that the column was thought to have achieved its purpose, and was suspended in 1970.

21 Publishing

The historical development of Australian book publishing has already been sketched. It has now (1973) reached a watershed and during the past years rapid changes have been taking place in ownership, targets, financial and editorial policies.

It can be said that in the foreseeable future, say for the next five years, owners of the larger publishing firms will try to avoid "risk" (in practical terms, general) publishing in favour of educational publishing, in which, however, the risk factor, because of competition and changing educational patterns, is increasing.

Fortunately some governmental action (→31: Literature Board) is taking shape which could well act as a brake on the decline of general publishing and may avoid a frightening situation where most Australian creative writing and general non-fiction could again be first published in the United Kingdom and the United States and merely distributed in Australia. A helpful trend is appearing also in the emergence of a number of smaller publishing firms whose survival or otherwise will exert considerable influence.

Another trend which might make publishing life more difficult is, however, an attempt to centralize school curricula and involve governments in the publishing of school textbooks and other material. In one Australian state (Western Australia) almost the entire range of primary and secondary schoolbooks are published by the state Education Department under conditions and prices with which commercial publishers cannot compete.

The recently established *National Curriculum Research Project* is almost certain to involve large-scale governmental publishing. It is likely therefore that educational publishing, within the next decade, will take a vastly different form from its present, on the whole profitable, stance.

Australian Book Publishers' Association (→4) annual statistics do give a profile of the development of Australian book publishing, with the qualification already referred to (→16). Another important qualification is that the statistics do indicate sales but not profits and returns on funds employed. The number of reporting publishers (increased from 17 in 1961 to 43 in 1970) reflects a genuine growth in Australia's book-publishing industry.

The following is a comparative summary of the relevant statistics for the respective years ending 30 June.

	1972 (48 publishers)	1973 (55 publishers)
Number of people employed in Australian book publishing	652	1,446
Total of wages and salaries paid to such people	$A 2,930,213	$A 7,042,502
Total sales (including exports, but not including royalties received or sales of rights)	$A 18,383,881	$A 24,450,966

	1971	1972	1973
Rights and other revenue	192,394	92,872	281,888
Value of all sales			
a) Educational*	9,645,702	9,155,980	11,064,756
b) Other than educational	8,976,206	9,320,783	13,668,098

Total number of new books and reprints, printed in Australia	1971	1972	1973
a) Hard-bound	1,688,468	1,531,365	1,057,120
b) Other than hard-bound**	6,580,982	4,385,905	6,554,597

Total number of new books and reprints printed outside Australia***	1971	1972	1973
a) Hard-bound	2,770,995	3,290,286	11,988,500
b) Other than hard-bound**	5,304,856	4,688,054	9,044,953
Total number of all books wherever printed	16,345,301	13,795,670	28,845,178

* For the purposes of these statistics an "educational" book is a school textbook; educational books at the tertiary level are included in category (b).
** This category covers all limp-bound books, mostly school textbooks; for figures on massmarket paperbacks →19 Paperbacks.
*** This category covers books designed in Australia but printed outside, mostly in Hong Kong and Singapore, as well as books contracted in Australia but designed and first published overseas and then "marketed" on a "closed market" in Australia.

Australia

The Commonwealth Bureau of Census and Statistics does not record the number of periodicals published in any given year; the National Library's *Australian Current Serials* (7th edition 1971) offers however a select list of over 1,500 current periodicals arranged broadly by subject.

There are eighteen metropolitan (i.e. issued in the capital cities and giving their respective states full coverage) and two national daily papers, and twelve metropolitan and three national Sunday papers in Australia. The papers with the largest circulation are the Sydney Sunday paper, *Sun-Herald*, 658,000 copies (1971) and the Melbourne *The Sun* 647,000 copies (1971). Non-metropolitan small-circulation newspapers are listed in the 1970 edition of *Press Radio and T.V. Guide* (Country Press Ltd 44 Pitt Street, AUS Sydney, 2000).

Bibliography

D.H. BARKER, *Australian book publishing*. (Unpublished thesis). University of Melbourne 1970. 190 pp.

THE BOOK TRADE. Current Affairs Bulletin. Vol. 27, No. 6. Sydney, University of Sydney 1966.

A. FABINYI, *On Australian publishing*. In: Meanjin Quarterly, September 1969, pp. 219–222.

A. FABINYI, *Development in the book industry*. In: Hemisphere 1968, pp. 64–69. Sydney, Commonwealth Office of Education 1968.

A. FABINYI, *Publishing in Australia*. In: Australian Book Review, April 1970, pp. 214–218. Adelaide, A.B.R. 1970.

G. FERGUSON, *Publishing in Australia*. In: Australian Book Review, April 1970, pp. 146–148. Adelaide, A.B.R. 1970.

F.S. GREENOP, *History of magazine publishing in Australia*. Sydney, Murray 1947. 300 pp.

22 Literary Agents

The only resident literary agent in Australia is a representative of
Curtis Brown Ltd
38 Stafford Street
AUS Paddington, NSN, 2021
Australian authors with international connections are represented by agents in the United Kingdom and United States.

The Australian Society of Authors provides an advisory service on publishers' contracts (→ 35).

As there is currently heavy emphasis in Australia on educational and scholarly books on the one hand and on publisher-conceived commissioned books on the other, the literary agent does not play a major part in the publishing process. He does offer authors useful advice, but is not often in the position to offer manuscripts to local publishers; he almost invariably offers important copyrights for first publication in the United Kingdom, covering the "British Traditional Market". Any book first published in Australia would also normally have rights for the same market.

23 Wholesale Trade

The essential function of the few Australian book wholesalers is to supply newsagents, and outlets other than bookshops not serviced direct by publishers; they play an important part in the distribution and stock control of mass-market paperbacks. Some wholesalers have sole distribution rights of particular United Kingdom paperback imprints.

The largest wholesale firm, and the only one with national coverage, having offices and warehouses in all capital cities, is the Forlib-Leutnegger chain.

Some wholesalers also act as library suppliers, that is, retailers selling books, normally bought from publishers at special wholesale discounts, to libraries at the various rates currently applicable to library purchases.

There is no wholesale "clearing house" in existence in Australia.

24 Retail Trade

The latest available estimate on Australian per annum book consumption expressed in Australian retail prices, according to the Australian Department of Trade Figures, was $A 10 per head in 1972. It rates second (after New Zealand) in the English-speaking world, and compares with an estimated per capita expenditure of $A 4 in the United Kingdom.

It would be reasonable to assume that the high rate of book consumption, which is mainly generated by the increased educational and institutional demand of a growing population (Australia has doubled her population since 1933) would be the basis of a flourishing retail book trade. Indeed, until the mid 1950s large Australian bookshops, situated in the main thoroughfares of cities, carried a greater variety of books than could be seen anywhere else (with the possible exception of New Zealand) in the English-speaking world, and operated at a reasonable profit. The reasons for the then success but subsequent economic distress of Australian bookselling may be summed up as follows:

a) Till the mid 1950s even major bookshops were privately owned, or were owned by publishing companies with tight shareholdings who regarded them as essential outlets; now (1971) major bookshops are expected to meet the financial requirements so far as returns on funds invested are concerned of large public companies, in many cases conglomerates; as against this there has been some revival of the smaller "personal bookshop", many of them located in the suburbs.

b) Till the mid 1950s booksellers were able to "indent" books from overseas publishers giving them a profit margin of up to 45% on retail prices; since then the growth of Australian publishing as well as the "closing of the market" by the major British and American publishers, has reduced their margin, in some cases down to 25%; although prices of imported books have been increased in June 1971, this still does not restore pre 1950s margins.

c) Till the mid 1950s retail stock-holding booksellers had a virtual (and through the services given, well-earned) monopoly on the supply of textbooks to schools and books to public libraries; the expansion of schools and libraries has had, however, the concomitant of creating the new category of "library suppliers", resembling the British and American patterns, these outlets do not normally serve the general public, do not carry stock for general display, and are in the position to sell books at prices equivalent to the price in the country of origin converted at the current rate into Australian currency, well below the general retail price. Education departments and other institutions have taken to calling tenders on the supply of books, and these tenders are invariably below the prices available from stockholding booksellers; the "Statement of Terms" ($\rightarrow$2) has removed all price restrictions on tendering to government departments; in addition there is very heavy buying by universities and other tertiary institutions direct from British and American booksellers and wholesalers; Australia's oldest university places all its orders direct with the publishers.

d) In common with other western countries, Australia has had to contend with accelerating inflation. The Retail Price Index rose from 262 in 1950 to 621 in 1971. Average male weekly earnings rose from $ 22.23 in 1950 to $A 101 in 1973. Neither bookshop turnovers nor book prices (or the discount by publishers allowed thereon) kept pace with the increase; the cost of rentals, telephones and other overhead expenses moved ahead even faster.

The *Survey of Profitability of Booksellers in Australia* commissioned by the Australian Booksellers' Association (→4) and published in August 1970 disclosed that only 5% of all bookshops operate at a profit, 25% operate at a loss and the remainder waver around break-even point.

Another survey is in preparation. It is likely to show a further deterioration in the position, except, of course, that some of the bookshops which have operated at a loss in 1970 have by now closed their doors.

Until recently bookshops had to be listed in the *Directory of Australian Booksellers* before they received trade terms from publishers, and they had to comply with a number of conditions before being eligible for listing. This requirement was loosened up even before retail price maintenance was abolished and the number of books, particularly mass-market paperbacks and children's books, sold with other goods in department stores, news agencies and so forth, had become greater than those sold in established bookshops.

At present *A Guide to Retail Book Outlets in Australia* is being published by the Australian Book Publishers' Association (→4) which lists all the major bookshops in Australia, indicates the type of books they stock, as well as coding their approximate yearly turnover.

This directory, however, is a guide only, and publishers are neither obliged to supply those listed in the directory, nor to refuse to supply those who are not.

The most successful bookshops are the "campus bookshops" serving Australia's universities and colleges of advanced education; they are either owned by the universities themselves, the profits usually used for subsidized publishing, or are co-operatives distributing their profits pro rata to individual purchases.

Because of economic pressures a number of city bookshops, particularly those owned by overseas or conglomerate interests, have or are in the process of closing down. In the national capital, Canberra, (population 159,000) eight bookshops operated in 1969; in 1971 there were three, one of which is the campus bookshop.

The market for every kind of book in Australia will not only remain large, but will continue to grow as population grows and educational and library services undergo further much-needed improvement. But overseas publishers who eye this substantial and wealthy market must continuously keep in mind the rapidly changing pattern of retail outlets and particularly the fact that the "stockholding" bookseller is faced with exceptional difficulties. This has many implications and consequences, including added difficulties and cost for the publisher in promoting new books.

Bibliography

R. PAGE, *Australian bookselling*. Melbourne, Hill of Content 1970 (→3).

25 Mail-Order Bookselling

Apart from routine mail-order activities both by publishers and booksellers, there are only two firms in Australia, both connected with international publishing houses, which run mail-order book businesses of any size.

Major metropolitan newspapers occasionally make mail-order offers for a particular title, normally as a means of boosting circulation.

26 Antiquarian Book Trade, Auctions

With one exception all major booksellers have discontinued their second-hand and antiquarian book departments, and the trade, not organized in any local association, is conducted by a few individual booksellers.

Their stock-in-trade is "Australiana", the description covering both late 18th-century and 19th-century books relating to Australia as well as first editions and out-of-print copies of 20th century material. Both are scarce; not only is there a growing demand from the rapidly expanding Australian institutional libraries, but Australian collections are also being established in the United States and Canada. There is also a local demand for rare books as an "investment". There are, for obvious reasons, only a limited number of private collections, and few come on the market at any given time. These factors have brought about a spectacular increase in the price of Australian material. It is not unusual for a book published say in 1950 for $ 1.50, remaindered later at 50c, to sell now at up to $A 20. There are no auctioneers specializing in books only. Books come up for auction as part of deceased estates, but Christies of London, who now have a permanent representative in Australia, and Joel's of Melbourne occasionally run special book auctions.

Bibliography

C. BARRETT (ed.), *Across the years. The lure of early Australian books*. Melbourne, Seward 1948. 156 pp.

A. H. SPENCER, *The Hill of Content: books, art, music, people*. Sydney, Angus & Robertson 1959. 260 pp.

J. R. TYRRELL, *Old books, old friends, old Sydney*. Sydney, Angus & Robertson 1952. 300 pp.

27 Book Imports

The inter-relation and inter-action of imported books with the whole fabric of the Australian book trade has been made clear in preceding chapters. Book imports fall into the following categories:

Books imported direct from overseas publishers by booksellers for re-sale to book users.

Books imported by Australian branches of overseas publishers for re-sale, usually on a "closed market" basis, to booksellers.

Books imported by Australian publishers for first publication in Australia from overseas printers (mostly from Hong Kong) for re-sale to booksellers.

Books imported direct by institutions and individuals from overseas booksellers or publishers, for their own use.

Although statistics do not reveal under which of the above categories books enter Australia, imports from Hong Kong and Japan are overwhelmingly books not published in those countries, but printed there for Australian publishers.

The Commonwealth Statistician's book-import figures for the twelve months ended 30 June 1971 are as follows:

Country	Australian $ f.o.b.
United Kingdom	21,563,000
USA	17,876,000
Hong Kong	3,550,000
Japan	1,103,000
Netherlands	647,000
Switzerland	658,000
Germany (Fed. Rep.)	392,000
New Zealand	359,000
Czechoslovakia	218,000
Other countries	3,063,000
Total	56,029,000

As can be seen, books in English dominate the market. Nevertheless immigrant groups from European countries represent some demand for books in their native languages. Tertiary institutions and larger libraries have specialized foreign language collections, but the volume, partly due to the difficulties of securing material from such countries as Indonesia or Burma, is not large.

Australia

Before the end of the Second World War the Australian book, except for the occasional sale to specialized library collections, was unexportable. Neither was it possible to sell the British or American rights of a book first published in Australia; this situation did not change till 1946, when the first books already published in Australia came out in overseas English-language editions. (Concurrently Australian publishers were normally unable to buy British or American copyrights for Australian and New Zealand publication only.)

However, as the post-war development of Australian book publishing began to take shape, publishers have recognized that an export market is a pre-condition to both economic survival and the ability to secure high-quality manuscripts. To establish an export market for Australian books, or concurrently for Australian copyrights in the United Kingdom and the United States, has proved, having regard to the powerful publishing industries in those countries, a difficult task, tackled by Australian publishers with a great deal of individual and collective skill and energy.

The Australian Book Publishers' Association Book Export Development Committee (of which the present writer is currently [1973] chairman) works in co-operation and with the invaluable assistance of the Commonwealth Department of overseas Trade. It organizes Australian participation in such fairs and displays as Frankfurt (since 1961), Singapore, Tokyo, Djakarta, Mexico, Montreal, Kuala Lumpur, Cape Town, Bologna and others. It arranges visits to Australia for overseas booksellers and wholesalers. It contributes to the cost of catalogues, co-operative advertisements and the fares of the ABPA's official representatives.

The heavy cost involved notwithstanding, individual publishers do frequently travel overseas and some have already established offices in the United Kingdom and South East Asia.

Efforts have been made over a long period to secure governmental assistance towards the distribution to developing countries of low-cost educational books, but no such scheme is in operation yet. Nevertheless, here again individual publishers have brought out special low-priced educational and technical books for countries such as Singapore and Malaysia, as well as some of the newer African nations.

Others have entered into effective publishing arrangements in Australia or have designed in Australia or adapted from Australian material educational books not only for South East Asian countries but Uganda, Kenya, Puerto Rico and Japan.

Export figures according to ABPA statistics, with the number of publishers reporting in the particular year in brackets, are as follows:

Category	1961 (17) $A	1969 (42) $A	1970 (43) $A	1972 (48) $A
Value of export sales including sales of sheets and bound books	216,524	1,181,600		2,040,421
Rights and other revenues outside Australia	Not recorded	235,090	199,158	37,811
Total export		1,416,690	1,579,919	2,078,232

In 1972 export sales represented over 11% of total turnover.

29 Book Fairs

No international book fairs have been held or are being planned in the foreseeable future in Australia.

Some local book fairs of which the most notable was the Melbourne Moomba Book Fair (held yearly from 1955 to 1970) were orientated towards the individual book buyer and not the bookselling trade. Since 1962 the ABPA with the assistance of the Department of Trade and Industry has been participating in the Frankfurt Book Fair at a national Australian stand. For other overseas displays → 28.

30 Public Relations

The main public-relations effort goes into *Australian Book Week*, held usually in the last quarter of each year, and organized by the ABPA's Publicity Committee.

Australian Book Week normally produces special posters, holds window display competitions, produces special catalogues or news-sheets about Australian books, commands funds for the general advertising of Australian books, and has succeeded in bringing about an increasing coverage in the mass media. Newspapers' book-review columns are devoted to Australian books during Book Week.

There is constant discussion going on whether *Australian* Book Week, which concerns itself with the promotion of Australian books only, should be extended into a general promotion of books, but it has been felt that this aspect is covered by the annual *Australian Library Week* organized by the

Australian Library Promotion Council
State Library of Victoria
Swanston Street
AUS Melbourne, 3000

on which both the Australian Book Publishers' Association (→ 4) and the Australian Booksellers' Association (→ 4) are re-

presented. Library Week is not merely concerned with public relations for libraries but with reading in general, and uses, through posters and advertisements, slogans such as "Books are In" or "You have a Right to Read".

The most successful public-relations exercise is probably *Australian Children's Book Week* organized by the Children's Book Council of Australia, on which both publishers and booksellers are represented. It is held in July each year, when the winner of the Children's Book Award (→ 10) is announced, book lists are published, and children's book displays are held in all capital cities.

31 Bibliophily

Book collectors' societies exist in Melbourne and Sydney; they have no premises on their own, and their addresses vary from year to year, being usually the home adresses of office bearers.

There is (→ 26) a strong interest in the collection of Australian material, and the subject is receiving increasing attention.

Australia owes a considerable debt to three famous book collectors: David Scott Mitchell (1836-1907) who devoted thirty years of his life to collecting 10,000 volumes on Australia, New Zealand and the Pacific Islands, and left his collection to the N.S.W. Library, which bears his name; Sir John Ferguson (1881-1969), whose collection, now in the National Library, was the basis of his *Bibliography of Australia* (→ 15); and E. A. Petherick (1847-1917) who started his career as an assistant to the Melbourne bookseller George Robertson; in 1899 he prepared, for the London bookseller, Francis Edwards, the notable *Catalogue of books relating to Australasia*; he sold his collection to the Commonwealth (→ 15) and was appointed the first Commonwealth Government Archivist.

International Book Year 1972 was an important event in the Australian book world. The UNESCO International Book Year Committee, under the chairmanship of the writer, generated activities throughout the year, distributed posters and organized regional meetings. On behalf of the Australian government it invited the National Librarian of Kenya for a four weeks visit as a necessary gesture towards developing countries. Events culminated at the end of 1972 in the "Book Under Challenge Seminar", held in November 1972 in Canberra. The proceedings of this seminar are being published and will be available from 1974 from the

Australian National Commission for
UNESCO
P.O. Box 826
AUS Canberra City, A.C.T., 2601
As a follow-up to International Book Year an
Australian National Book Council
was formed in July 1973.

Bibliography

R. DAVIDSON, *A book collector's notes on items relating to the discovery of Australia, the first settlement and the early coastal exploration of the Continent.* Melbourne, Cassel 1970. 146 pp.

G. MACKANESS, *Art of book collecting in Australia.* Sydney, Angus & Robertson 1956. 184 pp.

G. MACKANESS, *Bibliomania: an Australian book collector's essays.* Sydney, Angus & Robertson 1965. 205 pp.

32 Literary Prizes

The Commonwealth Literary Fund was founded in 1908 at a time when government patronage of literature was not a generally accepted concept.
The Fund was administered by a committee of one representative each of the main political parties under the chairmanship of the Prime Minister, and is assisted on all literary matters by an advisory board appointed by the Government.
The Fund each year awards fellowships of up to $A 6,000 to writers to enable them to work full time on a literary project; it assists by way of subsidies and guarantees against loss or a combination of both publishers to bring out works of literary merit which may not appear to be commercial propositions; it organizes lectures on Australian literature; it gives a financial award to the winner of the Best Children's Book of the Year (→ 10), and provides pensions to creative writers who have achieved nation-wide reputation for their work. In 1972 it disbursed $A 330,000 a year.
The influence of the *Commonwealth Literary Fund* on Australian literature and book publishing could not be overrated. Some of the books now regarded as contemporary classics could have not been published without the Fund's assistance. The fellowships given were not only the highest in Australia in monetary value, but bestow a distinction on the recipients.
Early in 1973 the Commonwealth government abolished the *Commonwealth Literary Fund* as such and created, as part of its newly established *Arts Council* a *Literature Board* which presents a startling and exciting re-valuation in government patronage of literature, of authors, and of book publishing. The budget has risen from $ 333,000 to approximately $ 2,000,000. The number of fellowships to writers have been increased in number, and substantially increased in value and assistance to publishing which, under the *Commonwealth Literary Fund* scheme was in the shape of a guarantee against loss, is now being replaced by generous subsidies. Moreover the *Literature Board* is taking an interest in the viability of Australian bookshops, recognizing the fact that it would be pointless to subsidize publication of books unless those books have a readily accessible channel to reach the public.

It is giving assistance to organizations such as a *Booktrade Working Party* and is also involved in Australian responsibilities for book development in Asia.

The *Australian National University* awards an annual fellowship (covering accommodation and living expenses) in the "creative arts" which from time to time goes to an Australian author.

The *Adelaide Advertiser Contest* gives an award of $ 5,000 every second year for an unpublished work by an Australian writer.

The *Foundation for Australian Literary Studies Award* worth $ 500 is given annually to the author of the best book dealing with any aspect of Australian life.

The *Mary Gilmore Award* of $ 2,000 is awarded annually to books of significance to the life and aspirations of the Australian people.

The *Moomba Awards for Australian Literature* of a total value of $ 4,500 are given to published Australian books in various categories.

The *Miles Franklin Award* of $ 1,200 for a published novel portraying Australian life is probably the most prestigious Australian literary award.

The *N.S.W. Fellowship* of $ 4,500 is given to writers resident in New South Wales to undertake or complete a literary work.

The *Encyclopedia Britannica Award* of $ 10,000 usually goes every third year to an Australian writer.

The *Barbara Ramsden Award* goes to both the author and the editor of an outstanding work of quality writing and presentation, published each year.

The *N.S.W. Fellowship:* a grant of $ 5,000 per annum to a writer resident in New South Wales.

The *Stanford Writing Scholarship* is awarded by the University of Melbourne, biennially, $ 4,000 to enable young Australian writers to study at the Creative Writing Centre, Stanford University.

The *Sir Thomas White Memorial Prize*, $ 500,

awarded annually by the United Kingdom Society of Australian Writers.

The *Angus & Robertson Writers' Fellowship* $ 5,000, awarded annually.

In addition to those listed there are a number of other occasional or minor awards.

For the *Children's Book of the Year Awards*, → 10.

33 The Reviewing of Books

The main book-reviewing media in Australia are:

a) The literary sections or supplements of metropolitan newspapers.

b) The literary sections or supplements of news weeklies and fortnightlies.

c) Monthly or quarterly literary journals.

d) Trade and learned journals on specialised subjects.

e) Education gazettes and journals published by the various educational authorities.

f) Subject journals produced by independent teachers' and educational associations.

g) Radio and television.

Over the years there has been considerable improvement both by way of space given and choice of competent reviewers by the metropolitan newspapers, in their review sections and supplements on Saturdays and Sundays. The leading media are *The Age* in Melbourne, the *Sydney Morning Herald*, *The Advertiser* in Adelaide, and the nationally distributed *The Australian*. Because of the ratio of overseas and Australian book production, reviews of Australian books are in the minority; some of the papers reprint syndicated overseas reviews.

The leaders amongst weeklies and fortnightlies, with influential book-review sections, are *The Bulletin* and *Nation-Review*.

Australian Book Review, which, having completed its first decade as a monthly, has now been turned into a quarterly, is the only journal which attempts a comprehensive coverage of Australian literary output.

Amongst the literary quarterlies, the pride of place goes to *Meanjin Quarterly*, under the editorship of C.B. Christensen, now in its thirty-second year of publication. Other important quarterlies include *Southerly* (devoted entirely to literature); *Quadrant;* the *Australian Quarterly*; for in-depth reviews of books on international affairs the quarterly *Australian Outlook* is published by the Australian Institute of International Affairs.

The education departments of all states publish an official educational journal which carries book reviews as well as periodical lists of prescribed and recommended textbooks. The Commonwealth Department of Education and Science publishes *Education News*.

Names and addresses of Australian learned journals and trade journals are available from the National Library ($\rightarrow$ 15).

Radio and television services are provided by both the nationally owned but independent statutory authority, the Australian Broadcasting Commission (ABC, the Australian equivalent to the British Broadcasting Corporation), and by commercial stations (equivalent to the United States system of broadcasting).

The ABC provides a weekly radio review of books, but television coverage of books and literature is only a very occasional feature of both national and commercial broadcasting.

34 Graphic Arts

The *Printing and Allied Trades Employers'*
 Federation of Australia (PATEFA)
 136 Jolimont Road
 AUS East Melbourne. Victoria, 3002
includes a Book Producers' Group.

Large-scale commercial printing of books in Australia only began at the end of the Second World War, and by the 1950s Australia had a number of well-equipped book-printing and bookbinding plants, a pool of skilled operators, and a reasonable, if restricted, choice of typefaces, papers, binding and other materials.

By the early 1960s, however, a flow of Australian book work was diverted to Asian printers, whose production costs, because of their lower labour costs and favourable duty-free admission of materials, were up to 50% to 70% (on colour work) lower than what local printers were in a position to quote.

By 1969 the position of Australian book printers had reached such crisis point that the Commonwealth Government paid Australian book printers, as an interim measure, a bounty of 25% on their quoted prices. Although this measure has stabilized the book-printing industry at the 1968 level, both the number of plants and skilled operatives continued to decline.

In 1971 the Commonwealth Government referred the matter to the independent Tariff Board, but it is significant that in the terms of reference given it instructed the Board to have regard to the Government's policy not to impede by tariffs or quota restrictions the importation into Australia of books. At the time of writing (1973) it is impossible to foretell what measures the Tariff Board will recommend, and whether or to what extent these recommendations will be accepted by the Government.

In the meantime, although over 50% of all "Australian" books are now (1973) being printed outside Australia, mainly in Hong Kong and Singapore, the bounty paid to book printers has now risen to over $A 3,000,000 per annum. To put a ceiling on this expenditure the government decided to restrict the categories of books eligible to bounty; e.g. no book under 96 pages receives this assistance.

Be that as it may, the parlous state of the Australian book-printing industry has the consequence that except for on-the-job training, no effective facilities exist for training in book printing, as distinct for training in printing in general (→11).

Nevertheless, the same period saw the emergence of some outstanding book designers, even if a great deal of their work, although designed and possibly typeset in Australia, is printed elsewhere. The only existing organization of book designers is the *Imprint Society* (→11) of Melbourne, the address of which is that of the various office bearers elected annually.

This assessment of the book-printing industry should of course be taken in the context of 20 (Book Design).

Bibliography

Books are Different. A case prepared by the Printing and Allied Trades Employers' Federation on behalf of the Federal Book Manufacturers' Group. Melbourne, Patefa 1969.

D. M. BORCHARDT, *The spread of printing. Eastern hemisphere: Australia.* Amsterdam, Vangendt 1969. 45 pp.

35 Miscellaneous

a) *Authors*

The
> *Australian Society of Authors*
> *252 George Street*
> *AUS Sydney, 2000*

represents virtually every writer who publishes, or hopes to publish books in Australia. Their quarterly journal *The Australian Author* carries a continuous flow of articles on publishing trends.

Other literary societies include:
> *Fellowship of Australian Authors*
> *Commonwealth Council*
> *64 Young Street*
> *AUS Cremorne, N.S.W. 2090*

Branches in all Australian states, and
> *International P.E.N. Club*
> *Melbourne and Sydney centres*
> *Box 997*
> *G.P.O.*
> *AUS Sydney, N.S.W. 2001*

New Zealand

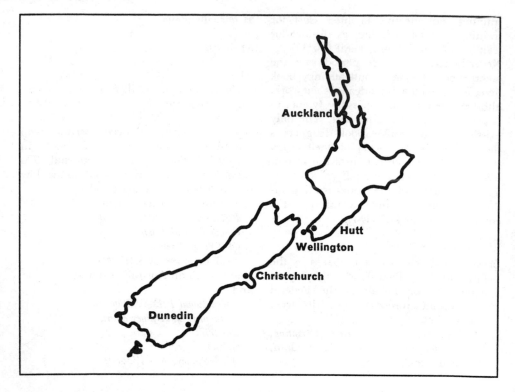

1 General Information

Area 265,149 km² (North Island 114,688 km²,
South Island 150,461 km²)

Population 2,821,000 (10 per km²)

Capital Wellington (179,300)

Largest towns Auckland (603,500); Christchurch
(260,200); Wellington (179,300); Hutt
(122,000); Dunedin (110,100)

Government A monarchical state, New Zealand is
also a constituent member of the Commonwealth. The supreme law-making body is the
General Assembly, which consists of the Governor General and the House of Representatives.
The powers of Parliament to make laws are
legally untrammelled

Religion Protestant 67.9%; Roman Catholic
15.9%; others and dissidents 16.2%

National language English

Leading foreign languages French and German are
taught in most schools but are not obligatory

Weights, measures Imperial in process of metrica-
tion

Currency unit New Zealand Dollar (N.Z. $) =
100 cents

Education Compulsory to 15 years of age. 28,821
(1968) students at six universities

Illiteracy Nil

Paper consumption a) Newsprint 32.6 kg per inhabitant (1970)

b) Printing paper (other than
newsprint) 11.1 kg per inhabitant (1970)

Membership UNESCO; ICBA

370

2 Past and Present

Planned settlement of New Zealand during the middle of the nineteenth century by English and Scottish companies and associations is the reason why the majority of the population derives originally from Great Britain. Strong familial and sentimental ties with Britain have resulted in the book trade in New Zealand being predominently British oriented. Although publishing in New Zealand has developed greatly during the past decade, the majority of books read in New Zealand are still imported, and most of these come from the United Kingdom.

Translations of scriptures and hymns for Maori converts, pamphlets about New Zealand, and transcriptions of Maori chants and traditions were the first areas of publication in New Zealand. In the last decade of the nineteenth century educational publishing began to develop and publishing of school texts has been a mainstay of New Zealand publishing, there being considerable growth in this area in the past ten years.

A recent development has been publishing in New Zealand by British publishing houses which have long maintained local representational offices. Also, there has been an increasing tendency in the past ten years for British publishers to set up wholesale warehouses in New Zealand and in some cases to close the market, i. e., to make their books available from their local warehouses only.

As a result of experimentation in the 1930s by small printing houses and private presses, specially in Christchurch and Auckland, book design since then has been up to the best world standards. Many poets and writers were encouraged by these small publishers who set high literary and design standards.

Retail bookselling in New Zealand, because of the 20,400 km from the main source of supply and the time taken for stock orders to be filled, has a history of large stockholding. The pattern of one or two large stock orders a year is now changing to one of smaller but more frequent orders. Improved shipping has been an obvious reason for this change, another being that the expectations and demands of customers are now stimulated by reviews and notices received by airmail.

Bibliography

D. B. Paul, *Organisation of the book trade*. In: N. Z. Libraries. Wellington. March-April 1955, pp. 31–39 and pp. 68–75.

D. B. Paul, *Publishing and bookselling*. In: An Encyclopaedia of New Zealand. Wellington, Government Printer. pp. 884–886.

F. Macmillan, *The spread of printing*, Eastern Hemisphere: New Zealand. Amsterdam, Vangendt 1969. 46 pp.

3 Retail Prices

Maintenance of a price and discount schedule has long been one of the main functions of the Booksellers' Association of New Zealand (→4). In 1961 the Trade Practices and Prices Commission, examining this schedule, found that the booksellers were operating a restrictive trade practice, and ordered that it cease. However, this decision was appealed against successfully, the Appeal Court finding that the booksellers' schedule encouraged an orderly trade to the benefit of the majority of book buyers. Because most books sold in New Zealand were imported, the price schedule was based on the discount allowed by the exporting publishers, this being adjusted to give a mark-up of approximately 40%. Privileged buyers are: libraries, which are allowed a 20% reduction on the retail price for indent orders and 10% on orders from a bookseller's stock; schools, which under the

Free Textbook Scheme are allowed 20%; students and teachers, who are given a 10% discount. Discounts from the retail price are not obligatory, but are at the discretion of the individual bookseller.

Bibliography

G. TAIT, *Price of books–a bookseller's view*. In: N. Z. Bookseller & Publisher No. 29, March-April 1971, pp. 14–16.

4 Organization

There are three individual associations and one co-operative association in the New Zealand book trade. They are
Booksellers' Association of New Zealand
P. O. Box 11377
NZ Wellington
Formed in 1921, the Booksellers' Association had 285 members and 45 associate members in 1971. It exists to foster, promote and encourage the development of retail bookselling and it operates a price and discount schedule which has resulted in an orderly and stable book trade.
Two smaller and more recent organizations are *The Association of British Publishers' Representatives Resident in N.Z.* (BPRA) which was formed in the 1950s and the *New Zealand Book Publishers' Association*, formed in 1962. Neither the Association of British Publishers' Representatives Resident in N. Z. nor the New Zealand Book Publishers' Association have fixed addresses, and the address of the secretary changes annually in each case. No doubt mail addressed c/o of the Booksellers' Association would be forwarded to the current address in each case.
In 1968, on the initiative of the *Booksellers' Association,* a co-operative organization, the *New Zealand Book Trade Organization* (NZBTO) was set up.
New Zealand Book Trade Organization
P. O. Box 11377
NZ Wellington

NZBTO is an incorporated society of representatives of each of the three above organizations and its primary function is to facilitate reading so that more people will gain delight and satisfaction from books. It has two lines of action: (a) short-term promotion activities of which an annual Christmas catalogue of books is the major work, and (b) long-term activities involving co-operation with those who use and enjoy books to discover and remove the barriers that prevent or discourage reading. NZBTO is financed by contributions from British publishers 45%; N. Z. booksellers 40%; N. Z. publishers 10% and Book Tokens N. Z. Ltd 5%. The secretary of NZBTO is also secretary of the Booksellers' Association.

5 Trade Press

There is only one book trade journal in New Zealand. It is
New Zealand Book World
P. O. Box 10082
NZ Wellington
Incorporating The *N. Z. Bookseller and Publisher*, the *N. Z. Book World* is published monthly 10 times a year with combined issues for December/January and February/March. Regular features include trade and library news items, book reviews, articles, lists of books from the National Bibliography, decisions of the Indecent Publications Tribunal and lists of books submitted to the Indecent Publications Tribunal. The first number appeared in June 1973.

6 Book-Trade Literature

Apart from histories of individual publishing houses and an article in *An Encyclopaedia of New Zealand* very little has been written on the book trade in New Zealand. Three works which merit attention are:
New Zealand Books In Print 1970, compiled by

B. Collie and published by the N. Z. Book Publishers' Association–the current and fifth edition of a book that is invaluable to the trade.

St. Perry, *The Indecent Publications Tribunal.* Wellington, Whitcombe & Tombs Ltd 1965. 169 pp. Deals with a particular aspect of the trade that has attracted attention throughout the English-speaking world.

New Zealand Writers' and Publishers' Year Book. Ed. by D. L. Double. Auckland. New Zealand Writers' Publications (C.P.O. Box 950).

→2, 3.

7 Sources of Information, Address Services

Information about the New Zealand book trade may be obtained from the
New Zealand Book Trade Organization
P.O. Box 11377
NZ Wellington
Addresses of libraries may be obtained from:
The Registrar
New Zealand Library Association
10 Park Street
NZ Wellington 1

8 International Membership

The Booksellers' Association is a member of the International Community of Booksellers Associations (→BTW I, International Section 4). New Zealand is a member of UNESCO.

9 Market Research

Since the late 1920s educationists have carried out several surveys of reading interests of schoolchildren, details of which may be obtained from the *New Zealand Council for Educational Research* (Education House, 178–182 Willis Street, Wellington). NZBTO (→4) initiated and financed a survey of teenage reading in 1969.

Bibliography

J. MACONIE AND G. TOWNSLEY, *Survey of teenage reading in New Zealand.* Wellington, NZBTO 1969. 38 pp.
Deals with a sample of 4,060 fourth-form children in 31 schools.

G. TAIT, *Changing reading patterns.* In: Education 9, Vol. 15, October 1966, pp. 3–10. Wellington, School Publ. Branch, Dept. of Education 1960.
Library issue figures in popular and serious categories related to population of one city over a ten-year period covering five years before television and five after.

G. TAIT, *Changing reading patterns in New Zealand.* In: The Bookseller, August 19, 1967, pp. 1,410–1,414. London, Whitaker 1967.
Same method used for issues from three libraries in three cities giving a sample of 17% of total population.

10 Books and Young People

An annual Children's Book Week, initiated by the
New Zealand Library Association
10 Park Street
NZ Wellington 1
is held each August. In some towns this is run solely by the public library and in others various community organizations co-operate with the library in arranging the week.

A regular list of *Children's Books to Buy* with short critical notices on each title is produced by the *School Library Service*, Private Bag, Wellington.

→9, 32.

Bibliography

A. PELLOWSKI, *The world of children's literature.* New York, Bowker 1968. pp. 342–346: New Zealand.

11 Training

For some years the Bookseller's Association (→4) ran a one-week residential training course every two years. Desire for a more formal training arose and currently the Booksellers' Association in conjunction with the Technical Institutes in Auckland and Wellington is operating a pilot training scheme preparatory to setting up a correspondence course through the Technical Correspondence School. It is hoped that this scheme will eventually develop into a three-stage structure resulting in a Junior Certificate in Bookselling, a Diploma of Bookselling, and finally a Diploma of Book Shop Management. This course is open to staff of publishing houses and wholesale houses as well as bookshop staff.

12 Taxes

Books are imported into New Zealand free of all customs duties and are not subject to any internal taxes.

13 Clearing Houses

Large rises in bank charges and postal rates led to the formation in 1971 of the
New Zealand Booksellers' Clearing House
P.O. Box 10340
NZ Wellington
Operating only within New Zealand, the Clearing House allows booksellers to pay up to 105 suppliers' accounts with one cheque.

14 Copyright

Under the Copyright Act, 1962, copyright comes into existence automatically upon completion of any original work. New Zealand is a party to both the International Convention for the Protection of Literary and Artistic Works (Berne Copyright Union) and the Universal Copyright Con-

vention, and consequently copyright in New Zealand extends to all countries which are parties to those Conventions (→BTW I, International Section 14).

15 National Bibliography, National Library

By the National Library Act 1965, the Alexander Turnbull Library, the General Assembly Library and the National Library Service were combined to form the
National Library of New Zealand
Private Bag
NZ Wellington
under the administration of the Department of Education. The
Alexander Turnbull Library
P.O. Box 8016
NZ Wellington
is a state research and reference library bequeathed to the nation in 1918. The original bequest has increased to approximately 112,500 books and many thousands of manuscripts. As from 1966 this library has assumed responsibility for the compilation and publication of the National Bibliography and for the centralized cataloguing of current New Zealand material. The
General Assembly Library
Parliament Buildings
NZ Wellington
provides library services for Parliament and since 1903 has been the principal depository for books and periodicals published in New Zealand. The library holds about 340,000 volumes. A new building to house the National Library is being planned.

16 Book Production

A total of 1,580 books and pamphlets were included in the National Bibliography for 1970, comprising 651 books and 929 pamphlets.

Subject group	Books	Pamphlets
General	14	23
Religion, theology, philosophy	16	44
Sociology, statistics	24	15
Political science	50	92
Law, public administration, social welfare	47	58
Education	38	74
Trade, communication, transport	16	27
Linguistics, philology	19	3
Sciences	104	102
Technology	40	85
Agriculture, forestry	39	137
Domestic science	6	15
Commercial management	16	29
Fine arts, etc.	29	52
Entertainment, sport	26	27
Literature	67	55
Geography, travel	47	46
History, biography	53	45
Total	651	929

18 Book Clubs

There being no New Zealand book clubs, British book clubs have attracted a small membership in New Zealand, two of the most popular being the Folio Society and the Readers Union.

19 Paperbacks

Sales of paperbacks in New Zealand occur noticeably more with young people than with old; indeed, many persons under the age of 25 will buy only paperbacks. Very little paperback publishing is done in New Zealand, partly because the small population does not provide a sufficient market for this sort of mass production and distribution. An interesting experiment has been the publication in paperback of facsimile editions of a dozen early New Zealand books that had long been out of print.

20 Book Design

→ 2.

21 Publishing

New Zealand has a vigorous publishing industry which is beginning to move into the export field. All publishing houses began either as printers or as booksellers, that is, they already had either the means of production or of distribution. The largest publishing house had both. An increasing part of New Zealand's educational book requirements are being published within the country and educational publishing has always been the backbone of the industry. New Zealand educational texts, specially at the primary level, are now being exported to Great Britain and the United States. General publishing of a high standard is produced by several small houses.

In 1969–70 there were 82 printing and publishing establishments in New Zealand employing 7,436 persons, and the total value of their production was NZ $ 57,703,000.

The main publishing centres are Auckland, Wellington, Christchurch and Dunedin.

23 Wholesale Trade

Geographic isolation from the world publishing centres has led to the development of half a dozen wholesale book houses. In the past ten years a growing number of publishers' representatives has begun holding partial stock of the houses they represent. Thus the more popular titles, at least, tend to be more readily available than formerly when booksellers would place import orders once a year. A growing proportion of book sales are from stock held by wholesalers or other stockists.

New Zealand

24 Retail Trade

Although overseas visitors frequently comment on the number and excellence of New Zealand bookshops, the retail trade is constantly trying to improve both its efficiency and its profitability. All bookshops are dependent on either, sales to institutions, or sales of goods other than books. The two main institutions are libraries and educational organizations, and other goods can be grouped mainly into stationery and toys.

Turnover statistics for the economic group "books, stationery, etc." extracted from the New Zealand Official Yearbook, 1970, are:

Year	Turnover m. NZ $	Percentage of total retail turnover	Turnover in NZ $ per capita
1966	41.2	2.6	15.2
1967	42.7	2.7	15.5
1968	45.9	2.8	16.4
1969	50.9	2.9	18.1

The Booksellers' Association (→4) has set up a committee to produce regular statistics and analysis relating to the volume, turnover and costs of the retail book trade in both total and the main parts of the trade. Not least of the reasons for the high standard of bookshops in New Zealand is that the libraries, with one or two exceptions, have put the bulk of their trade through the shops, enabling them to provide comprehensive book stocks and order services unequalled in comparable population groups.

25 Mail-Order Bookselling

Many bookshops run small mail-order departments, but constantly rising costs together with the small total population have guided the main development of bookselling along other lines.

26 Antiquarian Book Trade, Auctions

As may be expected in a country just over a hundred years old, the antiquarian book trade is very small, though reprints of early New Zealand books are increasing interest in this part of the book trade.

27 Book Imports

New Zealand imports some NZ $10,000,000 worth of books a year and in support of the UNESCO ideal these come in free of all import duty. The main countries from which these books and pamphlets are imported are:

Country of Origin	Value of Imports (1,000 NZ $)			
	1966–67	1967–68	1968–69	1969–70
Australia	1,105	1,199	1,407	1,684
United Kingdom	5,178	5,611	6,513	7,207
USA	2,838	2,642	2,225	2,446
All countries	10,032	10,616	11,492	13,127

An interesting recent development has been the increase in the importation of books from Hong Kong. These have risen from NZ $ 464 in 1963 to NZ $ 283,536 in 1969. As practically no books are imported from Hong Kong by booksellers, these figures relate almost entirely to books published by New Zealand publishers but manufactured elsewhere. This is causing some concern among New Zealand book printers.

28 Book Exports

The latest figures available show that New Zealand exported books to the value of NZ $ 502,799 in 1968–9. Of these, school texts accounted for NZ $ 107,387, but as there has been considerable activity in this field since then, it is likely that the book exports for the subsequent years will show a large increase.

376